POST-SOCIALISM IS NOT DEAD: (RE)READING THE GLOBAL IN COMPARATIVE EDUCATION

INTERNATIONAL PERSPECTIVES ON EDUCATION AND SOCIETY

Series Editor: Abraham Yogev

Recent Volumes:

Series Editor from Volume 5: David P. Baker

Series Editor from Volume 11: Alexander W. Wiseman

INTERNATIONAL PERSPECTIVES ON EDUCATION AND
SOCIETY   VOLUME 14

POST-SOCIALISM IS NOT DEAD: (RE)READING THE GLOBAL IN COMPARATIVE EDUCATION

EDITED BY

IVETA SILOVA
Lehigh University, PA, USA

United Kingdom – North America   Japan
India – Malaysia – China

Emerald Group Publishing Limited
Howard House, Wagon Lane, Bingley BD16 1WA, UK

First edition 2010

British Library Cataloguing in Publication Data
A catalogue record for this book is available from the British Library

ISBN: 978-0-85724-417-8
ISSN: 1479-3679 (Series)

Emerald Group Publishing
Limited, Howard House,
Environmental Management
System has been certified by
ISOQAR to ISO 14001:2004
standards

Awarded in recognition of
Emerald's production
department's adherence to
quality systems and processes
when preparing scholarly
journals for print

INVESTOR IN PEOPLE

CONTENTS

LIST OF CONTRIBUTORS

Olga Bain	George Washington University, Washington, DC, USA
Christine Beresniova	Indiana University, Bloomington, IN, USA
Kara D. Brown	University of South Carolina, Columbia, SC, USA
Eduard Dneprov	Russian Academy of Education, Moscow, Russia
Olena Fimyar	University of Cambridge, Cambridge, UK
Meg P. Gardinier	Cornell University, Ithaca, NY, USA
Magdalena Gross	Standford University, Palo Alto, CA, USA
Irina Horga	Institute of Educational Sciences, Bucharest, Romania
Robert J. Imre	The University of Newcastle, Newcastle, NSW, Australia
Tavis D. Jules	Globally Responsible Leadership Initiative, Brussels, Belgium
Zsuzsa Millei	The University of Newcastle, Newcastle, NSW, Australia
Monica E. Mincu	University of Torino, Torino, Italy
Diane Brook Napier	University of Georgia, Athens, GA, USA
Eleoussa Polyzoi	The University of Winnipeg, Winnipeg, MB, Canada
Heidi Ross	Indiana University, Bloomington, IN, USA

Anita Sanyal	University of Maryland, College Park, MD, USA
Iveta Silova	Lehigh University, Bethlehem, PA, USA
Noah W. Sobe	Loyola University Chicago, Chicago, IL, USA
Renee N. Timberlake	Loyola University Chicago, Chicago, IL, USA
Elizabeth Anderson Worden	American University, Washington, DC, USA
Ran Zhang	Peking University, Beijing, PRC
Wanxia Zhao	Indiana University, Bloomington, IN, USA

ACKNOWLEDGMENTS

When the Berlin wall fell in 1989, I was a high school student in Stuchka, a small Soviet town in Latvia named after Lenin's colleague Petr Stuchka, who founded the Marxist Party in Latvia, served as the head of the Bolshevik government during the Latvian War of Independence, acted as editor of major Latvian and Russian communist newspapers, and was the first president of the Supreme Court of the Soviet Union, among many other duties. His statue, once proudly towering near the House of Culture in my hometown, was hurriedly removed and the town renamed Aizkraukle, the historical local name of the hill used by the German knights in the Middle Ages. Amidst the major changes that followed, the one that particularly stood out to me as a young student was the cancelation of the end-of-the-year history examinations. What we had always known privately had finally become official: the history we learned was simply wrong and the new history was yet to be written. This moment of "in-betweeness" was both intimidating and exhilarating, and it was ultimately the moment that set the course for my academic and professional career. Straddling both Soviet and post-Soviet experiences, I became fascinated with observing, examining, and understanding postsocialist transformations and their impact on our past, present, and future.

As we celebrate (and commemorate) the 20th anniversary of the collapse of the Soviet Union in 2011, this book has both personal and professional meanings to me. Personally, it represents yet another attempt to grapple with the complexities and contradictions of the postsocialist transformations and I would like to thank my parents, grandmother (Omite), and my husband Neil for accompanying me on this fascinating journey. Professionally, it is an opportunity to theorize about postsocialism more broadly with colleagues who bring a variety of theoretical, methodological, and conceptual perspectives and speak from different geographical locations. It is an exciting and always thought-provoking exercise. Although our collective conversation may not necessarily have brought more clarity to our understandings of postsocialism (or globalization) today, it has definitely complicated our ongoing discussions by articulating questions that have been rarely asked before. I would like to thank all of the contributors to this book for engaging in this intellectual initiative so actively, critically, and passionately.

My graduate students at Lehigh University played an important role in helping me bring this volume together. I would like to give special thanks to William C. Brehm for helping me think through the labyrinth of essays and ideas that ultimately led to a coherent volume. Will also expertly managed the external review process while keeping me (and the authors) on schedule. I would also like to thank several graduate students who assisted with editing the published manuscripts, including Will Brehm, Tiffany Burke, and Michael Mead. Mike deserves special acknowledgment for taking on more editing than I could have ever expected (before even officially starting his graduate studies) and for admirably completing his work with careful attention to detail. While my children Maryam and Dmitry are convinced that it takes me too long to write books (after all, they can write and illustrate a book in just one weekend!), I thank them for their patience and enthusiasm for my work. Finally, I would like to thank Neil for all the support (both logistical and intellectual), and even more so, for many engaging conversations about (post)socialism and its future.

REDISCOVERING POST-SOCIALISM IN COMPARATIVE EDUCATION

Iveta Silova

Comparative education has always had an uneasy relationship with (post)socialism. In the United States, the relationship began during the Cold War, when the study of socialism occupied a central position in the field during the 1960s and 1970s. While its centrality was primarily driven by the geopolitical factors associated with the Cold War – including federal funding through the National Defense Education Act (NDEA) and the growth of area studies (especially Soviet studies) aimed at "keeping the United States ahead of the Soviet Union through education" (Noah, 2006, p. 10) – the study of socialism has eventually become mainstream in comparative education.[1] Contrastive analyses between education in the United States and the Soviet Union were center stage at the founding meeting of the Comparative Education Society (CES) in 1956 and constituted one-third of all articles published in *Comparative Education Review* in 1958 (Silova, 2009a). As Bereday and Pennar (1960) observed, "the market for writings on Soviet education" became "inexhaustible" during the 1960s (p. 3). In this context, the study of socialism has propelled the development of comparative education as a field. Wilson (1994) referred to this period as "the growth spurt of comparative and international education" (p. 464) and Steiner-Khamsi (2006) described it as "the development turn," which was characterized by "the greatest territorial gain" both in terms of geographic areas of comparative research (as reflected in the increasing focus on the study of education in nonaligned

Post-Socialism is not Dead: (Re)Reading the Global in Comparative Education
International Perspectives on Education and Society, Volume 14, 1–24
Copyright © 2010 by Emerald Group Publishing Limited
ISSN: 1479-3679/doi:10.1108/S1479-3679(2010)0000014004

countries) and higher education programs (as reflected in the growth of new degree programs across the United States).

However, such a close relationship with Sovietology came at a high methodological, epistemological, and ethical cost for comparative educa- tion – a discussion frequently avoided by comparative education today. The preoccupation of comparative education scholars with the study of educational systems in the socialist bloc and nonaligned countries margin- alized the study of education in other geographic areas.[2] Furthermore, it was accompanied by a methodological shift in comparative education where the original commitment to contextualized, historiographic comparative study was rapidly overpowered by an overemphasis on quantitative methodologies and positivist techniques (Silova & Brehm, 2010). Finally, the relationship between Sovietology and comparative education inevitably created serious tensions between academic scholarship and politics. As Sanders (1997) pointed out, "comparative education on both sides of the Iron Curtain was deeply involved in a sordid and ruthless propaganda war serving wider purposes of the Cold War policy" (p. 3). In the United States, the founding fathers of comparative education (William W. Brickman, Gerald H. Read, and George Z. F. Bereday) were accused by Soviet scholars of presenting "distorted interpretations" and "falsified facts" in their publications on education in the Soviet Union. For example, Malkova (1961) indignantly described the *The Changing Soviet School* edited by Bereday, Brickman, and Read (1960) as "a hostile, subjective, and, in many respects, malevolent book" (p. 69). Not surprisingly, American compar- ativists had similar criticisms for the scholarship of their Soviet colleagues (Brickman, 1961). Commenting on the political dynamics of comparative education in a divided Germany during the Cold War, Sanders (1997) cynically concluded, "this was ... a truly pathological case of permanent and institutionalized scientific schizophrenia" (p. 23).

Notwithstanding these complicated dynamics, the relationship between (post)socialism and comparative education did not stop with the collapse of the socialist bloc in 1989. As the Cold War ended and Sovietology became recast as transitology during the early 1990s, the study of what became known as post-socialism held yet another promise for comparative education. At the time when many transitology studies plunged into measuring the "progress" of former socialist societies toward the Western ideals of democracy (often assuming its linearity and inevitability), Cowen (2000) proposed a different, more revitalizing relationship between transitology and comparative education. Defining "transitologies" as complex mixtures of historical, political, economic, ideological, and sociological transformations, which reflect more or less simultaneous "processes of destroying the past and redefining the future," Cowen (2000) argued that "transitologies" have a great potential for the future of comparative education (p. 338). Instead of assuming that "the equilibrium conditions and the dynamic linearities of development of educational systems could be predicted," Cowen (2000) urged comparative education scholars to focus on "exploring moments of educational metamorphosis" (p. 333). In his conceptualization, transitologies could free comparative education for new epistemological and methodological explorations:

> ... transitologies should be part of a comparative education of the future, not merely because we do not understand them but because transitologies act for comparative education as lightning storms do on dark days. Transitologies are drama, they occur at remarkable speeds and often with stunning suddenness. They reveal to us, behind their drama and their rhetoric, the educational patterns that are ordinarily, in ordinary daylight as it were, difficult to see. Transitologies reveal new 'educational codings', that is, the compression of political and economic power into educational forms. (Cowen, 2000, p. 339)

With such a great promise for reconceptualizing the future of comparative education, "transitologies" experienced a brief moment of academic jubilation in the 1990s. By the 2000s, however, it became abundantly clear that the most "transitology" research was subsumed by more familiar globalization frameworks. Not only did the transitology research embrace a linear conceptualization of post-socialism (including the familiar stories documenting the progress from authoritarianism toward market economics and democracies), but also an increasing number of scholars began to focus on the perceived convergence of post-socialist societies toward the global norms (whether expressed in terms of European standards or the World Bank's political conditionalities). As Kapustin (2001) puts it, the paradigm of "transitology" has thus become "the second edition" of the modernization theories flawed with intellectual inconsistency and political inadequacy. With the accession of 10 former socialist countries into the European Union in 2004 and 2007,[3] some scholars "declared Eastern Europe to be fully 'transitioned,' socialism dead and gone, and liberal democracy a cure-all for the difficulties of global economic and political transformations" (Gilbert, Greenberg, Helms, & Jansen, 2008, p. 10). As a conceptual framework, post-socialism was thus officially relegated to the sidelines of comparative education (as well as other social science disciplines), while its frontiers came to be increasingly dominated by globalization debates.

This begs a set of serious questions for comparative education. Has the study of socialism and post-socialism finally exhausted itself? Or does it continue to hold value for comparative education? Are we better off switching attention to the study of globalization, which seems to be readily subsuming post-socialist processes within the established frameworks of modernity, or should we attempt to rediscover the complexity of over-lapping and often contradictory changes that are occurring in post-socialist contexts? Treating the term "post-socialist" not only as the geographic area of former socialist states but also as the broader post-socialist condition, this book argues that post-socialism is not dead. In fact, the chapters featured in this book highlight the prevailing relevancy of the concept two decades after the collapse of the socialist bloc. As Outhwaite and Ray (2005) explain, post-socialism "is not rendered redundant as a concept" simply because the socialist bloc collapsed and the former socialist nations have followed diverse paths of social development since 1989 (p. 23). Rather, post-socialist developments have become "among the most valuable resources available to social science" in a post-Cold War world (p. 2).

For the field of comparative education, the value of rediscovering post-socialism lies in the following promises. First, post-socialism provides a unique space to critically interrogate the nature of divergence and difference in the study of globalization in comparative education. As Stenning and Hörschelmann (2008) have argued, "a postsocialism which is ending, or must end, is a post-socialism of closures, fixated on the end of difference" (p. 329). Projecting the persistent diversity of post-socialism within globali-zation debates can thus yield fascinating insights into the complex processes of convergence and divergence, as well as entangled intersections of the "global" and "local." Second, post-socialism, as "part of a larger group of 'post' philosophies reflecting the uncertainties of our age" (Sakwa, 1999, p. 125), opens an opportunity for comparative education to accept Cowen's decade-old invitation to reengage in theorizing uncertainty as a conceptual category. The concept of uncertainty has a unique potential to free us from our persistent desire for predicting and controlling education reform trajectories and instead invites us to engage in challenging the evolutionary scheme of thought and questioning the established concepts of Western modernity. Rediscovering post-socialism in comparative education would thus allow us to "read our own contemporary and future worlds" (Cowen, 2000, p. 336) in new and unexpected ways.

THEORIZING POST-SOCIALISM IN THE AGE OF GLOBALIZATION

Since the collapse of the Soviet Union in 1991, the study of post-socialist transitions has often focused on reporting triumphant accounts about the monumental replacement of the Soviet system by Western political, economic, and social institutions, reflecting the principles of market economy, democratic pluralism, and human rights. Within a decade, policy rhetoric became remarkably similar across the region, signaling a move from socialist education policies to more Western-oriented ones. From the post-socialist countries of Central Europe to the post-Soviet republics of Central Asia, policymakers focused (at least in their rhetoric) on implementing "the post-education reform package," a set of policy reforms symbolizing the adoption of Western education values and including such "traveling policies" as student-centered learning, introduction of curriculum standards, decentralization of educational finance and governance, privatization of higher education, standardization of student assessment, liberalization of textbook publishing, and many others (Silova & Steiner-Khamsi, 2008).[4] In some cases, "the post-socialist education reform package" was imposed through the structural adjustment policies introduced by the World Bank and the Asian Development Bank. In other cases, however, it was voluntarily borrowed by policymakers in the former socialist state out of fear of "falling behind" internationally (Steiner-Khamsi & Stolpe, 2006, p. 189).

As Outhwaite and Ray (2005) observed, "everything was tossed up into the air" when the socialist bloc collapsed, but "it fell down again into relatively familiar [Western] structures and patterns" (pp. 23–24). With so much contextual diversity and difference across the post-socialist region (after all, new member states of the European Union such as the Czech Republic exist side by side with repressive autocracies such as Turkmenistan), why did education reform policies seem to have followed similar trajectories? Outhwaite and Ray (2005) further complicate the conversation by posing more questions to ponder about this particular phenomenon:

> How could futures which seemed so radically open, for better or worse, fall so quickly into familiar patterns? Were the apparent freedoms illusory, or just not exploited? Were the models adopted because they had proved themselves to be evolutionary or at least practically optimal, or just because they were familiar from the West and open to imitation? (p. 4)

Part of the explanation for the rapid adoption of these Western "standards" throughout the former bloc was undoubtedly the widespread perception that the whole telos of post-socialist transition was indeed a return to "Europe" and to "normality," with the EU accession processes accentuating the westernization trajectory. In fact, any deviation from the Western "norm" was immediately reflected in the emerging narratives of "crisis," "danger," and "decline," which widely circulated in the academic scholarship on political, economic, and social development in the former socialist region during the 1990s and 2000s (Silova, 2010). In fact, *Central Asian Survey* devoted an entire special issue of the journal to examining "the discourses of danger," pointing to the tendency of "the researchers, the development agencies, the experts" of Central Asia to socially construct the region as rife with conflict and danger (Thompson & Heathershaw, 2005, p. 1). Importantly, Shevchenko (2009) explains how the narratives of "crisis" became routinized in the post-socialist space by providing a framework for "forming alliances, building a sense of community, and maintaining moral boundaries" among post-socialist subjects (p. 174). These narratives have become at once "self-orientalizing" and normalizing, setting new frameworks for dealing with post-socialist change in both public and private spheres of post-socialist life (Shevchenko, 2009, p. 27).

What the emerging rhetoric of "crisis" has meant for education systems in the former socialist countries (and post-socialist scholarship more broadly) is that schools need to be normalized – redefined, recuperated, and re-formed – usually (but not exclusively) against the prevailing Western models (Silova, 2010). In this context, the West has been unproblematically presented as the embodiment of progress, providing "the normative affirmation of the Western modernity project" in academic terms (Blokker, 2005, p. 504). In comparative education, Perry's (2009) analysis of scholarly publications examining education change in the former socialist countries highlights the use of "normalizing" discourses, which construct conceptual dichotomies between education in the East and West. For example, these dichotomies portray "the West as tolerant, efficient, active, developed, organized, and democratic, and the East as intolerant, corrupt, passive, underdeveloped, chaotic, and undemocratic" (Perry, 2009, p. 177). More importantly, alternatives are presented through the familiar narratives of "progress," "hope," and "salvation," which the West is inevitably positioned to bring to the newly emerging societies of the post-socialist region. As Lindblad and Popkewitz (2004) explain, these modern narratives of "progress" and "salvation" invoke "social obligation to rescue those who have fallen outside the narratives of progress" (pp. xx–xxi). In other words, the promise of "salvation" for post-socialist schools and societies would be in abandoning the socialist past and embracing the logic of Western modernity.

Based on a linear and evolutionary conceptualization of social change (i.e., a direct movement from authoritarianism to "democracy"), most transition theory has "uncritically endorsed a revived modernization paradigm," promising a rapid convergence between the East and the West (Blokker, 2005, p. 2). In comparative education, one of the most visible embodiments of this convergence paradigm has been world culture theory.[5] Its main argument is that the rise of rationalized models of the nation-state and mass schooling in the 19th and 20th century has produced institutions that are increasingly more homogeneous across countries. These world models create "global scripts" or "templates" for national education arrangements, producing diffusion and standardization at an increasing rate (Meyer & Ramirez, 2000). Originally articulated in the 1970s, the world culture theory has experienced a rebirth after the collapse of the socialist bloc. Similar to Larry Diamond's claim that "the end of the Cold War and the collapse of communism discredited all models other than liberal democracy" (quoted in Friedman, 2000, p. 145), world culture theorists were now able to treat post-socialism as yet another case (and perhaps the most powerful one) to prove the inevitability of global convergence based on Western norms of rationality.

What the preceding discussion illustrates is that the post-socialist condition has indeed been incorporated into the existing frameworks of convergence theories. The persistent announcements of convergence reflect the way in which scholars in various disciplines (from political science to sociology) have tended to conceptualize social change, treating "non-Western societies as residual" and portraying "Western societies as the seat of historical change and the apex of social development" (Outhwaite & Ray, 2005, p. 201). In comparative education, the West (particularly the United States) has been proudly announced as "a forerunner in global institutional trends," setting new global standards of education quality and achievement (Baker & LeTendre, 2005, p. 17). With its persistent focus on specific types of global standards and norms (predominantly Western in origin and neoliberal in nature), world culture theory has inadvertently assumed a normative stance by offering a very particular "reading" of the world – a world governed by standardization, rationalization, scientization, and uniformity (Silova & Brehm, 2010); a world displaying "astonishing levels of sameness, and a considerable tendency to conformity" (Meyer, Drori, & Hwang, 2006, p. 49). Similar to modernization theories, its theoretical foundations have come to "valorize the institutional structure of the West while paying little attention to the costs of modernization" (Outhwaite & Ray, 2005, p. 94).

However, benchmarking post-socialism against Western norms is problematic on several levels. Such a perspective reduces difference to "relative backwardness" and diminishes geographic diversity to "a lagging temporality" (Stenning & Hörschelmann, 2008, pp. 320–321). Often critiqued for its inclination to overemphasize global convergence by focusing on dominant models (Finnemore, 1996), world culture theory (and globalization theories more broadly) tends to gloss over the cases of divergence and erase the instances of difference, while managing and controlling uncertainty. Within this framework, the post-socialist region is once again portrayed to be "on a journey somewhere":

> The transition recalls the earlier historical positioning of the region as "in between" east and west, a notion which not only redeploys the teleological construction of progress from east to west but also embeds the teleology (spatial and temporal) itself, focusing attention once again on the future and the west (then and there) rather than on the here and now of post-socialist Europe. In all of these ways, the diversity, depth and scale of the region's particular histories and geographies are erased as they become (just like) the west. (Stenning & Hörschelmann, 2008, p. 321)

Locating Divergence and Difference in Post-Socialism

Notwithstanding the claims of global convergence, post-socialism remains a space for increasing divergence and difference, where complex interactions between the global and the local persistently undermine all linear predictions. As Outhwaite and Ray (2005) argue, and as the chapters assembled in this book illustrate from different theoretical angles and geographical locations, the post-socialist world embodies "a paradox of homogeneity and difference" – "homogeneity, in that for the first time in history capitalism reaches across virtually the whole planet, yet difference in that its instantiation varies according to local circumstances and adaptations to the exigencies of postcommunism" (p. 201). In comparative education, scholars have approached the examination of this paradox from different theoretical perspectives. For example, numerous studies in educational anthropology and educational borrowing have demonstrated "loose coupling" (or divergence) between global norms and local meanings, ultimately questioning the universality of the world culture itself (e.g., see edited volumes by Anderson-Levitt, 2003; Steiner-Khamsi, 2004). Socio-historical conceptualizations of the global/local nexus (Schriewer, 2003) highlight on the one hand "the simultaneity of contrary currents," including the increasing world-level interconnection of communication in one single world-society, and the ongoing persistence of "culture-specific" adoptions, interpretations, and reformulations of world-level forces, on the other (p. 273).

From these historically and sociopolitically contextualized spaces, post-socialism appears to be both highly diverging and diverse, constituting "a complex and contradictory world of heightened uncertainty" (Outhwaite & Ray, 2005, p. 201). It points to the presence of "supplementary meanings," (Schriewer & Martinez, 2004, p. 32) "tensions between commonalities and differences," (Mitter, 2003, p. 79) and "educational mutations" (Karpov & Lisovskaya, 2001, p. 11). Indeed, when comparative research gives serious consideration to the uniqueness of the historical, political, social, and cultural contexts and carefully discerns the multiple (often overlapping) reform trajectories, post-socialist transformations assume characteristics of complex, dynamic processes, which inevitably result in multiple and often unpredictable outcomes (Silova, 2009b). To acknowledge the divergence and diversity of the post-socialist condition, Verdery (1996) proposes to use the framework of *transformation* (as opposed to the linearity of transitology) to describe a variety of post-socialist processes and outcomes (p. 16), while others explain the value of recognizing the multiplicity of "post-socialisms" as an equally meaningful conceptual category (Stenning & Hörschelmann, 2008, p. 326; Hann, Humphrey, & Verdery, 2002, p. 13).

In other words, when we take divergence and diversity as a starting point of comparative analysis (leaving convergence theories behind), westernization frameworks lose their explanatory power, failing to recognize sufficiently the essential ambiguity of post-socialist change. In this context, post-socialism becomes an intellectual space from which we can confidently challenge the established frameworks of Western modernity by critically interrogating "the nature of divergence and difference in the ubiquitous geographies of globalization, neoliberalism, and westernization" (Stenning & Hörschelmann, 2008, p. 314). It is from this conceptual space that the authors in this book attempt to grapple with the complexity of simultaneous transformation patterns of post-socialism – what Dürrschmidt and Taylor (2007, p. 168) called "a translusion" – including openness and closure, engagement and nonengagement, presence and absence, past and future, as well as here and there in complex configurations of social, political, and cultural practices.

Embracing the Uncertainty of Post-Socialism

By contesting a common expectation that post-socialist societies would inevitably converge toward Western norms, this book sees post-socialism as open, plural, and inevitably uncertain. Unlike early (positivist) accounts of post-socialist transitions, most studies in this book engage in "theoretical and conceptual complexification" (Dürrschmidt & Taylor, 2007, p. 159) of post-socialist transformation processes in order to grasp the nonlinear and often contradictory character of new educational configurations. Whether examining education policy rationalities in Ukraine, decentralization reforms in Romania, conceptualizations of "community" in Hungarian kindergartens, or changing narratives of history textbooks in Poland, most of the authors in the book lean on postmodern and post-structuralist frameworks of analysis to understand educational change. After all (and despite the criticisms of postmodernism as a theoretical model or historical thesis), it is not surprising that postmodern theory has resonated so widely in "a region where it often seems that almost everything has become shifting and uncertain" (Outhwaite & Ray, 2005, p. 11).

Postmodernism's appeal to the study of post-socialism lies in its distrust in metanarratives of any kind and an understanding – in fact, an expectation – that "a clean break with the past and an absolutely fresh beginning" is simply impossible (Jay, 2003, p. xvii). The theme of ruptures and continuities weaves throughout this volume highlighting the uncertainty and unpredictability of post-socialist transformations in contexts as diverse as Albania, China, Russia, Cuba, and Lithuania. It joins the discussion of *Uncertain Transition*, which Burawoy and Verdery (1999) initiated a decade ago when they examined how legacies of the past undergo novel and unexpected transformations as they move into the future. The chapters featured in this book reveal that post-socialist transformations have not become less uncertain two decades after the socialism collapsed. What they collectively emphasize is that the post-socialist space has become even more complex and the post-socialist processes remain ever so more incomplete, open-ended, and unpredictable. In a way, these post-socialist accounts echo Bakhtin's (1984) reflections about the impossibility of completing history:

> Nothing conclusive has yet taken place in the world, the ultimate word of the world and about the world has not yet been spoken, the world is open and free, everything is still in the future and will always be in the future. (p. 166)

The recognition of this state of incompleteness and uncertainty is a key to understanding the post-socialist condition. Instead of writing the clarity-seeking and closure-bound stories of success and failure of post-socialist transitions, the chapters in this book break away from modernism by providing interpretive understandings of "deviating cases" (Blokker, 2005, p. 519). They also engage in a critical revisiting of the metanarratives of globalization, while highlighting the role of agency in the reconfiguration of new educational spaces. By embracing the notion of uncertainty, they "challenge the tendency to collapse the post-socialist difference in universal(ising) accounts of change" and instead engage post-socialist pluralities to rethink categories and concepts of the global (Stenning & Hörschelmann, 2008, p. 330). As Stenning and Hörschelmann (2008) explain, such emphasis on pluralities is "hugely enabling, creating spaces for theorisations which are open, full of potential and marked more by beginnings than the endings so commonly associated with post-socialism" (p. 330).

(RE)READING THE GLOBAL

Each of the authors featured in this book joins the discussion of globalization and post-socialism from different geographical backgrounds, theoretical lenses, and methodological techniques. Yet, all authors share some commonalities as they attempt to complicate (rather than simplify) the post-socialist condition. Intimately familiar with the cultural, political, and historical contexts of the countries they are studying, the authors in this book offer nuanced interpretations of post-socialism's role in reorganizing populations and politics in the context of globalization. Speaking from particular contexts of their countries – both from within the post-socialist region of Southeast/Central Europe (Albania, Estonia, Hungary, Lithuania, Moldova, Poland, Romania, Russia, Ukraine) and outside (Cuba, Africa, the Caribbean, China, and Nicaragua) – they raise a series of questions that have rarely been asked before. What are the elements of continuities and discontinuities in various post-socialist settings and how do they interact in reshaping education policies and practices? What rationalities underpin the logic and define the purpose of education transformations in different post-socialist contexts? How do post-socialist policies function as political technologies to simultaneously promote and challenge the global norms? What are global norms actually understood, experienced, and interpreted in post-socialist contexts? And, more broadly, what insights do post-socialist analyses offer for our ongoing attempts to (re)read the global in comparative education?

Reflecting on this broad set of questions, the chapters in this book are organized into three parts. The book starts with an essay by Olga Bain who reviews scholarly discourses that have framed an understanding of post-socialist change and directed education reforms in the former socialist countries of Southeast/Central Europe and the Soviet Union. In her essay,

Education after the Fall of the Berlin Wall: The End of Histories or the Beginning of Histories?, Bain engages in discourse analysis to deconstruct how "educational change" has been framed in academic publications of post-socialist transformations during the last two decades. By utilizing the concept of *sensemaking* and using the lens of *translation,* she identified discourses that have entered academic scholarship from either outside the post-socialist region or outside the education area (e.g., such discourses as Revolution and Evolution, Transformation and Innovation, Crisis and Survival, etc.). Importantly, Bain also traces emerging scholarship that deconstructs framing of the same post-socialist educational phenomena by reflecting local and national searches for identity from within the post-socialist region. This is the first example (in what will become a series of similar accounts) of challenging the convergence paradigm by illustrating that the post-socialist scholarship today has come to display diversity, particularism, and multiplicity of voices. In Bain's words, the collapse of socialism in 1989 has in fact signified "the beginning of new histories." These new histories are examined in more detail in the following parts of the book, which focus on (1) examining new policy narratives, (2) redefining nations and identities, and (3) dealing more broadly with the implications of post-socialism globally.

Examining New Policy Narratives

While highlighting the diversity of themes and issues across different post-socialist contexts (Ukraine, Romania, Hungary, and Russia), the chapters in this part of the book are united by their attempt to understand the emergence of new education narratives across the region. What emerges from their analyses is the tensions of continuities and discontinuities, the modern and the postmodern, the Soviet and the European, the social and the economic in current policy debates across the region. These complex accounts of education reform efforts at various education system levels and geographical locations – the metamorphosis of policy rhetoric in Ukraine, reconceptualization of "community" through kindergarten curriculum reform in Hungary, as well as decentralization reforms in Romania and Russia – introduce doubt, highlight incoherencies, and ultimately unsettle the common sense embedded in official education narratives in post-socialist contexts.

In *Policy Why(s): Policy Rationalities and the Changing Logic of Educational Reform in Post-Communist Ukraine*, Olena Fimyar offers an alternative to mainstream policy studies analysis of educational policy by tracing the textual constructions of the models of individual, society, and the state as well as the definitions of education, upbringing, and educational governance in the Ukrainian context. Drawing on Foucault-inspired studies of education policy, she focuses her discussion of education policy in Ukraine around *policy rationalities* or *policy why(s),* including the rationalities of nation- and state-building, the rationalities of comparison and critique, and the rationalities of "catching-up" with Europe. Fimyar's analysis reveals tensions embodied in emerging hybrid rationalities of communism/neoliberalism – two distinct political projects that raise conflicts and incoherencies in both policy text and practice in Ukrainian education.

Zsuzsa Millei and Robert J. Imre continue the examination of post-socialist transformations through a Foucauldian genealogical analysis in their study, *Rethinking Transition Through Ideas of "Community" in Hungarian Kindergarten.* By analyzing the changing logic of the concept of "community" and "communitarianism" in three curriculum documents published during the socialist and post-socialist periods in Hungary, they find that the meaning of "post-socialist transition" needs to be radically redefined given its emergence well before the early 1990s and involving major reforms throughout the post-World War II period. Furthermore, Millei and Imre discuss whether the complex reconceptualizations of "community" and "communitarianism" could be directly linked to the transition of particular political ideologies – from socialism to neoliberal capitalism – or rather, whether they represent much smoother transitions to a new era after the fall of the Berlin Wall.

The theme of post-socialist complexities (as well as the one of unanticipated beginnings and ends) appears again in Monica Mincu and Irina Horga's chapter, *Visions of Reform in Post-Socialist Romania: Decentralization (Through Hybridization) and Teacher Autonomy.* The authors examine the meanings of decentralization in the context of post-socialist reforms in Romania. By drawing on an analysis of the contrasting perspectives expressed in policy documents and interviews with scholars, teachers, and school administrators, Mincu and Horga examine the circulation of decentralization reforms in what is generally considered to be a highly centralized country. They place Romanian education decentralization reforms in the larger context of the global trend toward marketization, which exists alongside Romanian political culture heralding the ideals of modernization and a "return to Europe." These contrasting discourses result in an intensification of bureaucracy (instead of local empowerment) and produce overlapping, and often contradictory, meanings among education stakeholders through complex hybridization processes.

The complex dynamics of the education decentralization processes is further discussed in the context of Russia's post-socialist transformation. In *A Framework for Understanding Dramatic Change: Educational Transformation in Post-Soviet Russia,* Eleoussa Polyzoi and Eduard Dneprov use Michael Fullan's education change framework to examine the initiation of education decentralization reforms in Russia during the 1990s. Drawing on interviews with 24 key respondents (including members of the Ministry of Education, teacher educators, university researchers, and members of advocacy organizations) and primary document analysis (including government, policy, and school documents), Polyzoi and Dneprov conclude that Russia's experience is more consistent with revolutionary rather than evolutionary transformation. Highlighting the rapidity of education change, the complexity of its political dynamics, as well as the constantly evolving nature of education reform vision, they propose a more nuanced account of the dramatic post-socialist change in Russia.

Redefining Nations and Identities

Recognizing the ambiguity and open-endedness of post-socialist transformation processes places the issue of social identities in a different light. This is exactly what the chapters assembled in this part of the book attempt to do by examining "the complex and shifting patterns of inclusion and exclusion" across a variety of post-socialist contexts (Dürrschmidt & Taylor, 2007, p. 108). By tracing the emergence of new forms of identities and the persistence of old ones, the authors examine contradictory responses to globalization and Europeanization forces, including mobilization around symbols of national, regional, and global identities. While the phenomena observed in each case may be different, as the chapters on Albania, Moldova, Lithuania, Poland, and Estonia vividly illustrate, the processes involved in redefining post-socialist nations and identities provide fascinating ground for comparative analysis.

In *The Semblance of Progress Amidst the Absence of Change: Educating for an Imagined Europe in Moldova and Albania,* Meg P. Gardinier and Elizabeth Anderson Worden examine how the promise of European Union (EU) integration has led to a reimagining of the purpose of schooling in Moldova and Albania. Once charged with producing loyal communist citizens, their schools and educational policies are now focused on producing democratic citizens of an expanded Europe. Drawing on case studies of civic education in Albania and Moldova, this chapter examines how educational discourses are reconstituting notions of national citizenship to fit within a broader pan-European identity. Gardinier and Worden argue that, despite the adoption of common European standards, the EU imaginary nonetheless produces divergent results in classrooms through the perpetuation of uneven power relations, the displacement of local needs, and the contradictory fusion of new principles and old practices. In these post-socialist contexts, the social imaginary is invoked to convey the semblance of progress amidst the absence of change.

In her chapter, *When Intolerance Means More Than Prejudice: Challenges to Lithuanian Education Reforms for Social Tolerance*, Christine Beresniova examines Lithuania's attempts to use education reform as a tool for imparting the democratic skills and worldviews necessary for EU accession. She finds that the internalization of new democratic norms proved to be more complicated than the unidirectional transmission expected by many elites, as students, parents, and politicians played a part in the way that educational reforms were understood, implemented, embodied, and even resisted. Although tolerance education was initially included in Lithuanian reforms with little fanfare, there has been an increasingly visible backlash against it, as it is increasingly viewed as an encroachment on the right of "Lithuanians" to strengthen their national identity after 60 years of Soviet occupation. By analyzing key educational policies in Lithuania, as well as international barometers for social tolerance, this study finds that the embrace of intolerance by many individuals and elites in Lithuania has inadvertently become a tool for challenging the EU attempts to define (and dictate) the values and norms of an independent nation-state.

In *Rewriting the Nation: World War II Narratives in Polish History Textbooks,* Magdalena Gross examines the processes of rewriting nationhood in educational narratives regarding the Second World War (WWII) in Poland. Using a mixed methods research design, she analyzes narrative change in state-approved history textbooks published between 1977 and 2008, thus covering the period of political transition from a communist to a democratic Poland. Her findings challenge the established trends in learning theory and international norms, which suggest that attention to diversity should have increased in history textbooks worldwide. In Poland, the analysis reveals the opposite trend – the global trends of diversity and tolerance have been subsumed by more persistent tropes of Polish cultural specificity. As the analysis of history textbooks throughout the 31-year sample suggests, WWII narratives continue to emphasize an ethnically homogeneous nation. In the post-socialist context, educating youth about WWII in Poland continues to be focused on reclaiming "Polishness" rather than on espousing global understandings and citizenship.

Shifting the discussion of identity formation toward "small" and widely dispersed nations, Kara D. Brown brings up the case of the Finno-Ugric identity, which was originally formulated by 19th century academics and nurtured as part of national identity movements and has been revived since the collapse of the Soviet Union in 1991. In *Transnational Vitality of the Finno-Ugric Identity in Estonia: The Role of Education and Advocacy in a New Geopolitical Context*, she explores how the Finno-Urgic identity has remained meaningful in the post-socialist context. Drawing on Schiffman's (2006) "linguistic culture" framework to understand the renewed relevance of the Finno-Ugric identity, Brown argues that the identity's continuing significance and renewed vitality stem from the new meanings that Finno-Ugric culture has taken on in the particular post-Soviet geo-political context. By focusing on Estonia's experiences, she provides fascinating insights into how Finno-Ugric linguistic culture functions to balance different priorities such as acting as a rich resource in developing Estonian national identity, in making statements of ethnic solidarity, and in providing new methods for language revitalization.

Global Implications of Post-Socialist Transformations

While the majority of the chapters in this book have focused on examining the dynamics of post-socialism in the countries of Southeast/Central Europe and the former the Soviet Union, the effects of the Cold War were clearly not confined to one geographical area. In fact, Hann et al. (2002) have argued that it is time "to liberate the cold war from the ghetto of Soviet area studies" (p. 20). The chapters in this part of the book extend the post-socialist analysis beyond the post-socialist education space of Southeast/Central Europe by discussing the impact and implications of post-socialism in places as diverse as China, Africa, Cuba, Nicaragua, and the Caribbean. Joining the conversation initiated earlier in the book, the authors continue the discussion of themes, which by now have become recurrent in this volume – those of the emerging contradictions between the global and the local, the persistent divergence and diversity, as well as ongoing ambiguity and complexity of post-socialism as experienced in more distant geographical locations. In many ways, these analyses imply that the conceptual category of post-socialism is becoming meaningful in a much broader geographical, historical, and epistemological sense. Perhaps, "we are all postcommunist now" (Sakwa, 1999, p. 713; Outhwaite & Ray, 2005, p. 24).

We begin our discussion of the global implications of post-socialism in China. In *The Reconfiguration of State–University–Student Relationships in Post/Socialist China,* Heidi Ross, Ran Zhang, and Wanxia Zhao examine the changing state–university–student relationship in China since the late 1980s. The discussion begins by an examination of interrelated educational trends that affect the state–university–student relationship in China, including globalization, "massification," and stratification of higher education; the redefined role of the state in university governance and management; higher education marketization and privatization; and the quest for meaning and equity in and through higher education. The main argument is that post-socialist transformations have brought complex reconfigurations of state–university–student relationships. During the "socialist" period, when universities had no independence from the state, the main relationship central to higher education learning was between the state and students. In the "postsocialist" period, the university–student relationship has become more significant. From the point of view of the state, the authors observe "appropriation and implementation of regulations shaping student rights and services are in partial contradiction with state policies to accelerate economic growth and bolster party authority." From the point of view of universities, they see "institutions grappling with how to deliver on forward looking structures and actions while navigating between the state's policy mandates and growing expectations and demands of its student and business stakeholders." From the point of view of students, they discuss "how constrained agency, uncertainty, and the power of the credential motivates social praxis." What is common to the relationship at these levels is the engagement of actors in "pragmatic improvisation," which, according to the authors, has become one of the salient features of post/socialism.

Moving on to Latin America, Anita Sanyal explores the case of post-socialist education transformations in Nicaragua. In *Socialist, Post-Socialist, and* Post-*Post-Socialist Transformations of Education in Nicaragua*, the analysis focuses on important political periods in the last 30 years by examining how reforms have been shaped by a complex interplay of international, national, and local political economic factors. Drawing on qualitative policy analysis and interviews with various groups of education stakeholders, Sanyal's findings highlight three specific dynamics of reforms. These dynamics highlight the complex nature of the reform processes, including the Nicaraguan government's relationship with and the role of international donor organizations, differing notions of "local participation" that signify the shifting role of civil society, as well as continuities and discontinuities of policy agents and process. While less commonly known to have been a full participant in the Cold War, Nicaragua's conflict with the United States during the 1980s was underlain by a socialist-capitalist struggle. Nicaragua's case thus presents an interesting example of socialism and post-socialism in the context of Latin America. It is also significant because of its current situation of having reelected the same government that was in power during the socialist period, thus reflecting a recent reemergence of the mix of capitalist and socialist elements in education.

In *Staying the (Post)Socialist Course: Global/Local Transformations and Cuban Education,* Noah W. Sobe and Renee N. Timberlake shift our attention to Cuba using a theory-driven synthesis of current scholarship on post-socialist educational transformation. Following the collapse of the Soviet Union in 1991, the Cuban economy came to a standstill in a matter of days as it lost Soviet financial subsidies and fuel imports. While the Castro regime has remained in power since, a significant feature of the post-socialist transformations has been the opening up of Cuba to tourism and the creation of what is referred to as a "dual economy." All of these changes have had a significant impact on nearly every sphere of life, including the country's education system, where, for example, the government has had to create an "emerging teachers program," a provisional teacher certification program, in order to compensate for the exodus of experienced teachers to the higher paying jobs in the tourism sector. Cuba's unique position vis-à-vis neoliberal and state socialist modes of governance challenges the claims that there are any predetermined "paths" of post-socialist political and economic transition. Furthermore, Sobe and Timberlake suggest it would be more meaningful to focus our analysis on the particular intersections and trajectories of both "local" and "global" transformations in understanding the specific of post-socialist, as well as in any other political, cultural, and social settings.

In *African Socialism, Post-Colonial Development, and Education: Continuity and Change in Post-Socialist Era,* Diane Brook Napier provides an overview of African socialism as an outgrowth of the wider ideological movement, linked to independence movements and postcolonial development in certain African countries (especially Tanzania, Zambia, and Zimbabwe). Drawing on critical review of the theoretical and empirical literature on African socialism, she discusses the role of the state in education transformations, revealing the failed promises of African socialism and global capitalism, and highlighting elements of continuity within a complex suite of factors that influenced postcolonial development in education and other sectors. This chapter offers important insights into the difficulties of implementing socialist and capitalist development policies in African countries in the context of global trends. Following a review of the contemporary debate over the prospects for socialism, capitalism, and democracy as vehicles for future postcolonial development in Africa, Brook Napier complicates the debate further by emphasizing the uncertainty of the optimal path for future development on the African continent.

While the African content continues to grapple with the complex relationship between socialism, capitalism, and democracy, the Caribbean seems to have taken advantage of the recent post-socialist reconfigurations by strategically repositioning itself in the new global order. In his chapter, *Beyond Post-Socialist Conversions: Functional Cooperation and Trans-Regional Regimes in the Global South,* Tavis D. Jules engages with the theoretical frameworks of neoinstitutionalism, regime theory, and lesson-drawing to understanding how post-socialist transformations created preconditions for deeper regionalization within the Global South at a time when the socialist bloc disintegrated in Southeast/Central Europe and the former Soviet Union. In the Caribbean context, post-socialist transforma-tions have thus triggered regional (rather than global) convergence, thus giving the Caribbean Community (CARICOM) a political advantage in negotiating the global and the local. Drawing on discourse analysis of policy documents published during the period of 1990–1996, Jules explains how national and regional ideologies aided educational reform among the CARICOM countries by providing a historical background to understand the impetus for education reform, and explaining the concept of lesson-drawing (as one of the policy mechanisms) used to facilitate the implementation of these reforms.

THE FUTURES OF POST-SOCIALISM: WHAT IS "NOT YET"

Sooner or later, when the generations brought up under socialist regimes disappear from the political scene, the category of postsocialism is likely to break apart and disappear ... many young people across a wide swathe of the region are already beginning to reject the term, which can be seen as a constricting, even insulting label, something imposed from outside that seems to imply constraints on the freedom of people in these countries to determine their own futures ... will post-socialism wither? (Hann et al., 2002, pp. 13, 15)

As we begin to ponder this important (rhetorical) question – *"Will post-socialism wither?"* – let us return to one of the issues raised in the introductory part of this essay, that is the question about the broader value of post-socialism to social theory. Speaking from diverse geographic areas, methodological perspectives, and subject matters, the chapters assembled in this book provide at least one collective conclusion: post-socialism is not dead. As a conceptual category, it is not likely to wither any time soon. In fact, the disappearance of post-socialism from social theorizing today would mark the end of divergence, difference, and uncertainty. Just as we cannot abandon the study of postcolonialism given the persistence of "the colonial presence" today (Gregory, 2004), dismissing post-socialism as a redundant conceptual category would be untimely for comparative education and social science more broadly. Post-socialism (just as other postmovements embracing the challenge of the uncertainty) provides a unique space from which we can challenge the metanarratives of globalization and interrupt their "clarity- and closure-seeking tendencies" (MacLure, 2006, p. 730). It is a space from which we can further complicate (not clarify) our under-standing of ongoing reconfigurations of educational spaces in a global context. And, as Stenning and Hörschelmann (2008, p. 318) suggest, and the chapters in this book collectively echo, post-socialism is "a challenge or an agenda for future debate" – whether theoretical or methodological – about global processes and their multiple effects on societies today, in the past, and in the future.

The questions raised by the study of post-socialism have important implications for comparative education. In addition to providing important comparative accounts of issues specific to post-socialist societies, it opens opportunities for us to engage in theorizing about globalization and its effects on education in refreshingly new ways. With its emphasis on contradictions and complexities, post-socialism suggests a (re)reading of the global through the lens of pluralities, discontinuities, and uncertainties. It proposes a (re)reading of the global that is free of its predetermined finality. Thus, post-socialism is not the study of already formed (neoliberal) policies and practices, but rather of a complex set of education phenomena in the early stages of its formation, when its fate "still belongs to the future, or rather, to one possible future" (Epstein, 1995, p. 331). We thus avoid focusing on, what Bakhtin (1986, p. 139) noted with regret as, the "ready-made and finalized," and rather examine what is constantly influx and shifting toward an open future. As Epstein (1995) articulated, "the 'not-yet' contains many possibilities absent in the 'already'" (p. 334). From this epistemological standpoint, comparative education has the potential to become more critically engaged and open to new theoretical and methodological possibilities.

Finally, returning to the question about the future of post-socialism itself, I would allow myself to disagree with viewing post-socialism as "a constricting label" that "seems to imply constraints on the freedom of people in these countries to determine their own futures" (Hann et al., 2002, p. 13). As the analyses presented in this book so convincingly illustrate, the post-socialist condition is in itself the embodiment of openness. It is an intellectual space, which permits us to "escape from incorporating into the future one of the key concepts which it [comparative education] took for granted in its past – the concept of equilibrium and equilibrium theorising" (Cowen, 2000, p. 339). In a way, post-socialism becomes the search for our new epistemological freedom(s). In a world trapped within modernity's rationalities, "to be postsocialist ... is not yet to be free. The mandate ... to protect against that condition of unfreedom has not yet expired" (Jay, 2003, p. xviii). This book therefore invites scholars to explore post-socialism (with all its contradictions and complexities) in hopes of discovering what is "not yet."

NOTES

1. Announced in 1958, the National Defense Education Act (NDEA) promoted the study of languages and regions deemed critical to U.S. national security during the Cold War. For more information on the role of comparative education during the Cold War, see the double issue of *European Education*, "Post Cold War Studies in Comparative and International Education," guest-edited by Steiner-Khamsi and deJong-Lambert (2006).

2. Historically, comparative education emerged as a field predominantly focused on the study of educational systems in Western Europe. Ironically, comparative education began to lose its European-centric focus during the 1960s as the research agenda shifted toward the study of education in the Soviet Union and the nonaligned countries in the context of the Cold War.

3. In 2004, eight former socialist countries joined the European Union (EU), including the Czech Republic, Estonia, Hungary, Latvia, Lithuania, Poland, Slovakia, and Slovenia. In 2007, Bulgaria and Romania joined the EU.

4. The features of "the post-socialist education reform package" are unique in that they combine (1) elements common to any low-income, developing country that implements the structural adjustment programs (SAPs) recommended by the international financial institutions (e.g., decentralization and privatization), (2) education reform aspects specific to the entire former socialist region (e.g., market-driven textbook provision, increased educational choice, standardized assessment systems), and (3) country- or region-specific components (e.g., conflict resolution in

the former Yugoslavia and gender equity reforms in Central Asia). Although the features of this "post-socialist education reform package" vary from place to place, they do exist (at least discursively) in most countries of the region (Silova & Steiner-Khamsi, 2008, pp. 19–22).

5. World culture theory originated in sociological institutionalism. Noticing an acute break with previous branches of institutionalism (the catchall term to capture all analyses that did not solely focus on the individual), John Meyer and other sociologists began classifying the theory "neo-institutionalism" to emphasize the break with the "old" institutionalists. In comparative education, neoinstitutionalism, world culture theory, and world society theory are often used interchangeably to describe the emergence of world culture and its lasting impact on education. For the purposes of this chapter, I will use the term "world culture theory" consistently throughout.

REFERENCES

Anderson-Levitt, K. M. (2003). *Local meanings, global schooling: Anthropology and world culture theory*. New York, NY: Palgrave Macmillan.

Baker, D. P., & LeTendre, G. K. (2005). *National differences, global similarities: World culture and the future of schooling*. Stanford, CA: Stanford University Press.

Bakhtin, M. M. (1984). *Problems of Dostoevsky's poetics*. (C. Emerson, Ed. & Trans.). Minneapolis, MN: University of Minnesota Press.

Bakhtin, M. M. (1986). *Speech genres and other late essays*. (V. W. McGee, Trans.) and (C. Emerson & M. Holquist, Eds.). Austin, TX: University of Texas Press.

Bereday, G., & Pennar, J. (1960). *The politics of Soviet education*. New York, NY: Praeger.

Bereday, G. Z. F., Brickman, W. W., & Read, G. H. (Eds). (1960). *The changing Soviet school*. Cambridge: The Riverside Press.

Blokker, P. (2005). Post-communist modernization, transition studies, and diversity in Europe. *European Journal of Social Theory, 8*(4), 503–525.

Brickman, W. W. (1961). The objectivity of a Soviet pedagogue. *Comparative Education Review, 5*(1), 72.

Burawoy, M., & Verdery, K. (1999). *Uncertain transition: Ethnographies of change in the postsocialist world*. New York, NY: Rowman and Littlefield Publishers.

Cowen, R. (2000). Comparing futures or comparing pasts? *Comparative Education, 36*(3), 333–342.

Dürrschmidt, J., & Taylor, G. (2007). *Globalization, modernity and social change: Hotspots of transition*. New York, NY: Palgrave MacMillan.

Epstein, M. (1995). *After the future. The paradoxes of postmodernism and contemporary Russian culture*. (Introduction by Anesa Miller-Pogacar, Trans.). Amherst, MA: Massachusetts University Press.

Finnemore, M. (1996). Norms, cultures, and world politics: Insights from sociology's institutionalism. *International Organization, 47*(4), 567–597.

Friedman, T. L. (2000). *The lexus and the olive tree: Understanding globalization*. New York, NY: Farrar, Straus, and Giroux.

Gilbert, A., Greenberg, J., Helms, E., & Jansen, S. (2008). Reconsidering postsocialism from the margins of Europe: Hope, time and normalcy in post-Yugoslav societies. *Anthropology News*, November, pp. 10–11.

Gregory, D. (2004). *The colonial present.* Oxford, UK: Blackwell.

Hann, C. M., Humphrey, C., & Verdery, K. (2002). Introduction: Postsocialism as a topic of anthropological investigation. In: C. M. Hann (Ed.), *Postsocialism: Ideals, ideologies and practices in Eurasia* (pp. 1–11). London: Routledge.

Jay, M. (2003). Foreword. In: A. Erjavec (Ed.), *Postmodernism and the postsocialist condition: Politicized art under late socialism* (pp. xv–xix). Berkley, CA: University of California Press.

Kapustin, B. (2001). The end of 'transitology'? *POLIS: The Journal of Political Studies, 4*, 6–26.

Karpov, V., & Lisovskaya, E. (2001). Reforms and mutations in Russian schooling: Implications for theory of educational transitions. Paper presented at the 45th Annual Conference of Comparative and International Education Society, Washington, DC, March 14–17.

Lindblad, S., & Popkewitz, T. S. (2004). *Educational restructuring: International perspectives on traveling policies.* Greenwich, CT: Information Age Publishing.

MacLure, M. (2006). The bone in the throat: Some uncertain thoughts on baroque method. *International Journal of Qualitative Studies in Education, 19*(6), 729–745.

Malkova, Z. (1961). An open letter to America: Be objectives, colleagues!. *Comparative Education Review, 5*(1), 69–72.

Meyer, J. W., Drori, G. S., & Hwang, H. (2006). World society and the proliferation of formal organization. In: G. S. Drori, J. W. Meyer & H. Hwang (Eds), *Globalization and organization: World society and organizational change* (pp. 25–49). Oxford: Oxford University Press.

Meyer, J. W., & Ramirez, F. O. (2000). The world institutionalization of education. In: J. Schriewer (Ed.), *Discourse formation in comparative education* (pp. 111–132). Frankfurt: Peter Lang Publishers.

Mitter, W. (2003). A decade of transformation: Education policies in Central and Eastern Europe. In: M. Bray (Ed.), *Comparative education: Continuing traditions, new challenges, and new paradigms.* London, UK: Kluwer Academic Publishers.

Noah, H. (2006). U.S. social and educational research during the cold war: An interview with Harold J. Noah by Gita Steiner-Khamsi. *European Education: Issues and Studies, 38*(3), 9–18.

Outhwaite, W., & Ray, W. (2005). *Social theory and postcommunism.* Oxford, UK: Blackwell Publishing.

Perry, L. (2009). American academics and education for democracy in post-communist Europe. In: N. Sobe (Ed.), *American post-conflict educational reform: From the Spanish war to Iraq* (pp. 169–188). New York, NY: Palgrave Macmillan.

Sakwa, R. (1999). *Postcommunism.* Oxford: OUP.

Sanders, T. (1997). Cold War and the politics of comparative education: The case of divided Germany. Presented at the Annual Meeting of AERA, Chicago, IL, March 24–28, 1997.

Schiffman, H. (2006). Language policy and linguistic culture. In T. Ricento (Ed.), *An introduction to language policy: Theory and method* (pp. 111–125). Malden, MA: Blackwell.

Schriewer, J. (2003). Globalization and education: Process and discourse. *Policy Futures in Education, 1*(2), 271–283.

Schriewer, J., & Martinez, C. (2004). Constructions of internationality in education. In: G. Steiner-Khamsi (Ed.), *The global politics of educational borrowing and lending.* New York: TC Press.

Shevchenko, O. (2009). *Crisis and the everyday in postsocialist Moscow.* Bloomington, IN: Indiana University Press.

Silova, I. (2009a). The changing frontiers of comparative education: A forty-year retrospective on *European Education. European Education: Issues and Studies, 41*(1), 17–31.

Silova, I. (2009b). Varieties of educational transformation: The post-socialist states of Central/ Southeastern Europe and the former Soviet Union. In: R. Cowen & A. Kazamias (Eds), *International handbook of comparative education* (pp. 295–320). Netherlands: Springer Publishers.

Silova, I. (Ed.) (2010). *Globalization on the margins: Education and post-socialist transformations in Central Asia*. Greenwich, CT: Information Age Publishing.

Silova, I., & Brehm, W. C. (2010). Unveiling masked ideologies: Examining the world culture debate in comparative education. Presented at the 54th Annual Conference of the Comparative and International Education Society in Chicago, IL, March 1–5, 2010.

Silova, I., & Steiner-Khamsi, G. (Eds). (2008). *How NGOs react: Globalization and education reform in the Caucasus, Central Asia, and Mongolia*. Bloomfield, CT: Kumarian Press.

Steiner-Khamsi, G. (Ed.) (2004). *The global politics of educational borrowing and lending*. New York: Teachers College Press.

Steiner-Khamsi, G. (2006). The development turn in comparative education. *European Education: Issues and Studies, 38*(3), 19–47.

Steiner-Khamsi, G., & deJong-Lambert, W. (Eds). (2006). Special issue: Post-Cold War studies in education (Part I). *European Education: Issues and Studies, 38*(3), 1–94.

Steiner-Khamsi, G., & Stolpe, I. (2006). *Educational import in Mongolia: Local encounters with global forces*. New York: Palgrave Macmillan.

Stenning, A., & Hörschelmann, K. (2008). History, geography and difference in the post-socialist world: Or, do we still need post-socialism? *Antipode, 40*(2), 312–335.

Thompson, C. D., & Heathershaw, J. (2005). Introduction: Discourses of danger in Central Asia. *Central Asian Survey, 25*(1), 1–4.

Verdery, K. (1996). *What was socialism and what comes next?* Princeton, NJ: Princeton Academic Press.

Wilson, D. N. (1994). Comparative and international education: Fraternal or Siamese twins? A preliminary genealogy of our twin fields. *Comparative Education Review, 38*(4), 449–486.

PART I
EDUCATION AND POST-SOCIALIST TRANSFORMATIONS IN SOUTHEAST/CENTRAL EUROPE AND THE FORMER SOVIET UNION

EDUCATION AFTER THE FALL OF THE BERLIN WALL: THE END OF HISTORY OR THE BEGINNING OF HISTORIES?

Olga Bain

INTRODUCTION

The fall of the Berlin Wall in 1989 is a symbolic event signifying in the most tangible way the dismantling of the "iron curtain" that, after decades of separating the East from the West, ended the division between the "two worlds." The dissolution of the Soviet Union on the last day of 1991 and the domino effect of liberal revolutions in what was at that time Eastern Europe were less symbolic yet momentous as they set a great number of all new and old nations to make profound changes in their polity, economy, and entire societal fabrics. Both from the political-economic and educational points of view, the region has been often viewed as an enormous laboratory for testing best policies and remedies. With the hindsight of 20 years, how has our knowledge of the changes and reforms in post-socialist education evolved? What cognitive frames – produced by either outsiders or insiders – shaped the understanding of educational change and also directed this change? What and how did "one world" learn? In other words, did the end of the cold war and the fall of the Soviet Union bring an "end of history"

Post-Socialism is not Dead: (Re)Reading the Global in Comparative Education
International Perspectives on Education and Society, Volume 14, 27–57
Copyright © 2010 by Emerald Group Publishing Limited
All rights of reproduction in any form reserved
ISSN: 1479-3679/doi:10.1108/S1479-3679(2010)0000014005

(Fukuyama, 1992), or did it just mark the beginning of histories? This chapter argues that, contrary to Francis Fukuyama's early 1990s prediction that economic, political, and social institutions (including education) were converging into one monolithic world order, the "one world" has come today to display – for better or worse – a variety of models and ways of doing and understanding things, including in education. The metaphor of the "beginning of histories" in the plural highlights the diversity, particularism, multiple voices, and meanings that have become the hallmark of today.

THE FOCUS ON EDUCATIONAL CHANGE AND REFORM

The early accounts of the unfolding of educational change in post-socialist countries were understandably ambiguous and difficult to generalize at the macro level of national systems or the region as a whole, while the documented change at the micro level of the classroom and school continued to be accumulated. With more certainty, the discourse on educational change in the countries formerly under state socialism developed around an unprecedented scale, scope, and speed of change and reform (Glenn, 1995; Cerych, 1997). The initial educational reform agendas in the post-socialist countries were considerably destructive, focusing primarily on the negation and removal of past practices. One of the earliest and most comprehensive conceptualizations of educational reforms was developed in Russia in the 1980s with some of the major reform objectives articulated with the prefix de-: *deideologization, depolitization, destatization*, and *decentralization* (Dneprov, 1993a; Eklof, 1993; Webber, 2000). The constructive agenda of *diversification, differentiation, humanization*, and *humanitarization* was also a radical departure from Soviet schooling emphasizing systemic reform of education from the bottom up.

The educational reform agendas in the countries of Eastern Europe in the early 1990s were remarkably similar. Cezar Birzea provided a comparative record of reform principles and priorities in 16 countries of the region during this period (Birzea, 1994). While some of the principles addressed the legacies of the past and were rectifying in character, the others envisioned new qualities in education for individuals and their societies. The variations in reform agendas appeared to be prompted by the specific additional agendas of the transition, such as nation-state building and ethnic-linguistic nationalism, or by the political balance in countries at the time leaning toward liberalism, neo-conservatism, or neo-traditionalism (Birzea, 1994).

The depth and scope of the change in education was radical and profound, prompting researchers to utilize the ideas of cyclical social revolution of Pitirim Sorokin and others (Sorokin, 1967; Brinton, 1965). In this model, the initial radical stage of liberalization is followed by the conservative stage – reform backlash, populist or nationalist agenda – in educational reform implementation (Dneprov, 1996; Karpov & Lisovskaya, 2005; Birzea, 1994).

Although the study by Birzea (1994) does not include a chronology of the enacted educational laws or the time of completed reform memoranda, the time and timing proved to be of significant importance in the educational change of the post-socialist countries. A case in point is that, on the heels of gaining independence and the free election of Russia's first President Boris Yeltsin, the first Russian Presidential Act of 1991 was the Education Act providing encouragement to the reform-oriented teacher movement and capitalizing on this bottom-up support. Countries that were latecomers to educational change might have either calculated the probabilities for the success of the reforms undertaken in neighboring states or experienced the peer pressure to launch similar reforms. This point indicates that a significant amount of learning from each other occurred across the countries of the region, irrespective of the biases that obscured such mutual learning and transfer. One significant source of such biases is related to the power of social construction of Eastern Europe by the West and thus the neglect of indigenous traditions and cross-border learning in the region during the transition.

Given the variation in educational developments in the countries of the region, were discourses for educational change across countries and educational systems significantly different or similar? What were the sources of these differences and similarities? Did similarities occur within time periods and span national borders? How did time and space get manipulated by various frames for educational change? What notable discourses and cognitive frames for insiders and outsiders of the region served to reconstruct explanations of educational transformation and further channeled change in education in certain directions? These questions guided the present inquiry of identifying and analyzing the scholarly frames for educational transformation in the post-socialist region.

METHOD AND STRUCTURE OF THE STUDY

A synthesis study offers a rare opportunity to generalize research from a plentitude of viewpoints. This study limits its purpose to identifying the prominent discourses that framed understanding and explanation of post-socialist educational change at different points of time in the past two decades and that shaped the directions of further reforms: What were the origins of these discourses and their relationship to the theoretical perspectives and assumptions regarding the large-scale social transformation in the region? What influence on the discourse formation did the insider/outsider categories of authorship have? And how did the relationship of observers toward the observed shape the discourses?

This approach draws on methods of discourse analysis and utilizes the concept of *sensemaking* and the lens of *translation* to deconstruct how educational change was perceived, framed, and made sense of at different points in the past two decades by insiders and outsiders of local contexts.

The concept of *sensemaking* (Weick, 1988, 1995) is particularly useful for this analysis as it helps to represent a process of cognitive framing of the educational change that is complex and ambiguous in its detail. Sensemaking is ongoing as the change unfolds. It is retrospective since it is grounded in the present cognitive mechanisms to explain the past, to predict the future, and to shape the expectations for the future. It involves identity construction and reconstruction. It is both belief-driven and action-driven as it shapes arguments and expectations and forms the basis for commitments or manipulation (Weick, 1995). Through sensemaking, the unknown situations are structured, labeled, and framed in certain ways, producing discourses and texts that do not only explain the current environment but also drive future actions. Such discourses become influential in directing the change itself.

The model of translation helps to look at sensemaking practice and discourse construction from another perspective. This model highlights the role of human agencies as negotiators of practice according to their own projects. It also probes the complex relationship between human practice and cognitive frames, labels, and texts. Proposed by Bruno Latour, the model of translation replaces the positivist causal model of diffusion in social practice, such as, for example, exerting power not because of having it but because of other agents' behavior through their own reconstruction of the practice (Latour, 1986). If the diffusion model assumes a norm in the linearly causal diffusion and interprets deviations from the causality model as some kind of inertia interfering with diffusion, the translational model focuses on the multiplicity of practice translations as a norm and explains the seemingly direct causality as an atypical confluence. One application of this model is to look at the educational change process through the lens of translation: How and why do reforms lead to unintentional results? If the reform targets students, their families, teachers, professors, and administrators as free agents, does it inevitably lead to multiple innovations? How do educational practices travel across borders: Has what is to be adopted already been adapted to the needs of the borrower before the borrowing is consummated? That is, to paraphrase, is the borrowing in the eye of the borrower? Do people find what they search for and do they search for what they find? Another application of the model is literally a translation of labels of educational practices from one language to another, and more generally from the languages of the former two worlds into a new common language.

The studies synthesized in this analysis were selected using the academic database Academic Search Premier-EBSCO and include those written over the past 20 years that focused on education in the region and that articulated an explicit discourse construction or theoretical perspective for framing the observed educational change. These studies include journal articles, books and book chapters, and additionally some often cited reports (such as those by the World Bank and the Organization for Economic Cooperation and Development). The selection was restricted to those in the English language – in part because of feasibility issues, in part because English became a new medium of communication for the region through which the region explained itself to the world and was explored from outside.

The analysis of discourses of educational change in the region that follows is split into two sections. The first identifies several frames for educational change that challenged preexisting theoretical perspectives. Most of these perspectives were originally developed outside either the realm of education – in economics, political science, and sociology – or outside the region itself, and were extended to extrapolate explanations for post-socialist educational change. Many of these scholarly perspectives are explicitly or implicitly prescriptive. Many tend to assume that there is one Western educational model that needs to be replicated in the countries formerly under state socialism, and that there is only one way of implementing this model.

The second part highlights what has been called emerging approaches to educational change. These approaches add significant nuances to the scholarship by redirecting the lens of inquiry from the object of study to the subject of study: How is the observed framed by the observer and with what effects on knowledge construction? What is seen by the observer as similar or different to other educational contexts, and why? How are articulations of educational situations constructed and then translated in different contexts? This shift of the focus to the social construction of meanings and their translation back into practices has the promise to further refine theories of educational change as applied to the post-socialist region. It also explicates identity and status-related relationships that may otherwise blind theoretical conceptions. These approaches directly explicate how distinctive meanings are constructed by local actors.

PAST PERSPECTIVES ON EDUCATIONAL CHANGE

The most powerful discourse for change in the region has been the discourse of transition. It originated as the Western technical assistance discourse of simultaneous economic and political transformation. It was reappropriated in the popular discourse with some additional connotations of the evolutionary, transient state of rebuilding the norm (Krzyzanowski & Wodak, 2009). It was conceptualized as an academic discourse, some of the most salient features and dilemmas of which are highlighted below. Several discourses for educational change originated from the transition studies.

Transition Studies and Processes: From Plan to Market

The countries of the former Eastern Bloc were quickly named countries in transition (World Bank, 1996) – transition from centrally planned economies to market economies and from fused party–state regimes to liberal pluralistic democracies. Transition or transitology studies originally focused on the development of market economies and liberal democracies in the societies of Southern Europe after World War II and of Latin America later (Przeworski, 1995). The twin goals of marketization and democratiza-tion in Eastern Europe in the early 1990s immediately became the focus of the established transitologists (Przeworski, 1995). The important difference was that these new transition countries had already undergone thorough modernization, had established high levels of industrialization and urbanization, and had educated their citizens (Hoen, 2004). Interestingly, it was the simultaneous economic and political reforms launched by Mikhail Gorbachev's *perestroika* and *glasnost* in 1985 that were credited with bringing the system of state socialism in the entire former Eastern Bloc to a collapse, unleashing the events in Eastern Europe and the former Soviet Union in one single snowball (Przeworski, 1995). For neither the earlier political reforms or revolutions (such as Khruschev's "thaw" in the USSR in 1953–1964, Gomulka's "thaw" in Poland in 1956, the Hungarian political revolution in 1956, and Czechoslovakia's 1968 attempt at political reform under Dubcek) nor economic reforms (such as in Hungary's "gouliash socialism" and in Poland of the 1980s) could undermine the reigning regime on their own (Hoen, 2004). This time the simultaneous economic and political reforms launched by *perestroika* and *glasnost* fostered the construction of a new political and economic order.

The academic debate in transitology studies in the 1990s centered on the speed and sequence of reforms. In terms of speed, the "shock therapy" reforms were contrasted with the gradualist approach. In terms of sequence, Eastern Europe and the Newly Independent States of the former Soviet Union were compared with the reforms in China. While in China, liberal economic reforms preceded moderate political adjustments and led to unprecedented economic growth, "the shock" of rapid economic liberalization following the radical change of political regimes in Eastern Europe and the Newly Independent States led to a deeper economic and societal crisis and a much more complicated economic recovery. The World Bank (1996) summarized this reform dilemma with regard to Eastern Europe and the Newly Independent States as "putting the cart in front of the horse." While academic debate on the speed and sequence of reforms followed the actual events rather than anticipated them, in reality technical assistance of the West to the East focused on a swift and radical "shock therapy"-style prescriptive package of economic reforms through privatization, liberalization, and stabilization. The accompanying metaphors referred to the Western "doctor" prescribing the Eastern "patient" to "take a bitter pill," to "take the strong medicine as the only cure," or to choose not to "pull slowly and faintly on a diseased tooth" as that would only "prolong the pain and agony" (as quoted in Wedel, 1998, pp. 21, 84). The expectation was that, as a result of implementing the "blueprint" of reforms, the market economies would emerge naturally and immediately and would lead to economic growth in the region (Blanchard, Dornbusch, Krugman, Layard, & Summers, 1992; Blanchard, Froot, & Sachs, 1994).

Post-Socialist Studies: Institutionalism and "Capitalisms"

The focus on institutional change in transitional post-socialist economies emerged as a response to the undue disregard of the historical legacies and institutional factors in the transitions – understood as both *normative*, as in the set of formal and informal rules and compliance procedures that guided calculative orientations, and *discursive*, as in the cognitive meaning frames that guided appropriate behavior (Campbell & Pedersen, 1996).

Such an analysis insisted on the evolutionary nature of the revolutionary and transformative process of transition – primarily because of the ongoing institutional change, which however was not assumed to happen in the end, thus removing the teleological reasoning from the analysis (p. 15). Yet, these studies prompted an interesting question of whether the historical legacies of state socialism alone determined the direction and speed of the transition.

Often cited works by David Stark and Laszlo Bruszt (Stark, 1996; Stark & Bruszt, 1998), a fruitful collaboration between an American economic sociologist and a Hungarian political scientist, opened up another perspective on post-socialist countries. Having documented the variation in reforms and in change processes in several countries in the region, the authors tested the assumptions of whether the transformation of post-socialist societies is (a) a project of the imitation of the West, "a void waiting to be filled with blueprints, therapies, and formulas" (Stark & Bruszt, 1998, p. 6), (b) a sure recipe for systemic underdevelopment under the weight of the legacies of state socialism, or (c) an innovation, when institutions not only constrain but also enable change. Stark and Bruszt deftly documented the innovative character of Eastern European capitalism, one of such examples is the common Eastern European practice of recombinant property, when actors discover and recombine resources creating "new property forms that blur the boundaries of public and private, blur organizational boundaries of firms," and blur the way the economic resources are governed, thus leading to the "emergence of a distinctively East European capitalism" (Stark & Bruszt, 1998, pp. 3, 5). The authors argue against the representation of socioeconomic change in the region as "transition" and as a part of the historical homogenization of the global sweep. Instead, they insist that "when we stop defining capitalism in terms of socialism, we see that, in our epoch, capitalism as a construct is analytically interesting only in the plural: *Capitalisms* must be compared vis-à-vis each other" (p. 3).

Approaching the 20th anniversary of post-socialist transformation and with the accumulation of new data, the transition thesis has been subject to revision and reevaluation. Empirical studies by Vladimir Popov, based on various longitudinal databases of economic, institutional, and political indicators for the region over the past 15 years, indicated that the speed and magnitude of reforms in the transition economies ("shock therapy" vs. gradualism) had a negligible influence on the success of the economic recovery of these countries, which experienced economic decline in the early transition years much in excess of the one caused by World War II (Popov,

2004, 2007). Dissatisfied with the arguments of past dependencies that had stressed the years under communism, the size of the economies, or over-industrialization as having little explanatory power, Popov explored why the economic recovery was much slower in the countries of the former Soviet Union (with the exception of the authoritarian states of Uzbekistan, Belarus, and Turkmenistan that were slow to implement economic reforms) compared with the Central European countries. In his studies, Popov found that, in addition to some poor populist policy choices, the major culprits for the lower economic performance of the Soviet successor states were the collapse of state institutions (leading to chaotic changes mainly through crisis management) and the distortions in the industrial structure and trade patterns prior to the transition. These findings prompted a shift of the research focus to the enabling and regulatory role of the state in advancing market institutions in a globalized world.

A question indirectly brought up by transitology studies hints at the sensemaking process that is critical for understanding educational change processes: How do the internal and external social actors make sense of the change process and of the changes already accomplished? How do these shifting discourses influence the direction, scope, and rationales for change, signaling whether the desired outcomes have already been achieved or not, or getting the outcomes modified? Part of this sensemaking process is determining whether and at what points in time the educational change has been constructed as "transition," "restoration," "revolution," "borrowing," "importation," "transformation," or something else.

Restoration

The discourse of restoration posits the past of state socialism as a historical accident and stresses the need to return to pre-socialist educational practices, to reconstruct the past as indigenous tradition, and to reclaim educational continuity. These reconstructions may be controversial. A case in point is the restoration of the pre–World War II Gymnasia as a selective academic track at the secondary educational level in several Central European countries (Cerych, 1997; Pritchard, 1998; Perry, 2005). The restoration of this educational form and its reconstruction in the process was to serve purposes that differed from the original: to create diverse educational opportunities and to replace the leveling effects of comprehensive schools during the years of state socialism. Over time, it raised public and expert concerns about equity. According to the Programme for

International Student Assessment (PISA) studies, which capture educational inequalities as measured within and between schools, educational inequalities are on the rise in post-socialist countries that have performed well on PISA achievement tests such as Hungary, the Slovak Republic, and the Czech Republic (OECD, 2007; Doyle, 2008). Ironically, the consistent top PISA performing countries boasted comprehensive schools and few educational inequalities and thus brought the comprehensive school back into focus (OECD, 2007).

Like other discourses, the discourse of restoration is a powerful tool for re/constructing identity – whether personal, local, national, or regional. Other restorative discourses of tribalism, kinship, or pastoralism found in some contemporary post-socialist countries of Asia and the Caucasus also look into the past to build new belief systems and identities that may have implications for educational practice. The scholarship on the separate impacts these discourses and emerging identities might have on education in post-socialist societies is surprisingly thin, and at best it only states widespread beliefs (at least among the Western researchers and consultants) that such pre-modern values and identities undermine the achievements of modern education. Although research on values and beliefs and their impact on education is difficult to operationalize and carry out, it appears that parental aspirations for modern schooling built in the socialist past continue to be driving demand for higher standards in education in post-socialist societies – even those emerging from civil war, with deteriorating state school systems, or with radically reduced years of mandatory schooling and under compulsory indoctrination by highly personalized regimes. The research in the Kyrgyz Republic in Central Asia, where traditionalist beliefs are re-emerging, found that parental aspirations and years of mother's education in particular are very strong positive indicators in determining attendance at preschool and the completion of secondary education for both girls and boys; the lack of gender bias distinguishes the post-socialist countries from most developing countries (Anderson, Pomfret, & Usseinova, 2004). Furthermore, it appears that liberal democratic structures themselves do not guarantee pedagogical liberalism as shown by the precedent of the Western powers using education to promote patriotism and feelings of national superiority after World War I (Janmaat & Vickers, 2007). The emerging national identities and values in the post-socialist countries may be advocated by a few, such as certain policy-makers or intellectual elites, and may diverge from the aspirations of broader social groups as is evident in post-socialist Moldova and Ukraine in recent times (Anderson, 2007; Janmaat, 2007). Additionally, multiple tensions may beset the new post-socialist states – between the proclaimed ideals of liberal democracy that encourage critical thinking and pluralistic views and the identity-construction processes that may use patriotism and the promotion of monolithic views to maintain social cohesion (Janmaat & Vickers, 2007).

Importation and Otherization

The discourse of importation places the preeminence of Western influences on schools and post-socialist societies at large. Similar to the imported values of Western consumerism that turned shops that "almost sought to exclude potential customers" into "seductive purveyors of goods," schools also are portrayed as subject to imported values (Elliott & Tudge, 2007, pp. 97–98). The focus thus is on the Western impact on schools in post-socialist nations, the resistance of schools to change (Elliott & Tudge, 2007), "passing the test," and the one-way transmission of expertise from Western advisors to local educators with the implicit idea of modeling schools after Western examples (Perry, 2005). Laura Perry found – through the comparison of perspectives of post-communist Czech schooling by Western scholars, on the one hand, and Czech scholars, on the other – that, in addition to the agreement between the two groups on the areas of needed reform, Western and primarily Anglo-American perceptions tended to offer a negative evaluation of Eastern European schools, thus perpetuating the sociocultural construction of Eastern Europe as opposite the West. In this otherization discourse, "the West is seen as tolerant, progressive, efficient, active, developed, organized and democratic, and the East as intolerant, corrupt, passive, undeveloped, chaotic and undemocratic" (Perry, 2005, p. 269). An interesting example in Perry's analysis of incongruent rationales for change concerns methods of instruction. The traditional Czech pedagogy was perceived by the English-speaking scholars as being too passive and teacher-centered, irrespective of the high achievement of Czech students on international tests, and was assumed to not be enabling students to become active citizens in a democratic society. In contrast, Western European authors indicated that the Czech "frontal" teacher-centered pedagogy was common to a number of OECD countries rather than due to its communist heritage; the rationale for change to a more active teaching method was premised on the goal of improving student achievement (already high) with no mention of the rationale of education for democratic citizenship. Meanwhile, Czech scholars regarded their educational system as sound and quite good, and some local authors saw a need to change the emphasis from encyclopedism to knowledge application and problem-solving (Perry, 2005, pp. 269–278).

Educational importation in this discourse may appear as logically effective in replacing "the old ways" of delivering post-socialist education – similar to the importation of a blueprint of economic reforms into the region from elsewhere as the only path to go. However, the striking differences and incongruence in perception and framing of educational change through importation discloses the cultural otherization of Eastern Europe. Otherization tends to divide educational scholarship into two realms: one is the realm of sophisticated and dynamic scholarship for domestic consumption, and the other one is for transferring idealized models of the self onto the "other" or for testing practices, which might be too controversial to implement in one's own home.

Revolution and Evolution

These two discourses indicate the radical departure and the overhaul of the very principles and forms of education similar to a revolutionary rupture, on the one hand, and a more gradual nature of change in education as a primary mechanism of intergenerational and intercultural continuity and integrity, on the other hand. Faced with the uncertainty and ambiguity concerning how exactly the change process might unfold on a daily basis, this change was simultaneously framed as mutation, assimilation, and evolution (Cerych, 1997). Educational change in post-socialist countries was constructed as a bottom-up, grass-roots movement based on individual, school, and local initiatives (Glenn, 1995; Froumin, 2005), and governments "generally followed rather than steered the bottom-up reform process" (Cerych, 1997, p. 78). Congruent with this impetus for change and building on the teacher movement in Russia, the Minister of Education Eduard Dneprov articulated the reform goals from the side of the classroom in 1988 and did not spare revolutionary rhetoric (Dneprov, 1993b, 1993c).

The symbiosis of both revolutionary and evolutionary strands in one discourse may seem peculiar to outsiders. It may be understood as an aversion to the "shock-therapy" style of economic reforms in the early transition, yet having the intention of reaching to the very foundation of educational practices and processes. This discourse also shows appreciation for the evolutionary transformation of attitudes and values in educational processes and for the role of education in intergenerational and intercultural continuity.

Transformation and Innovation

Most often educational change in the post-socialist countries is constructed by both insiders and outsiders as profound, far-reaching, irreversible, fast-paced, and transformative (Cerych, 1997). One of the most comprehensive accounts of the challenges in reforming education in the region is presented by Stephen Heyneman, which equally serves outsider and insider audiences by both explaining the scale and challenge of the educational reform in the region and conceptualizing the reform course (Heyneman, 1998). Renewal is not necessarily associated with the reinvention of the wheel, and does not appear shy of adapting and assimilating solutions and trends from elsewhere. There are numerous case studies from the region about adapting innovations – be it new programs in ecology, business management, economics, psychology, inclusive education for children with special education needs, new forms of adult education, multicultural methods of education, methods of civic education, or quality control mechanisms, to list a few. Innovations are also abundant: Locally developed models of university rankings that gauge ranking gain scores relative to their stronger or weaker resource endowments, community schools (*szkoła społeczna*) run by parents in Poland (Bodine, 2005), thought-provoking conceptualizations of higher education at the interaction of global, public, and academic dimensions (Kwiek, 2001), and many others. Innovation and experimentation in schools and higher education institutions were both feeding into and getting inspired by societal democratization. This might be a primary reason for the latecomers in educational reform to insist on room for their experimentation and reform ownership. Innovations after all appear to be rooted in progressive indigenous traditions that nurture national strength in education (Adamsky, 1995; Holmes, 2005; Webber, 2000; Sutherland, 1999).

The discourse of transformation is directly linked with the process of transition toward democracy and the market economy. Societal democratization liberalized individual and professional innovation. The logic of the new market-based economy produced a similar agenda in system-wide educational reform (Heyneman, 2010). Heyneman (2010) argues that it is the logic of the market economy rather than omnipotent globalization or the weakness of local institutions that prompted similar educational reform agendas in the diverse post-socialist societies.

Crisis and Survival

The discourse of educational crisis is prompted by setbacks in the political and economic transition and by the high societal price for these transformations: demographic collapse and its repercussions for education, street children, HIV and STD epidemics among youth, and the sky-rocketing youth suicide rates (Kerr, 2005; UNICEF, 2000; UN, 2007); the declining status of the teaching profession and low morale among teachers (Eklof & Seregny, 2005; Salitra, 2003); socioeconomic stratification of the society and the alternative schooling transfigured to serve the elites (Lisovskaya & Karpov, 2001; Bodine, 2005); political struggle that paralyzes educational reforms (Birzea, 1996; Kovacs, 2000); and the general societal crisis and the survival strategies of the marginalized teachers who nonetheless choose to serve their profession in a highly moral manner (Niyozov, 2004).

Indeed the scale of depopulation, shortage of funding for education, the deterioration of the teaching profession, and the hardships and vicissitudes of the large-scale societal change were critically alarming across many countries in the region and continue to be so in some. At the junctions of political muddling, weakened state institutions, nascent civil societies, and downward spiraling socioeconomic decline, the uncertainty of the possibility for improvement was particularly pronounced. Supported by the "undisputed" reality of statistical trends, the discourse of crisis emerged in Western scholarship. Some educational policy papers for domestic consumption in the post-socialist countries occasionally and purposefully resorted to the exaggeration of crisis in order to reach newspaper headlines, stir public opinion, and influence national policy-makers. Insiders in general tended to accept the crisis and learn to live on a daily basis coping with it. One of the powerful tools of such coping is estrangement of the crisis through "laugh-at-it" and "laugh through tears" mechanisms as reflected in educational folklore. Examples are the drastic shortage of funding for education captured as "new freedom, freedom from financing," and the constrains that enable innovation captured in "necessity is the mother of invention."

Glocalization

The glocalization discourse fuses the global and local/indigenous perspectives – captured through "spatial" metonymy: "global encounters in local contexts," "think globally, but act locally," or "the global village." Often framed by critical perspectives such as dependency theory, the glocalization framing of education in post-socialist countries produced more culturally oriented discourses calling for local ownership of international reforms and "traveling policies" and focused on microlevel educational case studies (Reeves, 2004; Bahry, 2005; DeYoung, 2005; Steiner-Khamsi & Stolpe, 2006). The glocalization framing of educational change in the region was produced mostly as a Western discourse sensitized to local needs and cultures.

Educational Borrowing

The discourse of educational borrowing evolves from the discourse of educational importation and distinguishes itself from the latter by assuming that the borrowing is a selective and adaptive process with the borrower an active agent rather than a passive receiver, not raw material waiting to be molded or to be imposed on by the imported models.

In the recent decade, there has been a resurgence of interest in educational policies that travel well across borders. This time global forces are taken into account, such as the influence of supranational organizations and agreements with clearly sanctioned incentives or without them (such as the European Union, the Bologna Process) (Phillips & Ochs, 2003; Phillips, 2004). This discourse stresses the process of packaging educational reform agendas developed by international donor organizations (such as the World Bank, International Bank for Reconstruction and Development, European Bank for Reconstruction and Development) for the latecomers in educational reform in the post-socialist countries of Central Asia, the Caucasus, and Mongolia. Acceptance of these reforms is said to be the condition for loan-lending by donor organizations (Berryman, 2000, Silova & Steiner-Khamsi, 2008). An additional component of this discourse is the circulation in international organizations and global fora of certain conceptual constructions such as multiculturalism, child-centered learning, outcome-based education, evidence-based practices, and two-tier higher education degree structures of the Anglo-American style. The speed and the scale of the global circulation of references to such practices indeed has reached a phenomenal level prompting some to utilize biological concepts of epidemiology, which may be presented as value-free or value-laden (Oushakine, 2007), and prompting others to use the science-derived language of diffusion, implying that the idea or the policy does not get transformed in the process of crossing borders. Studies on educational borrowing in the region focused on political and economic aspects of such borrowing when the powerful in local contexts, under external pressure, manipulate externally borrowed discourses (Silova, 2006; Steiner-Khamsi, 2006).

World System Convergence or Divergence

The studies of the expansion of modern schooling and the accelerating rates of school participation in modern nations as a consequence of changing political culture and values (Ramirez & Boli, 1987) indicate a convergence of formal structures of schooling around the world. This discourse has also advanced into research on educational change in the post-socialist countries. This research focus initially promised to provide further affirmation to the theory, although not with unequivocal explanatory power. For example, the study on private higher education in the post-socialist region confirmed the presence of local influences and the institutional behaviors and forms, inherited from the prior system, rather than global isomorphic effects (Levy, 2006). An interesting case study of higher education contraction in East Germany is portrayed as deviating from the global trend, although it was paralleled in other countries of the then Eastern Bloc through explicit strategies of manpower planning by the political elites (Baker, Köhler, & Stock, 2007). A recent study exploring education system regulatory policies in five European countries (Belgium, England, France, Portugal, and post-socialist Hungary) concluded that the policies themselves aim to create "evaluative states" or "quasi-market" governing systems and thus converge at the policy rhetoric level, but the realization of these policies varies considerably due to the interaction of institutional, political, and ideological constraints specific to each country (Maroy, 2009).

The increasing popularity among governments of learning competencies as provided by global benchmarking systems such as PISA under OECD auspices may point to the emerging global norm in measuring educational outcomes. Yet, each government might need to accommodate this norm to their own local attitudes, and even borrowing the discourse itself might ill-serve that purpose.

The UNICEF regional monitoring reports of post-socialist countries point to yet another global norm emerging in this region in the aftermath of transition – such as the high percentage of the youth population neither employed or enrolled in education at the time of the cataclysmic change in the 1990s, drug use, STD and HIV/AIDS epidemics among the youth, drop-outs, and street children – all of these emerged in these societies in the 1990s as costly side effects of the transition (UNICEF, 2000; Kerr, 2005; UN, 2007).

Education's Role in Social Reproduction or Social Transformation

Radical and indeed revolutionary change in education in the region poses an intriguing challenge to the dominant thesis of critical theory. Does education reproduce social relations in the larger society (Karabel & Halsey, 1977), or can it actually prepare individuals to challenge and overthrow the regime? It might also be possible that this question is not a dilemma at all, that "or" can be changed into "and." For it has been documented that the Soviet-style educational ideals that stress rationality, equality, and human power in reorganizing the social order turned out to be subversive to state socialism. The surveys of Polish students as early as the 1960s showed that engineering students, those most imbued with the value of rationality, were most radical in criticizing the socialist economy (Przeworski, 1995). The peaceful dissolution of the Eastern Bloc and of the Soviet Union in the 1990s resulted from exercising the very principles they were founded on – those of voluntary association and national self-determination. The first multiparty elections that revolutionized the political landscape of the country embraced the slogan of the 1917 revolution: "All power to the Soviets [Councils of Elected Representatives]!" This use of the very principles of the old social order but with the opposite intention – not for perpetuating it but creating its opposite – is symbolic of the outcry to the chasms created by the official language and actual life under state socialism. Both observers and reformers of Russian education documented how Russian educational reform had been prepared by the bottom-up teachers' movement and the enduring humanist tradition that survived Stalinism and Brezhnevism (Eklof, 1993; Adamsky, 1995). Eduard Dneprov, a notable Russian education reformer and the Minister of Education in the early years of Russia's independence, developed the thesis that a society can be changed through education – a thought that summarized the plans and aspirations of reform-minded educators in Russia (Eklof & Dneprov, 1993).

EMERGING APPROACHES TO EDUCATIONAL CHANGE IN THE REGION

Most discourses framing educational change in the post-socialist countries discussed above originated in the theories developed outside either education or the region itself, and then were extended to educational change in the post-socialist world. These educational extrapolations exposed the original theories to testing, questioning, and modification in some cases. The produced discourses may be viewed as sensemaking frames or snapshots against the backdrop of the ongoing change in education and the larger society. As such, these frames provided references for under-standing the current educational processes and shaped expectations and actions for their subsequent development. Some of the discourses were used either by insiders or outsiders, and others by both the groups. Some were replaced in a sequence reflecting the stages of transitioning economies, emerging democracies, and reshaped national identities, while others continued to be used. Some of the discourses based on the preexisting theories extrapolated into the post-socialist education appear problematic as revealed in the cultural otherization of the region as discussed above. This section discusses approaches that objectivate the observer and the observed in scholarly discourses for post-socialist education as emerging lines of inquiry. These emerging approaches are much more likely to be anchored in national and local searches for identity.

Revisiting Educational Transition through Sociocultural Geography

Transitology studies gradually went out of fashion with the countries in the region actively seeking acknowledgment of their accomplishments and of the differences in the degree and speed of transformation. In the global context, the societies besides the "transitioning" ones were paradoxically left out of the process of evolving and developing, and rather were restricted to the status quo. Similar to the Newly Independent States that emerged as a result of the collapse of the USSR in 1991 were Czechoslovakia and Yugoslavia, where identity formation had been addressed from early on by nationalist ideologies and linguistic nationalism (Birzea, 1994; Coulby, 2000; Coulby & Jones, 2001). The search for the differentiation and repositioning of the countries in the region relative to each other and relative to their external references shifted the accepted geographical boundaries or became highly politicized. Thus, in the search for distinctive identities, former Eastern European countries carefully constructed themselves as Central European countries (Wedel, 1998; Czarniawska, 2002). Such adjectives as post-Soviet stopped being used in self-reference as politically incorrect, although they continued to be used in the Western research discourse such as in the journal of *Post-Soviet Affairs*. The term *Visegrád countries* came into use circa 1991: it referred to Poland, Hungary, and at that time, the Czech and Slovak Federal Republic, and was reminiscent of their past in the Hapsburg Empire and their strong cultural and religious affinity with the West relative to other countries of the region (Wedel, 1998). The benchmarking of the economic and political transition progress of the countries in the region by such international organizations as the World Bank, the International Bank for Reconstruction and Development, and Freedom House replaced distinct national identifiers with "return to Europe." Acceptance to the European Union as a newly defined space with boundaries, desirable membership, and aid became a new destination.

The external benchmarking of the transition process and the social construction of geography produced new references and subdivisions of the countries in the region. These reference terms sometimes are discordant with the national self-identities in the making because of the evolving nature of these identities and the asymmetric positions of the "naming" and the "named." A case in point is the formation of the discourse of "new Europe" with reference to the Central European countries as a homogeneous entity, while "richness of diversity" is recognized as the political slogan for the Western European countries of the European Union (Galasinska & Krzyzanowski, 2009). However, the discourse of "diversity" of individual countries in Central and Eastern Europe may still be constructed using the same principle of "otherization" that builds divides within the region. Thus, it distinguishes Central European countries and their educational systems as closer to the advanced West from the Southeast European countries as the more backward "other" (Mincu, 2009). Geography as a sociocultural and geopolitical construct has come to dominate the mapping of the nations formerly under state socialism.

Globalization: Lost and Found in "Translation"

The studies that attempt to establish a dialogue among educators from both the transitioning world and outside it are rare and precious. Such is the volume edited by Ben Eklof, Larry Holmes, and Vera Kaplan that captures reflection on "oneself and the other," while formally focusing on educational reform in post-Soviet Russia (Eklof, Holmes, & Kaplan, 2005). The researchers from the former "two worlds" in this volume appear to be well-versed in discourses emanating from their former worlds and, in the best examples, cast enlightening views from inside looking out and from outside looking in. Thus, comparative international education as a learning model, generalized elsewhere as an ideal (Paige & Mestenhauser, 1999), is utilized in this volume as a meaningful practice.

This learning model rests in major part on translation – both linguistic and the one involved in defining social, economic, educational, and temporal local conditions that impart the discourse or the practice with its functional meaning. The concept of translation when introduced in social research in the 1980s (Latour, 1986) allows us to analyze and compare educational practices as socially reconstructed phenomena, which as they "travel" get transformed. This approach also allows us to take into account the outcomes of the transferred practices that are even "unintentional or unforeseen" at first sight.

One study focused on the concept of university autonomy, which when disembedded from its context (that is time and space) meant very little and began to be recognized as such only under specific conditions (Bain, 2003). In the 1970s to 1980s USA, this concept was brought into a focus vis-à-vis the rising controlling power of the states. In Europe and the USA in the late 1990s, it was manifested in the new accountability movement when accountability measures and governance "from a distance" were traded for greater operational decision-making and more power concentrated at the senior administration level of universities. In the recent Bologna documents, this concept appears to be a mixture of both academic freedom and academic values as well as the values of "effective," "transparent," and "responsible" decision-making under the new accountability. In late 1980s to 1990s Russia, the concept of university autonomy was deeply embedded in the entire socioeconomic and political reform with clear references to decentralization, national self-determination, and personal freedom (Bain, 2003). The concept got into the reform documents and the educational law without further explication, thus opening the opportunity for some risk-taking institutions of higher education in Russia to reinterpret and take advantage of it (Bain, 2003). Another study followed the cultural borrowing of the field of Western economics into newly established and existing Russian universities explicating intricate transformations (Suspitsyna, 2005). Yet another piece of research using the discourse and translation approach followed the paths of influence exerted by the recommendations of such global players as the World Bank and the OECD on the reform agenda in Russia formulated in 2000 and 2005 (Gounko & Smale, 2007).

Often taken for granted as commonly understood, various concepts of educational practice tend to differ depending on the space and the time of their construction. Even when one and the same word is used to signify such concepts, the larger context that framed its meaning is needed in order to do its reconstruction. It is a classic example when people may use the same words of educational policy parlance and yet misunderstand each other.

Among such concepts in post-socialist educational change are *modernization* of education, *educational vouchers* disguised under the principle of *"money follows students,"* and others. *Modernization* of education is often perceived inside the region as an euphemism for more reforms that came as a second wave in the late 1990s and early 2000s (Remizov, 2002), while donor organizations promoted educational modernization in its instrumentalist definition as serving the needs of the emerging market economy and thus filtering "wrong" from "right" and *relevant* skills (World Bank, 1996; Canning, Moock, & Heleniak, 1999; Berryman, 2000; Webber, 2000). The adjective *relevant* itself implied "relevant to economic needs" and was associated with the documents of the donor organizations of the time. Interestingly, some English-speaking educators resisted this new use of the word and its implicit value load and insisted instead that the adjective requires an explicit predicative structure "relevant *to what*?"

The *modernization* discourse is thus multifaceted: It is strongly linked with the neoliberal concepts of the knowledge economy and human capital formation where education primarily serves the economic needs and is considered a service industry. It is conceptualized in modernization theories of national development, particularly with regard to less developed nations, as having the built-in cultural superiority of the Western way and with the West as a modernizer. It is popularized as a cyclical process of updating, renewal, or rebuilding. Modernization of education in the post-socialist context emerged initially with regard to reforming vocational education and training (VET), that is, the educational subsector most immediately linked with work and employment and the one that was hit hardest by the economic decline during the transition. Both the discourse of the economic instrumentality of education and the fact that post-socialist societies were built as modernized states prompted educators in this region to rethink the future of education along postmodern conceptions by placing an individual and the society in the center of the relationship, not the economy and the state (Bain, 2001).

Were there any backward translations from educational practices in the post-socialist countries to the Western countries? There is the example of the concept of *humanization*, which was approximated in English as "child-centered learning and teaching." The former has been widely used in the Newly Independent States and other Eastern European countries and was found in the 1990s reform documents in Russia, Lithuania, Poland, and Bulgaria to name a few (Birzea, 1994). It is, however, contextualized in richer terms than its English translation allows. Thus, it is linked with the Russian practices of cooperative learning, student self-determination, and the activity-based approach that resurged in the 1980s, but drew on decades of enduring indigenous educational traditions (Dneprov, 1993a).

Similarly, the term *developmental education* is not easily translated into English from Russian. For example, the English paraphrase "teaching that is adapted to the pace of the child" (Elliott & Tudge, 2007, p. 104) only partially captures its meaning. The term is primarily associated with (a) Lev S. Vygotsky's zones of proximal development, where with adequate teacher support (captured in the English-coined "scaffolding") a child may develop conceptual grasps beyond its readiness or developmental stage – this discovery by Vygotsky contradicted the then-reigning approach by Jean Piaget that in order to be successful teaching should be adapted to a child's pace and ability level; Piaget's premise has served into the present days as a basis for ability testing and consequent student ability tracking. It is furthermore associated with (b) teaching aiming to assist a child's development and self-realization not just simply transmitting knowledge and values; (c) learning happening not only between a teacher and a child but also in a social group of peers; and (d) the activity approach in Russian psychology developed by Alexei N. Leontiev and Serguei L. Rubinstein in the 1920s to 1930s stressing that a child constructs his or her own learning process, that learning happens in activities and through active engagement of its participants, including meaningful problem-oriented and experiential learning techniques, and reflexive exercises on one's activity and contributions.

Some of these ideas are translatable into the recognizable techniques of progressive educators in the USA. However, it would be shortsighted to disregard that they have been developed into a distinct body of theories and practices by the Russian educators and to assume that there is not anything to learn from Russian educational practice. This assumption lies in particularly stark contrast with numerous educational practitioners world-wide that use Russian curricula and teaching methods.

Another example is the *community schools* (*szkoła społeczna*) in Poland that sprang up in the early 1990s and were run by parents (Laciak, 1998). The emergence of schools of various types as an alternative to the state-run system of schooling is typically presented as *school choice, educational market,* and *democratization* by Anglo-American authors (Glenn, 1995; Heyneman, 1997, 1998). Indeed, "school choice" primarily deconstructed as the individual expression of freedom fits well the decentralized and grassroots origins of the early 1990s Polish transition and the distrust toward the faltering state, but it fails to explain the communal nature of these new school organizations (Bodine, 2005). Community schools in

Poland are tracked by Polish scholars and American anthropologist to *środowisko*, a community defined beyond the neighborhood by ties of private friendships and trusted associations – a device for survival through private networks developed under the socialist state system, but also instrumental during the post-socialist change (Bodine, 2005; Wedel, 1992).

Non-state schools organized by parents emerged in other Eastern European countries, for example, as cooperative and independent schools in Russia where parents dissatisfied with the state's performance stepped up to the plate and organized schools with innovative and experimental approaches in pedagogy and school organization (Glenn, 1995). These schools appeared several years prior to the educational law legitimizing new types of schools. But the community school as a widespread communal movement was probably a distinct Polish phenomenon with institutional and financial support from the civic organizations and public resources (Bodine, 2005).

An interesting point of "translation" regarding such community and cooperative schools in the region is that they have been named *non-state schools*, not private schools. This was partly due to the emerging nature of this new alternative to state schools, partly due to the lack of laws differentiating between the non-profit and for-profit status of private organizations and the non-existence of share-holding in education at the time, and partly due to the fact that such schools were established not by private individuals but by social groups and associations. Because of the former two reasons, private status and educational privatization as such were too often associated with profit-making. Because of the latter, the Western concept of *school choice* closely corresponds with the Eastern European concepts of *diversification, school variety,* and educational *destatization*, or removal of the state as the sole provider of schooling. In reality, these terms from the policy documents followed the bottom-up innovations in the region – laws were developed to frame and regulate the bottom-up innovations, not to initiate them (Glenn, 1995), and the strategies for coping under the constraints of state socialism have been constructively used to channel innovative energies in post-socialism.

Time and Space Reconfigured

Postmodern studies claim the pre-eminence of space over time, pointing to the transformation of historical time into a spatial configuration. Time is thus often imparted some spatial attributes of spreading-out, contracting, intersecting, overlapping, fragmenting, and truncating. The merged concept of space–time ("here and now") is surprisingly synchronic, not diachronic or time-binding. Post-socialist discourses of education reveal, with a closer look, such experimentation with the space–time category.

The institutions of education existing prior to the imposition of the Soviet model have been reconstructed as idealized or decontextualized versions of themselves in order to serve as a new reference. By backward reconstruction, new types of schools re-emerged – for example, *Gymnasia*, highly selective secondary schools, were reinstalled in Russia and the Newly Independent States, referring to Russia's pre-Soviet prototype often only in name. In Central Europe, there has been a similar resurgence and idealization of the educational structures established prior to World War II, even though secondary comprehensive schools were only partially sovieticized and the *Gymnasien* of the Prussian educational model were retained in Poland, Czechoslovakia, and Hungary albeit at the upper secondary level. Such references to pre-socialist educational practices were impossible in nations and places with no formal or mass schooling prior to the Soviet model. The time vector might be reoriented toward the future in the case of an absence of reliable indigenous models. Some other variations on the theme of transformed time and space concern the "catching-up" thesis, rampant educational change, and revisiting past educational models.

The Catching-Up Thesis
The catching-up thesis is a variation on the reconceptualization of time with the built-in dominance assumption ("been there, done that") that presents change as a phased process from simple stages to advanced ones, as the only progressive and immanent model to follow. This assumption marginalizes local innovative capacities and contributions (Wedel, 1998). This logic restricts educators in the region to follow others' footsteps, fall into similar traps, and transplant remedies and solutions developed in other contexts, cultures, and traditions in their historical sequence, no matter how inadequate these could be. The most drastic scenario of educational "catching-up" was observed in the reunification (German *Einschluss*, literally "inclusion, locking within") of East Germany with West Germany. Stephanie Wilde argued that the changes in secondary education in Eastern federal states qualified as a decade of "non-reform" between 1990 and 2000 and that these changes resulted in the reproduction of the West German school structure already sharply criticized by German educators themselves in the late 1960s to early 1970s (Wilde, 2002). Similarly, the analysis of

trajectories from education to employment in the Eastern German federal states indicated that, far from "catching up" with the rest of Germany, the erosion of the dual system in the East might have a negative impact on the future of the Western German states. Indeed, the emerging problems and contradictions resembled those that beset British education and training a decade earlier (Evans, Behrens, & Kaluza, 1999).

Embracing Radical and Rampant Change
The region showed early on the eagerness to change radically and fast. Some commentators highlighted the depth and scope of such change (Cerych, 1997), although the goals were not always clearly articulated, and the search for constructive ideas and visions periodically emerged. The countries of Eastern Europe and Russia started transforming their higher education to fit into a two-tier Anglo-American model of higher education, and thus to induce change in the design of programs and curricula in the late 1980s to early 1990s. By doing so, these countries placed themselves "ahead of the pack" when the Bologna Process was initiated in 1999, when one of the major goals was articulated to differentiate tiers of study and to make the degrees awarded at each level more comparable. Some of the current debates on the challenges of implementing the tiers of study that the Bologna movement has produced are remarkably similar to earlier discussions in post-socialist countries (Crosier, Purser, & Smidt, 2007).

Revisiting the Past
There has been a lot of interest in rediscovering the historical events and interpretations that were obscured, rewritten or completely omitted to fit the theses of Marxist–Leninist ideology. This period of negation and collective repentance and rediscovery of the past often gave way to the search for new ideologies, particularly for those based on nationalism. While the process of nation-building has not been completed in many countries of the region, there emerged a more somber view of socialist history. In part, it was encouraged by consistently high results of students in the former socialist countries on international educational tests, such as Trends in International Mathematics and Science Study (TIMSS) and PISA. In part, it was encouraged by the search for continuing patterns in educational practice that affect schooling today – both as strengths and weaknesses of the system (Holmes, 1999, 2005).

CONCLUSION

The purpose of this chapter was to identify and analyze scholarly discourses and conceptions of post-socialist education over the past two decades. It is an attempt at conceptualizing the research in the field and at highlighting some promising and emerging lines of inquiry, social constructions, theoretical applications, and reflections that continue to challenge the status quo perceptions by both insiders and outsiders of the region. Through probing implicit assumptions and tracking changing approaches and shifting concepts, it is an attempt to map the more general route of translation between the former two worlds. The purpose was not to review as many studies on education in the region as possible, but rather to identify prominent discourses and their origins that shaped and continue to affect our understanding of the unfolding educational dynamics. It is acknowledged that some noteworthy discourses might be missing from this analysis.

Reflecting on research about research, it might be noted that research on education in post-socialist countries has outgrown its status of regional application as the curiosity from both sides about each other's education have been mostly saturated. The current body of research is more practice- and issue-oriented, theory-driven, or theory-testing, and offers research strands that will enrich scholarship on educational change. Furthermore, the discourses for educational change based on the extension of theories from outside of education or outside of the region challenged these very theories when developed for post-socialist educational change. The emerging lines of inquiry offer important nuances through focusing on relationships of the observer and the observed in the social construction of cognitive frames for educational processes. In particular, this emerging scholarship deconstructs cognitive frames for the same post-socialist educational phenomena, and thus tracks their meanings as embedded in larger societal processes. These approaches reflect local and national searches for identity rather than global agendas.

There was a striking similarity among the discourses for educational change across the post-socialist countries – especially at the early stages of transformation – when the goals of transformation were common, distinct self-identity and self-determination was at its prime, and a target educational model was only generally sketched. In other words, these discourses originated at times when transformation was constructed more as "transition from" rather than "transition to" (Neave, 2003). While similar discourses reflected some common innovative practices in education in the region, the precise configuration of educational forms and practices continued to grow, reflecting different policy choices, different timelines, and the embeddedness in the overall transition processes or a lack of it. Education has since increasingly become positioned at the intersection of global, cross-national, regional, domestic, community, professional, economic, political, cultural, and individual interests and influences. So has grown a repertoire of mechanisms for educational change and a variation in educational models in the post-socialist countries.

There are indeed many lessons to be learned and to reflect upon, and the most salient is that of revisiting the thesis that the fall of state socialism and the end of the cold war division of the world ends history. Contrary to the prediction of Fukuyama (1992), it marks the beginning of multiple histories that enrich each other, especially when there is the will to learn about them and to appreciate them. The emerging approaches to educational change are less likely to be located in global agendas, and rather reflect local and national searches for identity. Hence, the values are more particularistic, with less invocation of externally offered agendas.

REFERENCES

Adamsky, A. I. (1995). Democratic values in Russian education 1955–93: An analytical review of the cultural and historical background to reform. In: D. J. Chapman, I. D. Froumin & D. N. Aspin (Eds), *Creating and managing the democratic school* (pp. 86–99). London and Washington, DC: The Falmer Press.

Anderson, E. A. (2007). 'They are the priests': The role of Moldovan historian and its implications for civic education. *Compare, 37*(3), 277–290.

Anderson, K. H., Pomfret, R., & Usseinova, N. S. (2004). Education in Central Asia during transition to market economy. In: S. P. Heyneman & A. J. DeYoung (Eds), *The challenges of education in Central Asia* (pp. 131–152). Greenwich, CT: Information Age Publishing.

Bahry, S. A. (2005). Traveling policy and local spaces in the Republic of Tajikistan: A comparison of the attitudes of Tajikistan and the World Bank toward textbook provision. *European Educational Research Journal, 4*(1), 60–78.

Bain, O. (2001). Russia: Towards autonomous personalities. In: W. K. Cummings, M. T. Tatto & J. Hawkins (Eds), *Values education for dynamic societies: Individualism or collectivism* (pp. 60–78). Hong Kong: The University of Hong Kong Press.

Bain, O. (2003). *University autonomy in the Russian Federation since perestroika*. New York and London: Routledge Falmer.

Baker, D., Köhler, H., & Stock, M. (2007). Socialist ideology and the contraction of higher education: Institutional consequences of state manpower and education planning in the former East Germany. *Comparative Education Review, 51*(3), 353–377.

Berryman, S. (2000). *Hidden challenges to education systems in transition economies.* Washington, DC: The World Bank.

Birzea, C. (1994). *Educational policies of the countries in transition.* Strasbourg: Council of Europe.

Birzea, C. (1996). Educational reform and power struggles in Romania. *European Journal of Education, 31*(1), 97–107.

Blanchard, O., Dornbusch, R., Krugman, P., Layard, R., & Summers, L. (1992). *Reform in Eastern Europe.* Cambridge, MA: MIT Press.

Blanchard, O., Froot, K., & Sachs, J. (Eds). (1994). *The transition in Eastern Europe* (2 vols.). Chicago: University of Chicago Press.

Bodine, E. F. (2005). Radical decentralization and the role of community in Polish educational reform. *European Education, 37*(1), 83–102.

Brinton, C. (1965). *The anatomy of revolution.* New York: Vintage Books.

Campbell, J. L., & Pedersen, O. K. (Eds). (1996). *Legacies of change: Transformations of postcommunist European economies.* New York: Aldine de Gruyter.

Canning, M., Moock, P., & Heleniak, T. (1999). *Reforming education in the regions of Russia (World Bank technical paper No. 457).* Washington, DC: The World Bank.

Cerych, L. (1997). Educational reforms in Central and Eastern Europe: Processes and outcomes. *European Journal of Education, 32*(1), 75–97.

Coulby, D. (2000). Education in times of transition: Eastern Europe with particular reference to the Baltic States. In: D. Coulby, R. Cowen & C. Jones (Eds), *Education in times of transition* (pp. 8–21). London: Kogan Page.

Coulby, D., & Jones, C. (2001). *Education and warfare in Europe.* Aldershot and Burlignton, VT: Ashgate.

Crosier, D., Purser, L., & Smidt, H. (2007). *Trends V: Universities shaping the European higher education area.* Brussels: European University Association.

Czarniawska, B. (2002). Remembering while forgetting: The role of automorphism in city management in Warsaw. *Public Administration Review, 62*(2), 65–174.

DeYoung, A. (2005). Ownership of education reforms in the Kyrgyz Republic: Kto v dome hozyain? *European Educational Research Journal, 4*(1), 36–49.

Dneprov, E. D. (1993a). A concept of general (secondary) education. In: B. Eklof & E. D. Dneprov (Eds), *Democracy in the Russian school: The reform movement in education since 1984* (pp. 77–103). Boulder, CO: Westview Press.

Dneprov, E. D. (1993b). Bureaucratic tyranny (must be eliminated from the schools). In: B. Eklof & E. D. Dneprov (Eds), *Democracy in the Russian school: The reform movement in education since 1984* (pp. 36–41). Boulder, CO: Westview Press.

Dneprov, E. D. (1993c). Faith in the teacher: The energy of renewal for the school. In: B. Eklof & E. D. Dneprov (Eds), *Democracy in the Russian school: The reform movement in education since 1984* (pp. 42–46). Boulder, CO: Westview Press.

Dneprov, E. D. (1996). *School reform between "yesterday" and "tomorrow".* Moscow: Federal Institute of Educational Planning of the Russian Federation Ministry of Education and the Russian Academy of Education.

Doyle, A. (2008). Educational performance or educational inequality: What can we learn from PISA about France and England. *Compare, 38*(2), 205–217.

Eklof, B. (1993). Democracy in the Russian school: Educational reform since 1984. In: B. Eklof & E. D. Dneprov (Eds), *Democracy in the Russian school: The reform movement in education since 1984* (pp. 1–33). Boulder, CO: Westview Press.

Eklof, B., & Dneprov, E. D. (Eds). (1993). *Democracy in the Russian school: The reform movement in education since 1984.* Boulder, CO: Westview Press.

Eklof, B., Holmes, L. E., & Kaplan, V. (Eds). (2005). *Educational reform in post-Soviet Russia.* London and New York: Frank Cass.

Eklof, B., & Seregny, S. (2005). Teachers in Russia: State, community and profession. In: B. Eklof, L. E. Holmes & V. Kaplan (Eds), *Educational reform in post-Soviet Russia* (pp. 197 220). London and New York: Frank Cass.

Elliott, J., & Tudge, J. (2007). The impact of the west on post-Soviet Russian education: Change and resistance to change. *Comparative Education, 45*(1), 93–112.

Evans, K., Behrens, M., & Kaluza, J. (1999). Risky voyages: Navigating changes in the organization of work and education in Eastern Germany. *Comparative Education, 35*(2), 131–150.

Froumin, I. D. (2005). Democratizing the Russian school: Achievements and setbacks. In: B. Eklof, L. E. Holmes & V. Kaplan (Eds), *Educational reform in post-Soviet Russia: Legacies and prospects* (pp. 129–152). London and New York: Frank Cass.

Fukuyama, F. (1992). *The end of history and the last man.* New York: Free Press.

Galasinska, A., & Krzyzanowski, M. (Eds). (2009). *Discourse and transformation in Central and Eastern Europe.* Basingstoke: Palgrave Macmillan.

Glenn, C. L. (1995). *Educational freedom in Eastern Europe.* Washington, DC: Cato Institute.

Gounko, T., & Smale, W. (2007). Modernization of Russian higher education: Exploring paths of influence. *Compare, 37*(4), 533–548.

Heyneman, S. P. (1997). Educational choice in Eastern Europe and the former Soviet Union: A review essay. *Education Economics, 5*(3), 333–339.

Heyneman, S. P. (1998). The transition from part/state to open democracy: The role of education. *International Journal of Educational Development, 18*(1), 21–40.

Heyneman, S. P. (2010). A comment on the changes in higher education in the former Soviet Union. *European Education, 42*(1), 76–87.

Hoen, H. W. (2004). *Is there such a thing as "transitology"? Social economic research on transition in Central and Eastern Europe.* Paper presented at the 11th World Congress for Social Economics, June 8–11, 2004, Albertville, France.

Holmes, L. E. (1999). *Stalin's school: Moscow's model school No. 25, 1931 1937.* Pittsburgh, PA: University of Pittsburgh Press.

Holmes, L. E. (2005). School and schooling under Stalin, 1931–1953. In: B. Eklof, L. E. Holmes & V. Kaplan (Eds), *Educational reform in post-Soviet Russia* (pp. 56–101). London and New York: Frank Cass.

Janmaat, J. G. (2007). The ethnic 'other' in Ukrainian history textbooks: The case of Russia and the Russians. *Compare, 37*(3), 307–324.

Janmaat, J. G., & Vickers, E. (2007). Education and identity formation in post-cold war Eastern Europe and Asia. *Compare, 37*(3), 267–275.

Karabel, J., & Halsey, A. H. (Eds). (1977). *Power and ideology in education.* New York: Oxford University Press.

Karpov, V., & Lisovskaya, E. (2005). Educational change in time of social revolution: The case of post-communist Russia in comparative perspective. In: B. Eklof, L. E. Holmes & V. Kaplan (Eds), *Educational reform in post-Soviet Russia* (pp. 23–55). London and New York: Frank Cass.

Kerr, S. T. (2005). Demographic change and the fate of Russia's schools: The impact of population shifts on educational practice and policy. In: B. Eklof, L. E. Holmes & V. Kaplan (Eds), *Educational reform in post-Soviet Russia* (pp. 153–175). London and New York: Frank Cass.

Kovacs, K. (2000). Transitions in Hungary. In: D. Coulby, R. Cowen & C. Jones (Eds), *Education in times of transition* (pp. 76–87). London: Kogan Page.

Krzyzanowski, M., & Wodak, R. (2009). Theorising and analyzing social change in Central and Eastern Europe: The contribution of critical discourse analysis. In: A. Galasinska & M. Krzyzanowski (Eds), *Discourse and transformation in Central and Eastern Europe* (pp. 17–39). Basingstoke: Palgrave Macmillan.

Kwiek, M. (2001). Globalization and higher education. *Higher Education in Europe, XXVI*(1), 27–38.

Laciak, B. (1998). The development of non-public education in Poland. In: P. Beresford-Hill (Ed.), *Education and privatisation in Eastern Europe and the Baltic republics* (pp. 85–94). Wallingford, CT: Triangle Books.

Latour, B. (1986). The powers of association. In: J. Law (Ed.), *Power, action, and belief* (pp. 261–277). London: Routledge and Kegan Paul.

Levy, D. (2006). The unanticipated explosion: Private higher education's global surge. *Comparative Education Review, 50*(2), 217–240.

Lisovskaya, E., & Karpov, V. (2001). The perplexed world of Russian private schools. *Comparative Education, 37*(1), 43–64.

Maroy, C. (2009). Convergences and hybridization of educational policies around 'post-bureaucratic' models of regulation. *Compare, 39*(1), 71–84.

Mincu, M. E. (2009). Myth, rhetoric, and ideology in Eastern European education: School and citizenship in Hungary, Poland, and Romania. *European Education, 41*(1), 55–78.

Neave, G. (2003). On scholars, hippopotami and von Humboldt: Higher education in Europe in transition. *Higher Education Policy, 16*(2), 135–140.

Niyozov, S. (2004). The effects of collapse of the USSR on teachers' lives and work in Tajikistan. In: S. P. Heyneman & J. DeYoung (Eds), *The challenges of education in Central Asia* (pp. 37–64). Greenwich, CT: Information Age Publishing.

OECD. (2007). *PISA 2006: Science competencies for tomorrow's world*. Paris: OECD.

Oushakine, S. A. (2007). Vitality rediscovered. *Studies in Eastern European Thought, 59*, 171–193.

Paige, R. M., & Mestenhauser, J. A. (1999). Internationalizing educational administration. *Educational Administration Quarterly, 35*(4), 500–517.

Perry, L. B. (2005). The seeing and the seen: Contrasting perspectives of post-communist Czech schooling. *Compare, 35*(3), 265–283.

Phillips, D. (2004). Toward a theory of policy attraction in education. In: G. Steiner-Khamsi (Ed.), *The global politics of educational borrowing and lending* (pp. 54–67). New York: Teachers College Press.

Phillips, D., & Ochs, K. (2003). Processes of policy borrowing in education: Some analytical and explanatory devices. *Comparative Education, 39*(4), 451–461.

Popov, V. (2004). Circumstances versus policy choices: Why has the economic performance of the Soviet successor states been so poor? In: M. McFaul & K. Stoner-Weiss (Eds), *After the collapse of communism: Comparative lessons of transition* (pp. 96–129). Cambridge and New York: Cambridge University Press.

Popov, V. (2007). Shock therapy versus gradualism reconsidered: Lessons from transition economies after 15 years of reforms. *Comparative Economic Studies, 49*, 1–31.

Pritchard, R. M. O. (1998). Education transformed? The East German school system since the Wende. *German Politics*, *7*(3), 126–146.

Przeworski, A. (1995). *Democracy and the market: Political and economic reforms in Eastern Europe and Latin America*. New York: Cambridge University Press.

Ramirez, F. O., & Boli, J. (1987). The political construction of mass schooling: European origins and worldwide institutionalization. *Sociology of Education*, *60*, 2–17.

Reeves, M. (2004). Cultivating "citizens of new type": The politics and practice of educational reform at the American university in Kyrgyzstan. In: S. P. Heyneman & A. J. DeYoung (Eds), *The challenges of education in Central Asia* (pp. 365–385). Greenwich, CT: Information Age Publishing.

Remizov, M. (2002). Modernization versus modernization. *Russian Journal*. Available at http://english.russ.ru/politics/20020413.html

Salitra, K. (2003). Education of teachers for Polish schools at the beginning of the twenty-first century. *European Journal of Teacher Education*, *26*(1), 101–108.

Silova, I. (2006). *From sites of occupation to symbols of multiculturalism: Reconceptualizing minority education in post-Soviet Latvia*. Greenwich, CT: Information Age Publishing.

Silova, I., & Steiner-Khamsi, G. (Eds). (2008). *How NGOs react: Globalization and education reform in the Caucasus, Central Asia, and Mongolia*. Bloomfield, CT: Kumarian Press.

Sorokin, P. A. (1967). *The sociology of revolution*. New York: Howard Fertig.

Stark, D. (1996). Recombinant property in East European capitalism. *American Journal of Sociology*, *101*(4), 993–1028.

Stark, D., & Bruszt, L. (1998). *Post-socialist pathways: Transforming politics and property in East Central Europe*. Cambridge and New York: Cambridge University Press.

Steiner-Khamsi, G. (2006). The economics of policy borrowing and lending: A study of late adopters. *Oxford Review of Education*, *32*(5), 665–678.

Steiner-Khamsi, G., & Stolpe, I. (2006). *Educational import in Mongolia: Local encounters with global forces*. New York: Palgrave Macmillan.

Suspitsyna, T. (2005). *Adaptation of Western economics by Russian universities: Intercultural travel of an academic field*. New York: Routledge.

Sutherland, J. (1999). *Schooling in the new Russia*. New York: St. Martin's Press.

UN. (2007). *World youth report*. New York: The United Nations.

UNICEF. (2000). *Young people in changing societies, regional monitoring report No. 7*. Florence: UNICEF Innocenti Research Centre.

Webber, S. L. (2000). *School, reform, and society in the New Russia*. London: McMillan Press.

Wedel, J. (Ed.) (1992). *The unplanned society: Poland during and after communism*. New York: Columbia University Press.

Wedel, J. (1998). *Collision and collusion: The strange case of Western aid to Eastern Europe – 1993–1998*. New York: St. Martin Press.

Weick, K. E. (1988). Enacted sensemaking in crisis situations. *Journal of Management Studies*, *25*(4), 305–317.

Weick, K. E. (1995). *Sensemaking in organizations*. Thousand Oaks, CA and London: Sage Publications.

Wilde, S. (2002). Secondary education in Germany 1990–2000: 'One decade of non-reform in unified German education'? *Oxford Reviews of Education*, *28*(1), 39–51.

World Bank. (1996). *From plan to market: World Development Report 1996*. Washington, DC: The World Bank.

Examining New Policy Narratives

POLICY WHY(S): POLICY RATIONALITIES AND THE CHANGING LOGIC OF EDUCATIONAL REFORM IN POSTCOMMUNIST UKRAINE

Olena Fimyar

INTRODUCTION

This study of schooling is a diagnostic of the systems of reason as practices that simultaneously produce what is inside and outside.

(Popkewitz, 2008, p. 6)

The analysis presented in this chapter, as any other Foucault-inspired[1] study, is far from being an "easy" and straightforward reading with clear implications for policy and practice. The quote by Popkewitz cited above indicates the level of complexity that the chapter seeks to bring to the analysis of policy. To use Foucault's own words, this chapter aims to "unsettle" the taken-for-granted assumptions that inform our current understanding of the former Soviet space and its education as in need of "advice," "correction," and "guidance," which is generously offered by various organizations including the World Bank, the International and Monetary Fund, the Soros Foundations, independent policy consultants,

Post-Socialism is not Dead: (Re)Reading the Global in Comparative Education
International Perspectives on Education and Society, Volume 14, 61–91
Copyright © 2010 by Emerald Group Publishing Limited
ISSN: 1479-3679/doi:10.1108/S1479-3679(2010)0000014006

foreign scholars, philanthropies, and private, governmental, nongovernmental, and intergovernmental organizations.

By focusing not so much on the processes, actors, and discourses (which are the objects of analysis in what I will call here "mainstream policy studies"),[2] but on the "reason" and logic of education policy and by extension of the state, the study maps out a new terrain of inquiry, termed in this chapter *policy rationalities* or *policy why(s)*. Taking its many insights from Foucault-inspired studies of education policy (Besley & Peters, 2007; Doherty, 2006, 2007; Fejes & Nicoll, 2007; Fimyar, 2008a, 2008b; Lindblad & Popkewitz, 2004; Marshall, 1998; Masschelein, Simons, Bröckling, & Pongratz, 2007; Peters, 2001, 2004, 2006; Peters & Besley, 2007a, 2007b; Popkewitz, 2007; Tikly, 2003), this study sets itself a task of encouraging the reader to think "otherwise," and beyond the concepts, explanations, and imaginaries proposed by mainstream policy studies. The line of reasoning this study is particularly keen to disrupt is the opposition between Soviet legacies and Western/European values, the categories of thought that inform (and set limits to) political, policy, and academic debates in the countries of the former Soviet Union, including Ukraine.

POLITICAL AND POLICY CONTEXT OF UKRAINE: TOWARD A POSTSTRUCTURALIST CRITIQUE

In the world dominated by *neoliberal imaginary*,[3] Ukraine, as a country that has made a distinct (but as yet only rhetorical) break with its communist past, provides rich ground for the study of educational policy-making and changing approaches to government. Other characteristics that make Ukraine an interesting case for analysis are its strong regional, cultural, and linguistic differences – dynamics resulting from the country's history, diverse cultural and civilizational influences, and contemporary geopolitical position between Russia and the European Union (EU). In mapping the contours of the political and policy debate in postcommunist Ukraine, Riabchuk's study *Cultural Fault Lines and Political Divisions: The Legacy of History in Contemporary Ukraine* provides a good starting point and an insightful critique of what is currently known about Ukraine.

Riabchuk (2009) opens his work with an observation that despite a significant increase in the studies on contemporary Ukraine, especially after the so-called Orange Revolution of 2004, much of the knowledge about this country is still informed by conventional wisdom and commonsense logic rather than, what he calls, a "sober, competent, and comprehensive analysis" (Riabchuk, 2009, p. 18). In many of the existing studies, the political context of Ukraine is described as "divided between the pro-Russian east and the nationalist west." However, very few of these studies actually work towards defining the concepts constituting this "dubious formula" or questioning the assumptions underpinning such simplified and ready-to-consume imaginaries (Riabchuk, 2009, p. 18). The alleged east–west division of Ukraine gives some commentators enough grounds to envision a range of "apocalyptic" scenarios[4] for Ukraine, including the country's prospects of political break-up, societal unrest, or, what is even worse, a threat of civil war or war with neighboring Russia (Riabchuk, 2009, p. 18). The problem with such definition, analyses, let alone "apocalyptic" scenarios, is that they oversee diverse interregional divisions and dynamics and overshadow them with a simplified and limiting east–west dichotomy.

The understanding of Ukrainian politics as riddled with tensions, crises, and institutional turmoil is translated into the discussion of the educational policy context in Ukraine. An overarching theme that unites diverse studies in policy sociology, comparative and international education research, and anthropology (Fimyar, 2008b; Janmaat, 1999, 2000, 2008; Janmaat & Piattoeva, 2007; Koshmanova & Ravchyna, 2008; Krawchenko, 1997; Nikitin & Parashenko, 2009; Stepanenko, 1999; Sundakov, 2001; Wanner, 1998), as well as reports by the international organizations and the national research centers (MESU & UNDP, 2004, 2005; MESU, UNDP, IRF, & OSI, 2003; OSI & NEPC, 2006; UNDP, 2005; World Bank, 2004, 2005; Razymkov Centre, 2002), is that of educational crisis. Low quality, low efficiency, inadequate financing, and the lack of personnel, technological resources and physical facilities are problems organized in bullet points in the World Bank reports (2004, 2005, p. 7), and are some of the common concerns raised in all of these studies. The studies draw attention to other visible consequences of the educational crisis as well, including widening inequalities between rural and urban schools, mushrooming of private tutoring and non-state universities, widespread bribery, and corruption – developments that can have long-term social implications (Fimyar, 2008b).

The second stream of argument developed in these studies can be gathered under the name "an attack against the postcommunist state's inability to cope with the crisis." Political leadership of the country is criticized in the studies for the lack of commitment, expertise, vision, and strategy, as well as for the slow pace of reform and selective implementation of existing policies. Many commentators describe the Ukrainian education system as structurally "too centralized," and in terms of institutional practices, "too Soviet." The existing system of government in Ukraine did not escape these criticisms. The main problem in governmental hierarchy, the studies contend, is the duplication of authority, whereby various branches of government produce a large number of "quasi-legislative" policy documents that are poorly coordinated and implemented without much monitoring (Sundakov, 2001, p. 10). Kuzio and D'Anieri (2002) summarize this common practice in the following manner: "All CIS states – Ukraine included – have a penchant for drafting long documents that are then ignored or only partially fulfilled. These are more akin to letters of intent than contractual obligations" (p. 18). To sum up, the discussion of educational policy context in the existing literature is organized around two major themes: "educational crisis" and "an attack against the postcommunist state." These two themes will be revisited in the analysis section of this chapter.

Rationalities Explained

Borrowing from Popkewitz's quote cited in the beginning of the chapter, the main thesis of this study can be described as "a diagnostic of the systems of reason" in "the age of school reform" in postcommunist Ukraine from 1991 to 2008. In order to trace the "systems of reason," the chapter introduces the concept of policy rationalities to account for the structures beneath policy discourses that frame the logic and define the purpose of educational reform. In the course of analysis three sets of policy rationalities have been identified: (1) rationalities of nation- and state-building, (2) rationalities of comparison and critique, and (3) rationalities of (what I call) catching-up Europeanization.

The first set of rationalities, those of nation- and state-building, articulates the logic of educational reformation as a tool for building a new state and nation. The realization of this rationale is being achieved through institutionalizing what official discourses define as the "national idea" in education. This official term refers to the sets of pedagogical principles aimed at raising national awareness among Ukrainian students (Stepanenko, 1999, pp. 16–17). The second set of rationalities is that of comparison and critique. Their main function is to state, point, hint, or allude to the inferiority of the national vis-à-vis Western (or in some cases Soviet) standards, expertise, and overall level of development. The third set

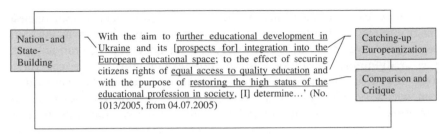

Fig. 1. An Example of the Synthesis of Rationalities. *Note:* Text translated from Ukrainian by author.

of policy rationalities is the most recently articulated logic of, what I call here, "catching-up Europeanization." According to this rationale, the need for reform is driven by the political aspiration of being reunited (and associated) with Europe (rather than Russia). As the analysis will demonstrate, reaching the level of development of other European countries, i.e., "catching up" with "Europe," has become a grand purpose of national development projects and a mantra of political and policy-making discourses.

It is important to emphasize that rationalities of nation- and state-building, comparison and critique, and catching-up Europeanization are not fixed entities and are differentiated here for analytical purposes only. In practice there is a great degree of interdependence and overlap between them. Policy agenda as it is formulated from the mid-2000s onwards is characterized by a growing interconnectedness between the three rationalities. Fig. 1, which quotes the preamble of the Presidential Decree "On Urgent Measures Aimed at Ensuring the Functionality and Development of Education in Ukraine," No. 1012/2005, provides an example of this increasingly synthesized policy agenda.

Conceptualization: Analytical Distinctions between
Rationalities, Discourses, and Texts

Before analysis proceeds any further, it is important to draw clear analytical distinctions between policy rationalities, policy discourses, and policy texts. By outlining conceptual differences between rationalities, discourses, and texts, this study attempts to avoid a commonplace approach of doing analysis at the surface of the policy text without paying due analytical consideration to the "systems of reason" that enable the production of the text, and make the text acceptable, convincing, and logical in a given context. By introducing a category of policy rationalities, this study argues that prior to directly engaging with the categories and discourses suggested by policy-makers – be it "globalization," "knowledge economy," "quality," "standards," or any other policy "solutions" – the first step of policy analysis should entail the study of policy rationalities.

This study argues that rationalities and discourses are positioned at different levels of policy analysis. Rationalities are not discourses per se, but are the formations beneath discourses, which constrain the content of what is said and thought in a particular area of social practice (i.e., educational policy-making) in a given period of time. However, rationalities do not only constrain what is thought, but also constitute an environment under which some discourses are established as true and others as false. In this meaning, rationalities can be understood as "conditions of possibility" for discourses to emerge, and be accepted or rejected in a particular context. The above definition of rationalities builds on the Foucauldian notion of "episteme," which he later substituted with "discursive formation" to emphasize the role of discourse in the production of knowledge (Dreyfus & Rabinow, 1982; Foucault, 2001, 2002).

Fig. 2 summarizes conceptual distinctions between rationalities, discourses, and texts. The three sets of rationalities – nation- and state-building, comparison and critique, and catching-up Europeanization – are presented at the bottom of the diagram. These rationalities provide a framework for what can be thought and said in the field of education policy in postcommunist Ukraine. All these thoughts, visions, and ideas are further organized into a series of discourses, or borrowing from Foucault's (1980, p. 133) new "regimes of truth" about "education," "development," "individual," "society," "state," and "government." In Ukraine these new "truth regimes" are articulated as discourses of "Ukrainization," "quality control," "globalization," "European integration," "national upbringing," "equal access," "standards," "modernization," "development," "educational crisis," "democratization," "decentralization," "standardized assessment," and "public-state governance" to name a few from a list that is far from complete. Policy texts, presented at the top of the diagram, are conceptualized as material representations, and as snapshots of discourses, which when outside the text, are in constant flux. The figures highlighted in gray use nation- and state-building rationale as an example of the trajectory of discourse formation.

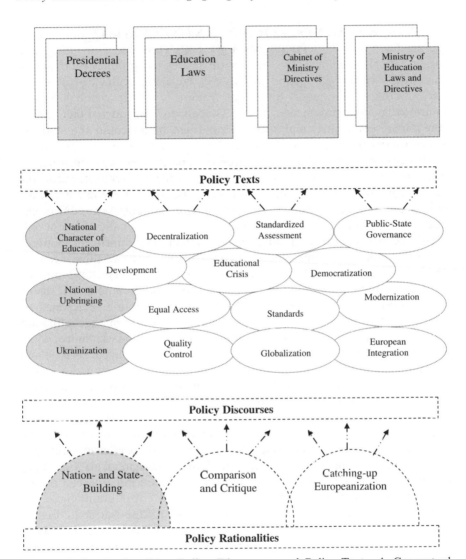

Fig. 2. Policy Rationalities, Policy Discourses, and Policy Texts: A Conceptual Mapping.

ANALYSIS: POLICY RATIONALITIES DECONSTRUCTED

The "Ideal," the "Real," and the "Strategy" for Getting There

Fourteen policy documents and 17 years of policy-making (1991–2008) represent textual and temporal borders of analysis.[5] The official authorship of the documents is limited to three state actors: the President, Parliament, and the Cabinet of Ministers. The documents authorized by the Ministry of Education and Science of Ukraine are not included in the analysis because in the majority of cases ministerial documents draw heavily and reiterate discourses emanating from the state actors above the Ministry.

Despite being written in different years and under different political leadership, all documents under analysis evolve around three lines of argumentation, which will be called here "ideal," "real," and "the strategy for getting there." The first "ideal" part of the narrative, so called for its pronounced "idealized" view of education and society, is underpinned by the rationalities of nation- and state-building. This line of argumentation defines the purposes of education and upbringing in newly independent Ukraine and maps out the models of the new ("ideal") citizen, society, and the state.

Having presented the ideal view of education – education how it *should* be – the documents move to describe the current, i.e., the "real", state of education – education how it *is* now. Many facets of educational crisis, its causes, and consequences are the themes that hold this part of the documents together. In advancing this narrative the argument spells out the gaps between the "ideal" and the "real" in Ukrainian education. Many discourses advanced in this part of the document are underpinned by the rationalities of comparison and critique.

The "ideal" and the "real" narratives contextualize the third line of argumentation, called here the "strategy," which spells out multiple tactics on how to achieve the desired "ideal" level of educational development. Among these multiple tactics, "modernization of educational structure and content," "new educational governance," "quality monitoring," and "new forms of assessment" are recognized as the most effective measures. In one way or another, all these measures are connected with the discourse of Europeanization, that is, the "strategy." To sum up, the analysis that follows traces the articulation of the three rationalities under analysis through the metaphors of the "ideal," the "real," and the "strategy."

Defining the "Ideal": The Models of a New Education, Individual, Society, and the State

We have witnessed during this process the emergence of a hybrid socialist-neoliberal (or perhaps "neoleninist") form of political rationality that is at once authoritarian in a familiar political and technocratic sense yet, at the same time, seeks to govern certain subjects, but not all, through their own autonomy.

(Sigley, 2006, p. 489)

Sigley's quote about the hybrid nature of the emergent governmental rationality in non-Western societies captures well the processes of discourse formation in postcommunist Ukraine. As a result of such unusual coupling of rationalities, Ukrainian political and policy discourses present a bricolage of ideas, concepts, and strategies that draw on opposing sets of values (traditional and postmodern) and contrasting approaches to government (communist and neoliberal). This hybridity of rationalities creates discontinuities at the level of policy text that are of particular importance in the study of policy.

The first "ideal" policy narrative, underpinned by the rationalities of nation- and state-building, opens with the definitions of education and upbringing and their role in building a new society and state. All these definitions advance the idea of educational development as the precondition for the emergence of the new ("ideal") type of society, individual, and state as envisaged by the policy-makers. This "ideal" policy narrative develops an argument about how education *should* function rather than how it *is* functioning under the current circumstances. Table 1 provides examples of such definitions.

The table demonstrates that during the 17 years of policy-making, the definitions of education may have been refined, but the idea of education as the basis for personal, societal, and state development has remained constant. In particular, the documents define education as "the foundation of [the] intellectual, cultural, spiritual, social, and economic development of society and the state," "a guarantee of [the] Ukraine's future," "a motive force for civil society development," and "a strategic resource for improving people's well-being, securing national interests and strengthening the authority and competitive ability of the [Ukrainian] state in the global arena."

Though policy-makers make every attempt to construct a view of education as an arena of consensus, tensions arise at the level of policy construction and drafting that need to be addressed in this analysis. The first tension is evident in the list of foundational principles of education.

Table 1. Defining "Education".

Education		
Definition	Goals	Values
Education is the foundation of [the] intellectual, cultural, spiritual, social, and economic *development of society and the state.* [It is aimed at] the *all-round* [*sic*] *development of an individual* as the highest societal value, development of his/her talents, intellectual and physical abilities, *upbringing* [nurturing] of *high moral values*, and the formation of citizens capable of *conscious social choice*, which is the basis for the development of the intellectual, creative, and cultural potential of the Ukrainian people, raising educational levels and satisfying the *economy's need* for qualified specialists. *(Law "On Education," No. 1060-XII, from May 23, 1991)*	*Education* consolidates the *national idea* and facilitates *national self-identification*, development of the Ukrainian culture, and learning the values of world culture and universal human achievements. *(Presidential Decree No. 347/2002 on National Doctrine of Educational Development, from April 17, 2002)*	*Education* in Ukraine is based on the principles of *humanism, democracy, national consciousness* [*sic*], *mutual respect between nations and peoples. (Law "On Education," No. 1060-XII from May 23, 1991)* *Education* in Ukraine is an *open social institution. (Presidential Decree "On the Urgent Measures Aimed at Ensuring the Functionality and Development of Education in Ukraine," No. 1013/ 2005, from July 04, 2005)*
Education is the foundation of personal, societal, national, and state development; it is a *guarantee of [the] Ukraine's future.* Education is *a determinant factor* behind political, socioeconomic, cultural, and scientific life of society ... Education *is a motive force* for civil society development. *(Presidential Decree "On the National Doctrine of Educational Development," No. 347/2002, from April 17, 2002)*	*Education* reproduces [*sic*] and enlarges the *intellectual, spiritual,* and *economic potential of society. (Presidential Decree "On the National Doctrine of Educational Development," No. 347/ 2002, from April 17, 2002)*	*Education* has a *humanist character* and is based on the cultural and historical values of the Ukrainian people, their *traditions, and spirituality. (Presidential Decree "On the National Doctrine of Educational Development," No. 347/ 2002, from April 17, 2002)*

Table 1. (*Continued*)

Education		
Definition	Goals	Values
Education is *a strategic resource* for improving *people's well-being,* securing *national interests,* and strengthening the authority and *competitive ability* of the [Ukrainian] state in the global arena. (*Presidential Decree "On the National Doctrine of Educational Development," No. 347/2002, from April 17, 2002*)	*Education* should assist in the formation of *the new system of social values* – open, diversified, spiritually and culturally rich, tolerant. [Education] ensures the formation of *a citizen and a patriot,* [and] the consolidation of society on the principles of *human rights and social equality.* (*Presidential Decree "On the National Doctrine of Educational Development," No. 347/2002, from April 17, 2002*)	

Discourses of "democracy," "humanism," and "tolerance," which continue to shape policy agenda in today's postmodern Europe, disagree vehemently with the discourse of "national consciousness [*sic*]" – the discourse of nationalism. Nationalism, a controversial yet inescapable concept of European modernity (Greenfeld, 1993, pp. 31–44, 133), has gradually fallen from official discourses in light of Europe's increasingly globalized and multicultural state. In Ukraine, however, discourses of "national consciousness," "national awareness," and "national self-identification" have recently re-emerged as central themes in education policy agenda. Ukrainian policy-makers see little conflict in the blending of postmodern and traditional (modern or premodern) value systems, and more examples of these apparently (in their view) unproblematic textual couplings will be presented later in this analysis.

A further tension evident at the textual policy level arises from the policy-makers attempts to affirm the primacy of the social and personal dimensions of education over the economic. For example, in the definitions of education as "the foundation of an intellectual, cultural, spiritual, social, and economic development of society and the state"; "a determinant factor behind political, socio-economic, cultural and scientific life of society"; and "the intellectual, spiritual and economic potential of society," the intellectual, cultural, spiritual, political, and social are prioritized over the economic. Though references to the "economic" are found in the expressions such as "economy's needs," "economic development," the "socio-economic life of society," and the "competitive ability of the [Ukrainian] state in the global arena," these are scarce and marginal in comparison to the text's consideration of social and personal dimensions. Most strikingly, the tension between the "social" and "economic," the two contrasting domains of social practice, is captured in the definition of education as the foundation of the "spiritual and economic potential of society."

Defining National Upbringing

"National upbringing" is another key concept extensively discussed in the "ideal" narrative. The concept of "upbringing" has a long history in Ukrainian education. Originally formulated as the core ideological objective of Soviet education, the pedagogical discourse of "upbringing" was aimed at cultivating the virtues of collectivism, diligence, respect of authority, and one party rule in generations of Soviet citizens. Once refined and stripped of its ideological baggage, the concept was reconstructed and renamed "national upbringing." Since this time, "national upbringing" has been successfully utilized by policy-makers as a tool for the construction of a new sense of national identity in new generations of Ukrainian citizens.

The definitions of "upbringing" advanced in the policy texts are presented in Table 2. In line with the above definitions of education, the concept of upbringing combines traditional and postmodern values, a combination the documents frequently refer to as both "organic" and "harmonious." The examples of traditional virtues include "respect for womankind" and "succession between generations," while postmodern virtues stress the importance of "active social choice," "mobility," and "competitiveness."

However, the above definitions of "education" and "upbringing" are not merely interesting from the point of view of the discourses embedded within them, but more particularly in consideration of the models of the "individual," "society," and the "state" inscribed in these definitions. Drawing on the examples from the policy documents, the analysis reconstructs the models of individual, society, and the state, and pinpoints the tensions between traditional and postmodern discourse inherent in the politics and policies of postcommunist Ukraine.

Table 3 maps out the models of the individual, society, and the state as embedded in the documents under analysis. The qualities that are perceived as desirable in an individual and society fall into two broad categories:

Table 2. Defining "National Upbringing".

National Upbringing		
Definition	Goals	Values
National upbringing is an *organic component of education*; it embraces all levels and structures of education. *(Cabinet of Ministers Decree "On the State National Programme 'Education' ('Ukraine XXI century')," No. 896, from November 3, 1993)* The main components of the *national upbringing* are *civic and patriotic education. (Presidential Decree No. 347/2002 on National Doctrine of Educational Development, from April 17, 2002)*	The main goal of *national upbringing* is the acquisition of *social experience* by the young generation, the inheritance of the *spiritual achievements* of the Ukrainian people, the development of high [sic] *culture of interethnic* relations, the formation in young people – irrespective of their national origins – individual characteristics of the citizens of the Ukrainian state, the development of *spiritual and physical perfection* [sic], and a moral, artistically aesthetic, legal, working and ecological culture. *(Cabinet of Ministers Decree "On the State National Programme 'Education' ('Ukraine XXI century')," No. 896, from November 3, 1993)*	The principles of *humanism, democratism* [sic], *unity of family and school,* the succession and inheritance of generations are the core bases of the *national upbringing. (Cabinet of Ministers Decree "On the State National Programme 'Education' ('Ukraine XXI century')," No. 896, from November 3, 1993)* The principles of universal morality: *truth, justice, devotion, patriotism, humanism, kindness, self-control, diligence, and judiciousness. (Law "On Education," No. 1060-XII, from May 23, 1991)*
National upbringing is an integral part and primary objective of education. National upbringing is aimed at the *formation and socialization* of responsible citizens and patriots with a high level of culture for	*National upbringing* ensures the *all-round* [sic] *harmonious development* and integrity of an individual and the development of talents and gifts, and the enrichment on this basis of the intellectual	*National upbringing* is aimed at bringing people to the *deepest layers* of the national *culture and spirituality,* the formation in children and young people of the national standpoints, ideas, views, beliefs based on

Table 2. (*Continued*)

National Upbringing		
Definition	Goals	Values
participation in international relations; it is also aimed at nurturing in Ukrainian youth a need and ability to live in a *civil society*. National upbringing assists in developing students' spiritual and physical perfection [*sic*], industriousness, moral, aesthetic, and ecological culture. *(Presidential Decree No. 347/2002 on National Doctrine of Educational Development, from April 17, 2002)*	potential of people. It nurtures spirituality and culture in the upbringing [formation] of a *citizen capable of independent thinking*, social choice, and action, aimed at the *flourishing of Ukraine*. *(Presidential Decree "On the National Doctrine of Educational Development," No. 347/2002, from April 17, 2002)*	*national and world culture. (Presidential Decree "On the National Doctrine of Educational Development," No. 347/2002, from April 17, 2002)*

premodern (or traditional, and encapsulating certain aspects of what could loosely be considered "modern") and postmodern (or neoliberal). In the model of an individual, examples of premodern qualities include a "respectful attitude to parents, womankind [*sic*], national culture, history, national sacred objects," while postmodern qualities include the ability to become or remain "autonomous," "self-sufficient," "mobile," and "competitive in the job market."

This clash between traditional and postmodern is most intensely perceptible in the definition of upbringing as the "socialization of responsible *citizens* and *patriots*." A law-abiding "citizen" and a "patriot" are two distinct subjectivities, and the emergence of the "patriot" in Western political thought (at the very least) chronologically preceded the emergence of the "citizen." In textual policy, however, they are articulated simultaneously, and this synchronicity is repeatedly described as both "organic" and "harmonious."

When addressing the second column of the table – society as it is envisaged by the policy-makers – it is clear that it is required to be both "spiritually and culturally rich," and additionally, "civil" or "civilized,"

Table 3. The Models of Individual, Society, and the State Embedded in the Definitions of "Education" and "Upbringing".

Individual		Society		The State
Premodern (Traditional)	Postmodern (Neoliberal)	Premodern (Traditional)	Postmodern (Neoliberal)	Postmodern (Neoliberal)
Patriot	Citizen	Tolerant and peaceful environment	Civil	Sovereign
With high [sic] moral, language, artistically aesthetic, legal, working, and ecological culture [sic]	Autonomous	Spiritually and culturally rich	Civilized [sic]	Independent
Has respectful attitude to parents, womankind [sic], national culture, history, national sacred objects	Self-sufficient		Legal	Democratic
Diligent Industrious	Mobile Independent thinker		Democratic Competitive in the global arena	Welfare Lawful
Spiritually and Physically Perfect [sic]	Qualified		Open	An integral part of the European and global community
	Specialist Creative Lifelong learn[er] Capable of conscious social choice and action Competitive in the job marketplace Aware of the link between the ideas of freedom, human rights, and individual responsibilities With a democratic worldview		Diversified Tolerant	

"legal," "democratic," and "open." "Spirituality," which is not generally a component of political vocabulary, potentially creates such a combination of characteristics and values problematic. The state, which is "sovereign," "independent," "democratic," "[a] welfare [state]," "lawful," and "an integral part of the European and global community," exhibits all the characteristics of postmodern neoliberal state.

What this study interprets as the tension between the "traditional" and "postmodern," postcommunist studies capture in the concepts of "ambivalence," "ambiguity," (Riabchuk, 2007, pp. 70–89) or "divided mentality" (Holloway, 2003, pp. 364–375); or formulate into a question: "Why [is] Ukraine [...] trapped between East and West?" (Riabchuk, 2007, pp. 70–89). These analytical descriptions reflect a deep-seated tension inherent in the Ukrainian nation-building strategy that seeks to construct two distinct forms of nation simultaneously: *ethno cultural*, which unites its populace on the basis of one language, history, and ethnicity; and *civic*, which binds the concept of national identity with concepts of civil rights, laws, and responsibilities (cf. Wilson, 1997, p. 148). These two distinct nation-building projects mobilize and demand distinct political vocabularies. While the first project makes an appeal to national spirituality – the sanctity of Ukraine's national culture, language, customs, and traditions; and respect for woman and the importance of intergenerational inheritance – the second calls for qualities that render an individual and the state competitive in the global market.

Defining the "Real": The Many Facets of "Educational Crisis"

[T]he state **does not fully realise** the Constitutional rights of the citizens to full general secondary education.[6]

The existing system of educational governance **does not fully accord** with the modern principles of democratisation, which recognise growing influence of public opinion upon governmental decisions, ability to react dynamically to the needs of society, re-distribution of the governmental functions between the state organs and the organs of self-governance.[7]

"Does not fully" and "is not yet" are the two most commonly found expressions in the opening of the second section of policy documents that are considered the "real" policy narrative in this analysis. The tone of the "real" policy narrative is very different from those outlined above. This narrative presents a notably pessimistic view of the various problems and crises in Ukrainian education as they are perceived by the policy-makers. In developing its argument, the "real" policy narrative points to the gaps between the "real" and the "ideal" conceptualizations of Ukrainian education. In the policy documents the "real" narrative unfolds in three stages. First, it engages with the "ideal" definitions of education; second, it maps out the facets of educational crisis; and finally, it reflects upon and criticizes the reasons behind these multiple crises. These three sections articulate a strong critique against the state's inability to effectively manage the multiple consequences of postcommunist transformation.

The "real" policy narrative opens with explicit references to the "ideal" views of education advanced in earlier policy texts, namely, "The State National 'Education' Programme" ("Ukraine XXI century", 1993) and the "National Doctrine of Educational Development" (2002). The only noticeable difference between the "real" and the "ideal" definitions of education seen in these texts is the use of "does not fully" and "is not yet" in front of the main verbs of the text outlining the "real" policy narrative. The above quotation provides an example of this: in particular, the statement from the National Doctrine of Educational Development, "[e]ducation *consolidates* national idea [*sic*]...," in the Cabinet of Ministers Order No. 396-r is restated as "Ukrainian education *does not fully consolidate* the idea of national statehood." Similarly, the definitions of education as "*a motive force* for civil society development" and education that is "*aimed* at all-rounded development of an individual" are restated as "[education] *does not fully assist* in the process of formation of civil society" and "*is not yet aimed* at all-rounded development of an individual." The full text of the quote from the Cabinet of Ministers Order No. 396-r reads:

> Ukrainian education *does not fully consolidate* the idea of national statehood and patriotism, [education] *does not fully assist* in the process of formation of civil society, democratisation, openness, and transparency. [...] Education and upbringing process *is not yet aimed* at all-rounded development of an individual, meeting his/her needs, upbringing of the conscious citizen, patriot, meeting the needs of society and the needs of the job market in competitive, experienced and responsible experts.[8]

The fact that the "real" policy narrative builds on and enters into a dialogue with the "ideal" narrative creates a condition for the emergence of *critique*, which is a relatively new development in educational policy-making in postcommunist Ukraine. The emergent culture of critique of political thought and policy strategy in a non-liberal context can be linked to Foucault's (1983) discussion of *parrhesia* or "truth-telling," which Foucault believes to be a deep-seated cultural practice and societal value in the West. The obligation to tell the truth, to be both critical and transparently reflective, cultivated through centuries of religious confessional and contemporary secularized (medicotherapeutic) practices, is an important premise in the "historical ontology" of the *liberal subject* (Besley & Peters, 2007, p. 55). The emergence of critique in the context of postcommunist Ukraine indicates that policy-making culture is undergoing major shifts, which is an integral part of the transformation of a former communist state into a neoliberal one.

Having reflected upon the "ideal" definitions of education, the "real" policy argument proceeds to uncover the features of the "educational crisis." Table 4 presents the citations that describe the critical state of Ukrainian education. "Deep crisis," "catastrophic lack," "ruination," "outflow," "violated rights," "rapidly falling prestige," "devaluation," "bureaucratization," and "impoverishment" are some of the expressions that permeate this critical and pessimistic perspective on education. In particular, the critique delineates five problem areas in Ukrainian education. These are (1) *the lack of teaching personnel*, (2) *the falling prestige of education*, (3) *the problem of the social protection of teachers*, (4) *the changes in the network of schools*, and finally (5) *the modernization of knowledge*.

The "real" policy narrative concludes by reflecting upon the four possible reasons for the crisis. The first and most significant reason is formulated as the *significant reduction in educational spending*. To appreciate the full scope of the problem of underfunding, the analysis will refer to Pleskovic, Åslund, Bader, and Campbell (2002), that contends that 10 years after gaining independence, state spending on education in postcommunist countries typically falls to "about *one-third* of its real level a decade ago," tremendously affecting teachers' salaries and the overall level of educational provision (Pleskovic et al., 2002, p. 19). Hence, education in former Soviet states suffered state funding cuts of almost 66%, demonstrating a major and unprecedented consequence of postcommunist transformation.

The second reason is formulated as the *nonimplementation of the policies on social protection*, in particular, "Articles 57 and 61 of the Law on Education (1060-12)" and, "Article 25 of the Law on General Secondary Education." The third explanation for the crisis according to the policy text is the *legacy of the Soviet system of education*. Two clear examples of this explanation are the "distortion of the goals and functions of education" and the "bureaucratization of all levels of [the] educational system," both of which are highlighted in the text. The fourth reason, underpinned by nostalgia for a big paternalistic state, can be described as *the weakness of state control* "over the adherence to the state standards and quality of education." This presents a further example of the ambivalent nature of postcommunist critique, which on the one hand denounces the legacies of

Table 4. Facets of "Educational Crisis" and the Reasons behind It.

The Facets of the "Crisis"	The Reasons behind the "Crisis"
[C]urrently *higher education in Ukraine is in deep crisis …* There is a *catastrophic lack of funding …* The *outflow* of pedagogical and teaching staff is *on its rise.* The interest in doing fundamental sciences *is falling.* The demands for the level of education and general culture *have fallen sharply; the lack* of textbooks, teaching manuals, and other teaching material is felt very strongly	The main reason for this is the *significant reduction in educational spending,* which has brought educational establishments, considerable number of students, pedagogical, and research staff *to the brink of impoverishment*
(Presidential Decree "On the Main Directions of Higher Education Reform in Ukraine," No. 832/95, from September 12, 1995)	*(Parliamentary Decree "On the Results of the Parliamentary Hearings 'On the Implementation of the Education Laws'," No. 210-15, from October 24, 2002)*
The *rights of the citizens* to general secondary education are *violated,* similarly as *the right of the pedagogical and research staff* to adequate level of social protection. *The prestige* of educational profession is *rapidly falling.* The level of the salary of pedagogical staff is *half the level of the salary in industry*	Low salaries of pedagogical staff, *nonimplementation* of the Articles 57 and 61 of the Law on Education (1060-12), Article 25 of the Law on General Secondary Education (651-14) impede professional development of teachers; it has become one of the main reasons of the low level of students' achievements and a major impediment toward an effective organization of teaching and upbringing.
(Parliamentary Decree "On the Results of the Parliamentary Hearings 'On the Implementation of the Education Laws'," No. 210–15, from October 24, 2002)	*(Parliamentary Decree "On the Results of the Parliamentary Hearings 'On the Implementation of the Education Laws'," No. 210 15, from October 24, 2002)*
The *modernization* of the educational content is being carried out *slowly,* the interdisciplinary and intersubject *links are weakening.* The network of general secondary, vocational and higher educational establishments of different forms of ownership is *in need of improvement.* The network of general secondary education establishments for gifted students: specialized schools, gymnasiums, collegiums, lyceums – is *developing slowly. The ruination* of the system of preschool and out-of-school	[It is a result of] *distortion of the goals and functions of education, bureaucratization* of all levels of educational system
	(Cabinet of Ministers Decree "On the State National Programme 'Education' ('Ukraine XXI century')," No. 896, from November 3, 1993)

Table 4. (*Continued*)

The Facets of the "Crisis"	The Reasons behind the "Crisis"
education *continues*. The schools in *rural areas are in crisis*. The achievements in the supply of pedagogical staff in the general secondary education *are falling*	
(*Parliamentary Decree "On the Results of the Parliamentary Hearings 'On the Implementation of the Education Laws'," No. 210–15, from October 24, 2002*)	There is *no thorough control* of the adherence to the state standards and quality of education (*Parliamentary Decree "On the Results of the Parliamentary Hearings 'On the Implementation of the Education Laws'," No. 210–15, from October 24, 2002*)

the Soviet regime, but, on the other, views a big state as desirable under the current postcommunist circumstances.

In all textual explanations the reasons behind the crisis and the nature of the crisis itself are presented as "processes without actors" (cf. Walters, 2005, p. 6). Constructing policy narrative in such an "impersonal" manner imparts the text with the quality of objectivity, which is a key characteristic of the policy text as a genre. However, "impersonal" narration also leads inevitably to "impersonal" critique. That is, critique that is limited to a critical evaluation of the processes but not the actors behind these processes; the identification of which is crucial for understanding and overcoming the crisis. The resulting critique, which accompanies the shift from communist to neoliberal regimes of government, is marked by a lack of specificity and a reliance upon sweeping generalizations; one of the most significant of which is to view a lack of "funding" as the sole reason behind the crisis and "the state" as the only actor responsible for the crisis.

Defining "The Strategy" on How to Get There: Catching Up with Europe and the World

Up until today, Ukrainian education **has not yet reached the European level** of education quality.[9]

The "strategy," which is the third policy narrative, outlines multiple tactics on how to bridge the "ideal" and "real" conceptions of education. The main objective of all of these tactics is "reaching the European level of education quality" (No. 396-r, 2006), which in the earlier policy text was formulated as "to bridge the gap between the national level of development and the living standards and the level of development of the developed countries of the world" (No. 377/2002, 2002). The "strategy" is the longest and most complex narrative in the comparison with the "ideal" and the "real," as this narrative seeks to target each and every subject, organization, as well as the system of education as a whole, to align the existing Ukrainian norms, capacities, and ethos with those in "Europe" and the "world." All discourses in the "strategy" narrative are underpinned by the rationalities of catching-up Europeanization.

The "strategy" narrative opens with an affirmation of the European aspirations of Ukraine, in which "Europe" is constructed as a new strategic partner and a guideline for Ukraine's reformation strategy. The idea of "partnership" is articulated through multiple references to "European integration" and "European standards," creating an impression of the certainty and irrevocability of the Europe-oriented reformation strategy: "taking into account the prospects of integration into European Union" (No. 1013/2005, 2005), "integration into the European and global space" (No. 396-r, 2006), "speeding up the process of integration of Ukraine's higher education into global structures" (No. 244/2008, 2008), "building a common European home [*sic*]" (No. 347/2002, 2002), "on the basis of the standards of the European Union member states" (No. 1013/2005, 2005), "according to the European standards of education quality stipulated in the European Quality Assurance Register for Higher Education," "the adherence of the national legislation to the international norms" (No. 396-r, 2006), "implementation of the objectives of the Dakar (1999), Prague (1998) and Seoul (1999) global educational forums and Bologna Declaration (1999)" (No. 244/2008, 2008), and "at the European and global educational arena" (No. 347/202, 2002).

The references to the work of international organizations, i.e., "[Ukraine's] involvement in bi-lateral and multi-lateral projects by UNESCO, UNICEF, the European Union, the Council of Europe, World Bank, international educational foundations, and other international organisations" (No. 347/2002, 2002), as well as its "participation in the international comparative studies of education quality monitoring" (No. 347/2002, 2002), are presented as highly positive tendencies. Above all, they are important signs of Ukraine's recognition in the European and global political arena. Through these and similar expressions, Ukrainian policy-makers forge a vision of an already extant alliance between "Europe" and Ukraine, despite the fact that the real prospect of Ukraine's official membership in the EU in the immediate future is essentially nonexistent (Sasse, 2010). Such ambition of domestic actors, which, despite their countries' remote prospects of official EU membership, nevertheless continue to gear their policies and reorient their political and social institutions in line with EU standards, can be termed "voluntary Europeanization."

In advancing its argument, the "strategy" narrative makes multiple comparisons between the previous and the current system of education, which in the "National Doctrine of Educational Development" is called a "new type of humanistic-innovative [sic] education." By referencing both the past and the future of education and by casting certain qualities of the education system as "old" and others as "new," the "strategy" narrative constructs a "cognitive map" of postcommunist transition whereby "old" is conceptualized as the point of departure, and "new," "modern," "latest," and "progressive" are the points of destination, for the national reform strategy. The logic of progression embedded in such "maps" builds upon oppositions between communist and neoliberal systems of rule. Conceptual binaries, which present two poles in the map of transition, give the actors a sense of direction and infuse a readily digested meaning into the process of educational reformation.

Table 5 traces the references to the "old" and "new" models of social organization within the four domains of power: *pedagogy, society, state,* and *governance.* According to the policy documents, the "old" system of rule is characterized by "authoritarian pedagogy," a "totalitarian state," an "industrial society," and a system of "state governance." These are now to be transformed into a "new" model of social organization, the main features of which are "humanistic-innovative [sic] education," the "civil society," the "information-technological [cf. knowledge] society," and a system of "state-public governance." In constructing the "cognitive map" of transition, the documents make use of traditional binary oppositions such as authoritarian/ humanistic, state/civil society, industrial/information-technological [knowledge] society, national nihilism/self-identification, monopoly/decentralization, and totalitarian/democratization to emphasize the differences between the communist and neoliberal systems of rule and approaches to government.

Apart from these traditional binaries, the documents introduce a new contextual binary of "person-oriented" vs. "process-oriented" governance (No. 347/2002, 2002). "Person-oriented governance," which alludes to the restriction of personal freedoms, is presented as an artifact of the "old" system. Contrasted with this, the "process-oriented governance" advances a view of the government as an activity aimed at the normalization and optimization of "naturally" evolving social processes, and is based on the

Table 5. "Cognitive Map" of Postcommunist Transition.

Old		New, Modern, Latest, Progressive
From	*Authoritarian pedagogy ...* • Devaluation of the universal humanistic values • Negation [repression] of the natural individual abilities • Disconnection of education from the national roots [*sic*]	*To* ... *New type of humanistic-innovative* [*sic*] *education* • Modern pedagogical techniques • New generation of pedagogical staff • National self-realization
	Industrial society ...	... *Information-Technological society* • Use of informational technology
	Totalitarian state ... • State monopoly • National nihilism	... Civil society • Democratization • Self-identification
	State governance ... • Person-oriented governance	... *State-public governance* • Process-oriented governance • Decentralization of governance • Self-governance • Autonomy • Educational leadership • Involvement of youth and woman in the governance of education • New financial mechanisms of educational development • International collaboration • System of monitoring • New economic foundation of education • New legislative basis

principles of minimizing outside interference and maximizing the individual subjects' ability to self-govern (cf. Dean, 1999, 2002; Rose, 1991, 1996).

Relevant to the map of cognitive transitions is the discussion started among Ukrainian academics who attempt to theorize the relationships between the state and society and therefore devise a new model of state governance. Drawing on the work of Habermas's *The Theory of Communicative Action* (1984), Korzhenko and Nikitin (2007) conceptualize the shift of governmental paradigms in postcommunist Ukraine, as a move from "monological" governance, based on a "subject–object" relationship between the state and society, to "dialogical" governance, which presupposes "subject–subject" relationships between those who govern and those who are governed (Korzhenko & Nikitin, 2007, pp. 80–82).

The title of Korzhenko and Nikitin's work (2007), "Theoretical and Methodological Foundations of the Formation of the New Paradigm of State Governance," as well as the title of the conference it was presented at, "The Reform Strategy of the System of the State Governance Based on the Principles of Democratic Governance: Conference proceedings with the contributions of foreign experts," presents examples of an ongoing effort among academics and policy-makers to rewrite the principles and foundations of the old system of state governance and signal the emergence of a new, fairer, and more just governmental paradigm.

CONCLUDING REMARKS

The main objective of this chapter was to identify core foundational principles, which underpin the logic and define the purpose of educational reformation in postcommunist Ukraine. Following the mode of inquiry suggested by Foucault (1991, 2007, 2008), further developed by Rose (1991, 1996, 1999, 2007), Dean (1999, 2002), Lemke (2000, 2001, 2007), Rose and Miller (2008), Sigley (2006) and other neo-Foucauldians, and then applied to the study of education policy by Tikly (2003), Besley and Peters (2007), Doherty (2006, 2007), Fejes and Nicoll (2007), Fimyar (2008a, 2008b, 2010), Popkewitz (2000, 2007, 2008), and others, this chapter introduced and employed the concept of "policy rationalities" in the study of educational policy-making in a postcommunist country using Ukraine as a case study. The concept of "policy rationalities," which is similar in many ways to Foucault's conception of "episteme" (Dreyfus & Rabinow, 1982; Foucault, 2001), Dean's understanding of the "telos of government" (1999, p. 17), and Popkewitz's "system of reason" of education (2008, p. 1), was used to refer to the structures beneath policy discourses that provide "conditions of possibility" for existing "regimes of truth" in education, and extension, in politics and society. As a unit of analysis distinct from "policy discourses," "policy rationalities" widen the field of inquiry so that it is not limited to the surface of the policy text, but rather engages with the cultural logic and political rationalities of a society transitioning from an authoritarian and centralized mode of government to a democratic, individualized, and market-based one.

By extracting the specificities of Ukrainian education policy discourses, and presenting such findings, as Ball, Goodson, and Maguire (2007, p. xi) describes, "forensically," the argument sought to introduce doubt, recognize contradictions, and "unsettle" common sense embedded in the official narratives of education, upbringing, as well as the models of individual, society, and the state. The analysis illuminated major tensions between the traditional and postmodern, as well as the social and the economic in the current educational policy debate in postcommunist Ukraine. These tensions were attributed to an emergent hybrid communist–neoliberal rationality that governs subjects in familiar authoritarian ways, but at the same time, at the level of discourse, seeks to cultivate their autonomy and self-governance (cf. Sigley, 2006, pp. 487–508). These tensions and inconsistencies embodied in the text are further exacerbated by the attempts of the political and policy-making elite to both "recapture Ukraine's past" and build a "spiritually and culturally rich" nation, while at the same time, "catch up with developed '"Europe"'" and thereby build a "modern and technologically advanced" market economy. Inevitably, the two distinct political projects envisaged here are prone to raise conflicts and incoherencies at the surface level of the policy text as well as within the process of policy implementation.

NOTES

1. I chose to use "Foucault-inspired" rather than "Foucauldian" or "neo-Foucauldian" as the authors cited in this chapter often do not categorize themselves in such terms. Many of these studies, as Dean (2010, p. 2) points out, are the result of deliberation on Foucault's methods and concepts in relation to individual lines of inquiry pursued by each of these authors.
2. The examples of mainstream policy research focusing on the countries of the former Soviet Union include the works by Bahry (2005), DeYoung (2005), Janmaat (1999, 2008), Janmaat and Piattoeva (2007), Koshmanova and Ravchyna (2008), Nikitin and Parashenko (2009), Reeves (2005), Seddon (2005), Silova (2005, 2006), Silova and Steiner-Khamsi (2008), Stepanenko (1999), Wanner (1998), and Zajda (2005).
3. Neoliberal imaginary is a term popularized by Appadurai (2001, p. 15), which is now widely used in sociology, cultural studies, and policy sociology. Here I draw on the work of Rizvi and Lingard (2010).
4. Riabchuk (2002) refers to two articles published in the early 1990s: one "The Birth and Possible Death of the Country" published in *The Economist* (7 May 1994), and another one, "S. Intelligence Sees Economic Fight Leading to Break up of Ukraine," which appeared in the *Washington Post* (25 January 1994) (p. 19).

5. The documents analyzed in this chapter fall into three categories:

(1) Presidential Decrees: "On the Main Directions of Higher Education Reform in Ukraine," No. 832/95, from September 12, 1995, "On Additional Measures Aimed at Ensuring Educational Development in Ukraine," No. 941/2001, from October 09, 2001, "On the National Doctrine of Educational Development," No. 347/2002, from April 17, 2002, "On Urgent Measures Aimed at Ensuring the Functionality and Development of Education in Ukraine," No. 1013/2005, from July 04, 2005, "On Additional Measures Aimed at Raising Education Quality in Ukraine," No. 244/2008, from March 20, 2008, "On Ensuring a Further Development of Higher Education in Ukraine," No. 857/2008, from September 25, 2008.

(2) Parliamentary Laws: Law "On Education," No. 1060-XII, from May 23, 1991, latest amendments from June 11, 2008; Parliamentary Law "On General Secondary Education," No. 651-XIV, from May 13, 1999, latest amendments from June 04, 2008; Parliamentary Law "On Higher Education," No. 2984-III, from January 17, 2002, latest amendments from March 12, 2009; Decree "On the Results of the Parliamentary Hearings 'On the Implementation of the Education Laws Aimed at Development of General Secondary Education in Ukraine,'" No. 210-15, from October 24, 2002.

(3) Cabinet of Ministers Decrees and Orders: "On the State National "Education" Programme ('Ukraine XXI century')," No. 896, from November 3, 1993, latest amendments from May 29, 1996; "On the Approval of Measures Aimed at the Implementation of the National Doctrine of Educational Development for 2002–2004," No. 1223, from August 19, 2002; "On the Approval of the Conception of the State Programme of Educational Development for 2006–2010," No. 396-r, from July 12, 2006; "On the Approval of the Comprehensive Plan of Measures Aimed at Educational Development in Ukraine for the Period until 2011," No. 1352-r, from October 16, 2008.

The documents were retrieved from http://zakon.rada.gov.ua and translated by the author.

6. Parliamentary Decree, "On the Results of the Parliamentary Hearings 'On the Implementation of the Education Laws'" No. 210-15, from October 24, 2002.

7. Cabinet of Ministers Order, "On the Approval of the Conception of the State Programme of Educational Development for 2006–2010," No. 396-r, from July 12, 2006.

8. See footnote 7.

9. See footnote 7.

REFERENCES

Appadurai, A. (2001). *Globalization*. Millennial quartet. Durham, NC: Duke University Press.

Bahry, S. A. (2005). Travelling policy and local spaces in the Republic of Tajikistan: A comparison of the attitudes of Tajikistan and the World Bank towards textbook provision. *European Educational Research Journal, 4*(1), 60–78.

Ball, S. J., Goodson, I., & Maguire, M. (Eds). (2007). *Education, globalisation and new times.* London: Routledge.

Besley, T., & Peters, M. A. (2007). *Subjectivity and truth: Foucault, education and the culture of self.* New York: Peter Lang.

Dean, M. (1999). *Governmentality: Power and rule in modern society.* London: Sage.

Dean, M. (2002). Liberal government and authoritarianism. *Economy and Society, 31*(1), 37–61.

Dean, M. (2010). *Governmentality: Power and Rule in Modern Society* (2nd ed.). Los Angles, Calif: SAGE.

DeYoung, A. J. (2005). Ownership of education reforms in the Kyrgyz Republic: Kto v dome hozyain? *European Educational Research Journal, 4*(1), 36–49.

Doherty, R. (2006). Towards a governmentality analysis of education policy. In: S. Weber & S. Maurer (Eds), *Gouvernementalität und Erziehungswissenschaft: Wissen-Macht-Transformation* (pp. 51–62). Wiesbaden: VS Verlag fur Sozialwissenschaften.

Doherty, R. (2007). Critically framing education policy: Foucault, discourse and governmentality. In: M. A. Peters & T. Besley (Eds), *Why Foucault? New directions in educational research* (pp. 193–204). New York: Peter Lang.

Dreyfus, H. L., & Rabinow, P. (1982). *Michel Foucault: Beyond structuralism and hermeneutics.* Brighton: Harvester.

Fejes, A., & Nicoll, K. (Eds). (2007). *Foucault and lifelong learning: Governing the subject* (1st ed.). New York: Routledge.

Fimyar, O. (2008a). Using governmentality as a conceptual tool in education policy research. *Educate: The Journal of Doctoral Research in Education* (Kaleidoscope Special Issue March 2008), *3*, 18.

Fimyar, O. (2008b). Educational policy-making in post-communist Ukraine as an example of emerging governmentality: Discourse analysis of curriculum choice and assessment policy documents (1999–2003). *Journal of Education Policy, 23*(6), 571–593.

Fimyar, O. (2010). The (Un)Importance of public opinion in educational policy-making in post-communist Ukraine: Education policy "elites" on the role of civil society in policy formation. In: S. Fischer & H. Pleines (Eds), *Civil society in Central and Eastern Europe: Successes and failures of Europeanisation in politics and society* (pp. 157–173). Stuttgart: Ibidem Publishers.

Foucault, M. (1980). *Power/knowledge. Selected interviews and other writings, 1972–1977.* New York: Pantheon Books.

Foucault, M. (1983). *Discourse and truth: Parrhesia* (Available at http://www.lib.berkeley.edu/ MRC/foucault/parrhesia.html.). Six lectures delivered on the UC Berkeley Campus in October and November of 1983. University of California, Berkley.

Foucault, M. (1991). Governmentality. In: G. Burchell, C. Gordon & P. Miller (Eds), *The Foucault effect: Studies in governmentality* (pp. 87–104). Chicago: University of Chicago Press.

Foucault, M. (2001). *The order of things (Routledge Classics): Archaeology of the human Sciences* (2nd ed.). New York: Routledge.

Foucault, M. (2002). *Archaeology of knowledge.* London: Routledge.

Foucault, M. (2007). *Security, territory, population: Lectures at the Colleège De France, 1977–78.* Basingstoke: Palgrave Macmillan.

Foucault, M. (2008). *The birth of biopolitics: Lectures at the Colleège De France, 1978–79.* New York: Palgrave Macmillan.

Greenfeld, L. (1993). *Nationalism: Five roads to modernity.* Cambridge, MA: Harvard University Press.

Habermas, J. (1984). *The theory of communicative action.* Cambridge, UK: Polity Press.

Holovatyy, M. (2003). *Sotsiolohiia polityky [Sociology of politics].* Kyiv: MAUP.

Janmaat, J. G. (1999). Language politics in education and the response of the Russians in Ukraine. *Nationalities Papers: The Journal of Nationalism and Ethnicity, 27*(3), 475–501.

Janmaat, J. G. (2000). *Nation-building in post-Soviet Ukraine: Educational policy and the response of the Russian-speaking population.* Utrecht: Royal Dutch Geographical Society.

Janmaat, J. G. (2008). Nation building, democratization and globalization as competing priorities in Ukraine's education system. *Nationalities Papers: The Journal of Nationalism and Ethnicity, 36*(1), 1–23.

Janmaat, J. G., & Piattoeva, N. (2007). Citizenship education in Ukraine and Russia: Reconciling nation-building and active citizenship. *Comparative Education, 43*(4), 527–552.

Korzhenko, V., & Nikitin, V. (2007). Teoretyko-metodologichni zasady formuvannia novoi paradygmy derzhavnogo upravlinnia v Ukraini *[Theoretical and methodological foundations of the formation of the new paradigm of the state governance in Ukraine].* In: O. Obolenskyj & S. Siomina (Eds), *Strategiia reformuvannia systemy derzhavnogo upravlinnia na zasadah demokratychnogo vriaduvannia: Materialy naukovo-praktychnoii konferentsii za mozhnorodnoi uchasti [The reform strategy of the system of the state governance based on the principles of democratic governance: Conference proceedings with the contributions from foreign experts],* (Vol. 1, pp. 80–82). Kyiv: NADU.

Koshmanova, T., & Ravchyna, T. (2008). Teacher preparation in a post-totalitarian society: An interpretation of Ukrainian teacher educators' stereotypes. *International Journal of Qualitative Studies in Education, 21*(2), 137–158.

Krawchenko, B. (1997). Administrative reform in Ukraine: Setting the agenda. Discussion paper, No. 3. Open Society Institute, Local Government and Public Service Reform Initiative, Budapest. Available at http://unpan1.un.org/intradoc/groups/public/documents/UNTC/UNPAN003981.pdf

Kuzio, T., & D'Anieri, P. J. (Eds). (2002). *Dilemmas of state-led nation building in Ukraine.* Westport, CT: Praeger.

Lemke, T. (2000). Foucault, governmentality, and critique. Presented at the Rethinking Marxism Conference. Available at http://www.andosciasociology.net/resources/Foucault$2C + Governmentality$2C + and + Critique + IV-2.pdf

Lemke, T. (2001). "The birth of bio-politics": Michel Foucault's lecture at the Collège de France on neo-liberal governmentality. *Economy and Society, 30*(2), 190–207.

Lemke, T. (2007). An indigestible meal? Foucault, governmentality and state theory. *Distinktion: Scandinavian Journal of Social Theory* (15), 43–64.

Lindblad, S., & Popkewitz, T. (Eds). (2004). *Educational restructuring: International perspectives on traveling policies.* Charlotte, NC: Information Age Publishing.

Marshall, J. (1998). Michel Foucault: Philosophy, education, and freedom as an exercise upon the self. In: M. A. Peters (Ed.), *Naming the multiple: Poststructuralism and education* (pp. 1–24). Westport, CT: Bergin and Garvey.

Masschelein, J., Simons, M., Bröckling, U., & Pongratz, L. A. (Eds). (2007). *The learning society from the perspective of governmentality.* Oxford: Blackwell.

MESU & UNDP. (2004). Competency-based approach in modern education: World experience and Ukrainian prospects (p. 112). Available at http://www.undp.org.ua/files/en_33582maket_competence_eng_ost.pdf

MESU & UNDP. (2005). Education quality monitoring: Development in Ukraine. Educational policy recommendations (p. 182), Kyiv. Available at http://www.undp.org.ua/files/en_42754monitoring_development.pdf

MESU, UNDP, IRF & OSI. (2003). Reform strategy for education in Ukraine: Educational policy recommendations (p. 280), Kyiv. Available at http://www.undp.org.ua/files/en_27489stateg_all_eng.pdf

Nikitin, V. A., Parashenko, L. I. (2009). New educational paradigm in transitional societies. *Journal of Research in Innovative Teaching* (Publication of National University), *2*(1), 26–32.

OSI & NEPC. (2006). *Education in a hidden marketplace: Monitoring of private tutoring. Overview and country reports.* New York: Open Society Institute.

Peters, M. A. (2001). Foucault and governmentality: Understanding the neoliberal paradigm of education policy. *The School Field, 12*(5), 59–80.

Peters, M. A. (2004). Educational research: "games of truth" and the ethics of subjectivity. *Journal of Educational Enquiry, 5*(2), 50–63.

Peters, M. A. (2006). Neoliberal governmentality: Foucault on the birth of biopolitics. In: S. Weber & S. Maurer (Eds), *Gouvernementalität und Erziehungswissenschaft: Wissen-Macht-Transformation* (pp. 37–50). Wiesbaden: VS Verlag fur Sozialwissenschaften.

Peters, M. A., & Besley, T. (Eds). (2007a). *Why Foucault?: New directions in educational research.* New York: Peter Lang.

Peters, M. A., & Besley, T. (2007b). Introduction. In: M. A. Peters & T. Besley (Eds), *Why Foucault?: New directions in educational research* (pp. 1–14). New York: Peter Lang.

Pleskovic, B., Åslund, A., Bader, W., & Campbell, R. (2002). *Capacity building in economics: Education and research in transition economies.* Washington, DC: The World Bank.

Popkewitz, T. S. (Ed.) (2000). *Educational knowledge: Changing relationships between the state, civil society, and the educational community.* Albany: State University of New York Press.

Popkewitz, T. S. (2007). The reason of reason: Cosmopolitanism, social exclusion and lifelong learning. In: A. Fejes & K. Nicoll (Eds), *Foucault and lifelong learning: Governing the subject* (1st ed., pp. 74–86). New York: Routledge.

Popkewitz, T. S. (2008). *Cosmopolitanism and the age of school reform. Science, education, and making society by making the child.* London: Routledge.

Razymkov Centre. (2002). The system of education in Ukraine: The state and prospects of development. *Analytical Report, 4*(28), 2–35, Kyiv: UCEPS.

Reeves, M. (2005). Of credits, kontrakty and critical thinking: Encountering 'market reforms' in Kyrgyzstani higher education. *European Educational Research Journal, 4*(1), 5–21.

Riabchuk, M. (2002). Culture and cultural politics in Ukraine: A postcolonial perspective. In: T. Kuzio & P. J. D'Anieri (Eds), *Dilemmas of state-led nation building in Ukraine* (pp. 47–69). Westport, CT: Praeger.

Riabchuk, M. (2007). Ambivalance or ambiguity?: Why Ukraine is trapped between East and West. In: S. Velychenko (Ed.), *Ukraine, the EU and Russia: History, culture and international relations, studies in central and Eastern Europe* (pp. 70–89). Basingstoke: Palgrave Macmillan.

Riabchuk, M. (2009). Cultural fault lines and political divisions: The legacy of history in contemporary Ukraine. In: L. M. L. Zaleska Onyshkevych & M. Revakovych (Eds), *Contemporary Ukraine on the cultural map of Europe* (pp. 18–29). Armonk, NY: M.E. Sharpe, Inc. (in cooperation with the Shevchenko Scientific Society).

Rizvi, F., & Lingard, B. (2010). *Globalising education policy*. London: Routledge.

Rose, N., & Miller, P. (2008). *Governing the present: Administering economic, social and personal life*. Cambridge, UK: Polity Press.

Rose, N. S. (1991). *Governing the soul: The shaping of the private self*. London: Routledge.

Rose, N. S. (1996). *Inventing our selves: Psychology, power, and personhood*. Cambridge studies in the history of psychology. Cambridge, UK: Cambridge University Press.

Rose, N. S. (1999). *Powers of freedom: Reframing political thought*. Cambridge, UK: Cambridge University Press.

Rose, N. S. (2007). *Politics of life itself: Biomedicine, power, and subjectivity in the twenty-first century*. Princeton: Oxford.

Sasse, G. (2010). Simply Ukraine: A nation, state and democracy without adjectives. Presented at the 8th Annual Stasiuk Lecture in Contemporary Ukrainian Studies, Robinson College, University of Cambridge. Available at http://131.111.162.162/slavonic/news/8th%20Annual%20Stasiuk.pdf

Seddon, T. (2005). Introduction. Travelling policy in post-socialist education. *European Educational Research Journal, 4*(1), 1–4.

Sigley, G. (2006). Chinese governmentalities: Government, governance and the socialist market economy. *Economy and Society, 35*(4), 487–508.

Silova, I. (2005). Traveling policies: Hijacked in Central Asia. *European Educational Research Journal, 4*(1), 50–59.

Silova, I. (2006). *From sites of occupation to symbols of multiculturalism: Re-conceptualizing minority education in post-Soviet Latvia*. Charlotte, NC: Information Age Publishing.

Silova, I., & Steiner-Khamsi, G. (2008). *How NGOs react: Globalization and education reform in the Caucasus, Central Asia and Mongolia*. Bloomington, CT: Kumarian Press.

Stepanenko, V. (1999). *The construction of identity and school policy in Ukraine*. Commack, NY: International Renaissance Foundation and Nova Science Publishers.

Sundakov, A. (2001). Public sector reforms in Ukraine: On the path of transformation. Discussion Papers, No. 18. Local Government and Public Service Reform Initiative, Open Society Institute, Hungary. Available at http://lgi.osi.hu/publications/dp/pdf/18.pdf

Tikly, L. (2003). Governmentality and the study of education policy in South Africa. *Journal of Education Policy, 18*(2), 161–174.

UNDP. (2005). Education modernisation in Ukraine: An analytical overview. Result of a National Survey of School Heads of Comprehensive Educational Institutions in Ukraine, 2004, Kyiv. Available at http://www.undp.org.ua/files/en_42754monitoring_development.pdf

Walters, W. (2005). *Governing Europe: Discourse, governmentality and European integration*. Routledge advances in European politics. London: Routledge.

Wanner, C. (1998). Educational reform. In: C. Wanner (Ed.), *Burden of dreams: History and identity in post-Soviet Ukraine* (pp. 79–120). University Park, PA: Pennsylvania State University Press.

Wilson, A. (1997). *Ukrainian nationalism in the 1990s: A minority faith*. Cambridge: Cambridge University Press.

World Bank. (2004). Ukraine-Equal access to quality education in Ukraine project. Project appraisal document (p. 5). Available at http://www-wds.worldbank.org/external/default/ WDSContentServer/WDSP/IB/2004/07/13/000104615_20040714143314/Rendered/PDF/ Project0Inform1ment010Concept0Stage.pdf

World Bank. (2005). Ukraine-Education reform project. Project information document (p. 138). Available at http://www-wds.worldbank.org/external/default/WDSContent Server/WDSP/IB/2005/05/06/000090341_20050506100702/Rendered/PDF/32175.pdf

Zajda, J. (2005). The educational reform and transformation in Russia. In: J. Zajda (Ed.), *International handbook on globalisation, education and policy research* (pp. 405–430). Dordrecht: Springer.

VISIONS OF REFORM IN POST-SOCIALIST ROMANIA: DECENTRALIZATION (THROUGH HYBRIDIZATION) AND TEACHER AUTONOMY

Monica E. Mincu and Irina Horga

INTRODUCTION

The revolutionary year 1989 was a symbolic cultural and economic watershed in European history. Much like its other Eastern European counterparts, Romania underwent a complex process of deep transformations, entering the so-called "transition period" from a communist planned economy and single-party system to democracy and a free market. The legal and institutional reforms to rebuild the state were accompanied by liberalization, restructuring, privatization, and macroeconomic stabilization – the strategies prescribed by the International Monetary Fund (IMF) worldwide. Almost 20 years after the collapse of communism, Romania has undertaken numerous and complex reforms of its social, economic, political, and educational arenas. Although it has been a member of the European Union (EU) since 2007, it is still considered a transition economy, working to reach the standards required by its integration into the

Post-Socialism is not Dead: (Re)Reading the Global in Comparative Education
International Perspectives on Education and Society, Volume 14, 93–123
Copyright © 2010 by Emerald Group Publishing Limited
ISSN: 1479-3679/doi:10.1108/S1479-3679(2010)0000014007

EU. The restructuring of the educational sector was as complex and ambitious a reform process as the various reforms of the state and of public services generally, and was strongly influenced by several international bodies, such as the World Bank, UNESCO, the Organization for Economic Co-operation and Development (OECD) and, most prominently, the EU. Indeed, it is particularly important to note that in the 1990s Romania was the Eastern European country with the most significant foreign support offered for the reform of its education system (Bîrzea & Fartuşnic, 2003). It depended heavily both in finance and policy initiatives on international assistance, principally from the World Bank, the EU, and the Open Society Institute.

Major steps toward decentralization began in 1994, in the form of both foreign assistance and national legislative measures. This year marked both the beginning of a World Bank reform program and the government's first attempts at reorganizing preuniversity education. Thereafter, a diversity of programs in the form of reimbursable and non-reimbursable loans was introduced to sustain decentralization as instructional and school autonomy (1998) and new financial regulations (1999 and 2007) (Table 1).

This chapter focuses on the meanings of decentralization in the context of post-socialist reforms in Romania. The main purpose is to examine the circulation of decentralization reform in what is generally considered to be a highly centralized country. Contrasting perspectives and hybridized ideas are noticeable in the critical investigation of key policy documents and from teachers' perspectives on reform drawn from in-depth interviews and focus groups. Post-socialist decentralization reforms in Romania should be seen in the larger context of state and education restructuring as a global movement and as part of the trend toward marketization (McGinn & Welsh, 1999). Romanian political culture, with its discourses on moderniza-tion and a "return to Europe," has offered a complementary, legitimizing base to the decentralizing reform of administration and education. In line with the recent history of these reforms, most interview participants view 1998 as the peak of real "institutional autonomy," followed by a decline or even a slow recentralization in subsequent years. They also refer to "self-assigned" or "reclaimed" autonomy, which every teacher can adopt "in their own class, once the doors are closed." Significantly, most agree that the latter type is essentially the same as in the communist period, prior to the 1989 political changes. We will thus investigate the contrasting perspectives expressed by scholars, teachers, policy documents, as well as the hybridized ideas which result in various visions of reform. The analysis of post-socialist changes, both as real and imagined processes, leads us to

Table 1. Legislative Context and Assistance Programs in Romania.

Legislative Measures	Foreign Assistance Programs
1994–1995: First measure in reorganizing the administrative and financial system of preuniversity level	Primary and Secondary Reform Program 1994–2001, World Bank (USD 50 million): Curriculum, Evaluation and Examinations, School-Based Management, Teacher Training
1998: National curriculum and a new system of teacher training, new evaluation procedures of student performances were deemed to increase school autonomy	EU Phare-VET (1995–1998) and EU Phare-TVET (since 2001 and until 2009) on Vocational Education
1999: The "official" introduction of the decentralization of educational financial systems	Reimbursable loans

• Early Childhood Education (Romanian Government + Council of Europe BIRD) |
| 2002–2005: New regulations in educational financial systems and preparatory measures for 2007 moment | • Inclusive Early Childhood Education (Romanian Government + World Bank) • School Infrastructure Rehabilitation (World Bank) |
| 2007: Updated and completed strategy for improving the competences of operating in a decentralized system [*Strategia de descentralizare a învăţământului preuniversitar*] from 2005, on an experimental base in 8 counties | • Rural Education (World Bank)

Non-Reimbursable Loans and Pre-EU Accession Facilities |
| 2008: Strategy for improving the competences of operating in a decentralized system [*Strategia pentru îmbunătăţirea modului de exercitare a competenţelor descentralizate în învăţământul preuniversitar*] | • Access to education for disadvantaged groups Phare 2004, 2005, 2006 • Second chance project • Primary and secondary teacher development Phare 2005/2006 • Modernizing professional and technical education Phare ROTVET 2006 |

conclude that the Romanian education transition should be seen as a complex process which has followed "unanticipated trajectories and has led to unknown destinations" (Silova, 2009, p. 298).

VISIONS OF REFORM: A THEORETICAL FRAMEWORK

Decentralization politics, as framed by references to Europe, European models, and more recently Europeanization as a process of "harmonization," has been introduced in Romania since 1989. In fact, decentralization emerged very early in policy debate as the only possible "vision of reform," serving as base for both coherent changes and various ad hoc corrections as well as giving a guiding sense to all sorts of chaotic and piecemeal transformations. Subsequently, decentralization has come to be variously promoted by different actors and foremost by international organizations, and as a result has informed every reform initiative over the last 20 years. After 2005–2006, it was upgraded to the status of a national policy, needing annual monitoring and special initiatives to increase "decentralizing competences in practice" (Ministry of Education, Research and Youth, 2008). The rationales to undertake decentralization have been variously identified over time, ranging from the "best model to be imported" policy – viewed as a quick fix solution to "rapidly pass through the primitive phase [of reform]" – to the best way to become "compatible with European standards" after EU accession. Decentralization policy should be seen both as the main impact of globalization on Romanian education (McGinn, 1997) and as a specific strategy to produce further modernization. In this sense, the Romanian case differs little from other Western or Occidental settings, since the pressures and the rationales for undertaking "further modernization" steps are currently seen as a part of the background for restructuring policies worldwide.

The analysis of decentralization reforms, and particularly the issue of teacher autonomy, must acknowledge global and institutional influences (Tatto, 2007, p. 7). It must also consider what is conceptualized as "imagined" or discursive globalization (Steiner-Khamsi, 2004, p. 7). Decentralization may also be understood as a major global travelling policy (Lindblad & Popkewitz, 2004) and restructuring strategy (Rizvi, 2004), although on practical grounds it implies both decentralization and central and state regulation over certain issues. The main ingredients of decentralization, its sources of inspiration, actors involved, and the dynamics of the borrowing and lending process need to be investigated as a result of complex processes of amalgamation, creolization (Anderson-Levitt, 2003), and hybridization (Popkewitz, 2000). In point of fact, "[the] concept of hybridization makes it possible to think of educational reforms as plural assumptions, orientations and procedures in which the practices of reform are effected" (Popkewitz, 2000, p. 6). It also "enables us to reconsider the relation[ship] of knowledge and power as not hierarchical, moving uncontested from the center nations of the world system to the peripheral and less powerful countries" (p. 6).

Another important perspective is the work of McGinn and Welsh (1999) on the three possible justifications to introduce and support decentralization: political legitimacy, professional expertise, and market efficiency. This is an important critical perspective which is particularly useful in understanding the Romanian transformations addressed in this study, considering both their nature as "real" versus "imagined" processes and their efficacy in promoting intended aims. Indeed, McGinn and Welsh (1999) point out that "these justifications are ideological, in that they are rooted in values and beliefs not justified by reference to facts" (p. 31). The reforms processes that these rationales underpin may vary in both "degree and kind of effectiveness" and may in fact present elements from all three categories of rationales, possibly leading to "results contrary to the interests of their proponents" (p. 31). Here, McGinn and Welsh (1999) suggest that, notwithstanding a rhetorical effect, the justificatory rationales may produce "real changes" not only coherent with but also in contradiction to the proposals they influence. The same view is held by Tyack and Cuban (1995). Their well-known thesis is that "tinkering is one way of preserving what is valuable and reworking what is not" (p. 5). In addition, they suggest viewing the hybridizing of reform ideas not as a fault, but as a virtue which may in fact lead to progress in the long run. Another view is that transformations may not necessarily involve progress but cycles of ups and downs, recursive patterns, and/or regressions to previous experiences or historical recurrences (Cuban, 1993). Given the political nature of the transformation processes, "post-socialist education transformations constitute complex, dynamic processes, which inevitably result in multiple outcomes" (Silova, 2009, p. 297).

We will therefore take a specific look at Romanian decentralization efforts as being underpinned by a hybridization of educational philosophies and thus resulting in contrasting policy meanings. The circulation of a "decentralization" concept reveals contrasting meanings also if we look at the internal policy debate (as reflected in key policy documents) and the perspectives of teachers and school directors on this issue (as analyzed through questionnaires and interviews). Our findings reveal that decentralization is primarily conceived as an evolutionary process (following linear trajectories) by ministry experts and in policy documents. Both from a technical perspective (from initiation to implementation) and from a cultural point of view (actors "need time" to properly understand it and adopt it). In practice, the picture is far more complicated given that the concept of "decentralization" takes on different meanings for different actors. Moreover, its profile is clearly discernable when confronting it with the three different justification types conceptualized by McGinn and Welsh (1999) – political legitimacy, professional expertise, and market efficiency.

METHODS AND DATA SOURCES

This study is based on a document analysis of some significant sources of production and dissemination of pedagogical knowledge as related to decentralization politics and teacher autonomy issues. We selected sources of documentation representative of official educational policy discourses widely disseminated within their national contexts and reflective of diverse political orientations. All these sources reveal pedagogical discourses closely related to the process of policy formation as they reflect the views of national experts charged with the reforming process. The sample of documents includes seven texts: official government documents, policy analysis of prominent scholars directly involved in the reform design and theoretical conceptualization (Bîrzea & Fartuşnic, 2003), and research documents prepared by relevant institutions such as the Institute of Educational Sciences (ISE), the Romanian Academic Society (SAR), and the National School of Political and Administrative Studies (SNSPA).[1] Table 2 summarizes the relevant information of each document included in the analysis.

In addition, drawing on the methodology of qualitative case studies (Stake, 2005), we conducted questionnaires and interviews with teachers and school directors and ran several focus groups on decentralization politics and teacher instructional autonomy topics in order to produce a complementary perspective. Most of our key informants were teachers with more than 20 years of school experience, both before and after 1989. In February and March 2010, we conducted 21 semi-structured interviews and organized a focus group with 21 teachers during a teacher training workshop held in Bucharest at the ISE. Of all participating teachers, 18 were women, revealing the feminization trend in Romanian education and reflecting the national ratio of female to male teachers composing the Romanian teaching body. Sixteen of the 21 teachers had entered the teaching profession before 1989, thus having more than 20 years of teaching experience (and with 3 teachers having more than 30 years). Of the five participating teachers who entered the teaching profession after 1989, only one had less than 10 years of teaching experience. The teachers worked in different types of school and at different school levels: Eight were primary school teachers, while nine worked as disciplinary teachers at lower secondary level and four as upper level secondary teachers. They came from both rural and urban areas and from all around the country. The semi-structured interviews were built around several issues: school autonomy, teacher autonomy, and school climate after the introduction of the reform of school autonomy. In some cases, the interviews developed as *conversational narratives*, asking our interviewees for narratives of their professional experiences. The data were then coded and sorted into the thematic categories which constituted our section on

Table 2. Selection of Documents.

Title	Criteria for Selection	Year	Author
Analiza structurilor de decizie în vederea descentralizării învăţământului românesc 1992–1995 [Analysis of decision-making processes as a premise to introducing educational decentralization]	Early research report investigating limits and possibilities of decentralization	1995	Ivan et al. (ISE)
Analiza structurilor de decizie în vederea descentralizării învăţământului românesc 1992–1995 [Analysis of decision-making processes as a premise to introducing educational decentralization]	Early research report investigating decentralization worldwide	1995	Sandi et al. (ISE)
Reforming the Romanian system of education: the agenda ahead	Study of prominent scholars directly involved in reform design and theoretical conceptualization	2003	Bîrzea and Fartuşnic
Descentralizarea învăţământului pre-univesitar [Decentralizing primary and secondary education]	First ministry report upholding decentraliza-tion as national policy	2005	Ministry of Education, Research and Youth
Descentralizarea învăţământului pre-univesitar, reactualizata 2007 [Decentralizing primary and secondary education updated to 2007]	Second report on decentralization as national priority	2007	Ministry of Education, Research and Youth
Nevoi şi priorităţi de schimbare educaţională în România – fundament al dezvoltării şi modernizării învăţământului preuniversitar [Needs and priorities of educational change in Romania as a premise to further modernization and development of primary and secondary education]	Major scholars' reform evaluation and relevant critical perspective on reform progress	2007	Miclea, Vlăsceanu, Potolea, Bîrzea, and Petrescu (SNSPA)
Effectiveness and efficiency in the Romanian primary school system		2008	SAR

Table 2. (*Continued*)

Title	Criteria for Selection	Year	Author
Strategia pentru îmbunătăţirea modului de exercitare a competenţelor descentralizate în învăţământului preuniversitar 2008–2013 [Strategy for improving the competences of operating in a decentralized system]	Third report on further upholding decentralization	2008	Ministry of Education, Research and Youth

teachers' perspectives. In addition to qualitative data, we administered a survey for school teachers. We have revised a questionnaire used by ISE researchers in 1995 with 30 school directors and inspectors to examine perspectives on teacher autonomy, adapting accordingly the scores assigned for each item. We administered the questionnaire to 20 teachers in 2010. This provided an opportunity for us to examine teacher opinions over time.

MODERNIZATION AS EUROPEANIZATION

The Chain of Transitions

As in other post-socialist settings, Romanian transformations are conceptualized by internal scholars mainly as a chain of several transitions without paying the required attention to the language that the concept of transition itself implies (Silova & Magno, 2004). A close look at the Romanian political post-socialist transformation demonstrates that a wide variety of transition mythologies and ideologies – in the role of salvation stories, normalizing practices, and devices to catch up with the "Western" European modernization path – have been at work from the outset. Moreover, the language of transition in Romania also implies that further steps toward modernization will be required.

In point of fact, "late modernization processes" were said to be in place since 1770, when a synthesis of ideas from the French Enlightenment and German Romanticism occurred and gave rise to what has been subsequently called an "ideological confusion" (Neumann, 2001, p. 39). In fact, political science considered that the contrasting pattern of a cosmopolitan versus

Herderian orientation was at the origin of the well-known opposition then playing out in Romania, a juxtaposition between a good/Western/ civic type of nation creation and a bad/Eastern/ethnic model. However, this oversimplification of the Eastern citizenship model has recently been radically questioned on empirical grounds (see Shulman, 2002). The process of national construction was influenced by the new political philosophies based first and foremost on mythologies such as "common origins" and "continuity," that is, *Daco-Romanianism.*[2] During the first half of the 20th century, the polarization of public themes around a cosmopolitan ideal, such as the "European idea," and an endogenous ethno-specificity became even more manifest. Public discourses supporting industrialization and urbanization processes were paralleled by the circulation of particularistic ideologies, such as *samanatorism* and *poporanism*, which were centered around traditionalist, populist, and agrarian ideas. This ideological juxtaposition marks the early pattern of contemporary transitions, thus labeling modernity *synchronization through cultural syncretism* and also the *import of forms without substance* (Maiorescu, 1967).

From the outset, the transition from communism to democracy and the free market was fueled by a renewed political myth of a "return to Europe" (Tismăneanu, 1999, p. 61; Silova, 2005, p. 129), and the steps taken toward further modernization were part of a "catching-up with Europe" project of modernity. This vision of reform updated old hopes and fears, and fed post-socialist national visions of progress as fitting within an evolutionary paradigm – a process which, although temporarily unspecified, would eventually lead to a clear end. The Romanian post-socialist political reconstruction, marked by the influence of new and old ideologies and political myths, was accompanied by similar phenomena in the education restructuring field (Mincu, 2009). In fact, decentralization policy played the role of a major "vision of reform," representing the best way to "catch up" with European and Western modernity.

Over the 1990s and until the EU accession (what Bîrzea and Fartuşnic label the *first transition*), education decentralization as a key education policy was endorsed as a main device to democratize and to "humanize and socialize" Romanian education. This process was intended to be in sharp departure from the communist education system read exclusively as a knotty heredity. As in the wider post-socialist area, Romanian education exhibited some similarly (negative) traits, mainly in terms of specific stratification dynamics between students (Shavit & Blossfeld, 1993). This problem was upheld by a collectivist pedagogical culture which largely contributed to systematically produce ad hoc hierarchies and an elitist class culture through the constant comparison between students and an excessive prevalence of cognitive aims (Oettingen, 1999). However, this was only part of the story, since education quality during socialism proved to be, in general, quite high as compared to other European countries and continued to be so after the collapse of the socialist bloc (Silova, 2009, p. 302). Romanian education, however, registered (as a rule) lower levels of performance, and quality remained stable or declined as compared to other post-socialist countries.

In spite of regional differences in education quality, the trend toward decentralization remained high on the agenda, and was a political priority particularly promoted by international donors in line with structural adjustment programs' philosophy and as part of a "reform package" (Silova & Steiner-Khamsi, 2008). In light of its lower education quality as compared to other countries in the area, Romania represents an emblematic case in point. In fact, decentralization was not primarily conceived of in public debates as a technical–administrative process – a reform of the governance – or as a strategy to increase education quality. It actually came to embody the qualities of an ethical principle, guiding education reform for the last 20 years. Decentralization was seen as a distinctive strategy to promote democracy, freedom, participation, and responsibility in education and, more generally, in society as a whole. This vision was founded on a premise: The pre-1989 pedagogical culture was inadequate, since teachers were not autonomous in their classes and schools, and the individualization of education processes was unworkable in a centralized system. In this sense, the teaching profession and the pedagogical culture, seen as mostly undemocratic, represented an important legitimating base to introduce decentralization (e.g., Sandi, Blendea, Isopescul, Ivan, & Radulescu, 1995, p. 10).

From a political and economic point of view, the first Romanian transition from a communist society to a democracy is now considered to be complete (Bîrzea & Fartuşnic, 2003), while the "cultural dimension," including education and the implicit goal of modernization (as full Europeanization), is yet to be attained. The main rationale for decentralization was the need to overcome what was perceived to be one of the most centralistic education configurations in the world. However, similar to the case of education quality in the Czech Republic (Perry, 2005), the perspectives of Romanian high officials, international organizations, and scholars, all claiming strong centralization, contrast with those expressed by teachers and school directors in interviews conducted by ISE researchers in the early 1990s. As we will show later in this chapter, teachers indicated that there was in fact weaker centralization than perceived by higher officials.

After EU accession, a *second transition* took place in Romania, a more general transition moving Western and Eastern parts of the continent alike toward a European knowledge society. In this context, decentralization continued to play a key strategic role. Measures were proposed at the school level in the fields of administration, management, and financing. And yet, while the professionalization of the teaching body had come to the forefront of the policy agenda, teacher pedagogical autonomy was not an explicit policy aim. There was a growing awareness of declining education quality over the previous 10 years and doubts about the efficacy of major (international) projects on education equity given the intensification of traditional disparities during the period, such as those between rural and urban schools and between students (Bîrzea & Fartunic, 2009, p. 78). After initial circulation as informal "visions of reform," the European regulative idea and the decentralization of education became, in the pre- and post-accession era, officially legitimized policies, almost seen as unique regulative principles in both the social and educational arenas.

Models, Normalization, and the Cultural Gap Theory

In the aftermath of the 1989 events, several questions emerged concerning democratic models as a specific method of modernization: Which model of democracy is best suited to our needs? Which are the best solutions and models in education? Ideological revival of some precommunist political orientations and even political parties, school structures, and interwar textbooks went hand-in-hand with the "best model to be imported" policy viewed as a quick fix solution to "rapidly pass through the primitive phase" (Bîrzea, 1994, p. 25). Some major scholars involved in political decisions declared that there were no models to reproduce, that it was "not easy to opt for a liberal or a centralistic model," and that "situations [were] very different" (Bîrzea, 1994, p. 25).

As in other countries (e.g., Italy), a modernization project through a search for "suitable models" as possible "dreams of salvation" (Tismăneanu, 1999) has been further sustained by myths of "normalization" (Romania in the process of becoming a "normal country") and ongoing patterns of perceived inferiority, such as the thesis of a "pseudo-modern" Romania (Ulrich, 2008). In the Romanian case, the inferiority pattern is best synthesized by a crucial dilemma: "Are we truly Europeans?" A mixed cultural heredity and history with oriental influences came to be seen as a problematic issue for modernists. A consolidated pattern of opposition between traditionalists and modernists is still visible in renewed contemporary distinctions. *Neo-traditionalists* close to the (extreme) Right and nationalistic movement make up the traditionalist side of this pattern. The modernist pattern is composed of the *pro-Oriental modernists*, originally traditionalists who opportunistically changed their views as an effect of the European integration process; the *moderate modernists* who value both international traditions and a slow "Europeanization" and who are mainly intellectuals affiliated with the liberal opposition; and the *post-modernists* – intellectuals with close literary associations, militating for modernization in terms of cultural "shock therapy" on the model of the "economic shock therapy" in vogue at the beginning of the 1990s (Blendea, 2004).

A major concern underlying models and normalization issues is the matter of the "cultural gap." As theorized by Kozma and Polonyi (2004), the cultural differences and specificities of the Eastern area as compared to Western Europe should be understood from the perspective of the "cultural gap." They maintain that "because of the decades behind the Iron Curtain, Eastern Europe has developed its own culture [apart from Western Europe]. The difference is not a modernisation gap (which could be avoided by enforced modernisation); instead it is a cultural gap" (p. 474). The idea posited here is that the traditional account of a "lack or insufficient modernity" cannot adequately explain people's behavior, knowledge, and values. The "cultural gap" perspective of Kozma and Polonyi (2004) implies that "[n]ew actors enter the region from outside and name the phenomena in English. They apply not only words but also concepts which they have brought in from outside. Once the phenomena have been internationally named, internal actors are expected to behave accordingly" (p. 474). Evidence of this perspective in action can be seen in the Romanian modernization project where decentralization in education is essentially a top-down project and based on borrowed solutions from elsewhere. One of the major consequences of this concept-borrowing is that a correct and efficient implementation of changes needs time: People need time to undertake a profound cultural change. The same conceptual framework has also been applied to Russian education and devolution-based reform, for instance. Kerr (2000) maintains that in order to overcome a "pattern of passivity, inertness, carelessness, and insensitivity, deference to [...] a 'command-administrative system'" together with the inability to make choices "may take far longer than Westerners are accustomed to allow when approaching changes in social life" (p. 150).

The cultural gap theoretical perspective proves to be quite diffused throughout the Romanian education system and Romanian scholars report that "[t]eachers are unwilling to completely change their way of work and their cultural pattern" (Bîrzea et al., 2006, p. 478). In the same vein, Vlăsceanu and Potolea (2002) consider that "[o]n average, only one in four teachers will have almost completely assimilated the new code of the curricular reform" (p. 15), and thus we should question our models, concepts, and their cultural appropriateness.

While we agree that Romanian restructuring as a borrowing process may indeed be analyzed in terms of "cultural gap," it may be argued that the same passivity is common to other traditionally centralistic countries with strong state control, such as Italy and France. Thus, recognizing a culturally specific trait of "the Eastern area" as one pertaining to a communist legacy would only continue a dichotomous, and controversial, line of reasoning between western and eastern parts of Europe. In addition, all kinds of top-down social and educational changes require time to be fully implemented (if they will ever be) in a wide range of cultures and societies. In addition, the sensible variables may not lie in such general categories as "post-socialist" society or Eastern European post-socialist mentality, but in more subtle and specific issues like the presence or lack of political consensus, or in implementing innovation in a homogeneous or heterogeneous society (McGinn & Welsh, 1999). As already mentioned, it may be a question of a bureaucratic mentality induced by a strong statist legacy, as is the case with contemporary Italy. The implementation of a school autonomy reform in Italy may also be analyzed in terms of a "cultural gap" with that of the preferred imported Anglo-Saxon model (Mincu & Chiosso, 2009). To sum up, a "cultural gap" may always be present when a borrowing process is at work. Interviews with Romanian teachers and scholars exhibit all these discursive patterns.

DECENTRALIZATION IN POLICY DOCUMENTS: A HYBRIDIZATION OF IDEAS

Hyper-Centralization as a Major Justification for Reform

In this section, we will draw upon a theory elaborated by McGinn and Welsh (1999) which is particularly useful in analyzing the effective changes and justifications for decentralization transformation in Romania.

Complaints about excessive centralization, as in the Romanian case, are the beginning of a process of shifting power from one group of decision-makers to another. The possible justifications for decentralization may be identified as political legitimacy, professional expertise, and market efficiency.

Most internal and external observers have reported a hyper-centralistic governance structure in the Romanian system of education (Bîrzea & Fartuş nic, unpublished, p. 9; Sandi et al., 1995, p. 2; SAR, 2008). A first evaluation of this was given by a World Bank report in 1991 (Ivan, Blendea, & Jemna, 1995, p. 14). Let us look now at two research reports regarding the 1992–1995 period (Sandi et al., 1995; Ivan et al., 1995) as one of the phases of investigation conducted by the ISE in Bucharest, which is the main research institution acting in support of the Ministry of Education. These documents analyzed the existing governing structures driving the decentralization reform and represent an important source of information through which to identify the early meanings and purposes of decentralization. The foreword to this study (Sandi et al., 1995) indicates that a comparative study on a larger number of countries worldwide has revealed a great "diversity of levels at which decisions are taken at central, regional and local levels, and of their modalities to be exercised in different arenas (planning, human resources, infrastructures, finance, curriculum etc) and that such decision structures cannot be understood without taking into account the context in which they have been generated" (Sandi et al., 1995, pp. 174–75). In addition, "governance reform must generate its own solutions that should be coherent with Romanian traditions and reality. At the same time it is necessary to engage with what happens elsewhere" (Ivan et al., 1995, p. 3). It is worth noting that the report underscores a necessary confrontation with internal traditions.

The report (Ivan et al., 1995) includes the results of a qualitative survey conducted in 1994 (30 school heads and inspectors) which reveals the perceived centralization of the Romanian education system: Almost 50% of decisions were taken at the ministry level, approximately 25% at the inspectorate level, almost 25% at the school level, and less than 2% taken by social partners and the community. The researchers comment that "most of the decisions pertain to the central level, the inspectorate-intermediary level plays the role of a 'transmission device'[...] School autonomy is *quite reduced* [italics mine] and the head teacher has a more nominal authority" (Ivan et al., 1995, p. 17); the community role is virtually lacking. We see here the first contradiction between the decentralization meanings as proposed by international actors and those locally understood by the school actors themselves.

Different levels and actors involved in the decision-making process (2010)

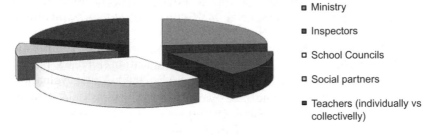

□ Ministry

■ Inspectors

□ School Councils

□ Social partners

■ Teachers (individually vs collectivelly)

Different levels and actors involved in the decision-making process (1995)

□ Ministry

■ Inspectors

□ School Councils

□ Social partners (parents and community)

Fig. 1. Different Levels and Actors Involved in the Decision-Making Process (1995 and 2010).

A replication of the same semi-structured interview with teachers and head teachers in 2010, adapted to include the level of teachers (significantly absent from the first study), reveals the actual perceptions of school actors on the state of the system. Ministry decisions were 24.17% of the total, inspectorate 15.39%, school council 31.96%, teachers 20.52%, and community 7.96% (Fig. 1).

Hybridization as Political Legitimacy and Market Efficiency Justifications

Early research reports (Ivan et al., 1995; Sandi et al., 1995) are particularly useful in revealing the initial conception and direction of the proposed decentralization. Two main traits characterize this early meaning. First, while the reports focus mainly on decentralization possibilities and rationales, they also consider the risks of decentralization which had emerged in other countries as well as the merits of a centralized organization (pp. 31–32). Second, in contrast with national and foreign experts and NGOs, the 1995 interviews present a different view of the degree of Romanian centralization, revealing a *moderate centralization* rather than the hyper-centralized one.

The early reports include justifications of *political legitimacy* – mainly visible from references to democratizing school life and transferring authority to community nonexpert members – and of *market efficiency*, claiming that the market is the best way to satisfy people's needs and, in a way, to create democracy. Some conditions need to be met in order to create an education market: Education content and quality must be diversified; consumers must be informed about options and also able to choose among them (McGinn & Welsch, 1999). In addition, a rather radical conception of decentralization regarding the autonomy of the school institution (devolution) in financial and human resource matters is clearly emerging as a seed of proper decentralization in an early vision of reform.

As already mentioned, calls for decentralization as underpinned by *political legitimacy* rationales of democratization are expressed in different ways:

> … the need to cooperate with the local community and involve parents in school matters … (pp. 18, 20)

> … the lack of a collegiate culture among teachers in a centralistic system … (p. 57)

> … Tayloristic-mechanical instructional processes: bureaucracy for both teacher and student, lack of initiative and the impossibility of individualising and diversifying instructional pathways … (pp. 20, 26, 57–58)

The early conception of decentralization also reveals *market efficiency* rationales, in line with McGinn and Welsh (1999, p. 44):

> … prioritising highly the need to identify alternative sources of finance … (p. 20)

> … students and parents seen as "key clients" and entitled to make choices between different alternatives …

This early sense of decentralization may be considered more balanced than later conceptions in that it takes into account both the limits and the possibilities of decentralization and also includes relevant qualitative data on the perceived degree of centralization, which contradicts the hyper-centralization hypothesis as the main justification adduced to introduce decentralization. Let us look now at policy documents characteristic of this phase, in which decentralization surged as a major national policy.

In the first document (Ministry of Education, Research and Youth, 2005) in which decentralization is dealt with in terms of national priority, the meaning (*vision* in the document) of decentralization is one in which "the role of the school is the main factor in decision-making, ensuring the participation of and communication with social stakeholders" (p. 2). The main aims of the decentralization process are identified in the 2005 ministry policy report and subsequently re-proposed in the 2007 and 2008 reports with reference to several underlying principles: institutional autonomy, public responsibility, institutional democracy, human resources valorization, subsidiarity, cultural diversity, and ethics in educational services. The major aims of decentralization are:

- raising efficiency and performance levels of educational institutions (making schools responsible for financial and human resources),
- democratizing the system of education mainly through community involvement,
- ensuring transparency in decision-making and the management of human and financial resources,
- ensuring access to and equity in education,
- enhancing the relevance of educational offerings as related to local needs and diverse student populations,
- stimulating innovation and public and professional responsibility.

This example confirms that the proposed reform continues to seek strong political legitimacy and is closely linked to a market efficiency rationale. This is clearly visible at the level of authority control, which is up to 40%–50% of local community competence in the experimental areas while in nonexperimental areas the control is of a professional type (teachers and school staff).

Hybridization through Theory Import for Legitimating Purposes

In line with the underlying evolutionary pattern of Romanian transitions, education transformations were, from the outset, conceived of as several phases, from the comparatively simple ad hoc "corrections" made in the beginning of the process, to the more complex and systemic strategies implemented from the end of the 1990s onwards. A conceptual schema of educational changes was understood to be at work, based on *initiation, implementation,* and *institutionalization,* corresponding to a logical sequence of deconstruction, stabilization, transformation, and then coordination.

Ministry officials constantly made legitimizing use of theories of change (specifically Fullan's (1993) "change forces" theory) in an oversimplified form and with an evolutionary vision, in order to give an apparent sense of coherence to piecemeal transformations and lack of internal policy agenda. This is somewhat ironic since the same documents include empirical evidence that contradicts this theoretical and legitimizing framework applied from above and *a posteriori*. For instance, an "implementation" phase of a national education reform cannot coincide with the implementation of various donor projects (of the World Bank and the EU) which have created "their own institutional system to administer the projects." In addition, a reform made through various foreign assistance donors, relevant "both as financial resources made available and know-how transferred," cannot be considered a "systemic reform," although it may cover a broad range of governance issues.

The reforms focused mainly on governance and less on pedagogical components. While the measures undertaken proved to be quite successful in changing the governance arena (introducing new mechanisms of control), the pedagogical and instructional component of reform was not a crucial issue (different reforms included smaller "components" of teacher training or curriculum development) and overall these were evaluated as less successful, or limited in scope by the experimental project. In this sense, the rural education project, introduced by the World Bank and seen as reflecting a more general, equity-driven orientation of Romanian reform, is currently considered by internal observers and ministry officials as rather unsuccessful (Bîrzea & Fartunic, 2009), since the discrepancies between rural and urban education as reported by assessment statistics have significantly increased. Undoubtedly, this data should also be understood in the larger economic context. Table 3 illustrates significant discrepancies between rural and urban students' performances as revealed by national test scores from 2000 to 2007.

Table 3.   Student Success Rates on National Examination Test (Capacitate – Completion of Lower Secondary Education).

	2000/2001	2001/2002	2002/2003	2003/2004	2004/2005	2005/2006	2006/2007
Total	76.3	76.2	74.9	66.9	57.6	59.6	62.7
Urban	85.7	84.0	83.3	75.7	68.3	68.4	70.5
Rural	62.2	65.0	63.2	55.0	43.6	48.0	52.8

Source: National Institute of Statistics INS, 2001–2008.

Table 4. Early School Leaving Rates in Romania (2001–2009).

2001	2002	2003	2004	2005	2006	2007	2008	2009
21.7	23	22.5	22.4	19.6	17.9	17.3	15.9	16.6

Source: Eurostat 2010, http://epp.eurostat.ec.europa.eu.

The quality of Romanian education as shown by international statistics is also dramatically declining. And this evidence presents quite a contrast when confronting it with the ministry officials' reports of the systemic and coordinated reform that is said to be now in place. Tables 4 and 5 depict a deteriorating and worsening tendency of dropouts when looking at the Romanian rates both longitudinally and comparatively.

Although the decentralization of educational governance has been mainly supported by (ineffective) foreign intervention rather than a national policy agenda, ironically, education reform came to be assessed as "ahead of economic reform" (Bîrzea & Fartuşnic, 2003, p. 87), since it "attained two goals not yet reached by economic reform, i.e. the decentralisation and liberalisation of the educational market" (p. 87). The sharp contradiction between the perception of education reform progress and the actual decline in education quality and equity is seen as somehow coherent with or less important than the reported success of decentralization.

Hybridization through "Technical" Harmonization

A major impact of the European integration process and further processes of pursuing compatibility with EU standards is that, in the future, "the policy process will be rather technical than political in nature" (Bîrzea & Fartuşnic, unpublished, p. 35). A proposed apolitical "technical" policy agenda is a serious matter of concern in that it implies an enduring dependency on international institutions (mainly the EU) setting standards and offering financial resources and conceptual frameworks. As some scholars suggest, if all the projected reforms had failed or reached only poor results, we would not blame the politics (the "lack of policy vision" as it is commonly termed), but the underdevelopment of original national research culturally bonded to the Romanian reality (Iosifescu, 2008). Let us give an example of how the EU influences Romanian views on teacher professionalism. Some scholars (Iucu & Pânişoara, 1999, 2000; Păun, 2002; Iucu, 2004) start from the premise that "in the past" – a rather unspecified time since it may refer to the post-socialist or even the socialist era – Romanian teachers

Table 5. Early School Leaving Rates – Comparative Data.

Year	Czech Republic	Estonia	Hungary	Latvia	Lithuania	Poland	Slovakia	Slovenia	Bulgaria	Cyprus	Malta	Romania	France	Spain	Portugal	UE-27
2000	5.5	14.2	13.8	19.5	16.7	7.9	5.6	7.5	20.3	18.5	54.2	22.3	13.3	29.1	42.6	17.6
2007	5.5	14.3	10.9	16.0	8.7	5.0	7.2	4.3	16.6	12.6	37.6	19.2	12.7	31.0	36.3	14.8

Source: Eurostat, 2009.

have not performed as professionals. Therefore, Iucu (2008) and many officials embraced the professionalization rhetoric: teachers must follow the European common principles of professionalism, adopting the three higher education cycles, promoting a lifelong learning strategy, sustaining teacher mobility, and promoting partnerships. It should be noticed that the European Network of Teacher Education Policies, an advisory association of ministry representatives working on harmonization of EU policies on teaching, is neither a decision group nor an expert group (Gassner, 2007). However, its meetings and activities receive great attention by Romanian academics and teaching staff. A technical policy agenda means foremost prioritizing compatibility with EU harmonization policy rather than identifying specific aims related to major constraints and difficulties emerging from internally and independently designed research projects.

Hybridization as Different Donors' Underlying Ideologies

In the education field, scholars remained reluctant for almost a decade when it came to recognizing the involvement of identifiable international "partners" (specific countries) and prominent scholars who offered advice in restructuring matters. Only recently Romanian officials admitted that international financing was not neutral but ideologically driven, financially conditioned, and that a real negotiation process on policy matters between the Romanian Education Ministry and international donors was lacking. But this is said to be a general trend in the Eastern European area. Three major donors, the World Bank, the EU, and the Soros Foundation Romania, have promoted different programs based on different ideas. As is well known, the World Bank (and its "structural adjustment programs") traditionally "emphasizes market mechanisms (alternative school books, external evaluation, free and competitive production of teaching aids)" in order to promote liberalization in education. The EU, through the "accession policy," favors harmonization and compatibility with the *acquis communautaire* based on "subsidiarity," an organizing principal which implies a consolidated and nationally relevant policy agenda. In a context in which different processes of hybridization are taking place, EU policy discourses are locally reproduced and overinflated as yet another dimension to be added to consolidated discursive practices. Arising from an early, vocationalist pattern of EU policy, there is also an added focus on preparation for competition in the European marketplace (Novoa, 2000).

Finally, the Soros Foundation Romania is enhancing the role of civil society and educational alternatives, and is promoting more bottom-up reform.

Reform of Governance versus Reform
of Instruction: Teachers' Perspective

Most of those interviewed appreciated that 1998–2000 saw the first and most developed experience to date of school autonomy. Several measures were undertaken to introduce a new school curriculum based on the principle of diversified educational provision and its local adaptation. In order to implement this, framework programs based on key competences and promoting interdisciplinary approaches were introduced and were linked to locally developed curriculum (SBC) and alternative textbooks. In addition, the hiring of local teaching staff and new financial mechanisms were trialed in selected schools. All these initiatives cumulatively produced one of the most advanced experiences of school autonomy yet seen in Romania. In the words of one teacher:

> At the end of the 90s we came to see the "light at the end of the tunnel" [the expression was very popular at that time]. Official documents from that time (plans, programs, teacher guides and additional material, in a word, the curriculum) were amazingly permissive and supportive of teacher professionalism. At stake was a flexible program developed by teachers themselves in line with their own visions and influenced only by the real situation in their classes/schools. [This program] proposed a change in the teacher's role as creator of curriculum and learning situations, as moderator and counsellor; it was about individualized educational pathways, about what the student actually does ... the teaching profession was almost on the road to becoming a liberal profession! (Teacher working since 1987)

After a brief moment of genuinely enhanced school autonomy from 1998 to 2000, however, many of our respondents reported that the school autonomy decreased, constrained by different realities. Instructional autonomy on paper was rather limited by weak curriculum autonomy in the form of SBC, in some cases reduced to a nominal one hour per week, to save teachers' jobs by completing their number of hours/lessons. One teacher criticized the illusory "autonomy" of new elective offerings:

> As a student, I remember that before 1989 I participated in all sorts of activities: music, dance, sports, theatre, because I liked to do it. Nobody forced me to do so. I cannot say the same about the "imposed" electives we are offering today. These are based on the type of school and the need to complete a certain number of teaching hours, not at all on the student's needs. So, where's autonomy? (Teacher and inspector, working experience previous to 1989)

Undoubtedly, financial constraints on Romanian schools made provisions to increase school autonomy, such as the textbook reform, irrelevant. One of the major limitations also came from the evaluation field, adapting instructional processes in class in line with the 1998 reform of national tests and standards. One teacher remembered this moment:

> My first year as a teacher was 1997. I found the old textbooks [reference to own schooling] slightly revised. I didn't feel comfortable; too many constraints: a fixed number of hours for each unit [text], lessons plans practically identical, like carbon copies. I felt like a grain of sand. The introduction of alternative textbooks gave me a feeling of more independence and responsibility. Unfortunately, it proved to be a false independence. [...] The introduction of the new curriculum focused on competences allowed me more freedom in making lessons plans and teaching content. Unfortunately, analysing the subjects for national tests, I understood that the focus was still on content and knowledge assimilation, and this fact does have an influence on my teaching practice. (Teacher in lower secondary school, 12 years of teaching experience)

Clearly related to this perceived "involution" after the 1998–2000 period of the policy of school autonomy, many teachers used different labels to express their disillusionment. They referred to the existence of a "simulated autonomy," "broken autonomy," and "endless transition" and to alternative textbooks as representing a part of a "fake autonomy," "some degree of unclear autonomy," or an "illusory autonomy." One teacher who had been working since 1987 complained that "[school autonomy at the time] was rather formal, occasional, relating to a few administrative and financial issues, and very little to the curriculum or the control of school councils or teacher-parents committees. In a word, a false independence."

In regards to a reform centered on local community and political legitimacy concerns, the teacher's role is another clear area of concern highlighted in our interviews:

> It is very rare that we have the chance to discuss our profession, and this means that we lack professional autonomy as institutionalised in association and organisations. Why is this? Because nobody "taught us" to do so. We come from a world – "the other world" I have been mentioning – in which individual autonomy and free association would have been punished. (Teacher, working since 1987)

Another teacher expressed a quite similar sentiment, "I can see that we are asked our opinion on an issue that doesn't exist: school and curriculum autonomy. [...] [Taking part in discussions] is useless, since we are only formally asked and our opinion is not taken into account by anybody" (teacher, working from 1974 in a wide range of schools and on different levels).

In terms of teacher workload, this situation has to be linked to a de facto increase in bureaucratization:

> The intensification of bureaucracy which accompanied education reform represents a terrible burden for teachers. We are no longer creating binders, but huge folders, for salaries or merit incentives or qualifications, for the methodological commission, for personal use, for the headmaster [main teacher in a class], for the quality commission, etc. – the more and bigger they are the better. If you have the bad luck to evaluate primary school teachers to assign merit qualifications, you examine two folders per candidate. We wonder how we can ever see the child from behind all that ... paper. We cannot but notice a serious alteration of the sense of the teacher mission: to communicate with children and have the necessary empathy to educate whole persons. This cannot be captured by a written report. (Teacher, 15 years of teaching experience in lower secondary schools)

Reforms of school autonomy in centralized countries such as Italy have been interpreted as an "eclipse of bureaucracy" (Landri, 2009). In the Romanian context, school autonomy goes hand-in-hand with an intensified bureaucracy. The prerequisite of "keeping track of teacher's activities" for all sorts of purposes should be interpreted as a clear trend toward a controlled or scripted professionalism. Only one teacher we interviewed considered it useful, while many others were very critical of this point. In addition, a scripted professionalism is also visible from the pattern of communication with higher authorities seen as "orders from above."

Another important theme and matter of concern is a "generational and meritocratic war," a form of contrived collegiality arising as a direct consequence of increased bureaucracy and the introduction of financial rewards which make it "more important to monitor an activity in its folders than to conceive of the activity in the first place" (teacher with 15 years of experience in lower secondary schools).

Most emblematically, Romanian teachers consider that classroom realities are only loosely linked with the realities of the "system." Here, we can observe a crucial issue at play: An *experienced and claimed autonomy* versus *an institutionally elaborated autonomy*. Indeed, the relationship between classroom realities and those intended by the education system are not considered to be significant for most teachers. This perception allows us to see a clear discontinuity between views and actions, between governance reform and instructional reform which concerns teachers in their classes. In addition, in a supposedly hyper-centralized education system, the opinion that "different schools may represent very different realities" is rather paradoxical as it actually gives support to a loosely linked thesis. This discontinuity between the two types of autonomy is expressed in the words of one teacher who also sees this reality in continuity with the educational practices prior to 1989: "Teachers can deploy a certain degree of autonomy in their class, depending on their intentions and competences. This has always existed. It is also the most important manifestation of school autonomy from which parents and students benefit, too" (teacher with experience prior to 1989).

A loosely coupled relationship between institutional autonomy (governance regulations) and instructional independence (a teacher-claimed autonomy) leads to a paradoxical outcome – "a dual evaluation":

> I have worked with pupils with special needs. So, a child in [his] third year of elementary school may be at the level of learning the alphabet. I can appreciate his progress with judgements "B" or "FB" [good or very good] in order to demonstrate to them their own progress, but in the catalogue I have to put an "S" [sufficient] because this is a third class catalogue. (Primary schoolteacher, 23 years of teaching experience)

The opinion that a certain degree of autonomy has always been possible is particularly interesting, but this should not always be considered a good thing. In some cases, teachers rightly maintain the need to have a system's supervision through inspection, which must be different from the "old system" and also in discontinuity with some prescriptive, "invasive" current practices. In other cases, they report that autonomy cannot be adequately promoted when resources are poor:

> The teacher has the freedom to do their job without control or external interference, except with regard to respecting the curriculum. But this is not always a good thing. As far as decentralization is concerned, as it is currently conceived, I think it will be mostly harmful. Administering poor resources in a local community less and less interested in education, with parents indifferent to the education of their children brings huge responsibilities for teachers, taking time from their main job, the education of their children. (Teacher, experience prior to 1989)

The issue of school and teacher autonomy has been often viewed in terms of there being "a lack of civic and moral values" or as a problem of corruption. This is the perspective that school "cannot work properly since it is part of a dysfunctional whole: the Romanian economy and society" (teacher working since 1979). The trajectory of reform as a recursive pattern rather than a linear-progressive pathway is to be found in the voice of a school inspector who underlines the contradictory process outcomes:

> In schools before 1989 there were students, teachers, and non-teaching staff, just as today. We tackled the same problems. But today things are upside-down: there is no value hierarchy, no rule of law. [And on autonomy ...] This word existed even before 1989, but now, like then, we are just talking about this theme and cannot persuade our

students that we are right, because we're ashamed we are asked to deliberately say wrong things. We arrived from where we came: we are talking about one thing and we are doing a completely different one! [...] Does anybody want us to really enjoy autonomy? (Teacher and school inspector, working since 1983)

The continuity with the past practices was also negatively discussed in reference to the legacy of collectivism. In fact, a teacher with 30 years of experience reported on a continuity of collectivism as upheld by families and their view on education matters:

Families must be educated to understand that the quantity of knowledge and the number of diplomas are not relevant criteria to measure the level of preparation, and that the competition between children should leave space for an evaluation of their own progress from one phase of development to another. (Primary schoolteacher, 32 years of teaching experience)

Here, we find a description of how a legacy of collectivistic culture produces constant hierarchies between students in class and finally an elitist ethos as documented by Oettingen (1999). This process allows for social stratification processes and preserves unaltered inequalities over time.

Another related concern is the influence of outside educational models. Some participants make references to overcoming the gap with European education or to the realignment of national education with European education. Most of them express critical opinions on the issue of borrowing models from abroad, claiming it arises from a clear lack of (national) vision. As one teacher and school inspector since 1983 explained, "Currently, the Romanian education system seems to have no major purpose. It has tried to copy some European models but without considering that these have emerged over time." Another teacher echoed this opinion, "I think we try Romanian school autonomy on the model of other's 'autonomies'. We are continuously 'reforming' without undertaking preliminary serious studies. Most of the time we are hesitant about what will come next" (primary schoolteacher).

CONCLUSION

As Popkewitz (2000) maintains, "national reform practices are simultaneously an overlay of a complex web of global and local relations" which should be rethought as one of hybridity: "that is, an overlay or scaffolding of different discourses that join the global and the local through complex patterns that are multiple and multidirectional" (p. 5). The perspective of hybridization proves particularly useful in analyzing the nature of imagined and real changes undertaken in the name of decentralization and school autonomy. Different "visions" of reform are to be considered outcomes of plural and complex processes of hybridization. We have identified different types: hybridization as political legitimacy and market efficiency justifications; hybridization through theory import for legitimizing purposes; hybridization through "technical" harmonization; and hybridization as different donors' underlying ideologies. In addition, there is a hybridization of ideas contained in the contrasting perspectives on the decentralization aims and limits of school actors and high officials.

The hybridization between different justifications, with the prevalence of political legitimacy and market efficiency, is articulated in a nutshell by internal officials themselves as *a production line and sport competition*: "There is in Romania an intensification of a corporate culture which has a deep influence upon the education system (standards, performance, incentives, competitiveness, market, and competition, all these leading-in the words of Kohn – to a hybridity between a production line and a sport competition" (Bîrzea & Fartuşnic, 2009, p. 84).

Several policy documents start from the self-legitimatizing premise that "decentralization is not an aim in itself" (Ivan et al., 1995; Ministry of Education, Research and Youth, 2005). In point of fact, a perceived discontinuity between "what happens in class" (a teacher's *claimed* autonomy) and "what happens in school and at the upper levels of the system" (*institutional* autonomy) may raise doubt that a governance decentralization has been indeed an ongoing end in itself, which doubt, paradoxically, became efficient in maintaining or even intensifying school bureaucracy. We also have to consider that at the beginning of the 1990s, school teachers and head teachers recognized a certain degree of school autonomy in spite of national and international experts' views supporting a hyper-centralization thesis as the main justification for introducing decentralization.

It is, however, undeniable that a certain progress of governance decentralization, as perceived by teachers, has been made. In fact, according to a qualitative instrument, school actors decided on 25% of education matters in 1994–1995, but more than 50% (as school councils and teachers themselves, collegially and individually) in 2010. This evidence is not, however, in contradiction with their rather critical views reflected in interviews. In fact, a certain formal decentralization of governance can be understood as only loosely connected with teacher autonomy at the school and class level and in continuity over time. Contradictory provisions, such as those between curriculum and evaluation, a disempowered teaching profession (the proposed reform is not one of a professional expertise) actually may have an impact on teacher autonomy in their class as rightly denounced by teachers themselves. In addition, a commonly held view by officials and prominent scholars alike that teachers are reluctant to fully engage in the top-down proposed changes, or are culturally unable to cope with them, contributes to further reproduce different visions of reform.

In order to situate our findings into the larger theoretical discussion on the failure of decentralization reforms worldwide (McGinn, 1997, pp. 47–48), we have to answer the following question: Why did Romanian decentralization reform have so little effect on education? A primary reason is that, from a governance point of view, the Romanian system of education was not (or is not) as centralized as was widely perceived; and indeed, decentralization reform has had little effect on what teachers are actually doing in the classroom. In addition, there are conservative forces that maintain the current system resistance to reform; in this case, the forces are not the teachers themselves, but rather the policy as conceived by officials and scholars, resulting in an intensification of bureaucracy and overlapping meanings produced through complex hybridization processes. Finally, the local community in a traditionally centralized country cannot influence education as projected by officials, as it lacks the required resources, authority, and technical skills to accomplish this task. As such, our analysis of post-socialist changes in Romania reveals various factors, such as real and imagined processes, contrasting perspectives, and complex hybridization outcomes which together compose the complicated and confused portrait of education reform in Romania since 1989.

NOTES

1. ISE: Institute of Educational Sciences [Institutul de Ştiinţe ale Educaţiei]; SAR: Romanian Academic Society [Societatea Academică Română]; SNSPA: National School of Political and Administrative Studies [Şcoala Naţională de Studii Politice şi Administrative].

2. *Daco-românism* (Daco-Romanianism), coined by V. A. Urechia, referenced the ancient territory of Dacia and, through it, the ideal of grouping together all territories inhabited by Romanians outside the Old Kingdom's borders.

REFERENCES

Anderson-Levitt, K. (2003). Introduction. A world culture of schooling? In: K. Anderson-Levitt (Ed.), *Local meanings, global schooling. Anthropology and world culture theory* (pp. 1–26). New York: Palgrave MacMillan.

Bîrzea, C. (1994). *Educational policies of the countries in transition.* Strasbourg: Council of Europe Press.

Bîrzea, C., & Fartunic, C. (2009). A doua tranziţie: Provocări pentru sistemul de învăţământ românesc [*The second tranzition: Challenges for the Romanian educational system*]. In: *Şansa României – oamenii. Reprofesionalizarea României II* (pp. 69–84). [*The chance of Romania: Its people. Reprofessionalising Romania II*Bucureşti: Institutul de Proiecte pentru Inovaţie şi Dezvoltare.

Bîrzea, C., & Fartuşnic, C. (2003). Reforming the Romanian system of education: The agenda ahead. In: E. Polyzoi & M. Fullan (Eds), *Change forces in post-communist Eastern Europe: Education in transition* (pp. 74–93). London: RoutledgeFalmer.

Bîrzea, C., Neacşu, I., Potolea, D., Ionescu, M., Istrate, O., & Velea, L.-S. (2006). National report: Romania. In: P. Zgaga (Ed.), *The prospects of teacher education in South-Eastern Europe* (pp. 437–485). Ljubljana: University of Ljubljana.

Bîrzea, C., & Fartuşnic, C. (unpublished). *Reforming the Romanian system of education: The agenda ahead* (pp. 1–37). Bucharest: ISE.

Blendea, P. (2004). Mandarinii culturali sau nevoia de schimbare culturală. Schiţa de opinie asupra unei dezbateri în curs [*The Mandarins and the need of a cultural change. An opinion on a current debate*]. *Sfera politicii, 112,* 52–55.

Cuban, L. (1993). *How teachers taught: Constancy and change in American classrooms. 1890 1990.* New York: Longman.

Fullan, M. (1993). *Change forces: Probing the depth of educational reform.* London: RoutledgeFalmer.

Gassner, O. (2007). *ENTEP and teacher education in a European perspective.* [Power point presentation]. Available at www.pef.uni-lj.si/bologna/dokumenti/posvet2-gassner.ppt. Retrieved on July 20, 2009.

Iosifescu, S. (2008). The dilemma of the cultural researcher: Are global answers suitable for local queries? In: A. Tat & S. Popenici (Eds), *Romanian philosophical culture, globalisation and education* (pp. 203–212). Washington: The Council for Research in Values and Philosophy.

Iucu, R. (2004). *Formarea cadrelor didactice. Sisteme, politici, strategii* [*Teacher training. Systems, policies, strategies*]. Bucharest: Humanitas Educational.

Iucu, R. (2008). *Cercetare şi dezvoltare in formarea cadrelor didactice aplicaţii pentru procesele de dezvoltare profesionala.* [Research and development in teacher education.] Paper presented at Conference "Profesionalizarea carierei didactice din perspectiva educaţiei permanente" [The professionalisation of teaching career from the lifelong learning perspective], Bucureşti, May 23–24, 2008.

Iucu, R., & Pânişoara, I.-O. (1999, 2000). *Formarea personalului didactic.* [Teacher training.] Research reports 1 & 2. National Council for Teacher Education, Bucharest.

Ivan, G., Blendea, P., & Jemna, M. (1995). *Analiza structurilor de decizie în vederea descentralizării învăţământului românesc 1992–1995* [*Analysis of decision-making processes as a premise to introducing educational decentralisation*]. Bucureşti: ISE.

Kerr, S. (2000). When the center cannot hold: The devolution and evolution of power, authority and responsability in Russian education. In: T. Popkewitz (Ed.), *Educational knowledge: Changing relationships between the state, civil society and the educational community* (pp. 131–152). Albany, NY: State University of New York Press.

Kozma, T., & Polonyi, T. (2004). Understanding education in Europe-East: Frames of interpretation and comparison. *International Journal of Educational Development, 24*(5), 467–477.

Landri, P. (2009). Temporary eclipse of bureaucracy. The circulation of school autonomy in Italy. *Italian Journal of Sociology of Education, 3,* 76–93.

Lindblad, S., & Popkewitz, T. (Eds). (2004). *Educational restructuring: International perspectives on travelling policies.* Greenwich, CT: Information Age Publishing.

Maiorescu, T. (1967). În contra direcţiei de astăzi în cultura română [*Against the nowadays direction in culture*]. In: T. Maiorescu (Ed.), *Critice, I.* [*Critical Studies, I*Bucureşti: Editura pentru literatură.

McGinn, N. (1997). The impact of globalisation on national education systems. *Prospects, 27*(1), 41–54.

McGinn, N., & Welsh, T. (1999). *Decentralization of education: Why, when, what and how?* Paris: IIEP/UNESCO.

Miclea, M., Vlăsceanu, L., Potolea, D., Bîrzea, C., & Petrescu, P. (2007). *Nevoi şi priorităţi de schimbare educaţională în România – fundament al dezvoltării şi modernizării învăţământului preuniversitar* [*Needs and priorities of educational change in Romania as a premise to further modernisation and development of primary and secondary education*]. Bucharest: SNSPA.

Mincu, M. (2009). Myth, rhetoric, and ideology in Eastern European education: Schools and citizenship in Hungary, Poland, and Romania. *European Education, 41*(1), 55–78.

Mincu, M., & Chiosso, G. (2009). Imagined globalisation in Italian education: Discourse and action in initial teacher training. In: T. Tatto & M. Mincu (Eds), *Reforming teaching and learning. Comparative perspectives in a global era* (pp. 23–39). Rotterdam: Sense and WCCES.

Ministry of Education, Research and Youth. (2005). *Descentralizarea învăţământului pre-univesitar* [*Decentralising primary and secondary education*]. Bucharest: Ministry of Education, Research and Youth.

Ministry of Education, Research and Youth. (2007). *Descentralizarea învăţământului pre-univesitar, reactualizată 2007* [*Decentralising primary and secondary education updated to 2007*]. Bucharest: Ministry of Education, Research and Youth.

Ministry of Education, Research and Youth. (2008). *Strategia pentru îmbunătăţirea modului de exercitare a competenţelor descentralizate în învăţământul preuniversitar 2008–2013* [*Strategy for improving the competences of operating in a decentralised system*]. Bucharest: Ministry of Education, Research and Youth.

Neumann, V. (2001). *Ideologie şi fantasmagorie: Perspective comparative asupra istoriei gândirii politice în Europa Est-Centrală* [*Ideology and fantasy. Comparative perspectives on the historical political thinking in East-Central Europe*]. Ia: Polirom.

Novoa, A. (2000). *The restructuring of the European educational space – changing relationships among states, citizens and educational communities.* In: T. Popkewitz (Ed.) Educational knowledge. Changing relationships between the state, civil society and the educational community (pp. 3–27). Albany, NY: State University of New York Press.

Oettingen, G. (1999). L'autoefficacia in una prospetiva transculturale [*Cross-cultural perspectives on self-efficacy beliefs*]. In: A. Bandura (Ed.), *Il senso di autoefficacia: Aspettative su di sé e azione* (pp. 173–208). [*Self-efficacy in changing societies*Trento: Erikson.

Perry, L. (2005). The seeing and the seen: Contrasting perspectives on post-communist Czech schooling. *Compare, 35*(3), 265–283.

Popkewitz, T. (2000). Globalisation/Regionalisation, knowledge, and the educational practices. Some notes on comparative strategies for educational research. In: T. Popkewitz (Ed.), *Educational knowledge. Changing relationships between the state, civil society and the educational community* (pp. 3–27). Albany, NY: State University of New York Press.

Păun, E. (2002). *Profesionalizarea cariei didactice. Standarde profesionale pentru cariera didactică* [*The professionalisation of the teaching career*]. Bucureşti: CNPP.

Rizvi, F. (2004). Theorizing the global convergence of educational restructuring. In: S. Lindblad & T. Popkewitz (Eds), *Educational restructuring: International perspectives on travelling policies* (pp. 73–94). Greenwich, CT: Information Age Publishing.

Sandi, A. M., Blendea, P., Isopescul, V., Ivan, G., & Radulescu, E. (1995). *Analiza structurilor de decizie în vederea descentralizării învăţământului românesc 1992–1995* [*Analysis of decision-making processes as a premise to introducing educational decentralisation*]. Bucureşti: ISE.

SAR. (2008). *Effectiveness and efficiency in the Romanian primary school system*. Bucharest: SAR.

Shavit, Y., & Blossfeld, H. P. (Eds). (1993). *Persistent inequalities: Changing educational attainment in thirteen countries*. Boulder, CO: Westview Press.

Shulman, S. (2002). Challenging the civic/ethnic and west/east dichotomies in the studies of nationalism. *Comparative Political Studies, 35*(5), 554–585.

Silova, I. (2005). Retourner en Europe [*Returning to Europe. The use of external references in reconceptualizing minority education in post-Soviet Latvia*]. In: M. Lawn & A. Novoa (Eds), *L'Europe Réinventée. Regards critique sur l'espace européen de l'éducation* (pp. 129–162). [*Fabricating Europe: The formation of an education space*Paris: L'Harmattan.

Silova, I. (2009). Varieties of educational transformation: The post-socialist states of Central/ Southeastern Europe and the former Soviet-Union. In: R. Cowen & A. Kazamias (Eds), *International handbook of comparative education,* (pp. 295–320). Dordrecht: Springer.

Silova, I., & Magno, C. (2004). Gender equity unmasked: Revisiting democracy, gender, and education in post-socialist Central/Southeastern Europe and the Former Soviet Union. *Comparative Education Review, 48*(4), 417–442.

Silova, I., & Steiner-Khamsi, G. (2008). *How NGOs react: Globalisation and education reform in the Caucasus, Central Asia and Mongolia*. Bloomfield, CT: Kumarian Press.

Stake, R. (2005). Qualitative case studies. In: N. Denzin & Y. Lincoln (Eds), *The Sage handbook of qualitative research* (pp. 443–466). Thousand Oaks, CA: Sage.

Steiner-Khamsi, G. (2004). Globalisation in education: Real or imagined? In: G. Steiner-Khamsi (Ed.), *The global politics of educational borrowing and lending* (pp. 1–7) New York: Teachers College Press.

Tatto, M. T. (2007). Introduction: International comparisons and the global reform of teaching. In: M. T. Tatto (Ed.), *Reforming teaching globally* (pp. 7–18). Oxford: Symposium Books.

Tismăneanu, V. (1999). *Fantasmele salvării: Democraţie, naţionalism şi mit în Europa post-comunistă* [*Fantasies of salvation: Democracy, nationalism, and myth in post-communist Europe*]. Iaşi: Polirom.

Tyack, D., & Cuban, L. (1995). *Tinkering toward utopia. A century of public school reform*. Cambridge, MA: Harvard University Press.

Ulrich, C. (2008). Education and globalisation in "pseudo-modern" Romania: The issue of difference. In: A. Tat & S. Popenici (Eds), *Romanian philosophical culture, globalisation and education* (pp. 165–188). Washington: The Council for Research in Values and Philosophy.

Vlăsceanu, L., & Potolea, D. (2002). *Şcoala la răscruce- schimbare şi continuitate în curriculumul învăţământului* [*School at a crossroad: Change and continuity in the compulsory education curriculum*]. Bucharest: Center Education 2000 + .

RETHINKING TRANSITION THROUGH IDEAS OF "COMMUNITY" IN HUNGARIAN KINDERGARTEN CURRICULUM

Zsuzsa Millei and Robert J. Imre

INTRODUCTION

Community is the most rugged concept of ours. A few decades ago this concept flowed even from the water tap, everybody used it whether they needed it or not, quite often with a hidden agenda. After the transition, community became a dirty word, it was attacked rightfully or wrongly, then its usage was avoided, recently they want to bury it forever. (Karikó, 2008, p. 123, authors' translation)

The meaning of "community" in Hungary has undergone several conceptual shifts during socialist and post-socialist transition periods. Looking through the prism of kindergarten curriculum documents published during the 1970s through the 1990s, there are easily identifiable and multiple shifts in the usage of the concept of "community" which are not in alignment with the major ideological shifts of the post-socialist transition. The ideological foundations of kindergarten education theory were highly sensitive to change and reconceptualization under socialism in Hungary. In the immediate postwar era in which "dictatorship" presided over "need," the early period of "state socialism" was characterized by "bureaucratic state

Post-Socialism is not Dead: (Re)Reading the Global in Comparative Education
International Perspectives on Education and Society, Volume 14, 125–154
Copyright © 2010 by Emerald Group Publishing Limited
ISSN: 1479-3679/doi:10.1108/S1479-3679(2010)0000014008

coordination" and "centralized redistributive intervention" (Stark & Bruszt, 1998). At this time, education theory closely followed the changes in central political ideology typically established by the Hungarian Socialist Workers Party (Sáska, 2004). The state viewed kindergarten education, through its role in the character formation of its subjects, as a first step in transforming society. The second period of socialism, the "reform socialist" period, started after 1968 and was marked by "the state's partial withdrawal from the productive realm" (Lampland, 1997, p. 5). The withdrawal brought the rise of the so-called "second" economy and, as a result, the diversification of economic and social practices similar in nature to that of capitalist systems (Haney, 2002), such as partial commodification (Lampland, 1997). In this new sphere, experts took over some of the state's disciplinary functions, as in the cases of other countries around the globe (Haney, 2002; Rose, 1999). For example, in Hungarian kindergarten education, the work that gained influence was that of those experts who had returned to Marx's original solutions to govern everyday living. The return to Marxian ideas without the distortion of the previous totalitarian period marked a reform era (Sáska, 2004). The aim was to make kindergarten education human- and child-centered, to infuse education with a particular socialist (collective) humanism and with an absolute respect for others (including a focus on individual abilities, needs, and capacities). This process was the beginning of the creation of an increasingly flexible curriculum in kindergarten education that was coupled with growing teacher autonomy aimed at fostering "modernization."

The post-socialist transition of the 1990s fashioned a particular under-standing of "community." In the context of post-socialist reforms focused on decentralization, autonomy, and self-administration, the goal was to create an autonomous, self-governing kindergarten as a part of the public education system. Kindergarten was to become a self-governing educational "service" that would meet the individual educational needs of children. "Community" was reconceptualized as "group" and its pedagogical role was narrowed to serve the development of the self and of a positive self-concept.

What is interesting about the Hungarian case is that the shift in the pedagogical utility of "community" did not neatly coincide with the collapse of the socialist system, but rather preceded the post-socialist transition processes of the 1990s by at least a decade. This chapter seeks to explain why Hungary began converging toward neoliberalism alongside other Western nations well before socialism collapsed. To achieve this goal, this study attempts to unearth and compare ideologically driven understandings of "community" in Hungarian kindergarten curriculum documents published in 1971, in 1989 (right before post-socialist transition), and in 1996 (post-transition) in order to reflect on the nature of transition in Hungary. We understand the emergence of particular understandings of "community" as answers to political problems of governance. By outlining the shifts in the conceptualizations of "community" we aim to explore which political problems the changing kindergarten curricula attempted to address and whether these shifting conceptualizations of kindergarten can be linked directly to the shifting of particular political ideologies – from reform socialism to neoliberal capitalism – or do they rather represent much smoother transitions to a new era after the fall of the Berlin Wall.

This chapter offers a comparison of three curriculum documents of Hungarian kindergarten education. We have selected these documents because they brought major changes to the ways in which kindergarten education was conceptualized in Hungary. The first document, *Az óvodai nevelés programja* [*Educational program for kindergartens*] (Bakonyi & Szabadi, 1971), departed from the earlier curriculum document in major ways, with the introduction of child-centered teaching and a flexible curriculum. It was fashioned by a political ideological shift in socialist Hungary that translated thinking(s) about kindergarten and the delivery of kindergarten education. The second document is the 1989 *Az óvodai nevelés programja* [*Educational program for kindergartens, or New Program* hereafter] (Keresztúri, Kereszty, & Kósáné, 1989), which first saw light of day after five years of development. This document contains the inclusion of the findings of new pedagogical research that had emerged in the 1980s. The third document is the 1996 curriculum text, *Az óvodai nevelés országos allapprogramja* [*The Hungarian core program of kindergarten education*, or *Core Program* hereafter] (Oktatási és Kulturális Minisztérium, 1996), which was conditioned by the changes of a transitory Hungarian society arguably heading toward democratization, market economy, and the reinforcement of civil society.

This study involves a historical refocusing and a conceptual retooling. It uses genealogy in a Foucauldian sense as an alternative method of history writing (Foucault, 1980). Foucault (1994) used genealogy as a method for the history of thought and analyzed "the conditions under which certain relations between subject and object formed or modified, to the extent that these relations are constitutive of a possible knowledge" (p. 314). Consequently, by following Foucault's method, this chapter interrogates the ways in which particular ideologies produced knowledges about "community" that, in turn, formed ideas about kindergarten education and ways of educating children. These histories of "community" in socialist and post-Cold War Hungary are not the product of a preexisting idea that runs through history, but rather are embedded in ideas that were constituted according to different rationalities (inherent in political ideologies) offering solutions for the government of subjects. There exists a body of work examining different understandings of community and communitarianism. We discuss these as background to our study, offer a comparative picture, and then depart from them and consider the conditions that created the possibilities for particular understandings of "community" to emerge in Hungarian kindergarten education.

This study "de-centers" from its subject ("the child") and examines the documentary data that were shaped by its historical–political discursive field. It discusses themes to describe the conditions that allowed the production of particular ideas about the "community." In this way, as Foucault (1980) argues, the genealogy of the subject "get[s] rid of the subject itself [...] to arrive at an analysis which can account for the constitution of the subject within a historical framework" and thus without the necessity to examine an "empty subject as it runs throughout the course of history" (p. 117). Using genealogy in comparative research is a somewhat new methodology that has the potential to help our understanding of various "phenomena in historical terms but not in terms of a metanarrative of linearity, continuity, or rational progress" (Carney & Bista, 2009, p. 194). It focuses on the knowledges and technologies assembled for the education of the young child in which particular ideas of "community" are constituted (Foucault, 1988). The analysis in this chapter focuses on particular documents[1] that had a central importance in kindergarten education in state socialist and post-Cold War Hungary. Through the examination of the data, "community" emerges as a historically contingent idea fashioned by the available discourses of a given time. This methodology is similar in concept to a "vertical case study," described by Vavrus and Bartlett (2006), that situates a local phenomenon and its "interpretation within a broader cultural, historical, and political investigation" (p. 95). During the analysis, we look for significant discursive themes that fashioned "community" in particular ways by outlining the idea, the purpose, and some methods of education in their broader intellectual, ideological, historical, and political contexts.

COMMUNITY AS AN "ANSWER"

A core problem with discussions of "community" and/or communitarianism revolves around the issue of universalism and particularism. This means that communitarianism, as a political philosophy, has among its greatest concerns the problem with rational moral subjects employing some form of universal understanding of "reason" to develop a right and just society. Most prominent communitarians such as Charles Taylor (1989, 1991, 1994), Alasdair MacIntyre (1981, 1988), Amitai Etzioni (1993, 1996), and others such as Michael Walzer and Michael Sandel, developed their theories in specific contexts using examples of real political situations to emphasize the various challenges as well as supports for versions of communitarianism in liberal nation-states in the modern period. Many of the communitarians mentioned here developed their ideas as a critique of influential liberal thinkers, most especially Isaiah Berlin and John Rawls. For example, Charles Taylor's version of communitarianism placed strong emphasis on a kind of linguistic particularism as a way of supporting Quebecois nationalism. The liberalism–communitarianism debates in Canada revolved around the lengths to which the contemporary liberal nation-state could accommodate a "distinct society" within a federal nation-state.[2] For Taylor, this is a practical example of a kind of communitarianism that ought to be supported since it is so intimately linked to the identity of Quebecois. From this normative position, Taylor has consistently argued that the Francophone community in Quebec needs to be supported in all sorts of ways, politically and socially, as this provides a basis for progressive social order. We discuss the various challenges to this in greater detail below.

Another kind of communitarianism, related to Taylor's approach in many ways, is present in the large body of work developed by Amitai Etzioni. Etzioni has developed a communitarian critique of liberal democracy in a somewhat different fashion in that his principal approach was that of a sociologist examining human organizations. While Taylor developed a philosophical position to rival both Canadian multiculturalism and an ostensibly American liberalism, and to shore up the special status of Quebec as a "founding nation" among other founding nations within Canada, Etzioni has consistently sought to bolster what is ostensibly a particular style of idealized democratic organization found in the United States through his support of local democratic organizations. The capacity to elect school district representatives, local sheriffs, local government officials, and local "functionaries" who perform tasks at town district levels (i.e., dog-catchers, library organizers, etc.) might appear separately in other nation-states, but nowhere in the world does this capacity exist to the level it does in the United States. Etzioni has been primarily concerned with, especially in the post-Cold War period, countering the encroachment of a neoliberal understanding of democratic politics through a communitarianism that seeks to support these kinds of local initiatives. This "localization of politics" through Etzioni's reliance on organizational behavior of a particular kind has developed a communitarianism that seeks to counter the individualism and atomization that he believes is one of the great dangers of liberal democracy. In this way, Etzioni is not challenging liberalism, nor does he seek to counter democratic activity in which some version of the "majority of the polity" can express itself politically. Instead, he seeks to strengthen small versions of communities without opting out of liberal democratic practice or claiming special status for linguistic or religious practice. This is very much unlike the Canadian versions of both Taylor's communitarianism as well as the entrenched liberal-pluralism as expressed in Canada's unique multicultural policies.

Another version of communitarianism that has some prominence in the field revolves around Alisdair MacIntyre's earlier discussions of the concept of civic virtue. For MacIntyre, human communities offered the highest form of political life; employing Aristotle's term, he described this as the "good life." As such, MacIntyre, in reviving Aristotle's work but interpreting the question of civic virtue as a still modern one, was concerned most with how moral arbiters can define what we do in our lives. Politics and morality are essential elements of communities for MacIntyre, and he sought to redevelop the preoccupation with moral rationality so strongly rejected by modern philosophers of the Existential movement on through contemporary postmodernism (from Nietzsche, to Sartre, to Derrida, and so on). MacIntyre's concern with Aristotelian virtue ethics is a particular type of focus on communitarianism and communities and how individuals ought to behave in modern societies. MacIntyre's work was an attempt to focus on the "good person" and to develop a normative theory around that concept.

Our goal here is to understand the ways in which the concepts of "community" change over time at particular locations and under different ideological regimes. In the United States and Canada, the development of communitarianism was in large part a response to the work on theoretical concepts of justice made most prominent by John Rawls. Communitarians who identified as such were all concerned with countering those of Rawls's (1993, 1999[1971]) arguments positing that the concept of justice with a neutral procedural approach was a foundation of modern society. Rawls's work in developing this version of the "veil of ignorance" and the variety of ways in which to use the "justice as fairness" concept prompted the communitarian philosophers to develop their critiques. As such, there is a rich and diverse array of communitarian thinkers, and their philosophies provide us with a number of choices regarding the understanding of the concepts of "community" and the myriad of implications to be found therein.

In addressing the specifics of our problem at hand, that is, the identification of the changing concepts of "community" and communitarian ideals in Hungary, we posit two tracks of analysis. First, since communitarianism is concerned with questions around philosophical universalism and particularism in the Aristotelian and Platonic senses of the terms, this allows us to problematize those questions of community that are not linked to the immediate critique of Rawls's position. We can engage in discussions around what the broad terms of "community," as a structural concern, as well as "communitarianism," as an ideological challenge, mean in specific situations in Hungary and the Hungarian early childhood education system at various times. Second, since communitarianism at a certain level of discourse presents us with a normative set of concerns around specific and particular self-identified groups of individuals operating within the confines of both formal and informal versions of civil society, we can problematize how this can operate in Hungary and make an attempt to analyze specifically Hungarian components of this "ideology" of community and communitarianism by posing them next to other prominent versions of the broader theory of communitarianism.

For example, one could argue that a "modern" version of Hungarian feminism – in terms of questioning gender roles and gendered participation in political and civil society – can be seen as having developed in the 1950s and 1960s, even if it is/was not specifically referred to as "feminism" in the context of women's movements in Hungary. Similarly, the emphasizing of "community," at various times explored in this chapter, can be seen as contributing to broad ideas of community, and possibly to "communitarianism," as an ideology seeking to carve out an independent approach to civil society within Hungary itself. Essentially, we are concerned with how "community" was conceptualized in Hungary under various transitions, and how this can possibly contribute to contemporary theoretical understandings of "communitarianism."

LAYING THE FOUNDATIONS FOR SOCIALIST KINDERGARTEN

After centuries of being a feudal-capitalist state and part of the Austro-Hungarian empire, Hungary became a socialist country after World War II. Prior to the socialist government begun in 1949, proletarian rule was established in 1919 under the leadership of Béla Kun. Though this leadership made powerful attempts to transform Hungarian feudal society, the socialist republic that emerged with the destruction of the Austro-Hungarian Empire at the end of World War I was only short-lived. In the wake of the Treaty of Trianon and the establishment of the nation-state politically in the interwar years, Hungary was cast into the throes of ideological conflicts that often led to violence and open conflict. Education became a way in which to ensure a kind of social order and thus played a large role in the establishment of the new political regime each time leadership changed. As such, early education and the place of children in Hungary remained highly valued and highly politicized.

The political regime in the post-WWII period also saw early education as an integral part of the socialist agenda, viewing it as a part of society that contributed greatly to the socialist transformation of the state (Bakonyi, Földesi, & Hermann, 1963; Vág, 1979). The early period of "state socialism" was marked by agrarian reform, nationalization, the secularization of schools, and the introduction of a planned economy. The demographic characteristics of the country rapidly and extensively changed as well; heavy industrialization took place in which two-thirds of working-age women became employed in production by 1971 (Hermann & Komlósi, 1972). Satisfying the needs of working mothers, however, made up only part of the agenda of early education. The agenda for kindergarten education was also motivated by a dominant political raison d'etre: to create the foundations for the "standard program of personality" (Vág, 1979) and to form the characteristics of individuals ensuring they become socialist citizens (Robinson & Robinson, 1971). The development of a particular form of community played an essential role in shaping socialist citizens and fulfilling the dominant political raison d'etre.

The Hungarian kindergarten system has a long, rich, and pioneering history that shows a great and rapid expansion and a strong intellectual tradition (OECD, 2004). From 1938 to 1975 there was a more than a threefold increase in the number of kindergartens (Kardos & Kornidesz, 1990). By 1985, 91.3% of three- to six-year-old children were taught in 4,823 kindergartens where 96.2% of teachers had the required two years tertiary training at diploma level (Kardos & Kornidesz, 1990). The child–teacher ratio was 12.7 at this time (Kardos & Kornidesz, 1990). An important political period providing some of the foundations for the development of the socialist kindergarten system was the 133 days of Proletarian Rule in 1919 under Béla Kun. According to Vág (1979), this period brought forth a particular set of early education conceptualizations in which kindergarten not only preserved its educational nature, but also played an integral role in public schooling for the first time. The proposal for the compulsory enrollment of three- to six-year-old children in "playschools" (kindergartens), the representation of "playschools" as the first step of schooling, the governmental ownership of "playschools" (they were nationalized), and the introduction of a uniform socialist pedagogy all reflected the heightened importance and changed role of "playschool" (Vág, 1979). In the short life of the Proletarian Rule, however, the full transformation of the kindergarten system could not take place.

During subsequent political shifts to the far right[3] after the Proletarian Rule, kindergartens were reconceptualized as institutions primarily providing care. Placing kindergartens under the responsibility of the Ministry of Internal Affairs in 1936 and later under the Ministry of Welfare signaled this change in understanding (Hermann & Komlósi, 1972). The centers were overcrowded and the educational function of kindergarten was displaced by a new focus on the nationalistic and militaristic "habituation" of the children (Kövér, 2004). After the "Liberation"[4] of Hungary from fascist rule by the Soviet Army and its allies, and as part of the process of socialist nation-building, kindergartens and schools were nationalized (collectivized) in 1948 and were taken over by the Ministry of Cultural Affairs responsible also for all other schooling. This shift meant the rethinking of kindergartens as educational institutions that "must lay the foundation of education" and "prepare the children for school" (Hermann & Komlósi, 1972, p. 6).

By the early 1950s, the structural groundwork of the kindergarten system was laid and included guidelines for the development of its governance and institutional aspects. The 1953 Kindergarten Law No. III (Magyar Népköztársaság, 1953) aimed: (1) to protect working mothers' rights to work; (2) to further solidify the interests of the family; and (3) to ensure children's development and education. The law secularized kindergarten, regulated its funding and the operation and establishment of new centers, centralized its programming, laid down the requirement of employing only trained teachers,[5] and legislated the establishment of ethnic kindergartens in particular areas of need[6] (Magyar Népköztársaság, 1953). First of all, the law outlined:

> The function of kindergarten education is the education and care of children of kindergarten age in accordance with the goals of socialist education, and their preparation for primary education. Kindergarten education must establish the basis for the healthy, hardy, patriotic, self-confident, courageous, disciplined and multi-laterally educated man [sic]. (Braham, 1970, p. 44)

The law was followed by the introduction of a pedagogical guide for kindergarten teachers in 1957. This text, *Nevelőmunka az óvodában: Útmutatás óvónők számára* [*Education in kindergarten: A guide for kindergarten teachers*] (*Guide* hereafter) by Balogh, Hermann, Szabó, and Szabó (1957), filled the need for a coordinated national plan. The *Guide* clarified the role of education and teaching to take place in kindergartens (Kövér, 2004). Broad educational aims were broken down into smaller, more detailed aims determined according to the age-specific capabilities of children. Critics evaluated the *Guide* as overly prescriptive and as rigidly centered on goals that aimed too high and without the consideration of children's manifold and growing capabilities and readiness for learning (Bakonyi et al., 1963; Hermann, 1963, 1965; Hermann & Komlósi, 1972). In a similar vein, the *Guide* also ascribed methods that disregarded children's actual capabilities. Not surprisingly, it could be argued that this plan mirrored the logic of socialist command economic planning and the dictatorial and highly centralized regime of the first phase of "state socialism."

While up until 1960, education was under the shadow of rational economic planning, by the 1960s the opinions of the professional class of social scientists were becoming increasingly important, and the socialist state legitimated their voice. At the end of the 1960s, the educational sphere was strengthened in organizational terms as well. Professional public life began to shape public opinions and to have a structure, and the range of possibilities for the integration of professional interest and voice became broader (Báthory, 2001). The Hungarian Pedagogical Association was re-founded in 1967 and the 5th Congress on Education was organized in 1970. Professionals at the Congress raised attention to the need for educational reform and outlined its nature. The push for reform led to the 1972 Party Decision that marked the beginning of the education system reform still in process today in Hungary (Báthory, 2001). Indeed, the integration and increased voicing of educational interests in itself has led to the rearrangement of power relations in the arena of educational policy-making (Halász, 1981). Increased attention was paid to ideological questions in education and a new decentralizing economic policy was adopted in 1968 that tended to reinforce social inequalities.

During the 1960s, answers to questions raised in the process of education reform were found by returning to Marxian ideas and to the development of a Marxian pedagogical science. As Sáska (2006, p. 16) summarizes, during this time, in the background of "socialist didactics, educational theory and educational psychology, the character forming school and community education ... the young Marx's vision about the society of equals and the full development of personality, and the attraction to the anti-capitalist reform-pedagogical movement" are all present. Rubinstein was revived and widely used as well. It was argued that he translated the ideas of communism truly into the language of psychology (Pléh, 2002). Makarenko's ideas on psychology and pedagogy still remained strongly influential as well. His thoughts on pedagogical reform also brought the child in to the center of pedagogy and educational research, more specifically, he sought to research and develop ways to professionally serve children, who were considered the "present of our future" (Sáska, 2006). A form of liberalism and the effects of the environment on children's psychological development seeped in to thinking about "the child" in kindergarten education. As a result, a "middle way" of educational thinking was conceived that allowed for a particular child-centeredness. Professionals defined the needs of children through scientific research and the focus of teaching shifted to fulfill children's "natural" needs. This focus replaced the teaching of a curriculum that was defined by politicians and economists or that drew upon knowledge selected by the elite.

These critiques generated a movement toward the inclusion of more and more spontaneous activities and child-centeredness. The culmination of this shows in the 1971 *Az óvodai nevelés programja* [*Educational program for kindergartens*] (*Program* hereafter) (Bakonyi and Szabadi). The child's interests and independent thinking were also taken into consideration in the *Program*. Conceived as a document "connected with the worldwide 'pedagogic revolution'" (p. 11), it emphasized the importance of children's capacity to acquire and elaborate on knowledge and to think creatively, and it stressed the need for children's activity (Hermann & Komlósi, 1972). Indeed, in order to respond to the reform thinking of the Hungarian pedagogical sphere, and to critiques of the earlier curriculum as well as global changes, the *Program* shifted the emphasis from academic teaching to the development of personality (Hermann & Komlósi, 1972) and addressing children's "real" needs, two areas argued to be closely aligned with the new socialist pedagogy and the formation of the "socialist human" ideal. In 1972, the Hungarian Communist Party declared that kindergarten's work in preparing children for schooling was an uppermost political task (Kövér, 2004). This acknowledgement of the importance of kindergarten further reinforced its role as a first step in public education.

Parallel to these shifts and connected to the development of the *Program* during the 1960s, increasing efforts were invested in exploring the psychological laws of learning and knowledge acquisition with the explicit aim of determining how education could support the purposeful ideological formation of young "socialist humans" (Kövér, 2004). For this reason, children's worldview was placed at the center of psychological inquiry (see Elkonyin, 1964; Lénárd, 1959; Mérei, 1945) in order to understand the processes of and possibilities for children's ideological thinking, the development of their worldview, and the educational processes that might facilitate developing these areas (Hermann, 1963, 1966). Another important stream of studies was concerned with the relations of society and consciousness (in a Marxian understanding) and the foundations of community behavior (Mérei, 1948). This body of research was incorporated into the *Program* and helped to create a balance between community concerns and children's individual differences, considered to be a crucial problem for the socialist transformation of society (Hermann, 1965). It also supplied solutions for the optimal use of individual talents and capabilities for the purposes of community interests (Hermann & Komlósi, 1972).

The development of the *Program* took five years and a great collaborative effort. It was used for more than two decades but was updated several times. It is a key text of educational rethinking, one that marks an important shift in kindergarten education and that appeared at the start of "reform socialist" period in Hungary (Millei, 2009). "Reform socialism" is the latter part of socialism in Hungary that brought new relationships between the government and its subjects (Stark & Bruszt, 1998). A shift in thinking about the government of individuals is apparent in the *Program*. Instead of governing the population through investing sovereign power in a centrally designed and minutely detailed curriculum and in methods for the regulation of young citizens, this reform embodied a shift that represented a sensitivity to individual needs – albeit an "individualism" defined by an expertise that balanced it out with a retained focus on the community's interests. Moreover, "community" was constructed as an avenue through which to serve individual children's needs in particular ways.

THE IDEA OF SOCIALIST "COMMUNITY"

Keeping the first edition of the Program (1971) at the center of analysis, we briefly outline some discursive themes in regard to the concept of "community" and "the child." To aid in de-centering "the child" from its discursive context this analysis also includes references to other documentary data.

The *Program* starts with a chapter that discusses the aims and tasks of kindergarten education. While the *Guide* of 1957 focused on the institution of kindergarten and its role and responsibilities (structural foundation), the

Program's main focus was the "kind" or the nature[7] of education delivered as an integral part of socialist education (focus on pedagogy). According to the *Program*, kindergarten ought to continue the care role of the family and extend it in to the school environment. The family and the kindergarten are both responsible for the education of three- to six-year-old children that helps them "to 'feel good,' [that develops] routine activities and [forms their] personalities corresponding to society's expectations" (p. 9, authors' translation). This passage calls for a longer elaboration and the contextualization of the terminology used.

The aim of socialist education, according to Bakonyi et al. (1963), is derived from the identification of the needs of a future socialist society and how forming particular characteristics of "man" can serve this. Drawing on Makarenko, the prominent Soviet pedagogue, they explain: "Where could the aims of education come from? Naturally, it cannot originate from elsewhere than from our society's needs" (Bakonyi et al., 1963, p. 12; authors' translation). In this way, Bakonyi et al. (1963) continue, the aim of individual development of "man" is in a dialectical relationship with society's development. This relationship, they argue, by drawing on Marxian explanations,[8] minimizes conflict between the person and society and therefore provides the foundations for proper relationships and individual happiness.

As the *Program* states, the aim of kindergarten education is "to facilitate the harmonious development of children's versatile (multilateral) capabilities" (p. 9, authors' translation). It is argued by Engels (Bakonyi et al., 1963) that a man needs to be versatile to help overcome the capitalist division of labor and consequently to facilitate the building of a classless society. By having versatile capabilities every man is ready to use his abilities and skills in all possible ways to fulfill society's shifting needs and his own individual inclinations (Bakonyi et al., 1963). It is important to note that the idea of "versatility" articulated here is different than that of "flexibility." "Versatility" means that new abilities and skills are not developed as simply a *reaction* to demands, as in flexibility, but rather are *already* developed – to be used at one's disposal as the desire or need arises. So having the abilities and skills developed in one's "versatility" opens up possibilities; it is not a matter of merely adapting as reaction to given opportunities and circumstances.

The *Program* also identifies the age at which a child finishes kindergarten as still a "beginning and unfixed stage of the process of becoming a socialist man" (p. 9, authors' translation). Therefore, kindergarten is an integral part of socialist education, as it lays down particular foundations necessary for the development of the socialist "man." These foundations are: (1) physical health and health care, and the development of practices to ensure these; (2) community feeling, behavior, and pursuits; and (3) experiencing, learning about, and connecting to the realities of life. In these foundations the *Program* pragmatically defines the experiences that will lead to the formation of a healthy and happy "man" who appreciates community values and living.

One of the themes that underpin these foundations is the interrelationship and mutual determination of the individual child and children's community. Under the second area of the *Program*, for example, it is stated: "to be in a community should become children's natural form of life, and they should seek it out as an internal need" (p. 10, authors' translation). In other words, a preference for a community living and values should become a characteristic of the child's personality. If this characteristic is acquired the child feels better in the community of children, because he or she belongs to this group (rather than being with adults or alone). The children's community holds children together with specific duties and responsibilities. The kindergarten teacher's role, as it is assigned in the *Program*, is to develop the children's community through particular methods so that the child feels he or she belongs. As claimed by Madarász (1963), in this way, the process of community formation essentially becomes one with socialist education itself, that is, with the well-rounded formation of personality and teaching through the community.

The development and strengthening of the children's community are also directly manifested in the development of the individual and the formation of her or his personality (Madarász, 1963). Drawing on Makarenko's (1949) work to explain this further, the *Program* argues that the teacher is unable to form a child's personality without the help of the children's community. The two run parallel. Not only are teachers responsible for education, but children also teach each other, and both avenues of teaching are equally important.[9] Moreover, community teaching also involved the idea that the teacher is not solely responsible for the development of the community, but that individual children, with their *individual* opinions and activities, are also effective in forming the community (Hermann & Komlósi, 1972).

In this way, and if looking at education in its whole process as fashioned by Marxian ideas, the education of children is embedded in the dialectical and dynamic relationships among people (younger and older), education, and society. This vision implies that, in order to create a classless society, a mass of people should be educated to gain socialist characteristics. At the same time, the socialist person is not only the foundation but also the product of societal relations (Szarka, 1962). Moreover, it is argued by utilizing Makarenko's (1949) work, that being a member of a community is the only form of life that enables the full development of the individual because it teaches the child – and (as it is assumed) the child feels happy only in this particular community. This notion of community is prevalent at all levels and in most texts of education, including kindergarten education, and it powerfully shapes constitutions of "the child."

The role of education is, in corollary to these arguments, to make children experience their "objective" dependence on the community (Madarász, 1963). If a child is a contributing member of the community then he or she must experience that the community works on his or her behalf and vice versa. However, as added by Bakonyi et al. (1963), is the notion that in order for community to provide this experience it should be lively and positive. Thus, the teacher's role is to intentionally develop a happy community in the kindergarten. Additionally, Bakonyi et al. argues that the feeling of collective belonging also teaches the child responsibility, in the form of giving up individualistic desires, and that this further reinforces the child's dependence on the community. Only this kind of community, they continue, has the potential to resolve the antagonistic contradiction between the needs of the individual and the needs of the community. Privileging either over the other might lead to individualism and egoism or asceticism, all of which were seen in socialist writings as detrimental to the development of the individual as well as to the community (Bakonyi et al., 1963). Developing the community and the need for the individual to feel dependent on the community, thus, are also claimed to lead to the development of society by overcoming (what they perceive to be) a fundamental problem of capitalism, that is, individual greed trumping community interests. Moreover, it is stated (Bakonyi et al., 1963) that the characteristics of a community personality, community behavior, and activity with or for the community only develop in children if they live in a community. Thus, education emphasizes community to a great extent, embodying the slogan used by Hermann and Komlósi (1972): "in the collective, by the collective, for the collective" (p. 13).

"The child" is constituted by this discursive context as in a continual process of acquiring a socialist personality through the experience of "belonging" to a happy children's community. The child's characteristics are formed through belonging to the community and, in a dialectical relationship, the community is shaped through the child becoming a certain kind of individual and therefore changing his or her relationship with the community in a positive manner. This pedagogy, or character formation through the community, employs the Marxian idea about the dialectical relationship between the individual and society, that is, changes in the individuals composing society change the relationship of the individual and society and therefore change society. "The child" is thought about as primarily belonging to children's communities, shaped in collaboration with other children and the teacher, and as acting as a devoted and active member of that community. "The child" is also constituted as possessing a form of individualism that needs to be "tamed" (through belonging to children's communities) so that he or she is also able to serve the community's needs. Being a responsible member of children's community also entails that "the child" becomes the educator of other children. "The child" is fashioned to posses particular feelings that enable him or her to become a productive member of the future socialist society and, at the same time, to develop that society by being that type of person.

The present and the future are equally important for "the child" fashioned by this discursive context. "The child" is thought about as not only a "man" in the making, but also as a "man-child" in the present, his or her identity thus envisaged as *in the process* of acquiring certain characteristics. In other words, not having all the characteristics that a socialist person should have does not make "the child" less than a "man." As Vág (1979) explains by drawing on Makarenko's ideas, a "man" can be mis-educated but that does not mean that he or she cannot be re-educated to have a socialist personality, even if education experienced was misguided in the first five years of the person's life (or even for more); the person can be re-educated at any age of his or her life (p. 181, authors' translation). Thus, as Makarenko argues, no education, or learning, or experience is fatalistic. The endpoint of education is represented by the acquisition of personal qualities and characteristics ensuring the child becomes a "public-spirited man interested in the well-being of the immediate and larger community" (Hermann & Komlósi, 1972, p. 10).[10]

REFORMS LEADING UP TO REGIME CHANGE

The 1972 Party Congress opened up alternative ways of thinking about education, initiated top–down reforms, and officially facilitated the development of various pedagogical research agendas. During the 1970s there was a threefold focus on curriculum development for public education and two separate camps of researchers emerged (Báthory, 2001). One of the groups espoused "traditional pedagogies" with a focus on the "human" and often drew from the socialist human ideal, the importance of students' morals and worldview, socialist work school, curriculum and curriculum reform, and various concepts of education and teaching. The other group was composed of social scientists concerned about society as a whole, and, more specifically, on the division of labor, social mobility, equal opportunity, selection, and elitism. The difference between these groups facilitated greatly the development of pedagogical research and influenced educational reforms in Hungary in the long term.

Public education during the 1980s was infused with three ideals: decentralization, the expansion of school's self-governing autonomy, and "alternativism" (Báthory, 2001). Reform ideas, which originated from the ground up instead of dictated from above, also began to take hold. Coupled with the appearance of these ideas, the professional body was "liberated" from its bureaucratic leadership. These changes paved the way for the new 1985 law on education and for the reshaping of the pedagogical research field. The Party avoided dealing with the complex problems related to education and therefore reinforced the aims of the 1972 policy that represented only a narrow agenda for reform, one entailing curriculum and methods reforms, but not bringing wider structural changes in to the system to address societal problems. Enabled by the partial withdrawal of the Party from addressing complex educational issues, educational research departed from the translation of socialist ideology to educational theories and practices and instead adopted a social science perspective that included international comparisons and critical attitudes. The result was the development of a global professional approach to education replacing the earlier provincial approach based on party ideology and decisions. A great number of new conceptions, plans, and working documents came to light at this time and prepared the scene for the 1985 law incorporating these new ways of thinking. One of these conceptions built both on this shift in thinking and the shift in values taking place in the 1980s as a result of changes in economy and broader society (Báthory, 2001). This conception eroded the previously ideologically positioned pedagogy and exchanged it with a new program based on the "self-worth" of individuals: autonomy, self-regulation, self-evaluation, initiative, risk-taking, responsibility, creativity, and competency. This new value system openly sketched out a radically new pedagogy. But it is important to note, as Báthory (2001) summarizes, that these changes resulted from the acceptance of a value system that had *already* begun to take hold rather than from the development of something truly new: "really, the value system was not new, but rather the courage to state it openly [was new] ... under the umbrella of education bureaucracy" (p. 43, authors' translation).

The ideological shift was also felt in everyday pedagogy, which allowed some undercurrents of teachers' thinking to come to the fore. Bakonyi's 1980 research explored teachers' beliefs about human characteristics. The research demonstrated that teachers had always been able to divide the ideological from the humanist aims of education in relation to the character formation of students. In fact, it argues that this division became even more pronounced by 1980. During Bakonyi's project, teachers were asked about the most important human characteristics and their lists failed to represent the concrete type of human ideal as positioned in the particular historico-political context (a socialist human ideal). In contrast, they listed an inventory of characteristics assembled from various humanist traditions. The Party's decreased concern about education created the conditions for the publication of a wide range of often critical educational research. By 1985, as Ottó Mihály, a prominent education policy analyst in Hungary, states, the Central Party was scattered in its political vision, which allowed concessions for the free expression of professional critique and decision-making. And thus, professionals gained a certain level of autonomy at this time:

> [A]lmost everything could be done in this country. Those who state in the 1990s that they could not publish during the 1980s, did not tell the truth. There was nothing left in the drawer in this field [education and pedagogy]; if that was the case, those secrets would have appeared during the 1990s. But it did not happen. Those who did not start their publication with stating that the Russians and Kádár should go to hell, could write what [they] thought. I can state quite firmly that "negative reaction" or "retribution" were not present anymore. (Interview with Ottó Mihály, Báthory, 2001, p. 229; authors' translation)

An increased level of autonomy was also taking hold in other reform areas of public education in the 1980s (Sáska, 2002–2003). First, the teaching profession became more autonomous, as expressed above, which therefore also brought autonomy for non-professionals and more independence for schools. Second, the local authority of settlements became responsible for administering the local society independently, and third, student organizations gained increased autonomy. Taking into account these changes, the 1980s is considered to mark the changing point of systems within education and to be the starting point of democratic development (Báthory, 2001). And to even further extend the start of the transition as in the context of our study, "the process of decentralisation, self-administration, and creation of local authorities [that] established the conditions of political change after the collapse of socialism" (Sáska, 2002–2003, p. 35) had already been in action in the 1970s.

During the 1970s, the early forms of socialist type processes of decentralization manifested quite particularly in Hungary through the distribution of authority to lower levels of bureaucracy, now enabling them to administer centrally legislated law and to realize party decisions, but with no possibility of independent decision-making. In addition to this particular type of devolution, voices of representatives of experts became stronger in defining educational policy and curricula. These processes were different to reforms taking place in the West facilitated by supporters of democracy (Sáska, 2002–2003). These reform movements culminated in the 1985 Education Law that enabled kindergartens (and all schools) to be autonomous (except in regards to funding), to develop their educational program in a local collaborative manner according to a central framework, and to evaluate and regulate themselves (Sáska, 2004).

The 1985 law brought important new developments in legislation related to kindergartens. For the first time in its history, the kindergarten system became an element of the public school system and was considered a professionally independent educational institution (Magyarné, 1999). The law not only ensured the rights and responsibilities of individuals and communities (child, teacher, parents, and broader society), but also enabled their active participation and sometimes even called for the compulsory participation of individuals and groups in processes of educational institutions. In addition to guaranteeing the rights and responsibilities of teachers, the law secured and regulated their professional autonomy, a full departure from the earlier focus on regulating teachers' ideological views (Magyarné, 1999).

This law opened a legal way for the presence and spread of alternative pedagogies that differed in aims and methods from state education (Báthory, 2001). Studies of Halász (1980, 1981) on school climate had illustrated that alternative pedagogies were present in 10% of schools prior to the 1985 law, demonstrating the relative autonomy schools by this time and that, basically, the law was functioning to legitimate these developments. Additionally, most socialist ideology was also removed from the subsequent reformulated curriculum framework for kindergartens published in 1989. Regardless of the significant reforms introduced in the 1980s, however, living with the rights and responsibilities remained quite difficult for teachers – due to this central curriculum framework, the lack of autonomy in financial matters, and because of pedagogical prescriptions (Kelemen, 2000).

THE WIND OF CHANGE – "NEW PROGRAM"

The 1989 *Az Óvodai Nevelés Programja* [*New Program*] (Országos Pedagógiai Intézet) drew on the traditions of the 1971 *Program* and incorporated numerous pedagogical research results and considerations, especially in the area of cognitive development, and included a novel emphasis on the interplaying of social and cognitive development. These changes were coupled with an increased focus on the child as an individual, which was based on knowing the child in her or his individuality and competencies. The understanding of the child as an individual, however, was still defined on the basis of belonging to a community, in that, the recognition of the child's individuality served the formation of accepting relationships based on this knowledge. Similar principles to those of "Developmentally Appropriate Practice" (Bredekamp, 1987) are also interwoven in the document, further emphasizing the individual differences in lifestyle and developmental progress. Although some major changes occurred in response to some of the concepts in the *New Program*, leading to some highly contentious structural and conceptual issues (Keresztúri, Kereszty, & Kósáné, 1990a, 1990b), the main outline and content of the document nevertheless remained very similar to the *Program* of 1971.

The *New Program* advocates an informal routine with a continuous daily schedule that accommodates children's individual needs. The kindergarten teacher can also make decisions independently in the classroom, departing from the guidelines and timing of prewritten plans and instead working through playful experiences organized in subject areas. This more relaxed pedagogical approach, one accounting for individual differences and open to teacher adaptation, is also manifested in the use of certain words all through the program's text, such as "possible" in place of "must," or referring to the "provision" of techniques, methods, and points of view instead of the "prescription" of particular ways of teaching (Keresztúri et al., 1990a).

The concept of "teaching" was exchanged with "learning," shifting the focus even further to the individual child. "Learning" incorporates not only the intellectual, but also the social learning that happens when spontaneous activities arise from the internal motivation of the child and our shared between student and teacher. The importance of knowledge acquisition was exchanged with the development of competencies (Keresztúri et al., 1990b). Instead of stressing content learning, the emphasis of the *New Program* was shifted to the playful learning of intellectual processing.

The *New Program* changed the desired relationship between "parents" and the kindergarten. Here, the teacher not only "persuades" and "enlightens" parents but also "discusses" issues with parents, provides them with "information," and receives "advice" from them (Keresztúri et al., 1990a). This more democratic relationship entails that pedagogical knowledge and families' child raising experiences should be used together and complement each other in the interest of the child for whom both parties are equally responsible. Also, according to the *New Program*, this relationship should be based on the "tolerance" toward different families' cultural backgrounds and child raising practices.

In sum, the *New Program* shifted the balance between the child and children's community to the individual child, his or her competencies, needs, interests, and internal motivation. The explicit socialist ideology contained in previous programs was also erased from the document. The earlier use of community in the education of children remained but took a somewhat different form. While the community was a "field" of pedagogy in the *Program* – and teachable curriculum and the children's community was a "teacher" of the child – in the *New Program*, however, community is considered as only a "frame" for education, one in which "socialization" and "social learning" take place through the relationships formed through play, work, and learning. Now that socialization played a dominant role in shaping the idea of community, community was reconceptualized on social psychological grounds as a "social group" with particular "dynamics," "social interactions," "accommodation to each other," and "cooperation." Similarly, we see that the role of kindergarten teacher has changed between programs – from the teacher being the leader of the community (and intentionally forming it by being a leader) to a less explicit role, in which, rather than *build* the community, the teacher *influences* it through her own warm relationships with or feelings toward children.

The community was subordinated to the individual in a sense that its role was narrowed to serve the development of the self and positive self-concept. And the community's role in forming "community characteristics" in individuals was cut out from the *New Program*. Evaluation was an aspect of education that the *Program* considered to be:

> ... an important community forming agent. On the one hand it demonstrates to the child how much her or his behaviour corresponded with the requirements of the community ... [E]valuation should happen from the perspective of the community with the protection of the interests of the community ... good deeds should be judged in relation to the community. (pp. 66–67)

In the *New Program*, however, evaluation remained in the frame of community, but its role was reduced such that it only concerned the child finding his or her place in the group.

Although in both documents, the "individual treatment in the community" occupies a lengthy section (five pages in the *Program* and nine in the *New Program*), there is a great, fundamental difference between what the two documents have to say on this topic. While the *Program* argues that individual treatment has a major role in forming and developing the community, and the development of community characteristics of personality, the *New Program* states that the individual treatment of each child ensures that they will attain particular kind of memberships in their kindergarten group based on their individual characteristics. This idea, together with the shifts in the conceptual understanding of community, leads to a fundamentally different understanding of the concept and role of "community" in young children's education.

AFTER TRANSITION

With the new 1990 Constitution the principles of self-governance were laid down: "voters of the community, the town, the capital and its districts, and the county have the right of local self-governance ... realizing local public power in the interest of the inhabitants" (1990 Constitution §42; quoted in Sáska, 2002–2003, p. 38). Processes of decentralization, autonomy, and self-administration had been on their way from earlier developments, and now they took a legal form leading school reform. The aim of the public education reform of the 1980s – captured in the National Pedagogical Institute's (NIP) 1984 program – started to be realized with the creation of the autonomous, self-governing kindergarten as part of the public school system. This type of kindergarten, as discussed in the NIP program, was planned so that it would decide on its own activities and inner frames of organization, would shape its own program, elect its leader and employees, decide on its inner hierarchy, and be "able to consider and integrate the requirements of those to who they offer educational-pedagogical services" (NIP, 1984; quoted in Sáska, 2002–2003, pp. 39–40). Thus, the kindergarten was launched on its way to become a self-governing educational "service."

The 1991 Law on Public Education made local councils responsible financially for the kindergarten (Magyarné, 1999). The councils' role was to provide access to kindergarten education to all three to seven year olds, but they had no influence on educational program development and delivery of kindergarten education except to provide the funding for specialist programs approved by the council (Pethő, 1993). Prior to the councils fulfilling this role, they were able to choose in what ways they secured kindergarten education, a liberty that allowed a disregard for pedagogical considerations (Pethő, 1993). But now the explicit role of kindergarten had shifted from serving state ideology to serving communities' needs as understood on economic terms. A massive structural reshaping of the kindergarten system began due to its changed funding structure (Villányi, 1998) and also because of the law allowing the establishment of kindergarten for non-state bodies (Magyarné, 1999). Kindergartens of the same districts were drawn together under a head kindergarten, private kindergartens were established, and churches and alternative pedagogical programs established their own kindergartens. Small towns merged their kindergartens with the school to make it viable. Another important change that the 1991 Law brought was making kindergarten education for five year olds compulsory.

Beginning in the 1980s many kindergartens were experimenting with alternative pedagogical programs. The *New Program* served as a frame for kindergartens developing their pedagogical methods. This freedom facilitated kindergartens to experiment and develop their own programs (Pethő, 1996). The 1993 and 1996 Laws changed the regulation of curriculum content, which lead to the publication of the *Óvodai Nevelés Országos Allapprogramja* [*Core Program of Kindergarten Education*] (*Core Program* hereafter) (Oktatási és Kulturális Minisztérium, 1996). The *Core Program* is a slim framework that is constrained to the outlining of the principles and values of kindergarten education, the fundamental tasks of kindergarten education, the principles for organizing kindergarten life, the nature and form of class activities, and a set of statements characterizing the development of the child to becoming school ready. The programming work became a two-level process after the publication of the *Core Program*. First, the *Core Program* had to be incorporated in to the particular kindergarten's program that ensured that the developed program was aligned with the principles and values in relation to legislations, the rights of ethnic minorities, children's rights, and those responsibilities that Hungary signed in international agreements (Pethő, 1996). The development of local educational programs constituted the second level of programming wherein the kindergarten either developed their own unique program or adapted a program from a series of programs offered nationally in a quality assured pool. The local educational program had to be approved by the teacher body of the kindergarten and passed by the funding body after going through an expert appraisal. The kindergartens received three years to develop or adopt their local programs.

THE DEATH OF "COMMUNITY" –
THE CORE PROGRAM

In agreement with Szécsényi (2009) and Karikó (2008), the changes from the 1971 to the 1996 kindergarten programs in regards to the concept of "community" can be briefly summarized as such: community interests dominated before the transition while individual interests became overriding after the transition. As the discussion outlined so far, this shift was quite smooth and long lasting, and began to appear at least a decade before the fall of the Berlin Wall rather than manifested as a radical change over a short period of time during transition.

Educating through the community has at least four meanings according to Báthory and Falus (1997, p. 314): (1) education in the community or with community actions; (2) the development and training of social relations; (3) the development of community feeling and concept; (4) gaining community characteristics of personality. The 1971 *Program* utilized all four understandings as equally important. In the 1989 *New Program*, the second meaning became dominant, but the other three meanings were still kept and utilized in pedagogical methods. In the *New Program*, educating in the community gained an understanding closer to socialization. The 1996 *Core Program* remains silent about three of the meanings and only discusses the second one: social relations and socialization.

The word "community" appears only twice in the document. The first appearance is under the section "Image of the Kindergarten." Here it is described that the kindergarten provides the child with various activities to be carried out in the children's community. In this way, the community delivers a special avenue for learning through social relations. The other appearance of "community" is also in reference to social relations, that is, community enables the development of these relationships. In comparison to the earlier understandings of "community" in the preceding two documents, the concept of community shown here is a much impoverished one.

To further demonstrate the shifts that occurred since 1971 we have compared the aims of the three programs in regards to the concept of community. As the 1971 *Program* states, "kindergarten education is the elemental part of socialist public education system ... a beginning point in the process of becoming a socialist human" (p. 9). It considers "community feeling, behaviour and pursuit" (p. 10) as a field of education that underpins all pedagogical methods. In the 1989 *New Program*, the explicit identification of the ideological foundation is lost; there is no mention of the role of kindergarten in socialist education. "Community and social development" (p. 8) is reconceptualized as a task of education and the emphasis falls on the formation of tradition, the ability for children to form relationships, and on the founding of attitudes to work, independence, and socially accept-able self-actualization that emphasizes individual interests (önérvényesítés). In the 1996 *Core Program*, the task of education is rethought as a "socialization" process that has minimal relation to community in its earlier meanings, and it is rather the opportunity of simply *being together* that contributes to children learning morals and develops their will to learn. As the *Core Program* states, "practising common activities based on common experiences ... [is what] promotes the development of children's morals (such as sympathy, helpfulness, unselfishness, attentiveness) and their will (including self-reliance, self-discipline, persistence, and awareness of the task and rules)" (p. 12, authors' translation).

CONCLUSION

There remains much to be done in this field of examining how transitions occur in a variety of societies around the world and what that might mean for comparative education studies. We have added to this part of the literature through an analysis of the shifts in the understanding of concepts about and around the idea of "community" in Hungarian kindergarten education. Socialist education policies, and their use of "community" and the particular version of Hungarian communitarianism outlined in this chapter, provided a solution to two particular problems at the conclusion of both world wars. In the first Socialist Republic of 1919, Béla Kun's administration sought to take Hungary out of the feudalism that was still so prevalent in the nation and to develop an education system that would lift everyone up. This was necessary for a number of reasons, not the least of which was that the liberal-capitalist model of individual competition could not function in a semi-agrarian state. With the demise of the nationalists of Horthy and the Fascists of Szálasi at the conclusion of WWII, the establishment of the new Socialist Republic by the Hungarian Socialist Workers Party sought the answer for a similar problem that faced Hungarian society in the interwar years. Industrialization, and the creation of a functioning economy while reconstructing the nation after a devastating war, needed a healthy, educated, and regulated populace. Rather than view the Hungarian education system of the time as an ideologically bound structure trapped in socialist rhetoric, we should instead view it as an attempt to solve particular societal problems given specific limitations. One might even go so far as to conclude that Hungarian communitarianism was always a status quo oriented theory in its attempt to maintain specific political and ideological loyalties, while solving the sociopolitical problem of creating a developing economy during the post-WWII reconstruction. Thus, Hungarian-communitarianism was its own variant of a goal-oriented problem-solving theory, a communitarianism not unlike those described above in this chapter, such as Charles Taylor and Amitai Etzioni's.

The broader conclusion here is that there appears to be a greater closeness to global shifts in the Hungarian curriculum in the post-WWII period leading up to the post-Cold War transitions than is widely perceived. This allows us to question the effects of globalization in the 1970s and 1980s in that it appears that Hungary, as an example of a nation-state in the "Soviet bloc," was already involved in a transition of its education policies well before the 1990s and that particular periods of reform were enacted through education policies beginning to transform prior to now famous transitions of the early 1990s. The transition did not begin immediately when the Berlin Wall was taken down, nor did it move very far from considerations of community and communitarianism in the main field of philosophy dealing with these ideas. For example, considerations of the "good person" and what constitutes the "good life" in Aristotelian terms, and questions surrounding the normative construct of individuals are prevalent, not merely present, in the Hungarian documents.

Taking our conclusion further, we suggest there needs to be a greater criticism of "transitions" in comparative education literature as well as greater thought toward general "transitology" involving political science, sociology, and history. Perhaps the larger question is why there was so much convergence taking place in Hungary regarding the move toward neoliberalism well before there was talk of a transition? As our examination of the documents demonstrates, progressive Hungarian educators were involved in the same shift as progressive educators in the United States and were subject to the same social forces in the 1980s. And it is the recognition of this phenomenon that leads us to the bigger question for comparative education studies: Why?

NOTES

1. The documentary data collected and used as primary data contain curriculum, pedagogical, policy, and academic texts produced in the given time periods and locations.

2. Quebec is a separate province with clearly defined territories (at least according to the provincial governments – First Nations peoples in Quebec and other parts of Canada have continued to challenge this in various ways). Throughout the post-World War II period, Quebec has pressed the federal government as well as other provinces to redefine their role in the federation. Quebec makes decisions on immigration, has a separate language policy of Francophone instruction at all levels of education, has claimed language status in greater Canada, and maintains a high level of decision-making for all aspects of governance within Quebec. The avowedly separatist Bloc Quebecois political party was at one point in time, from 1993 until 1997, the official opposition due to it having the second largest number of seats in the Parliament of Canada.

3. The Cultural Minister under Miklós Horthy, Bálint Hóman, promoted national unity instead of the coexistence of multiple "national" ideologies and he initiated the organizational restructuring of schooling. He also withdrew funds from kindergartens. The ideal of a uniform national ideology above everything, even over religious ethics, governed education and professional training at this time (Mészáros, Németh, & Pukánszky, 2004).

4. The liberation of Hungary from under Fascist rule by the Soviet Army and its alliances.

5. Training of preschool teachers included three years of specialized high school training at that time. This was changed in 1959; training was elevated to an academic level with the establishment of three Training Institutes for Preschool Teachers where two years of tertiary level training took place (Hermann & Komlósi, 1972).

6. These kindergartens were established in areas where the dominant part of the population belonged to an ethnicity other than Hungarian, for example, Slovak, Slovenes, Serbian, German-Slovenes, or Roma.

7. While the guide emphasized kindergarten as a particular institution with its structure, employees, organization, and so on, the *Program* focuses mainly on the nature of education delivered in kindergartens.

8. In the *Economic and Political Manuscripts of 1844*, Marx argues that alienation from certain parts of our lives – other people, things, and activities – is the cause of human unhappiness and dissatisfaction. Therefore, by bringing his ideas to bear on the concept of education, Bakonyi et al. (1963) argues that education's aim is to bring up humans in relationship with society.

9. There are several examples of children teaching children in Bronfenbrenner's (1970) *Two worlds of childhood: US and USSR*. For example, children in school usually were asked to sort out the culprit's punishment in their groups. The group assigned punishment for the child at fault, but also collectively developed strategies how to help this child so that in the future the group would not suffer as a result of similar actions.

10. Education through the community is a vital element of the socialist kindergarten and more substantial work is required to discuss in more details how the ideas of community education fashions "the child" as the subject of kindergarten education.

ACKNOWLEDGMENT

We would like to thank Iveta Silova for her invitation to contribute to this special edition and Mike Mead for meticulously editing our piece.

152   ZSUZSA MILLEI AND ROBERT J. IMRE

REFERENCES

Bakonyi, P., Földesi, K., & Hermann, A. (1963). *Pedagógia az óvónőképző intézetek számára* *[Pedagogy for training institutions of kindergarten teachers]*. Budapest: Tankönyvkiadó.
Bakonyi, P., & Szabadi, I. (1971). *Az óvodai nevelés programja [The national program for kindergarten education]*. Budapest: Tankönyvkiadó, Országos Pedagógiai Intézet.
Balogh, E., Hermann, A., Szabó, E., & Szabó, F. (1957). *Nevelőmunka az óvodában: Útmutatás óvónők számára [Education is kindergarten: A guide for kindergarten teachers]*. Budapest: Ministry of Cultural Affairs and Education, Tankönyvkiadó.
Báthory, Z. (2001). *Maratoni reform: A magyar közoktatás reformjának története, 1972–2000 [Marathon reform: The history of the reform of Hungarian public education, 1972–2000]*. Budapest: Ökonet Kft.
Báthory, Z., & Falus, I. (1997). *Pedagógiai Lexikon II. kötet [Cylopedia of Pedagogy, II. Volume]*. Budapest: Keraban Könyvkiadó.
Braham, R. L. (1970). *Education in the Hungarian people's republic*. Washington, DC: Government Printing Office.
Bredekamp, S. (Ed.) (1987). *Developmentally appropriate practice in early childhood programs serving children from birth through age 8*. Washington, DC: National Association for the Education of Young Children.
Bronfenbrenner, U. (1970). *Two worlds of childhood: US and USSR*. Harmondsworth, UK: Penguin Education.
Carney, S., & Bista, M. B. (2009). Community schooling in Nepal: A genealogy of education reform since 1990. *Comparative Education Review, 53*(2), 189–211.
Elkonyin, D. B. (1964). *Gyermeklélektan [Child psychology]*. Budapest: Tankönyvkiadó.
Etzioni, A. (1993). *The spirit of community: The reinvention of American society*. New York: Simon and Schuster.
Etzioni, A. (1996). *New communitarian thinking*. Charlottesville, VA: University Press of Virginia.
Foucault, M. (1980). Two lectures. In: C. Gordon (Ed.), *Power/knowledge: Selected interviews and other writings, 1972–1977* (pp. 78–109). New York: Pantheon Books.
Foucault, M. (1988). The political technology of individuals. In: L. M. Martin, H. Gutman & P. H. Hutton (Eds), *Technologies of the self: A seminar with Michel Foucault* (pp. 145–162). London: Tavistock Publications.
Foucault, M. (1994). The ethics of the concern for the self as a practice of freedom. In: P. Rabinow (Ed.), *Michel Foucault ethics subjectivity and truth* (Vol. 1, pp. 281–302). London: Allen Lane, The Penguin Press.
Halász, G. (1980). *Az iskolai szervezet elemzése [School organization study]*. Budapest: MTA Pedagógiai Kutató Csoport.
Halász, G. (1981). Adalékok az iskola környezetének és légkörének vizsgálatához *[Additions to the study of school climate and school environment]*. Pedagógiai Szemle, 7–8, 581–587.
Haney, L. (2002). *Inventing the needy: Gender and the politics of welfare in Hungary*. Berkeley, CA: University of California Press.
Hermann, A. (1963). *Óvodáskorú gyermekek tájékozottsága az világban [Orientation of kindergarten children in the world]*. Budapest: Tankönyvkiadó.
Hermann, A. (1965). Az óvoda és az óvónőképzés *[The kindergarten and teacher training]*. In: G. Simon (Ed.), *Nevelésügyünk húsz éve, 1945–1964: Tanulmányok a magyar népi demokrácia neveléstörténetéből. [20 years of our education policy, 1945–1964: Studies from the history of Hungarian Peoples' Republic's education*. Budapest: Tankönyvkiadó.

Hermann, A. (1966). *A világnézet megalapozása az óvodában [Foundation of ideology in kindergarten]*. Budapest: Országos Pedagógiai Intézet.

Hermann, A., & Komlósi, S. (1972). *Early child care in Hungary.* London: Gordon and Breach.

Kardos, J., & Kornidesz, M. (Eds). (1990). *Dokumentumok a magyar oktatáspolitika történetéből II. (1950–72). [Documents from the history of Hungarian education politics II. (1950–72).* Budapest: Tankönyvkiadó.

Karikó, S. (2008). A közösség újragondolásához: Akarunk-e és tudunk-e még közösséget alkotni? *[To the re-thinking of community: Do we want or can we create community?].* Iskolakultúra, *18*(5–6), 123–131.

Kelemen, E. (2000). Oktatásügyi változások Kelet-Közép-Európában az 1990-es években *[Changes in education policy in Eastern-Central-Europe in the 1990s].* Magyar Pedagógia, *100*(3), 315–330.

Keresztúri, F., Kereszty, Z., & Kósáné, O. V. (1989). *Az óvodai nevelés programja [The national program for kindergarten education].* Budapest: Országos Pedagógiai Intézet.

Keresztúri, F., Kereszty, Z., & Kósáné, O. V. (1990a). Az új nevelési program kritikai elemzése *[Critical analysis of the new kindergarten program].* Óvodai Nevelés, *3*, 85–90.

Keresztúri, F., Kereszty, Z., & Kósáné, O. V. (1990b). Mi az új az óvodai nevelési programban? *[What is new in the new program?].* Óvodai Nevelés, *2*, 44–46.

Kövér, S. (2004). Kell-e mennünk Európába?-A magyar és európai óvodai rendszer kapcsolata és sajátos vonásai 1828–1998 között *[Should we go to Europe? The relationship of Hungarian and European kindergarten systems and their particular features between 1828–1998].* Neveléstörténet, (3–4). Available at http://www.kodolanyi.hu/nevelestortenet/ index.php?rovat_mod=archiv&act=menu_tart&eid=30&rid=1&id=123

Lampland, M. (1997). *The object of labor: Commodification in socialist Hungary.* Chicago: University of Chicago Press.

Lénárd, F. (1959). A gyermeki világkép és a világnézeti nevelés *[The worldview of the child and ideological education].* Pedagógiai Szemle, *59*(9), 835–845.

MacIntyre, A. (1981). *After virtue.* Notre Dame, IN: University of Notre Dame Press.

MacIntyre, A. (1988). *Whose justice, which rationality?* Notre Dame, IN: University of Notre Dame Press.

Madarász, M. (1963). Közösségi nevelés-egyéni bánásmód *[Community education – Individual treatment].* Óvodai Nevelés, *XVI*(207), 207–220.

Magyar Népköztársaság. (1953). Kisdedóvási törvény (Kindergarten law). Óvodai Nevelés, *6*(4), 82–83.

Magyarné, S. I. (1999). *Neveléstörténet [History of education].* Pécs, Hungary: Comenius, Bt.

Makarenko, A. (1949). *Válogatott pedagógiai tanulmányok [Selected studies in pedagogy].* Budapest: Tankönyvkiadó.

Mérei, F. (1945). *A gyermek világnézete. Gyermeklélektani tanulmány [The worldview of the child. A study in child psychology].* Budapest: Anonymous.

Mérei, F. (1948). *Az együttes élmény [The community experience: A social psychological experiment with children].* (2nd ed.). Budapest: Officina.

Millei, Z. (2009). Early education and "the child" as sites of politics: A comparative study of Hungary and Australia. *ANZCIES 09: Conference Proceedings of the 37th Annual Conference,* Armidale.

OECD. (2004). *Early childhood education and care policy: Country note for Hungary* (Available at http://www.oecd.org/document/56/0,3343,en_2649_39263231_1941752_1_1_1_1,00.html. Accessed on September 15, 2008). Paris: OECD Directorate for Education.

Oktatási és Kulturális Minisztérium. (1996). *Az óvodai nevelés országos alapprogramja [The Hungarian core programme of kindergarten education].* Budapest: Ministry of Culture and Education, Magenta Kft.

Pethő, Á. (1993). Az óvoda helye és szerepe a közoktatási törvény tükrében *[The place and role of kindergarten in the new law on public education].* Óvodai Nevelés, 46(8), 264–266.

Pethő, Á. (1996). Az óvodai nevelőmunka szabályozása: Egy új dokumentum született *[Regulating teachers' work in kindergarten: A new document was born].* Óvodai Nevelés, 49(8), 288–289.

Pléh, C. (2002). Öröklés és környezetelvű nevelés az 1970-es évek fordulóján *[Education according to genetics and the environment on the turn of the 1970s].* Magyar Pszichológiai Szemle, 1, 39–50.

Rawls, J. (1993). *Political liberalism.* New York: Columbia University Press.

Rawls, J. (1999[1971]). *A theory of justice.* Oxford: Oxford University Press.

Robinson, H. B., & Robinson, N. M. (1971). Foreword. In: A. Hermann & S. Komlósi (Eds), *Early child care in Hungary* (pp. ix–x). London: Gordon and Breach.

Rose, N. (1999). *Powers of freedom: Reframing political thought.* Cambridge, UK: Cambridge University Press.

Sáska, G. (2002–2003). The age of autonomy. *European Education, 34*(4), 34–55.

Sáska, G. (2004). Az alternatív pedagógia posztszocialista győzelme *[The post-socialist triumph of alternative pedagogy].* Beszélő, 12, 20–30.

Sáska, G. (2006). A reformpedagódia alakváltozása az 1945-ös 'kis' és az 1947 utáni 'nagy' rendszerváltást követő időszakban *[The shaping form of reform pedagogy in the period after the 1945 'small' and 1947 'great' regime change].* Magyar Pedagógia, 106(4), 263–285.

Stark, D., & Bruszt, L. (1998). *Postsocialist pathways: Transforming politics and property in East Central Europe.* Cambridge: Cambridge University Press.

Szarka, J. (1962). Az ember felemelésének programja *[The program of man's advancement].* Pedagógiai Szemle, 1(7), 28–35.

Szécsényi, I. (2009). A közösség szerepe az egyén szocializációjában *[The community's role in the socialisation of the individual].* Fejlesztő Pedagógia, 20(3), 53–64.

Taylor, C. (1989). *Sources of the self: The making of modern identity.* Boston, MA: Harvard University Press.

Taylor, C. (1991). *The malaise of modernity.* Massey Lecture Series. Concord, Ontario: Anansi.

Taylor, C., & Gutman, A. (Eds). (1994). *Multiculturalism: Examining the politics of recognition.* Princeton, NJ: Princeton University Press.

Vág, O. (1979). *Az óvoda es óvodapedagógia [Kindergarten and kindergarten pedagogy].* Budapest: Tankönyvkiadó.

Vavrus, F., & Bartlett, L. (2006). Comparatively knowing: Making a case for the vertical case study. *Current Issues in Comparative Education, 8*(2), 95–103.

Villányi, G. (1998). Az óvodai nevelés helyzetéről: Az óvodai nevelés országos allapprogramjának implementációja *[Update on kindergarten education: The implementation of the Hungarian core programme for kindergarten education].* Fejlesztő Pedagógia, 1, 26–30.

A FRAMEWORK FOR UNDERSTANDING DRAMATIC CHANGE: EDUCATIONAL TRANSFORMATION IN POST-SOVIET RUSSIA

Eleoussa Polyzoi and Eduard Dneprov

INTRODUCTION

In 1991, the Soviet Union collapsed and, one after another, the Soviet Republics – including Georgia, Moldova, Belarus, the Baltic States, and Ukraine – began to secede from the Union. The main priority of the new Russian government, under the leadership of President Boris Yeltsin, was to move from a planned to a free-market economy within a new democratic framework. The new government also promised to initiate significant educational reform. At first, educational change across republics, united by their collective rejection of the communist ideology, was characterized by a striking uniformity. However, as the republics began to set their own course, their educational reform agendas began to take on an increasingly distinct character (Rust, Knost, & Wichmann, 1994).

As Birzea (1994) notes in his analysis of the transition of post-socialist nations from a totalitarian to an open and democratic system, one of the

Post-Socialism is not Dead: (Re)Reading the Global in Comparative Education
International Perspectives on Education and Society, Volume 14, 155–179
Copyright © 2010 by Emerald Group Publishing Limited
ISSN: 1479-3679/doi:10.1108/S1479-3679(2010)0000014009

easiest ways to fill the vacuum not yet filled by new self-regulating mechanisms is to search in the past, to seek out old securities in the face of an uncertain future. However, Anweiler (1992) cautions that "the emerging new systems of education in the post-communist societies cannot simply start their reconstruction at the status-quo ante, before the communist regime came to power" (p. 38). This is particularly true in the case of Russia and other former Soviet republics, which experienced more than 70 years of communist rule. Russia's experience with educational change has been particularly chaotic and protracted in nature. The events of 1991 set the stage for a major contradiction within the Russian educational system. The inconsistency between the overwhelming administrative rigidity, which was a legacy of the centralized communist structure, and the new principles of democracy made change inevitable.

This chapter explores the initiation of educational transformation in Russia in the decade following 1991 where change was dramatic and immediate. Since educational transformation in Russia has unfolded within a more compressed timeframe than in North America, the Russian experience provides a unique opportunity for the investigation of educational change – a "living laboratory," qualitatively different from the United States or Canada where change occurs within an essentially stable societal context.

This study is conceptualized within Fullan's (2001) framework of educational change, which has utility for helping us understand events in Russia. However, we propose a revised framework to better account for the dynamic character of dramatic and sudden change, typical of former Soviet countries. According to Fullan (2001), most researchers acknowledge three broad phases to the process of educational change: initiation, implementation, and institutionalization. Whereas initiation (or mobilization) consists of the process that leads up to and includes a decision to adopt or proceed with change, implementation involves the first attempts to put an idea or reform into practice. In contrast, institutionalization refers to whether the change gets built in as an ongoing part of the system or disappears by way of a decision to discard of or through attrition (Fullan, 2001, p. 69). This exploration focuses primarily on the first phase of the change process: *initiation* of educational reform. According to Fullan (2001), successful initiation or mobilization for educational change is dependent on a number of factors, including support from central administration, the sense of moral purpose guiding the change process, the degree to which the teachers embrace the change, policies and funds that support and enable it, the existence of innovations that fuel it, the pressure groups that encourage it,

Fig. 1. Factors Affecting Initiation of Education Change. *Source:* Polyzoi, Fullan, and Anchan (2003, p. 6). Permission to reproduce by Routledge/Falmer Press.

information networks that facilitate it, and external change agents that stimulate it (see Fig. 1).

Although Fullan's schema is rich in detail and multivariate in approach, there are certain dynamics of the change process which it does not address. In particular, educational change in Russia has not typically proceeded in a linear fashion. Systems in transition, including many post-Soviet countries, are initially characterized by the coexistence of old and new structures, one from which a country is currently emerging and one toward which it is moving. The greater the differences between a system's initial and final states (i.e., the less common or overlapping elements they share), the more difficult the transition process will be. If the two states are highly disparate, chaos will result. In order to facilitate change, a "bridge" or intermediate state must be constructed with common features spanning the old and the new (Venda, 1991, 1999). In addition to capturing, more fully, the organic nature of large-scale reform in politically, socially, and economically volatile settings, our revisions to Fullan's (2001) framework provide a more complete account of the unique preconditions that precipitate large-scale change; that is, they acknowledge the importance of the stage-setting that allows the initiation of major national reform to proceed with such speed and breadth. Both of these additional dimensions, more characteristic of revolutionary change, will be addressed in this study.

METHODOLOGY

The findings presented in this chapter are based on lengthy interviews with 24 key individuals, including members of the Ministry of Education, teacher educators, university researchers, and members of advocacy and school reform organizations. Interviewees were selected because of their role in the educational system and in its transformation. The authors deliberately selected a wide variety of participants, in accordance with the concept of "shared meaning of change" (Fullan, 2001, p. 9). A number of interviewees also furnished important primary (government, policy, and school) documents related to the process of educational transformation. These documents addressed selected innovative programs, provided statistical data on various aspects of the educational system, and described legislative changes that had been introduced in Russia since 1991.

The authors acknowledge that this study is based on research in a small geographical area (Moscow) and with a limited number of interviewees. In addition, the interpretations of events reflect the authors' own perspectives and, of necessity, are informed both by the individuals interviewed and by the specific time period during which the interviews were conducted. Nevertheless, in the short time available, a wealth of primary information was collected from individuals who played a key role in the reform movement in Moscow, particularly during Russia's initial transition period.

The format for the interviews involved a common, open-ended, unstructured questionnaire, upon which the researchers elaborated with additional probes as the interview unfolded. The following questions served as a guide for the interviews: How have the political, economic, and social changes that have taken place in Russia since 1991 affected the educational system? What factors prompted the onset of these changes? Is there a vision that characterizes these changes? Who are the educational decision and policy makers? Are parents empowered to make decisions in schools? Who are the key individuals/organizations/government bodies that have pushed for/initiated/supported change? What problems have you encountered in the transformation of the Russian educational system? What have been the barriers and facilitators of change? What does the future hold for Russian education?

These questions were overlaid with probes which helped clarify: the perceived need for and clarity of educational change; the influence of the past (including the role of prerevolutionary models of education); the heritage of the communist regime and the importance of "reculturing" (see Hargreaves & Fullan, 1998); the reciprocal relationship between cultural (norms, habits, skills, and beliefs) and structural change (physical environment, organizational arrangements, finance, governance, curriculum, training, etc.); the complexity of the change that is required; external factors that press for and advance change; the influence of the West in facilitating change; the role of reform organizations; and the degree to which change is supported by its direct participants, including teachers, parents, administrators, students, business community, churches, private schools, and others.

The interviews ranged from 1–2 hours in length, with approximately 50–55 hours of material recorded. About one quarter of the interviewees spoke English. The services of an interpreter (a journalism student from Moscow State University) were used in those cases where the interviewee spoke only Russian. Data analyses involved examination of the transcribed interviews and extensive notes and documents acquired by the principal researcher. The Russian experience was then matched against the initiation stage of Fullan's (2001) framework in order to understand Russia's transformation as a "change" process.

THE CONTEXT: PUBLIC DISCONTENT WITH AN EDUCATIONAL SYSTEM IN NEED OF REFORM

The genesis of educational reform in Russia does not date from the dissolution of the Soviet Union. It began much earlier. When Mikhail Gorbachev came to power in 1985, it was increasingly becoming clear that the Soviet educational system was in need of restructuring. As reported in the Russian newspaper *Izvestia* (1988), the whole country had "slipped onto the sidelines of world progress scientifically, technologically, economically and socially" (p. 3).

During the decade preceding *perestroika*, Russian education was characterized by a marked decline in the quality of teachers and teacher training, by authoritarian and inflexible teaching methods, by a static and bureaucratic administrative structure which left little room for teacher initiative, and by outdated textbooks whose content was overlaid with increasingly discredited communist ideology. In addition, research and development related to the reality of teaching was almost nonexistent, and teachers' working conditions were abysmal: teachers' salaries were lower than those of industrial skilled workers, basic school supplies were difficult to obtain, and school buildings (particularly in the rural areas) lacked running water, central heating, and indoor plumbing (Kerr, 1991, 1995). These conditions prompted a reexamination of the Russian educational system and precipitated the initiation of major change.

In 1984, one year before becoming leader of the Communist Party, Mikhail Gorbachev served as chair of a commission examining educational reform. This commission's recommendations included the national establishment of a compulsory computer-literacy course at the high-school level, the improvement of in-service training programs, and minimal raises in teacher salaries. However, these "muted" measures were characterized as nothing more than reform "by the bureaucrats for the bureaucrats" (Kerr, 1991). By 1987, Gorbachev had begun talking openly about his program of *perestroika* (restructuring) in terms of a revolutionary shift in how Soviet citizens were to begin thinking about themselves and their role in the world. During this early period, the educational media – particularly the *Teacher's Gazette* (*Uchitel'skaia gazetta*), edited by V. F. Matveev – played a critical role in supporting a spontaneous grassroots campaign that questioned the fundamental assumptions underlying the Soviet educational system. The educational media, a barometer of teachers' sentiments, became an important means through which community pressure for change was exerted (Nechaev, 1999). For example, the *Teacher's Gazette* regularly printed critiques by teachers, school administrators, prominent intellectuals, and scientists, and served as a critical venue for public expression and dialogue (Dimova, 1999).

Between 1987 and 1989, against a backdrop of increasing public complaint, several main developments took place which pushed the debate on education forward. First, in 1987, Eduard Dneprov, a maverick educational reformer, founded a semiautonomous School Ad Hoc Research Group (VNIK-SHKOLA) to develop a new "conception" of general education (Dneprov, 1999a). Second, a new Creative Teachers Union (independent of the state-sponsored educators' trade union) was founded which gave teachers a more forceful professional voice and the potential to affect national policy. Third, the structure of educational research and development in the USSR (which had been within the purview of the Academy of Pedagogical Sciences and its constituent research institutes) was subjected to a major overhaul in order to make allocation of contracts more equitable, research output more productive, and the quality of studies more responsive to educators' current needs (Kerr, 1990).

However, the old bureaucratic counter forces in education turned out to be too strong and resistant to change. Although the long-awaited meeting of the Congress of Education Workers in December 1988 proved that many teachers supported the position outlined by VNIK-SHKOLA (Dneprov, 1999a), real power still remained in the hands of conservatives. The visionary proposals introduced in 1998 by Dneprov's VNIK group were so carefully scrutinized and repeatedly rewritten by the bureaucracy, that it became difficult to recognize their original liberal thrust. Matveev and his reform-minded colleagues were forced out of the *Teachers Gazette* in 1989. The reform movement had minimal representation on the newly created Council on National Education. The expected reform of the Academy of Pedagogical Sciences did not take place. The old guard had succeeded in obstructing any plans for major educational reorganization.

The direction of the political winds in the USSR, however, was not always predictable. In 1991, the Soviet Union dissolved; Boris Yeltsin became leader of the new Russian Socialist Federated Soviet Republic (RSFSR), and the educational critic and reformist Dneprov was suddenly catapulted into the role of RSFSR Minister of Education, bringing with him the small team of reformers who had founded VNIK-SHKOLA. In his first few days in office, Dneprov fired hundreds of officials and moved swiftly to introduce his new conception of education (Kerr, 1991). Key terms such as "humanization," "differentiation," "democratization," and "pluralization" defined the guiding principles of this vision (Rust, 1992).

After the introduction of the Law on Education in 1992 (slightly revised in 1996), the government was silent on educational matters. However, many gaps remained in the federal laws, regulations, and policies governing education, and regional and local policies became even more diverse, creating an increasingly confusing and chaotic situation. In the summer of 1997, the government announced a new program of educational reform. The announcement was eagerly anticipated by Russian teachers, administrators, educational consultants/entrepreneurs, as well as central bureaucrats (Kerr, 1998). Teachers were angry about salary arrears and concerned about the effects of social and economic upheaval on their schools. Administrators were confounded by unfamiliar financial procedures and uncertain about their legal authority. Educational consultants/entrepreneurs were anxious about the lack of federal and regional support for truly new educational approaches and fearful of a return to a centralized system. Central bureaucrats were infuriated by the increasing educational autonomy of the regions, and apprehensive about the potential impact that regional diversity might have on higher education (Kerr, 1998). Initially, the commission responsible for drafting the new reform proposal expressed a desire to reaffirm the principles articulated in the original work of the VNKIK-SHKOLA under Dneprov's leadership. However, in the autumn of 1997, stronger centrist factions emerged within the commission. By December, educational financing and the payment of educators' back salaries became overriding issues. Further action on the reform proposals was delayed by the Duma in May 1998, following strikes staged by teachers, students, and professors in sympathy with the Siberian miners' demonstrations. The final version of the reform document clearly favored a more conservative vision and one oriented primarily toward economic concerns (Kerr, 1998).

ANALYSIS OF THE RUSSIAN EXPERIENCE USING FULLAN'S CONCEPTUAL FRAMEWORK

In considering educational reform in Russia, one must acknowledge the complex historical legacy of the Soviet educational system. Soviet education was characterized by a rigid, federally controlled, common school curriculum which emphasized the acquisition of factual knowledge in highly specialized subjects, leaving little room for individual pedagogical initiatives. Textbooks were provided by a state publication monopoly, and educational needs were guided by a centralized manpower planning strategy. Since the dissolution of the Soviet Union, the nation has been influenced by a plethora of competing social, political, and economic forces – sometimes enabling educational change, sometimes derailing or obstructing it – but always dynamic in character.

What follows is a discussion of Fullan's eight-factor schema as it applies to the Russian experience of the initiation of change. Since the landscape of educational reform in Russia is so remarkably complex, this discussion will focus on one of the most pressing issues identified by the OECD Team in their 1998 report, namely, the decentralization of the Russian educational system. The 1992 Law on Education (and subsequent amendments) have provided the legislative framework for this major policy shift. Although tensions unavoidably accompany any decentralization effort, it was widely believed by Russians that only through such restructuring could innovative ideas, curricula, teaching methods, and programs evolve. Although the following analysis is not to be understood as precluding other related levels of reform, it will necessarily assume a macro-perspective, and change will be considered primarily at the national level rather than at the level of school division, school, or classroom (Polyzoi & Nazarenko, 2004).

Advocacy from Central Administration/Bureaucratic Orientations: Laying the Foundation for a New Educational Vision

According to Fullan (2001), "initiation of change never occurs without an advocate, and one of the most powerful [of these] is the chief district administrator ... [however] ... administrators can be equally powerful at blocking change" (p. 58). In Russia, although one cannot credit any single individual with the role of chief advocate, it is clear that strong advocates of educational change exerted influence at the highest level of government; the most influential of these were Eduard Dneprov and his reform group. Before his 1990 appointment as Minister of Education, Dneprov realized that the radical change of the educational system was necessary in order to adapt to the emergent forces of democratization and liberalization and to develop civic education and students' capacity for critical thinking. To this end, Dneprov's allies sought to break the totalitarian bureaucracy and to rapidly "de-monopolize" and "decentralize" administrative and curricular authority. The New Law on Education, ushered in by Dneprov in 1992, laid the foundation for a new vision of education in Russia.

However, just as there were early forces that advocated for reform from central administration, there were also counter forces that made its realization difficult. Although Dneprov's 1992 Law on Education was seen by some as an enormous accomplishment, others took a different view. According to Johnson (1997), Dneprov's insistence on a "big bang" to force the reform through was perceived as a politically questionable strategy. The rapid decentralization, thus, only served to aggravate administrative and financial chaos at the regional and local levels. Faced with bitter resistance and increasingly caustic personal and political attacks from conservative educators, Dneprov was forced to resign as Minister of Education in December 1992.

In Russia, "advocacy from central administration" and "bureaucratic orientations" appear to be intimately linked. Fullan (1999) defines the latter as the perspective brought by central administrators to the decision to introduce an innovation or change. Such adoption decisions may be characterized either by an opportunistic (bureaucratic) approach or by a genuine problem-solving orientation that responds to a real need. Cynics might argue that reform in Russia was introduced by bureaucrats motivated by political expediency. Others might claim that the true driving force behind Dneprov's reform movement was a strong sense of "moral purpose" (Fullan, 1999), a desire to modernize the inefficient Russian educational system. There is probably some truth to both views. Pinski (1999) adds a further layer of explanation: "The 'winds of freedom' in the early 1990s helped push Dneprov's new conception of education through. However, the principles embodied in his law lacked the details needed to effectively transform the system." Dneprov, realizing the urgency of consolidating his "conception" into law, hoped that its framework would be fleshed out at a later time through a series of amendments. However, this became increasingly difficult as economic conditions rapidly deteriorated and the Duma's conservative elements gained influence. In what Dneprov refers to as the "Communist revenge," the Communist majority succeeded in blocking further attempts at educational reform (Dneprov, 1999a).[1] In spring 2000, Russia was preparing for national elections; and although a Communist government was considered a possibility, many believed that a return to the former Soviet model of education was now an impossibility.[2]

Role of Teachers Unions/Teacher Advocacy: The Birth of Russia's Educational Reform Movement

Fullan (2001) acknowledges that national teacher unions in North America have become strong advocates of reform, and indeed can be powerful initiators. However, he cautions that "most teachers do no have adequate information, access, time or energy [to initiate change]; and the innovations they do adopt are often individualistic [rather than broad-based or wide-reaching]" (Fullan, 2001, p. 60). The implication is that advocacy from district administrators and/or union leaders is necessary for district-wide changes.

The official teacher's trade union that existed for many years in the Soviet Union was never seen by Russian teachers as an organization that served their interests but, rather, as a government agency of control (Krugliakov, 1999). The *perestroika* period saw the emergence of over 400 independent teacher organizations, whose common interest was to engage teachers in discussion about new forms of education which collectively came to be known as the *pedagogy of cooperation* – perceiving the teacher as a guide rather than a taskmaster, treating students with respect, engaging in honest dialogue with other teachers, and encouraging variety in teaching (Kerr, 1991). Many of these organizations soon adopted the name "Eureka Club," and a new movement was born, led by journalist and physics teacher Alexander Adamsky. By 1988, the *Teachers Gazette* began to provide wide coverage of the club's activities. Shortly thereafter, the clubs banded together to form the *Creative Union of Teachers*, which ultimately included most of the country's well-known innovators and activists, including S. Lysenkova, V. Davydov, B. Bim-Bad, V. Karakovskii, and A. Tubelski (Kerr, 1991). Upon gaining legal status in the spring of 1989, the Creative Union began to link with foreign groups such as *Phi Delta Kappan* in the USA and, by the early 1990s, emerged as an important provider of in-service training for Soviet teachers. Eureka illustrates a phenomenon unique to the USSR: an independent approach to in-service delivery – training created for teachers by the teachers themselves. By fall 1991, several thousand teachers had participated in Eureka seminars offered throughout the country (Kerr, 1991). The difficulty of teacher unions in Russia to effectively mobilize their members (Johnson, 1997) is understandable, considering the fact that political consciousness was hardly nurtured during Communist era. Nevertheless, the sporadic strikes in the spring of 1995, the one-day national strike in the fall of the same year, as well as the strikes which immediately preceded the economic crisis of August 1998 demonstrated some nascent, albeit minimal, political consciousness among teachers.

It is indisputable that the *Creative Union of Teachers* succeeded in energizing more reform-minded educators who, in turn, had the potential to effect change in their own schools. However, escalating economic hardships and the realization that the reform measures would ultimately require a complete "reculturing" of the educational system (Fullan, 1993)[3] forced many teachers to pull back, despite early enthusiasm for the principles of democratic education and the "pedagogy of cooperation." The government's 1997 announcement of its new program of educational renewal was met with significant resistance. As one educator angrily commented in a front page editorial of the *Teachers Gazette* on December 23, 1997:

> We are swamped by a tidal wave of catastrophes ... crushing debts, salaries unpaid for months on end, work stoppages and hunger strikes. ... And what have we here – yet more reform? ... Will reform bring the school its long-lost revenues, or take away its remaining kopeks? Will reform help us cope with the deception we have experienced; can we take yet more empty promises seriously? (quoted in Elkof, 1997, p. 1)

To teachers who felt betrayed by the government, the word "reform" had become anathema by 1998 (Pinski, 1999). The teachers' situation was complicated by the deteriorating conditions of the schools (collapsing facilities, lack of material supplies and absence of funds for capital repairs), as well as by the serious physical health problems experienced by the majority of students in Russian schools. For example, many children would come to school physically weak, due to malnourishment; others had vision problems, serious tooth decay, skeletal deformities, and heart and circulatory problems (Kerr, 1996). In addition, the continued exodus of young, bright teachers and the consequent aging of the teaching body aggravated an already critical situation (Kerr, 1996).

New Policy/Funds to Support Decentralization: Inadequate Capacity Building

One of the major elements of the 1992 Law on Education was the devolution of selected administrative and fiscal responsibilities from central to regional and local authorities. In moving toward a decentralized system, it is necessary, Fullan (1999) warns, to "strike a balance between too little and too much structure" (p. 51). Too much structure produces rigid rules, highly channeled communication, loss of flexibility, and stunted innovation; too little structure, on the other hand, promotes rule-breaking, loose relationships, random communication, and confusion. The analogy by Brown and Eisenhardt (as cited in Fullan, 1999) illustrates this principle well: "If there are no lights, traffic is chaotic. If there are too many lights, traffic stops. A moderate number of lights creates structure but still allows drivers to adapt their routes in surprising ways in response to changing traffic conditions" (p. 5). One might argue that, in Russia, there was too little structure, so that the groundwork for effective decentralization was not adequately prepared. Fullan (1999) emphasizes the importance of "local capacity building" as a prerequisite to successful change. He defines this as "directly and indirectly providing opportunities for advancing the knowledge, skills, and work of local school and district personnel [in order to] create powerful learning communities" (p. 57). He admonishes, "Knowledge ... must be developed not borrowed ... capacity building includes the continual flow and integration of the best ideas available ... rather than the transfer of products" (pp. 68–69). In Russia, legislation was enacted *before* the regions had a chance to develop appropriate decentralized administrative structures for its effective implementation (OECD, 1998, p. 27).[4] As a result, the system was beleaguered by lack of financial coordination, legislative ambiguity, and administrative inexperience. All new administrative obligations devolved to the regions; yet, most regions had limited skills in management, budgetary planning, negotiating with teachers unions, defining the new roles of city and district educational heads, and identifying the retraining needs of teachers. Although they could not legally refuse their new responsibilities, some regions learned to outwardly conform to the official decentralization policy without truly changing. While there were some success stories of regional and local self-management, there were also failures involving problems ranging from wage misappropriation to bureaucratic conflict and inertia (OECD, 1998, p. 46). This situation seriously threatened public confidence in the law and raised doubts about the authority of a federal government, which passes legislation it can neither implement nor enforce (OECD, 1998, pp. 35–36).[5]

Fullan also points out that any new policy must be accompanied by sufficient funding to ensure its effective initiation. In Russia, the funding required to support the decentralization of the educational system was not fully coordinated with budgetary capacity. Regions (some less affluent than others) were left to pay for educational programs which the federal government was simply unable to support. Tax administration in Russia is typically "bottom-up," that is, revenues are collected locally and may be withheld at that level. Regional authorities, therefore, were in a position to bargain over revenues to be released to the federal government, using their control over local resources and tax revenue as leverage (OECD, 1998, p. 35). However, regions had few incentives to forward tax revenues to the federal government (OECD, 1998, p. 36). Education was often pitted against other social programs for available funds. Regional inequities intensified emergent local disparities in the quality of education (OECD, 1998, p. 37). Paradoxically, a policy originally designed to promote educational equity through increased choice and regional differentiation helped to create its opposite (OECD, 1998, p. 79). In Russia, decentralization was initiated, but local capacity was not sufficiently developed to take advantage of the new government's proposal.

Existence and Quality of Innovations/Pressure Groups: The Limited Reach of Pedagogical Reform

In Russia, the process of educational decentralization brought about some interesting pedagogical innovations concentrated mainly in schools with established records of scholarship (i.e., gymnasia and lycées)[6] or in schools that had entered into partnerships with foreign schools and professional associations (OECD, 1998, p. 54). Many of these schools were directed either by members of Dneprov's original reform group or by independent innovative thinkers. Among these talented individuals were Alexander Naumovich Tubelsky (1999), President of the Association of Innovative Schools and Centres and Director of the School of Self-Determination in Moscow; Alexi Borisovich Vorontsov (1999), Director of the Moscow

Association for Developmental Education[7] and Principal of the Experimental Teaching Complex #1133 in Moscow; Anatoli Arkadievich Pinski (1999), Director of the Association of Russian Schools, President of the Association of Moscow School Directors, and Director of School #1060 in Moscow; Alexandra Mihalovna Lenartovich (1999), Principal of School #1321, "Kovcheg," a unique "integrated" special-needs school in Moscow; Anatoli Georgievich Kasprjak (1999), Principal of Moscow Pedagogical Gymnasium; and Evgeni Alexandrovich Yamburg (1999), Principal of the elite Gymnasium #109 in Moscow.

The late 1980s saw the emergence of private consultants and experimental training groups, which offered training alternatives based on the pedagogical models of these innovative schools (Kerr, 1991). One of the earliest was the Eureka group, part of the innovative school movement which provided seminars and training sessions for teachers in Russia and the former USSR since 1990. Several other organizations, such as the Centre for Cultural Policy and the new Association for Developmental Education, were also active in providing educational training opportunities. These – as well as many other local and private entrepreneurs – organized workshops for teachers to facilitate the sharing and exchange of ideas and to offer training in new pedagogical paradigms, alternative teaching techniques, and imported models of education (based primarily on Montessori and Waldorf philosophies).

Although it is arguable that these organizations served as influential pressure groups for the transformation of Russian education, they too fell victim to a struggling economy. Dwindling enrollments forced some consultants either to dissolve or to extend into outlying regions and other countries in search of new clients.[8] In the final analysis, economic conditions compromised whatever initial enthusiasm teachers exhibited for reform. When Tubelsky was asked what was happening to the innovators' movement – was it spreading and developing or had it died – he lamented, "It hasn't died, but I think it's dying" (as cited in Kerr, 1995).

Fullan (2001) notes that the role of the community in the initiation process may take the form of "exerting pressure for a solution to a problem, opposing a potential innovation or adoption, or doing nothing" (p. 61). In Russia, it is clear that the innovators' movement was influential in pressing for educational change and in introducing teachers to new pedagogical models and offering them training opportunities to prepare for unfamiliar challenges. However, the influence of this movement had not reached the majority of teachers within the decade following the collapse of the Soviet Union. Although there were pockets of change and exciting innovative programs, the majority of Russian classrooms remained traditional; even, in Brodinsky's words (1992), "as the winds of change sweep all around them" (p. 379).[9]

According to Pinski (1999), Russian parents were *not* perceived as a significant community pressure group. In an interview with the primary author, Pinksi explains: "In the last decade of the innovative school movement, you will find brilliant pedagogical personalities: highly talented teachers, school directors, and scientists. However, you will rarely find the voice of parents." Although parental political activism and empowerment have been minimal, a new relationship between parents and schools *was* beginning to emerge by the late 1990s. The first important step in this direction was the affirmation of the parents' rights to select the school they wished their children to attend, including the option of private schools. Parents of children with special needs were particularly active in school governance. For example, parents whose children attended Kovcheg School in Moscow recognized that both the regular school system and the segregated special-needs schools were harmful to children. In 1991, they founded a unique school in which 80% of the student population was either deaf, had cerebral palsy, autism, epilepsy, developmental delays, asthma, behavior problems, or was classified as "at-risk" for failure; 20% had no special needs. A. M. Lenartovich, Principal of Kovcheg School (which she describes as a "thorn" in the side of society) declined to register Kovcheg as a special-needs school, in order to avoid the negative effects of "labeling." Although not "integrated" in the North American sense, this school was considered to be quite innovative (Lenartovich, 1999).

Fullan (1999) stresses the importance of parental involvement as a means of fostering a "client orientation" for schools. As personal interactions between parents and schools expand and become institutionalized, greater trust and mutual engagement will begin to evolve. Parental involvement ensures that the school ultimately becomes responsive to the real needs of the community (p. 46). This is precisely the type of relationship that is nurtured at Kovcheg School in Moscow.

Access to Information: Minimal Knowledge Sharing
among Regions and Municipalities

Fullan (2001) discusses "access to information" in terms of teachers' contact with innovative ideas, which is essential to the success of any change effort. In Russia, "access to information" may also refer to data about the evolving educational system, which the government requires in order to monitor the effects of current policy and to make informed decisions about future reform. In the traditional USSR educational system, the data that were gathered concerned quantitative characteristics, for example, numbers of schools, students, teachers, graduates, school buildings, boarding facilities, etc. By the late 1990s, the information base provided only limited data on the efficiency of schools, the quality of teaching, the cost effectiveness of the system, and the extent to which the design and delivery of new programs met changing market needs (OECD, 1998). Hindered by the rigidity of the vertical administrative structure, "knowledge sharing" among regions and municipalities was limited. In some cases, schools located in the same city *rayon* often were left to solve common problems independently. Clearly, more effective networking would have benefited teachers and administrators who, up to then, worked in isolation. This would have facilitated the development and adoption of the best educational programs and teaching practices (OECD, 1998).

External Change Agents: Russia's Ambivalent Relationship with the West

Fullan (2001) classifies as external change agents those regional, state, or national bodies, external to the district, which stimulate or support change, particularly in the initiation phase (p. 60). For the purposes of this study, since the unit of analysis is the nation, external agents may be defined as those that impact the change process from outside the Russian Federation. In the decade following the fall of communism, there is evidence that substantial international activity was taking place in Russia at all levels of the educational system, from the highest administrative offices of government to the individual classroom. However, the overall impact of these external agents on the national direction of reform was less clear.

When Dneprov introduced the 1992 Law on Education, he realized that the goal of modernization required the integration of the Russian educational system into the world community. Accordingly, the Law contained a provision regarding networking with international partners, such as the World Bank, the Carnegie Foundation, the United States International Agency (USIA), the British Council, and the Soros Foundation. Even prior to 1992, one of Dneprov's early initiatives as a Minister of Education was the establishment of ties with the Oslo-based International Movement toward Educational Change (IMTEC), now known as the International Learning Cooperative on Educational Reform.[10]

The Soros Foundation played a particularly significant role in Russia in the preparation of new *civics* courses and materials, including textbooks in the decade following the collapse of the Union. Various international agencies assisted with the development of university-level distance educational programs. For example, in Krasnoyarsk, the regional Centre for the Development of Education offered a number of courses jointly with the Open University in the United Kingdom (OECD, 1998, p. 75).[11] There was even opportunity for international cooperation in the development of Russian educational standards. In the Vologda region, for example, a Dutch–Russian testing center was established. Using modern technology, the center created and administered examinations for a range of school subjects and was responsible for collecting, analyzing, and reporting student data to regional education officials. The center also organized a number of successful workshops for other regions interested in developing similar procedures (Kaliningrad, Stavropol, Saki) (OECD, 1998, p. 95). The British Council also began to play an important role in educational reform in both central Russia (Moscow and St. Petersburg) and remote areas of the Federation (e.g., Omsk, Krasnoyarsk, Volgograd, Tomsk, and Irkutsk). Projects ranged from curriculum development, educational management, and in-service training, to vocational education, special education for at-risk children, and the educational rights of ethnic minorities (Lenskaya, 1999).[12] Specific British Council projects, underway in 2000, included (a) At-Risk Children in the Nizhny Novgorod Region, cosponsored by Kibble Education and Care Centre, Scotland; (b) Developing Technology Education in the Nizhny Novgorod region, cosponsored by University of York in Northern Ireland; (c) Competency-Based Vocational Education and Training (a modular approach to teaching) in the Omsk region, cosponsored by the Scottish Qualifications Authority in Glasgow; (d) Retraining Teachers in Civics Education in the Krasnoyarsk region, cosponsored by the Citizenship Foundation in London, England; (e) In-Service Training for Educational Administrators in the Krasnoyarsk region, cosponsored by Kent Advisory Service in Kent County, Great Britain; (f) National Professional Qualification for Head Teachers in the Sochi region, cosponsored by the Gloucestershire Education County Council; (g) English Language In-Service Training for Secondary School Teachers (KINSET Project) in the Krasnoyarsk region, with participant outreach in Omsk, Sochi, and Volgograd, sponsored by the British Council; and (h) English Language Examination Project (SPEX): Development of New School Leaving Examinations in English in St. Petersburg, sponsored by the British Council.

Russia's relationship with the West, however, remained ambivalent. Despite significant international activity in such areas as management, curriculum, training, assessment, and distance education, the majority of individuals interviewed for this study did not perceive these interventions as significantly having shaped the nature of the innovations that took place in Russia. Although funding partners for projects were actively being pursued, there was tacit, if not obdurate, resistance on the part of many Russian educators to the adoption of "western-style" models of education.[13] Fullan (1999) provides evidence that, if knowledge is imposed rather than "grown," it will fail (p. 17). He adds, "... successful reforms in one place are partly a function of good ideas and largely a function of the conditions under which the ideas flourished. Successful innovations ... fail to be replicated because the wrong thing is being replicated – the reform itself, instead of the conditions which spawned its success" (p. 64).

DISCUSSION

The objective of this chapter is not to provide an exhaustive analysis of the experience of change, but rather to explore the utility of Fullan's framework for helping us understand Russia's post-1991 initiation of change. The data clearly support the value of Fullan's framework. Educational reform in Russia began before the dissolution of the Soviet Union, when it was evident that the educational system was rapidly deteriorating. Fuelled by the spirit of *perestroika* and supported by the increasing presence and voice of the educational media, the innovative school movement, led by Dneprov, was born. Although Dneprov's 1992 Law on Education laid the groundwork for significant educational change in the Russian Federation, bureaucratic counter forces seriously hindered its progress. Initial teacher support for change had been compromised by devastating economic hardships. Teacher enthusiasm had given way to disillusionment, and public confidence in the government's ability to effect educational change had been shaken. Reform had been adversely affected by the absence of appropriate local adminis- trative infrastructures to support the decentralization of administrative and fiscal responsibilities to regional educational authorities.

While the new Law on Education (1992) enabled the emergence of a number of unique innovative programs, directed by talented and progressively minded school principals (Polyzoi & Nazarenko, 2004), many of these programs became victims of the ensuing economic crisis. As a result, many school principals were compelled to explore creative ways to survive, such as charging parents supplementary tuition fees for specialized courses (e.g., music, theatre, English language), renting out parts of their schools to generate revenue, encouraging parental involvement, offering yearly in-service teacher training, and marketing their own curricular materials (Lisovskaya & Karpov, 2001; Polyzoi & Nazarenko, 2004). Knowledge sharing, as it relates to innovative school programs among regions and municipalities, was limited, hindered by the rigidity of the educational system's vertical administrative structure. In addition, although numerous international partnerships developed between Western and Russian educational institutions, the impact of the West on the reforms taking shape in Russia remains unclear.

Although educational reform as a conscious targeted political action by government was concluded in 1992 with the introduction of the Law on Education, educational reform as a large-scale spontaneous process of internal change continued to gain strength in Russia. Situated between the obstructive economic and conservative political polarities, Russian education in the decade following the dissolution of the Union showed a measure of resiliency and resolve. Despite devastating economic hardships and waning political involvement (complicated by quasi-reformists and regressive political tendencies), an emergent progressive educational movement in Russia began to move forward, albeit with difficulty. This was due largely to the efforts of a motivated, inspired pedagogical community, innovative teachers and administrators, and committed regional directors throughout the Federation.

However, despite the richness and multidimensionality of Fullan's framework, its structure does not sufficiently address the dynamics of the change process. Systems undergoing transition are initially characterized by the coexistence of old and new structures. The greater the differences between a system's initial and final states (i.e., the fewer elements they share), the more arduous the transition process will be. In order to ease the change process, a "bridge" or intermediate state must be constructed with common features straddling the old and the new (Venda, 1991, 1999). As Russia struggled to move from a highly centralized, teacher-directed educational system to a liberal, democratic, and child-centered curriculum, educators began searching for a more widely acceptable centrist position (Kerr, 1996). The window of opportunity for dramatic change, which opened immediately following the collapse of the Union, slowly began to close. Over the next decade, change began to be more measured and cautious, as the reform movement's tendency toward retrenchment attests – perhaps in an attempt to bridge the "revolutionary leap" initiated by Denprov in his 1992 Law on Education.

In addition, Fullan's model does not address the unique preconditions that prompted dramatic change in post-Soviet countries – the political, economic, and social forces that catapult nations into mobilizing for major reform. Birzea (1995) incorporates these preconditions in his four-phase model of educational transformation: *deconstruction, stabilization, reconstruction,* and *counter-reform.* The first two of these stages may be understood as preceding Fullan's "initiation" stage. In the USSR, the deconstruction period was initiated by Gorbachev during the era of *perestroika.* It was at this time that the first steps toward dismantling the Russian educational system were taken. Once the Marxist–Leninist ideology had been discredited, schools had little choice but to deconstruct their outdated ideology-driven educational system. Curricular innovations, first proposed by the Soviet ministry in 1998, were extended in the early 1990s. Indeed, Russia's attempt to stabilize these reforms began with the introduction of the Law on Education in 1992. Although this law provided an important framework for educational transformation, attempts to move forward with substantive educational reconstruction have been hindered by a number of other factors, to which Birzea (1995) alludes. According to Birzea (1995), change in the post-Communist countries is dependent on reform in other domains: economic, ideological, and political. Dneprov (1999a) supports Birzea's views:

> Russian educational reform has been unable to break through the economic barriers which have increasingly paralyzed the education system. The ideological breaking away has, in some ways, been even more problematic because it challenges the values, attitudes, and mentalities of the Russian people. Pedagogical models that emphasize conformity, the collective, and centralized control are inconsistent with those that emphasize individual choice, self-development, and independent thinking. In addition, reform in Russia is aggravated by the political context, in particular, the recent attempt by the various Communist factions within the Duma, within the decade following the collapse, to fuel the fires of opposition, to repeatedly impeach President Yeltsin, to resurrect the nostalgic past by rekindling feelings of nationalism.

This is what Birzea (1995) refers to as the counter-reform stage – the emergence of residual communism that serves to block or retard the pace of national reform.

In conclusion, Fullan's conceptual framework, while rich in detail, does not directly address the revolutionary nature of change, and is comparatively linear in its approach. Birzea's transformational framework provides a dynamic overlay more consistent with an organic picture of the Russian change process. Taken together, these two complementary models of change provide an enhanced understanding of the transition process, particularly when change is sudden and dramatic as in the case of former Communist countries in Eastern and Central Europe. The confluence of these two models produces a dynamic picture of change that is much richer and more complex than either could yield by itself. As Fullan (1999) aptly explains:

> The first ... step is to understand what makes social forces move forward in turbulent environments. ... [This] involves understanding the complex interactive flow of change, establishing conditions that will turn this complexity into advantage, and then looking for, fostering, reinforcing, and celebrating emerging outcomes that are valued, while discouraging those that are not. ... Good outcomes are not as random as they may seem ... there are orientations that we can work on that make it likely that positive patterns will frequently emerge. (p. 79)

As we learn more about rapid and dramatic change at the national level in Russia, as we discover which forces are relevant in successful reform, and as we appreciate the complexity of a dynamic, living, and continuously evolving system, we are in a better position to direct and shape change in positive ways. Although – given our current knowledge of educational change theory – harnessing these forces may be difficult, this study represents the beginning of a framework for thinking about change, particularly as it pertains to nations that undergo dramatic and sudden transformation.

NOTES

1. Johnson (1997) observes that the "politics of personality based on arcane and bitter personal rivalries and ambitions" within Russian bureaucracy (p. 223) impede attempts to advance reform. The controversial OECD Background Report (Bolotov, 1995) is one example that merits some attention: In October 1995, a team of experts at the Ministry of Education, in response to a request by the OECD team, prepared a background document which provided a candid analysis of accomplishments, mistakes, and new challenges in Russian education. However, despite its professional nature, the survey and its authors were viciously criticized in an incident that seems to have been linked to political struggles within the education establishment. "... the attacks were full of insinuations and innuendo about personal motivations that reminded some observers of the ... form of political denunciation perfected in Soviet time. The most serious charge was that its distribution represented an attempt to discredit the Yeltsin government in the eyes of the West and undermine him in his race for president of the Federation" (Vaillant, 1997, p. 3). As a result, the distribution of the background report was limited and controversial information deliberately left out of the final OECD report prepared by the official European examination team (Lenskaya, 1999).

2. On March 26, 2000, Vladimir Putin, former Head of the KGB, was elected president of the Russian Federation. His military successes in the Chechnyan war made him immensely popular among Russians who felt that he could effectively

guide the country out of its economic turmoil. Appointed as Yeltsin's successor, Putin believed that Russia could move forward only if it combined the principles of a market economy and democracy with the realities of Russian history, culture, and society.

3. Teachers were beset with a constellation of confusing, often competing, new demands. For example, they were required to be more accountable to parents and administrators, who began, increasingly, to question their work (Krugliakov, 1999). The growing influx of new curricular materials challenged teachers who were unused to making independent decisions about instructional design and curriculum development. The new law and its accompanying legal requirements (e.g., the regular evaluation of teachers' work) introduced new pressures and placed increasing burdens on teachers (Kerr, 1995).

4. Fullan (1993) distinguishes between *cultural* change (norms, habits, skills, and beliefs) and *structural* change (physical environment, organizational arrangements, roles, finance governance, curriculum training, etc.). Although "reculturing is much more difficult than restructuring" (Fullan, 1999, p. 66), change in one domain typically serves as a catalyst for change in the other.

5. For example, the new law and subsequent decrees stipulated that education was to receive no less than 10% of the GNP (by the early part of the 2000, it was only at 8%); that all students were to receive free full secondary education through grade 11 (this was compromised by the introduction of tuition fees in private and selected state schools); that teachers' salaries were to match those of government employees earning the equivalent of US$110 per month (salaries for junior teachers at that time reached only US$8 per month; for senior teachers it was US$40 per month (Kromov, 1999; Ignatov, 1999). In 1995, the federal government honored only about 67% of its own education bill to the regions. As a result, it was necessary to carry over wage arrears into the following fiscal year (OECD, 1998, pp. 35–36).

6. Gymnasia and lycées are academic secondary schools that prepare students for university entrance.

7. The Association for Developmental Education promoted Davydov's ideas concerning the use of Vygotskian psychology as a basis for classroom teaching (Davydov, 1995; Vorontsov, 1999). The model is conceptually sophisticated, but in most schools its implementation took on a form not radically different from a traditional classroom (Kerr, 1995). Davydov's model was more readily accepted by Russians because it originated in Russia (i.e., was not borrowed or adapted from Western pedagogy) and was based on the concept of "social constructivism," popular in North America today. Developmental Instruction garnered support from the Ministry of Education; since 1992, when Davydov and his colleagues began to disseminate the model in a well-elaborated and practical format, it has spread to more than 42% of all Russian primary classrooms. The popularity of this model supports the belief that, in educational reform, small steps are easier for teachers to work with than major conceptual leaps that lack specificity (Kerr, 1996; Vorontsov, 1999).

8. Eureka even began offering summer programs for pupils and teachers in England, the USA, and Cyprus. Many of these special workshops were regularly advertised through the pedagogical press (Kerr, 1995).

9. Curricular innovation within the decentralization process involve providing teachers with greater choice of course materials. For example, there was an opportunity to incorporate locally devised inputs into the school program, to help foster a sense of local identity, and inform pupils about valuable aspects of their local heritage and institutions. Whereas the federal authorities prescribed a main core curriculum (60%) that reflected the great Russian national heritage, regions had the opportunity to contribute about 30% of the curricular content, focusing on such regionally distinct areas as ethnicity, language, history, folklore, crafts, etc. Individual schools (which may have wanted to extend programming in the English language, the arts, or the sciences) had control over the remaining 10% (OECD, 1998, pp. 20, 88). The challenge was to preserve the overall unity of various regions, while simultaneously accommodating the great diversity of their peoples (OECD, 1998, p. 35).

10. In fact, it was Dneprov's openness to Western contacts during his tenure as Minister of Education that, some believe, contributed to the increased alienation of many of his original supporters, and ultimately to his resignation from office (Johnson, 1997).

11. Moscow's University of the Russian Academy of Education, the first private university to receive official state accreditation (in 1995) was initially modeled after the United Kingdom's Open University concept (Bim-Bad, 1999).

12. Each region was responsible for seeking out an international partner from the United Kingdom. It was only though the devolution of finances from the federal government that the regions had become able to initiate and fund such projects independently (Lenskaya, 1999).

13. Innovative programs, they argue, are inspired by internal sources – talented educators who recognize the need to challenge the traditional school system and to offer the youth of Russia an alternative for the twenty-first century.

ACKNOWLEDGMENTS

This chapter is an adaptation of an article entitled "Harnessing the forces of change: Educational transformation in Russia" that appeared in Polyzoi, Fullan, and Anchan (2003, pp. 13–32). Copyright permission is granted by the publisher. The study was funded by the Social Sciences and Humanities Research Council (SSHRC), internal University of Winnipeg grant. The authors would like to thank the individuals who participated in the study and who gave so generously of their time.

REFERENCES

Anweiler, O. (1992). Some historical aspects of educational change in the former Soviet Union and Eastern Europe. In: D. Phillips & M. Kaser (Eds), *Education and economic change in Eastern Europe and the former Soviet Union* (p. 29). Wallingford, Oxfordshire: Triangle Books.

Bim-Bad, B. M. (1999). Interview by the primary author. *Moscow*, March 22, 1999.

Birzea, C. (1994). *Educational policies of the countries in transition.* Strasbourg: Council of Europe Press.

Birzea, C. (1995). *Educational reform and educational research in Central-Eastern Europe: The case of Romania.* Paper presented at the IBE International Meeting on Educational Reform and Educational Research, Tokyo, Japan.

Bolotov, V. A. (1995). *The reform of education in new Russia: A background report for the OECD* (unpublished). Available at http://www.indiana.edu/~isre/NEWSLETTER/vol6no2/OECD.htm

Brodinsky, B. (1992). The impact of perestroika on Soviet education. *Phi Delta Kappan, 73*(5), 378–385.

Davydov, V. V. (1995). The influence of L. S. Vygotsky on education, theory, research, and practice. *Educational Researcher, 24*(3), 12–21.

Dimova, I. (1999). Interview by the primary author. *Moscow*, April 5, 1999.

Dneprov, E. (1999a). Interview by the primary author. *Moscow*, March 25, 1999.

Elkof, B. (1997). From the editor: The state of Russian education. *ISRE Virtual Newsletter, 6*(1), 1.

Fullan, M. (1993). *Change forces: Probing the depths of educational reform.* London: Falmer Press.

Fullan, M. (1999). *Change forces: The sequel.* London: Falmer Press.

Fullan, M. (2001). *The new meaning of educational change* (3rd ed.). New York: Teachers College Press.

Hargreaves, A., & Fullan, M. (1998). *What's worth fighting for out there?* Toronto, Elementary School Teachers' Federation; New York, Teachers' College Press; Buckingham, Open University Press.

Ignatov, A. M. (1999). Interview by the primary author. *Moscow*, March 18, 1999.

Izvestia. (1988). Moscow, Russia, December 24, p. 3.

Johnson, M. S. (1997). Visionary hopes and technocratic fallacies in Russian education. *Comparative Education Review, 4*(2), 219–225.

Kasprjak, A. G. (1999). Interview by the primary author. *Moscow*, April 6, 1999.

Kerr, S. T. (1990). Will glasnost lead to perestroika? Directions of educational reform in the USSR. *Educational Researcher, 19*(7), 26–31.

Kerr, S. T. (1991). Beyond dogma: Teacher education in the USSR. *Journal of Teacher Education, 42*(5), 332–349.

Kerr, S. T. (1995, October). *Teacher's continuing education and Russian school reform.* Paper presented at the Conference of the American Association for the Advancement of Slavic Studies, Washington, DC. Available at http://weber.uwashington.edu/~stkerr/concrut.htm

Kerr, S. T. (1996). *The re-centering of Russian education.* Comments as part of a roundtable at the American Association for the Advancement of Slavic Studies, Boston, MA. Available at http://weber.u.washington.edu/~stkerr/aaass.html

Kerr, S. T. (1998). The new Russian education reform: Back to the future? *ISRE Virtual Newsletter, 7*(1), 1–6. Available at http://www.indiana.edu/~isre/NEWSLETTER/vol7no1/Kerr.htm

Kromov, K. M. (1999). Interview by the primary author. *Moscow*, March 18, 1999.

Krugliakov, K. M. (1999). Interview by the primary author. *Moscow*, March 18, 1999.

Lenartovich, A. M. (1999). Interview by the primary author. *Moscow*, April 8, 1999.

Lenskaya, L. (1999). Interview by the primary author. *Moscow*, March 26, 1999.

Lisovskaya, E., & Karpov, V. (2001). The perplexed world of Russian private schools: Findings from field research. *Comparative Education, 37*(1), 43–64.

Nechaev, N. N. (1999). Interview by the primary author. *Moscow*, March 25, 1999.

OECD. (1998). *Reviews of national policies for education: Russian education.* Paris: Organization for Economic Co-operation and Development.

Pinski, A. A. (1999). Interview by the primary author. *Moscow*, March 30, 1999.

Polyzoi, E., Fullan, M., & Anchan, J. (Eds). (2003). *Change forces in post-Soviet Eastern Europe: Education in transition.* London: Routledge/Falmer Press.

Polyzoi, E., & Nazarenko, T. (2004). Comparative analysis of four case studies of educational reform in Russia – Strategies of survival and change. *World Studies in Education, 5*(2), 65–80.

Rust, V. D. (1992). An interview with Edward Dneprov: School reform in the Russian Republic. *Phi Delta Kappan, 73*(5), 375–377.

Rust, V. D., Knost, P., & Wichmann, J. (1994). Education and youth in Central and Eastern Europe: A comparative assessment. In: V. D. Rust, P. Knost & J. Wichmann (Eds), *Education and the values crisis in Central and Eastern Europe* (pp. 281–308). Frankfurt: Peter Lang.

Tubelsky, A. N. (1999). Interview by the primary author. *Moscow*, April 1, 1999.

Vaillant, J. (1997). *A provocative report: The reform of education in new Russia* [A background report for the OECD; Review of government report]. Available at http://www.indiana. edu/~isre/NEWSLETTER/vol6no1/OECDreview.htm. Retrieved on November 3, 1999.

Venda, V. (1991). Transformation dynamics in complex systems. *Journal of the Washington Academy of Sciences, 81*(4), 163–184.

Venda, V. (1999). Interview by the primary author. Winnipeg, Manitoba, Canada, May 5, 1999.

Vorontsov, A. B. (1999). Interview by the primary author. *Moscow*, March 26, 1999.

Yamburg, E. A. (1999). Interview by the primary author. *Moscow*, April 6, 1999.

Redefining Nations and Identities

THE SEMBLANCE OF PROGRESS AMIDST THE ABSENCE OF CHANGE: EDUCATING FOR AN IMAGINED EUROPE IN MOLDOVA AND ALBANIA

Meg P. Gardinier and Elizabeth Anderson Worden

INTRODUCTION

For Moldova and Albania, two of the poorest countries in Europe, the promise of European integration has led to a reimagining of the purpose of schooling in the context of post-authoritarian national reform. Once charged with producing loyal communist citizens, schools and educational policies in these countries are now focused on producing democratic citizens of an expanded Europe. Drawing on extensive qualitative research, this chapter explores how educational discourses in these countries are reconstituting notions of national citizenship to fit within a broader pan-European identity. This shift has significant implications within and beyond the borders of these countries.

As transnational European values and norms are being incorporated into national policies, curricula, and teacher practice, "new identity positions and practices" (Soysal, 2002, p. 60) are engendered in different ways.

Post-Socialism is not Dead: (Re)Reading the Global in Comparative Education
International Perspectives on Education and Society, Volume 14, 183–211
Copyright © 2010 by Emerald Group Publishing Limited
ISSN: 1479-3679/doi:10.1108/S1479-3679(2010)0000014010

We argue that the possibility of future European Union (EU) integration is not necessarily a stick or carrot that drives reform, but rather it serves as a powerful imaginary force that comes to life in particular educational arenas. As these states venture to reimagine themselves through their alignment with Europe, the EU imaginary serves as a mechanism for creating a forward-looking sense of national momentum that represents a break with their authoritarian pasts. In both Moldova and Albania, however, important national-level debates and demands are being displaced in the interest of transnational belonging.

We investigate both policy and teaching practice, and like others in this line of research (Silova, 2002; Steiner-Khamsi, 2002), our findings suggest that the adoption of common European standards at the policy level is actually producing divergent educational results in classrooms. As Moldovan and Albanian policy-makers adopt European principles of democratic citizenship, human rights, and social inclusion, the appropriation and application of these ideals at the school level varies. This disconnection has important implications for researchers, policy-makers, and practitioners.

Below, we begin with a brief overview of related literature, followed by our methodology and a discussion of the case studies. For the Moldovan case, we examine the EU imaginary and the role of European actors in the recent reform of history and civic education. For the Albanian case, we expand our scope to understand European integration in the context of general preuniversity education reform since the collapse of the communist regime. In both cases, particular attention is paid to the disconnect between policy goals and teachers' practice as well as to the lingering legacies of the countries' former regimes. We conclude with a discussion of the productive nature of the European social imaginary, which under certain circumstances has led to the perpetuation of problematic power relations, the displacement of local needs, and the contradictory fusion of new principles and old practices.

THEORETICAL PERSPECTIVES

The construct of the social imaginary is gaining ground in comparative and international research on educational policy and practice. In the face of increasing globalization and internationalization in the field of education, researchers are seeking new tools to investigate the changing relations among nation-states, their constituent societies, and transnational actors that often influence domestic dynamics. For Rizvi and Lingard (2010), "The state now represents a site increasingly influenced not only by transnational institutions, but also by global ideologies that constantly seek to steer the social imaginaries of policy actors everywhere, but in ways that are mediated by national traditions and local politics" (p. xii). Thus, attention to the role of social imaginaries is crucial in comparative and international education policy research. At a fundamental level, Rizvi (2006) argues, "It is through the collective sense of imagination that a society is created, given coherence and identity, and also subjected to social change, both mundane and radical" (pp. 195–196). Our study thus focuses on the shared notion of European identity as a pervasive social imaginary that produces discursive and material results in the two postcommunist societies of Moldova and Albania.

With the significant influence of European integration on education policy reform in these two countries, the concept of the European social imaginary provides a powerful lens through which to investigate and understand particular dimensions of education for democratization. In newly democratic states like Moldova and Albania, public schools play an important role in the creation and maintenance of a democratic citizenry. Moreover, education serves an important legitimizing function in democratic and democratizing societies. In the context of EU-based policy development, "education has a new prominence as the arena in which identity and legitimacy can be created" (Novoa & Lawn, 2002, p. 4).

The construction of citizenship identities is therefore a primary function of educational systems. In the European context, these identities are what hold together the "imagined community" (Anderson, 2006) of Europe. Researchers contend that it is in localized educational debates, such as over various versions of contested histories, that the production of European identity is most salient (Soysal, 2002). In local structures "is where Europeanization (the creation of Europe, if you will) happens and where European space is enacted: mainly outside intergovernmental structures and formal EU institutions, and through informal institutional processes. Through these processes a revised representation of Europe is communicated and contested" (Soysal, 2002, p. 59). Soysal's (2002) research on select history texts has shown that the notion of European citizenship is constructed through the adoption of shared civic ideals, values, and norms rather than through traditional approaches celebrating the particular national practices and local historical roots of individual European nation-states. In other words, "European identity" is constituted and legitimated in and through "claims to universality rather than particularisms" (p. 61).

Just as local educational debates constitute new notions of a European educational space, so too does the European imaginary frame local level educational affairs. National history texts "increasingly situate the nation and identity within a European context, and in the process, the nation is being reinterpreted and recast anew" (Soysal, 2002, p. 61). This process of "externalization" is common in education reform efforts, as local actors seek external legitimacy for contested domestic reforms. Steiner-Khamsi (2002) argues that "using references as sources of authority – internal or external, domestic or international – is endemic to education, which is under constant public pressure to legitimize its practices, values and forms of organization, since in the domain of education, each and every citizen feels entitled to act as 'natural expert' and stakeholder" (p. 70). The present study of Moldovan and Albanian policy and civic education curricula builds on these findings, providing additional empirical data on the EU imaginary as an important factor influencing the course of postcommunist education reform.

We argue that the European social imaginary is productive in many senses. As noted above, it serves as a powerful legitimizing discourse in Moldova and Albania as policy-makers seek to differentiate national identity from the communist past. In the educational sphere, civic education employs the European social imaginary as a means of recasting national identity within a modern European frame. As a result, national citizenship education incorporates European discourses of democracy, human rights, social inclusion, and other normative principles. Furthermore, international actors increasingly define and prescribe concepts of European citizenship, such as "lifelong learning" (Novoa & Lawn, 2002; McNeely, 1995). In recasting these national discourses, "a specific voice and identity is evolving; a particular production of a modern governing European rationale is established and circulated" (Novoa & Lawn, 2002, p. 7). The European social imaginary is thus playing a major role in "making policies authoritative, in securing consent and becoming legitimate. ...[It] bring[s] together factual and normative aspects of policies, and enable[s] people to develop a shared understanding of the problems to which policies are proposed as solutions" (Rizvi, 2006, p. 198). As we discuss below, these productive aspects of the social imaginary introduce challenging dilemmas for educational reform as an aspect of democratization.

METHODOLOGY

This study is grounded in extensive ethnographic fieldwork in both Moldova and Albania. These EU borderland states make a rich comparison because they share similar political, social, and economic challenges, such as corruption, poverty, and migration that have intensified during the recent period of democratization. Both countries are looking toward EU membership as a desirable future goal and have developed policies to support their accession. Yet, while Moldova and Albania share aspirations toward joining the European community and face similar authoritarian legacies, they have strikingly different ethnic, religious, and political compositions. By studying these two contexts together then, our under-standing of the EU imaginary in education policy and practice gains a greater depth and richness than if we were to consider them individually.

Theoretically, this research in Moldova and Albania is situated similarly to Steiner-Khamsi and Stolpe's (2006) research in Mongolia. As Steiner-Khamsi and Stolpe (2006) argue, "For the 'strong cases' of convergence, that is, for systems from which one would not expect convergence toward an international model," comparative researchers will gain a richer under-standing of the local impact of foreign educational borrowing (p. 3). Like Mongolia, Moldova and Albania offer strong cases to examine European "harmonization" at the policy level alongside divergence of educational practice at the local level. With so many years under authoritarian regimes, one would not expect democratic citizenship education to become a dominant model for Moldovan and Albanian education reform, and yet, such Western models are precisely the ones that have come to the forefront in these post-socialist societies. Moldova and Albania thus serve as unlikely cases of European educational diffusion, and as a result, demand deeper investigation.

The analysis presented here is part of larger independent studies of education reform and policy localization in Moldova and Albania.[1] Teachers and classroom practice are a critical component of the study because textbooks and curricula cannot be studied in isolation; teachers interpret and control these materials in their classroom (Luke, de Castell, & Luke, 1989a, 1989b; Apple & Christian-Smith, 1991). Also, teachers' beliefs and experiences often influence their teaching regardless of what is mandated in the curriculum (Keddie, 1971; Cuban, 1986). The focus on teachers is therefore a key in fully understanding the European imaginary as a facet of the implementation and adoption of educational reforms in these case studies.

The Moldovan section of the chapter is based on 36 interviews with high school history teachers, seven interviews with current and former national ministry of education officials, and 70 hours of formal classroom observation conducted during three research trips over five years, from 2003 to 2008. The teachers taught at four sites in central, southern, and northern regions of Moldova, as well as the capital city, Chisinau. The school sites were selected for comparable demographics, size, and language of instruction (Romanian). Interviews were conducted in Romanian, audio-recorded, and transcribed by a research assistant. Quotations and excerpts included in this chapter were translated by the researcher.

The Albanian section is based on 40 intensive interviews, 40 hours of school observation and participant observation in numerous educational meetings, and trainings and conferences for a total of 32 months between 2003 and 2009. Interviews were conducted with national education officials, staff in international and nongovernmental organizations, foreign educational consultants, program managers, school directors, and teachers. Participants were selected through a purposive sampling approach. Three school sites were selected for extended observation based on their participation in democracy-related projects,[2] their location in an urban center or periphery, and their accessibility.[3] Teacher interviews were conducted in Albanian with the help of a translator and then transcribed into English. All other interviews were conducted in English, transcribed, and analyzed by the researcher.

MOLDOVA

Situated on the eastern edge of the EU between Romania and Ukraine, the Republic of Moldova continues to transition from communism to democracy. This ethnically diverse state [4] is often considered to be the poorest country in Europe. Moldova is at the crossroads of two worlds, an observation that comes to light each spring with the celebration of two national holidays on May 9: Victory Day and Europe Day. While the former commemorates the Soviet victory over Nazi Germany in 1945, the latter celebrates unity in Europe.

On May 9, 2008, there were parades, outdoor concerts, and ceremonies honoring fallen soldiers. In the capital city of Chisinau, World War II veterans wearing jackets adorned with Soviet medals strolled under the EU flags that lined the central boulevard. Crowds gathered for ice cream and conversation at Pushkin Park where the entrance was decorated with rings of yellow marigolds to symbolize the EU emblem. Although the Moldovan government often fluctuates between Europe and Russia's sphere of influence (see March, 2007; Mungiu-Pippidi, Munteanu, 2009), enthusiasm for an EU future abounds. Since the Moldovan parliament adopted an EU integration strategy and established a ministry to oversee its implementation in 2005, politicians have peppered their speeches with references to the EU and to the reforms required for membership. Former President Vladimir Voronin, for example, encouraged reform before the integration process: "We have to implement European standards and criteria here, in our society, before knocking on Europe's door and asking to join the great European family" (Tomiuc, 2007).

The Moldovan Ministry of Education has also talked of these "standards" and "criteria." Since independence in 1991, Moldovan educators have looked to their European peers for guidance, training, collaboration, and models of reform. As exemplified by the 2006 adoption of the Bologna Process, belonging to and being accepted by the EU educational community has become a guiding principle in recent initiatives. Primary and secondary school curricula are also influenced by trends and models borrowed from Europe. This section of the chapter focuses on one aspect of the national curriculum: democratic citizenship education. Throughout interviews, ministry officials, school administrators, and teachers alike recognized the importance of preparing young Moldovans to participate in a democratic society. They frequently discussed the need to create democratic and European citizens who are informed and "think critically," as well as the importance of pedagogical methods that promote these skills, such as developing "interactive lessons" or "encouraging debate" (personal communication, October 4 and 15, 2004; November 3, 13, 16, and 17, 2004; December 11, 2004; May 19, 22, and 28, 2008; June 4, 19, and 26, 2008). Yet, like the layering of Soviet and European holidays, new practices and beliefs have not replaced existing practices but rather have been added onto them. As in Latvia and other post-Soviet states, the Moldovan educational system is rife with a "hybridity" of educational discourses (Silova, 2002).

In the case of Moldova's citizenship education, prescribed European educational practices have not entirely replaced existing ones. For Moldovan educators, being part of and accepted by a larger educational community provides legitimacy and signals progress. Becoming "European" is a future goal, but not necessarily something that is practiced. For history teachers, there is also a difference between "Europe" and the "EU." Whereas belonging to Europe symbolizes the break with their Soviet past, belonging to the EU is something less immediate and attainable, as in the minds of many teachers, the government impedes the country's future EU membership. For these teachers, adopting a European style of teaching was perceived as a sign of social progress even when it did not reflect their current national status.

The following section illustrates the ways in which Moldovan education officials and teachers looked toward Europe in developing citizenship education and how following a European model fostered a sense of belonging – real and imagined. These perspectives are then contrasted with their actual practice in terms of both policy implementation and pedagogy.

Ministry Officials: Legitimacy and Belonging

Because currently there are no standardized courses on history in Moldovan schools, the subject has become de facto citizenship education. The National History Curriculum includes citizenship education among its goals "to re-establish the national consciousness; to contribute to the development of notions of identity, individual and collective" (Ministerul Educatiei si Stiintei, 1999). With guidance from the Council of Europe and the European Standing Conference of History Teachers' Associations (EUROCLIO), the Moldovan Ministry of Education recently reformed the national history curriculum. On September 1, 2006, the Ministry of Education replaced the existing history curriculum, *History of the Romanians*, with the new one, *Integrated History*. The former was controversial because the central narrative excluded minority populations and whitewashed darker periods of history, such as the Holocaust (Ihrig, 2008; van Meurs, 2003; Solonari, 2002). The new curriculum aimed to de-emphasize national history by placing it in the context of global history and increasing emphasis on citizenship education. From its earliest development in 2003, it met with public resistance, skepticism, and fierce criticism from university professors, journalists, and historians. Critics accused the new curriculum of glorifying Soviet achievements and denying citizens' ethnic Romanian identity. Proponents, such as officials from the Council of Europe and Ministry of Education, defended the new curriculum claiming it fostered multiculturalism and tolerance, and it promoted citizenship (Anderson, 2005; van der Leeuw-Roord & Hiubert, 2002).

The new history curriculum and subsequent controversy provided a space to investigate how "Europe" plays out in educational reform. Both policy-makers (i.e., ministry officials) and teachers adopted pedagogical jargon and attitudes that mirrored their European counterparts. For the ministry officials, being accepted by the larger European education community was an important part of their profession. In this regard, *Integrated History* was in keeping with larger – and perceivably better – professional trends in Western Europe. Angela,[5] a ministry official who worked on the Integrated History project, was interviewed both in 2004 during the development of *Integrated History* and in 2008, two years after its implementation.

When asked why the Ministry implemented the curriculum despite the controversy, she responded, "Well, it is from the Council of Europe" (personal communication, October 15, 2004). Another official replied that the adoption of the new curriculum was "inevitable because all of Europe is doing it" (personal communication, November 3, 2004). Oleg, a senior official who was a proponent of the curriculum in its earlier stages, recalled that he had to convince the government to support the project. He made his case by stating that "an integrated course is the norm in the entire EU – in France, in Germany, and even in Bulgaria!" For Oleg, instilling "European values" was an important part of reforming the education system after communism. He discussed the need to reform the ideological content of the previous curriculum; in his view, "European values" was the alternative to "Soviet ideology" (personal communication, July 30, 2008).

Angela often discussed her collaborations with education professionals outside of Moldova. In 2008, she recalled her visit to the George Eckert Institute for International Textbook Research in Germany. With funding from George Eckert, she traveled to the Institute in 2003 and met with "experts from all over Europe" who helped develop the "recommendations and concepts for Integrated History" (personal communication, June 4, 2008). Professional seminars, meetings, trainings, and travel abroad were important components in developing the new curriculum. Nina, another official from the Ministry who visited the George Eckert Institute in 2003, thought that *Integrated History* was the "new" way to teach history and that it was progressive because it encouraged "critical thinking" skills (personal communication, November 3, 2004). Nina thought it was most important to keep up with advanced pedagogy and belong to the European community of educators. This was more important than potential funding because, according to a Council of Europe official, the Council gave only "seed money" for the project and the Moldovan government was responsible for funding the project further (personal communication, June 11, 2008). Angela from the Ministry confirmed this and noted with regret that the government had not been able to support the project fully (personal communication, June 4, 2008). The subjective rewards of legitimacy and European belonging were thus more important to officials than the monetary benefits of adopting the Council's recommendations.

In 2006, the *Integrated History* curriculum became mandatory in all schools. Yet in the spring of 2008, most teachers continued to use the same textbooks as in 2004. New textbooks were written and published for grades five through eight only, and opponents complained that these books were full of mistakes – from factual mistakes to simple typographical errors.

Despite supporting the initial concept, the Council of Europe criticized the final version of the books for their "general lack of reference to the history and culture of national minorities" (Council of Europe, 2008, p. 32). For high school (grades nine through twelve), the teachers used the old books – *History of the Romanians* and *Universal History* – together. Problematically, there was little overlap between the two books and little if any integration between the former's national-centric content and the latter's universal (global) perspective. There was no indication that the new books would be published for the upper grades, and when asked about this issue, Angela responded that she "hope[s]" the government will give them more money for completing the project (personal communication, June 4, 2008). Despite not having the new textbook, the teachers were required to teach an integrated history, now simply called History,[6] but had received little if any training on how to combine the two histories. Most teachers received no training at all. Those who had some sort of training had been part of an earlier pilot program in 2004.

Despite the Ministry's talk of improving pedagogy in the history classroom, they failed to support all teachers in the endeavor. In addition, the Ministry again relied on external actors to direct education policy. Since Moldovan independence in 1992, foreign actors have developed, guided, supported, and/or funded education reform. The most prominent example is the World Bank's "General Education Project," a $16.8 million project implemented in 1997 (World Bank, 1997). The Council of Europe's involvement has perpetuated a Soviet-style control[7] where directives come from outside of Chisinau. Moreover, the Council's involvement may be viewed as stifling local debate. In their recommendations for the new textbooks in 2002, the Council wrote:

> As a first step, we recommend to end the distinction within the school subject history between national and general (world) history and name the school subject straightforwardly history. [...] In such a way further debates about changing the name of the national history course on history can be avoided and such decision will also remove the contentious name of the present national history course. (van der Leeuw-Roord & Hiubert, 2002, p. 31)

This potential suppression of local decision-making and debate through externalization corresponds to the way in which Moldovan educators talk about their nation. In 2008, when asked to describe Moldova and the people of Moldova, interviewees used similar language, describing Moldova as an occupied place with a government that comes and goes while the people of the land remain. They felt that the government did not represent them, and that government decisions were influenced by larger and more powerful states. In the words of one respondent, "often times, we dance to somebody else's tune" (personal communication, June 27, 2008). By following recommendations from the Council of Europe and uncritically adopting European reforms, Moldovans are again dancing to somebody else's tune.

History Teachers: Social Progress Yet Not Reality

The history teachers' language shifted noticeably between the 2004 and 2008 interviews. In 2004, before Integrated History was implemented, teachers spoke about the history textbooks with great reverence. Some thought that the textbook was the teacher's "most important tool" (personal communication, November 7, 2004). Teachers often spoke about history as a "science," and they emphasized teaching children the "truth" (personal communication, October 1, 2, 8, and 19, 2004; November 6, 15, and 24, 2004; December 11 and 19, 2004). Those who spoke about multiple interpretations of history were the exception. In 2008, almost all the teachers touched on the importance of conducting "interactive" lessons, teaching "critical thinking," and of using "multiple sources" in their classrooms (personal communication, May 13, 19, 22, 26, and 28, 2008; June 2, 3, 6, and 20, 2008). For some, increased internet availability had played a role in this shift of language and pedagogical style; several teachers reported that they used the internet regularly for lesson plans, teaching ideas, and historical sources. Other teachers adopted this new language as a result of regional professional development programs.

Further investigation, however, revealed that despite the talk of new teaching styles and pedagogy, teachers' classroom practice did not always reflect the new models. Ana was one of the most popular teachers at her high school in central Moldova. She was the faculty sponsor of the Model United Nations (UN) club and other student activities. Although Ana described her teaching style and classroom as democratic, open, and different from her fellow teachers, in practice, Ana's "democratic" style basically entailed being more personable with her students. During observations of Ana's classes in 2004, the researcher sat quietly at the back of the classroom. On the first day of observation in 2008, however, Ana pulled the researcher to the front of the class to sit together at her desk in front of the students. She introduced the researcher, declared that they had a "democratic" classroom, and then demonstrated this democracy by inviting her students to ask the researcher about anything they wished to know. In subsequent classes, Ana was considerably more open than her peers. She laughed frequently with her students, and they hung around her classroom during free time throughout the day. Beyond Ana's personable approach and claims of having a "democratic" class and teaching style, though, the actual content of her lessons seemed similar to that of other teachers. There was an emphasis on recitation from the textbook, and students did not use additional materials or outside sources (personal observations, May 12 and 13, 2008).

Other teachers demonstrated a similar disconnection between the new models and their actual practice. Victoria, a young teacher in Chisinau, invited the researcher to observe one of her classes for which she had prepared an "interactive" lesson. Her 8th grade students had prepared a skit about Steven the Great in a courtroom scene. Eight students were the main actors and the rest of the class formed the jury. The main actors had dressed for the part and were busy rehearsing their lines before the class began. The skit was called "interactive" because the students moved around the classroom, but the majority of the lesson involved the students all reciting carefully memorized lines. When Victoria asked the jury for comments or debate, a few students read prepared speeches from their notebooks (personal observation, May 22, 2008). Thus, despite adopting the language of new interactive teaching methods, these teachers still relied on more traditional forms of instruction that required students to carefully reproduce text-based information.

More importantly, many of these teachers continued to assert that there is one "true" version of history, and they continued to maintain the same end goal for teaching history. When asked about the purpose or importance of teaching history, many teachers – both in 2004 and 2008 – responded that the goal of teaching history is to create patriots, to develop love of country, or to not repeat the mistakes of the past (personal communication, October 2, 8, 9, 19, and 20, 2004; November 6, 7, and 16, 2004; December 11 and 19, 2004; May 19, 20, 22, and 26, 2008; June 2, 3, and 20, 2008). Although teachers talked about critical thinking, the overall goal for history instruction was not to create critical thinkers or to instill a sense of European belonging. In fact, some of the teachers' goals, and the methods used to achieve them, undermined or negated the development of students' critical thinking skills – skills considered to be a primary component of new models of democratic citizenship education.

From the perspective of most of the history teachers in this study, Moldova's natural course is with Europe; the Soviet Union, in contrast, had been a deviation from their country's destiny. They considered themselves to be a European people, and thus adopting a new pedagogy was a means of identifying themselves in opposition to their Soviet past. New teaching styles were aligned with Europe; old teaching styles were aligned with the Soviet Union. Teachers described history education in the former USSR as "false" or taught with a "forced ideology" (personal communication, November 7 and 28, 2004; December 11 and 19, 2004; May 19 and 26, 2008). As Oleg noted, "European values" had taken the place of "Soviet ideology" in more recent times. Education in the Soviet past was often discussed in opposition to contemporary education. Ana from central Moldova described history teaching in the USSR as "a very ideological history" for which "teachers did not have the possibility to change something [or] to think freely" (personal communication, December 11, 2004). As described above, Ana now considered her classroom to be democratic and open – the opposite of the old style.

Although the teachers thought that adopting European modes of teaching was a sign of social progress, when asked about future EU membership or how Romania's EU accession has affected their lives, their answers were less straightforward. EU membership seemed less attainable than incorporating "European" values. For some, like Victoria, a teacher in her late 20s in Chisinau, the EU may not necessarily be better. "I don't know if it's good or bad that Romania is part of the EU," she noted, "A coworker of mine lives there and she told me that prices are really high [...] I don't know what's better" (personal communication, May 28, 2008). For another teacher in southern Moldova, Romania's accession may be a step forward for Moldova. She remarked, "I see this as a step toward civilization, progress and development [...] I see this as a step towards the disappearance of borders and differences, to be a people. It is to rise on the stairs, because the EU is a step further" (personal communication, May 26, 2008).

For other teachers, talking about the EU (not "Europe") provided a space to complain about their government. Many Moldovans have a deep rooted distrust of the state (Cash, 2007; Anderson, 2005). Natalia and Simona, two history teachers in southern Moldova, thought that the government impeded their country's entry to the EU. When asked if the EU had made a difference in her life, Simona responded that it only made it more difficult to travel to Romania because Moldovans now need visas (personal communication, May 26, 2008). Natalia thought that Romania's integration may force the government to "step things up a bit," but that Moldova should have "both feet in Europe already" – i.e. not one foot in

Russia, one foot in Europe (personal communication, May 26, 2008). Natalia also expressed her discontent with the government; she remarked that the "government publicly says that you are heading towards Europe! All they think about is their own pockets," implying that the government, like the Ministry of Education, may not live up to its promises (personal communication, May 26, 2008).

For these teachers, the reality of EU membership is uncertain, but the EU imaginary signified an important break from the Soviet past and a positive direction for the future. For the Moldovan policy-makers, as in Albania, the EU imaginary served as an important force in creating a public sense of belonging and legitimacy, despite inconsistency in the actual implementation of reforms.

ALBANIA

Like Moldova, Albania is a relatively small country (population 3.2 million) considered one of the poorest in Europe. Situated in the heart of Southeast Europe, Albania is bordered by Italy to the west, Greece to the southeast, and Macedonia, Kosovo, and Montenegro to the north. Unlike its northern neighbors, however, Albania was never part of the former Soviet Union or the former Yugoslavia. Instead, for over four decades following World War II, Albanians were subject to a brutal totalitarian regime, with the vast majority living in poor rural and mountainous communities isolated from the world and enveloped in an ideological cocoon. During this time, schools served as an instrument of Marxist indoctrination. Teachers, portrayed as a source of guiding light for "the new socialist man" (Musai, 2005, p. 85), were often sent to remote villages in order to propagate the centralized educational policies of the ruling party.

With the fall of communism, Albanians were cautiously hopeful. Policy-makers looked to the West for economic assistance and guidance for democratic reform, as former adversaries were greeted with new respect. International donors and organizations such as the World Bank, UN agencies, the US government, and Soros Foundation arrived in Albania bringing a plethora of foreign educational models for democratic reform. These trends have continued for the past two decades as Albania has sought to move closer to its European and American allies.

On April 1, 2009, Albania officially became one of the newest members of the North Atlantic Treaty Organization (NATO). Celebrations were held around the country and especially in the Albanian capital, Tirana.

The Prime Minister, Sali Berisha, blanketed the city with NATO and Albanian flags and banners. Not long after, his reelection campaign slogans highlighted the achievement, stating: "Today NATO, tomorrow EU."

In schools, lessons about NATO and the EU were actively promoted. Albanian students dutifully downloaded information from the internet for lessons about NATO and the EU. In a ceremony commemorating the death of Arben Broci, a student who demonstrated for democracy during the tumultuous fall of communism, the Minister of Education, Fatos Beja, proclaimed the following at a prominent secondary school in the capital city:

> This is a historic day for your school, dear pupils, you should be very proud of your school ... You're born in a time when Albania is changing, we are very proud of Arben Broci and what his friends have done. We should never in any way forget our heroes; we should remember together our heroes. [...] Today we are only two days before a very important event. We enter NATO, and this is one of the objectives that the youth of 1991 had, and this is also what Albanians want. [...] We have also signed an agreement on stabilization and association with the EU that makes Albania a part of the whole continent just like the other countries [he points to the EU flag displayed in the school's lobby]. And this came about because of what Arben Broci and his friends did, so that all of us will honor Arben Broci and all of us have the obligation to hold this name high. (Personal observation, April 1, 2009)

Public ceremonies, rhetoric, and slogans such as these animate the collective imagination of Albanians with dreams of EU membership and belonging. By aligning a constructed history of democratic struggle with the latest struggles for EU and NATO membership, political figures conflate popular ideas about freedom, democracy, security, and progress with Westernization, Europeanization, and EU membership. Enveloping themselves (and their policies) in a protective cloak of modernity and supranational European identity, politicians reinforce the public perception that their goals are the shared goals of all the people.

This section examines the policy context of Albanian aspirations for EU membership, particularly in relation to educational reform. As described below, EU accession is the principle policy aim of the current Albanian administration under Sali Berisha. Within this context, the "harmonization" of national policies with European standards is a top priority. For the educational sector, this approach to harmonization is less of a mandate than in other areas such as public finance, defense, and judicial reform. Nonetheless, aligning with European education standards is a powerful goal that "comes to life" in a variety of ways. In the construction of new educational policy, the development of new curricular content, and in the overt and implicit new roles prescribed for teachers, the cultivation of

European belonging serves as perhaps the most powerful force under-pinning contemporary educational reform in Albania. Yet by striving to maintain the appearance of European belonging through the adoption of legitimated educational standards, policy-makers may actually be evading more immediate social, political, and economic challenges.

European Integration and the Albanian Educational Policy Context

The road leading up to EU integration and NATO membership has been a long time in the making. Since 1992, Albanian schools have been in a process of reform. What began with the removal of ideological and militarized content in school texts and curricula has evolved into a complete overhaul of the educational system, including its financing, governance, and curricular content. According to one key policy-maker involved in this long-term effort, political integration with Western Europe has for years served as an important motivating factor for policy reform in Albania. From his perspective, the education sector should be the first to be integrated with modern European and American standards, Indeed, he believes schools should "live 20 years ahead" of the rest of society, providing a "beacon" for broader social and democratic change and progress (personal communication, July 18, 2007).

By 1995, laws governing the educational system were updated and the subject of human rights was introduced in preuniversity education. The World Bank, E U, and Soros Foundation provided USD 30 million to build the capacity of educators and foster the reconstruction of schools – many of which were dilapidated from years of neglect and damaged during the last days of the dictatorship (Center for Democratic Education (CDE), 2006). Despite these efforts, in 1997 and 1998, school reconstruction and reform experienced a setback due to civil unrest and violence resulting from the collapse of government-endorsed pyramid schemes in Albania (ironically under the current Prime Minister, Sali Berisha). Soon after, the arrival of thousands of Kosovar Albanian refugees further slowed the educational reform process.

Despite these setbacks, education policy reform efforts accelerated in the new millennium. In 2001, Albania adopted the United Nations framework of the Millennium Development Goals for poverty reduction and education and health sector reform. The focus of education policy reform during the next few years reflected international norms of providing "quality education"[8] and "building capacity" in the education system. The National

Strategy for Socio-Economic Development (NSSED) was approved in 2001 and endorsed by the World Bank, the United Nations, and bilateral donors. From 2003 to 2006, the Albanian Ministry of Education drafted reforms that helped Albania resemble other European systems of education. In particular, the National Strategy of Education, approved in 2004, restructured the levels and years of schooling according to the practices of member countries of the EU and the Organization for Economic Cooperation and Development (CDE, 2006).

In 2006, the Albanian government adopted the World Bank's "Educational Excellence and Equity Project" (EEEP) at a value of USD 75 million. This program aims to assist with the implementation of the National Strategy of Education, to improve the quality of learning and the conditions of schools, and to reduce student attrition during the years 2006–2010 (CDE, 2006). Its general focus is on "modernization" and "rationalization" of the Albanian education system.

Alongside these ongoing education policy initiatives, Albania's EU aspirations have been building throughout the last decade. In 2008, the National Strategy for Development and Integration (2007–2013), or NSDI, was passed by the Albanian Council of Ministers. In the words of Prime Minister Sali Berisha, this document "combines the principal agendas of the Government of Albania" [and ...] "for the first time the perspectives for sustainable economic and social development, integration into the European Union and NATO structures, as well as achievement of [UN] Millennium Challenge Goals are harmonized in a single strategic document" (Albanian Council of Ministers, 2008, p. 3). While the main aspects of the NSDI focus on Albanian economic, political, security, legal, infrastructure, and diverse sector reform and development, educational and youth-related goals are also embedded in its priorities. For example, the NSDI calls for the following in relation to educational reform and restructuring:

- "Curriculum modernization to meet labour market needs" (p. 63).
- "Promotion of European principles, preparing young people through education and youth exchange programmes on democratic citizenship, human rights and volunteering culture" (p. 64).
- Promotion of social inclusion to ensure "the integration, development and equality of children at schools" as well as the "enforcement of compulsory education" (p. 69).
- Ensuring "a modern national education system, which will stimulate sustainable economic growth, will raise competitiveness in the region and beyond, and will help consolidate citizen consciousness" (p. 74).

- Developing "standards for teachers and the status of their profession" and "student achievement standards and objectives based on performance" (p. 74).
- Ensuring that educational opportunities at all levels are provided without discrimination (p. 75).

A comprehensive analysis of the implications of this national strategy is beyond the scope of this chapter; however, the importance of EU integration as a policy target of cross-sector reform in Albania is abundantly clear in this document. In sum, "harmonization" with European standards has become the crux of Albanian governmental policy, including education reform.

Another important aspect of new policy frameworks, in terms of their role in fomenting the collective imagination of Albanians, is the pervasive use of external "performance targets" as "indicators" of reform and modernization. Soysal (2002) has noted that "for the potential member states, Europeanness serves as a test of their compatibility for convergence and stipulates measures as inscribed in the nondescript question, 'who belongs?'" (p. 55). By embracing European models and educational indicators as their principle approach to educational reform, Albanian policy-makers seek to signal and legitimize their aspiration to join the European community. Table 1 developed for the World Bank project and included in the NSDI (Albanian Council of Ministers, 2008, p. 75), provides a typical example of how such frameworks are represented in Albanian reform strategy documents.

While perhaps providing a useful monitoring mechanism for politicians and bureaucrats, indicator charts and frameworks such as this concurrently reinforce and substantiate the popular local belief that Albania has to "catch up" with the rest of Europe. In this way, European belonging becomes equated with the achievement of parity in select education system indicators.

Like the adoption of European models for curriculum reform, the adoption of particular performance indicators for Albanian education reform is based not on locally determined priorities and social and economic needs, but rather on the direct importation of externally defined measures. Such a policy gesture not only signals "harmonization," but it also serves to indicate a sense of equality among those belonging to the community of "Europe." In his discussion of "imagined communities," Benedict Anderson (2006) points out that the nation is imagined as a "*community*, because, regardless of the actual inequality and exploitation that may prevail in each,

Table 1. Selective Basic Education System Performance
Targets in the Albanian System.

Performance Indicator	2006	Target 2012	EU 2004
School expectancy for 5-year-olds (years)	11.1	14	17.4
Average annual total compulsory instruction time for 7–8 year olds (hours)	570	660	750
Net enrollment rate in secondary education (%)	55	75	85
Percentage of females aged 15–24 years in education and training	33	50	66
Total public expenditure on education as share of total public expenditure (%)	10.7	12.0	10.8
Share of total education expenditure allocated to recurrent non-salary purposes (%)	10.0	13.0	19.9
Average number of 15-year-old students per computer in public sector schools	900	100	10
Mean performance of students aged 15 years on PISA mathematics literacy scale	381	425	495

Source: Annex 3 – Results framework and monitoring, Project Appraisal Document, Education Excellence and Equity Project, World Bank, May 2006.

the nation is always conceived as a deep, horizontal comradeship" (p. 7). In a similar way, the collective imagining of membership in the "European community" is equated with progress to be measured by European standards. Identification with the supranational imagined community of Europe affords Albanian policy-makers a certain legitimacy and authority that may otherwise elude them locally. However, by importing external frameworks for reform rather than conducting deep needs assessments into the most salient issues in their own educational system, policy-makers may be overlooking important aspects of needed reform and circumventing public debate around poignant local issues.

*EU Belonging as Imagined and Enacted in Curriculum
and Classroom Practice*

Through this discussion of education policy, it is clear that preparing students for their roles as citizens and workers in a democratic market-based society is cast in the wider context of European membership rather than in a narrow focus on Albanian national citizenship. Looking "closer-to-the-ground" (Bartlett, 2003, p. 186), we can identify new roles and identities for

Albanian teachers, along with new curricular content and prescriptive discourses on classroom practice that are embedded in the policy documents. For example, at the curricular level, there is increased emphasis on key European principles of social inclusion, tolerance, diversity, equality, nondiscrimination, human rights, democracy, rule of law, and nonviolent conflict resolution. From a pedagogical perspective, the emphasis of reform documents is on the cultivation of critical thinking, student- or child-centered teaching, working in small groups, and interactive methods. For example, the National Education Strategy recommends the following (emphasis mine):

> The current student workload is high compared to OECD guidelines and benchmarks. The curriculum reform should consider the *quality of learning* rather than the quantity, allowing more time for students to *experiment, research, reflect and synthesize information.* (Albanian Ministry of Education and Science [MOES], 2005, p. 11)

Embedded in these concepts and approaches are new forms of teacher–student relationships that de-center the teacher as the font of knowledge, requiring a more "open" classroom and thereby a more "interactive" pedagogy. The "ideal teacher" is no longer expected to simply lecture from the text; instead, teachers must become facilitators for interactive dialogue and student inquiry. Likewise according to these models, the new "ideal student" is no longer expected to recite back the words from the text in perfect reproduction, but rather to engage in more active approaches to learning such as experimentation, analysis, reflection, and synthesis. Along with these methodologies of teaching and learning, the power relations of the classroom and implicit notions of what makes a successful teacher are shifting, causing uncertainty for many.

Professionals at the National Institute of Curriculum and Training are concerned with these national policy directives, but they are also responsive to the needs and requests of local school directors, educational inspectors, and regional educational directorates. They are responsible for shaping the new curriculum for public schools, as well as for conducting the teacher training that is mandated to help prepare teachers to deliver the new subjects in accordance with pedagogical models focusing on interactive, student-centered pedagogy. In speaking with these professionals, democratic citizenship education is seen as infused throughout various subjects including history, sociology, social and legal education, and civics. While concepts of rights and responsibilities and issues of respect and tolerance are important aspects, during interviews in 2008–2009, there was more attention placed on interdisciplinary and cross-curricular models of critical thinking and student choice.

According to Andi, one of the main professionals at the Institute in the area of citizenship education, "There are only two philosophies of education – one that says the truth is known by those at the top and there is only one truth, thus the task of education is to fully appreciate that truth. The other is that truth is something that people come to know together through dialogue, interaction, and debate" (personal communication, April 8, 2009). Negotiating with proponents of these two philosophies, one representative of the former regime and the other evoking new models of education for democracy, posed an ongoing challenge for these professionals.

At the school level, teachers also spoke of the educational importance of human rights and responsibilities, tolerance, equality, and nondiscrimination. For Rozafa, a social education teacher with nearly 30 years of experience, teaching students about rights and responsibilities was a major shift toward democratic education. She explained in reference to changes after 1994:

> We knew in theory what human rights were and we were applying those rights, but later we learned that the true rights were when you gave teachers and students freedom to participate in every activity; to give them equal rights and possibilities even though not everybody had the same capacity to do things, but at least they all had a chance to participate. (Personal communication, April 14, 2009)

In her classroom, Rozafa demonstrated both her embrace of teaching about human rights and her comfort with the idea that discrimination did not exist within her school. After explaining that her school was a "periphery school" with students of diverse backgrounds coming from the mountainous villages in Northern Albania, as well as from minority Roma and Egyptian[9] communities within the capital city, she noted that "despite this [mix of student backgrounds and status], we co-exist well together, without discrimination" (personal communication, April 14, 2009).

During classroom observations, Rozafa seemed very proud of the level of tolerance in her school. After one eighth grade class, she pointed to the two Roma girls in her classroom and explained that they were very good students. When Rozafa asked one of the Roma students how she was treated in the school the girl stood up sheepishly and replied, "I have never experienced discrimination here." One could argue, however, that simply this act of pointing her out in front of an outsider and other students could be considered differential or discriminatory treatment. This interaction thus kept me wondering how exactly concepts like "equality" and "discrimination" were defined within the school, particularly by teachers like Rozafa who have participated in numerous trainings for human rights, democratic citizenship, and conflict resolution. Did their language of nondiscrimination and equality match their classroom practice?

Juxtaposing these viewpoints at various levels of the Albanian education system, we find an array of shifting meanings and practices associated with notions of democratic citizenship education. While national policy documents aim to bring the Albanian system in line with "the rest of Europe," professionals at the Institute of Curriculum and Training struggled more with the legacy of authoritarianism embedded in both mentalities and educational structures. Faced with the challenge to restructure curricula, teacher programs, training, and evaluation, these professionals experienced daily struggles to concretize new models of democratic education amidst significant obstacles. At the school level, despite years of training and a sincere commitment to teaching about human rights, tolerance, and nondiscrimination, teachers such as Rozafa nonetheless struggled with relinquishing their authoritarian role and fully accepting differences among students.

In terms of educating future democratic citizens, teachers took their role very seriously, but were also constantly aware of the constraints posed by local school conditions, relationships with parents, and their insecurity about the impact of local and national elections on their schools. According to Albana, a middle school teacher, "We teachers have an extraordinary role, most of all with our behavior and also by teaching [pupils] what they should do. We are the ones that contribute the most to their character" (personal communication, May 19, 2009). For Albana, the way to teach students was to create an open environment in the classroom and help guide them to take greater and greater initiative.

At the high school level, however, such openness was more difficult. For Eda, a high school sociology instructor teaching several different classes back-to-back and running the social science department, her role as a teacher was complex and changing. Even with many years of experience, she still felt uncertain about the long-term security of her current position. Only a few years earlier, she had been summarily fired from a different school when the political leadership changed. These kinds of shifts and pressures are being exacerbated by the uncertainty over the new reform policies and expectations placed on teachers. Thus, while seasoned teachers like Eda and Rozafa desired change and were working hard to bring new ideas and concepts to their classrooms, they were nonetheless frustrated by a lack of transparency regarding reforms and the lack of support structures for them in their schools. If teachers such as these seasoned professionals have struggled to implement reforms, we must question whether and how other teachers, particularly those in more rural and economically disadvantaged areas, will find the resources to transform their pedagogical practices and adopt these new European models.

DISCUSSION

In the disconnection between policy and practice, and between global models and local realities, we find that what is actively being imagined is distinct from what is being realized and enacted on the day-to-day practical level in schools and policy implementation. Considering this, we must ask: Is there a displacement of local needs or local perspectives that is being overshadowed by the larger vision of the EU imaginary? What purposes does this social imaginary play in these historically situated contexts?

We find that in Moldova and Albania there is a displacement of local interests being actively obscured by the uncritical adoption of European standards and normative frameworks. Furthermore, we find a problematic reproduction of power relations in both countries. In Moldova, there is a legacy of following directives from external actors. In its days as part of the former USSR, directives came from Moscow; today they come from the Council of Europe and other international organizations. Thus, in contrast to reform rhetoric around decentralization and localized decision-making, we see a persistent deferment of policy decisions to larger (external) authorities. Moldovan educators still feel they are dancing to somebody else's tune.

In Albania, despite a fervent effort to harmonize national policies with EU, NATO, and UN mandates, the legacy of authoritarianism is still an obstacle to the full implementation of educational reforms. The teachers we encountered were concerned about their job security, fearing that sudden shifts in political leadership could result in their immediate removal. Adding to their anxiety, teachers faced increasing pressure from parents, students, and local administrators to improve student performance on new standardized exams. Their role as the traditional pillar of unquestionable knowledge in the classroom had rhetorically shifted to one of facilitating a democratic, student-centered, interactive climate for critical thinking. Furthermore, embracing norms of social inclusion and nondiscrimination, teachers spoke of treating all students equally. Yet many teachers acknowledged and lamented the disparities among students caused by their negative attitudes, lack of interest and motivation, and inadequate preparation for school due to personal or socioeconomic factors. Teachers also recognized the problems caused both by so-called "hidden dropouts,"[10] and by students at risk for dropping out of school due to factors such as family traditions and economic need (e.g., Roma students who are often taken out of schools at an early age for marriage or employment). The deep divisions between students are often glossed over in efforts to demonstrate new normative standards of equality, social inclusion, and nondiscrimination. Moreover, the needs of struggling students and mechanisms of support for teachers to address these deep disparities are in fact undermined by the pressure to perform and achieve projected standards.

The push to address the social exclusion of minorities is yet another example of how well-intentioned reform policy can create unintended consequences. Policy-makers must ask: What are the most significant bases of social exclusion in the country? In Albania, social and educational exclusion results primarily from poverty, and particularly, the migration of poor rural students coming into crowded urban schools. Yet international priorities focused primarily on a small, but extreme, subset of Albania's poor: the Roma and Egyptian communities. While the deep marginalization that exists for these communities must be addressed, these needs should not overshadow the demands of educational equity for all of Albania's poor. Questions of educational inequality ultimately demand a deeper level of response grounded in local realities rather than narrowly defined international priorities.

Furthermore, while educational policy documents call for increasing school autonomy, enhancing teacher professionalization, and improving transparency by decentralizing educational decision-making, the Albanian and Moldovan teachers in this study still in many ways "dance to somebody else's tune." They may adopt the language of reform while maintaining more traditional classroom practices. In many classrooms, group work was still individualized work; discussion resembled rote recitation; and grades measured the reproduction of information rather than students' ability to critically analyze, evaluate, and apply their knowledge. This situation is similar to the findings in Larry Cuban's (1986) study of U.S. teachers attempting to integrate new technologies into their classroom. He concluded:

> Teacher repertoires, both resilient and efficient, have been shaped by the crucible of experience and the culture of teaching. Policy-makers need to understand that altering pedagogy requires a change in what teachers believe. Getting professionals to unlearn in order to learn, while certainly not impossible, is closer in magnitude of difficulty to performing a double bypass heart operation than to hammering a nail. (p. 109)

While teachers' beliefs regarding Europe may be changing amidst the prevalence of the European social imaginary, the structural reform of their schools and classrooms is slower to change, causing teachers to continue to rely on what is most familiar to them. Thus, we found that the European social imaginary introduced new discourses that found their way into education policies, curricula, and classroom practice in distinct ways. Yet while teachers aimed to adopt the new content and pedagogies prescribed by European models, some nonetheless continued to employ habitual approaches of instruction that bolstered rather than decentered their traditional authority in the classroom.

CONCLUSION

This chapter has used the concept of the social imaginary to analyze the ways in which the goal of EU integration serves as a powerful imaginary force that comes to life in policies, curricula, and classroom practice. The social imaginary is important because it is productive: investment is being made in this vision; policy is being formed; textbooks are imported, translated, and newly developed; teachers are being trained; new educational structures are being constructed; and significant resources – financial and human – are being allocated on the basis of an imagined future of European integration. Research on the EU as an imaginary force illuminates some of the productive power behind these new policy initiatives as well as the ongoing production of identity in Moldova and Albania. But, a closer look at how particular actors then attempt to participate in an imagined European identity reveals a disparity between the goals and principles of EU belonging (such as social inclusion, democracy, and equality) and the everyday circumstances and political contexts in which education occurs in these countries. Similarly, there is a displacement in some cases between the prioritized goals of EU membership and the needs of local actors – resources may be misallocated on the basis of abstract principles and external standards, while local circumstances demand more basic needs in the form of better school structures, effective professional support, and adequate materials for all students, including those from marginalized communities, minority language groups, or with special needs. As in other postcommunist societies (see Polyzoi & Cerna, 2001), while some significant reforms have taken hold, legacies of the previous era remain embedded in educational institutions and mentalities. The new "hidden curriculum" may be again one of a top down "dance to somebody else's tune" model rather than the idealized model of participatory, democratically organized schools that empower new European citizens and future democratic leaders. While an imagined Europe promises a community predicated upon shared principles of democracy, human rights, equality, and inclusion, particular actors may nonetheless invoke European belonging for very divergent purposes. In sum, through an analysis of these cases, we are reminded to look critically at how the productive elements of the social imaginary can be utilized to convey the semblance of progress amidst the absence of change.

NOTES

1. Meg P. Gardinier conducted the research in Albania while Elizabeth Anderson Worden conducted research in Moldova.

2. These schools, and particular teachers, were identified with the assistance of a local nongovernmental organization that conducted a peer mediation and conflict resolution project in these and other schools. Two additional schools were identified through their participation in an international organization pilot project on minority human rights and educational inclusion.

3. Gaining access to Albanian schools was a significant undertaking that entailed two months of painstaking negotiation. This experience, though not within the scope of the current chapter, speaks to the level of politicization of the education system and the absence of transparency in educational decision-making.

4. According to the 2004 census, Moldova's population of 3.5 million is comprised of the following ethnic groups: Moldovan/Romanian 78.2%, Ukrainian 8.4%, Russian 5.8%, Gagauz 4.4%, Bulgarian 1.9%, other 1.3% (CIA World Fact Book Online, 2010).

5. All names have been changed.

6. For the sake of clarity, we will continue to refer to this textbook and curriculum as *Integrated History*.

7. During the Soviet period, "the USSR Ministry of Higher Specialized and Secondary Education [had] administrative control over all universities, correspondence, divisions, institutes, and technicians – in short, over all teachers, textbooks, teaching aids, and curricula in all branches of history above the elementary level" (Heer, 1971, p. 36).

8. The concept of "quality education" is heavily laden with normative implications. Regarding "quality education" in Albania, Dhamo (2003) points out: "The over-use of the term 'quality in education' in daily rhetoric is not sufficient reason to believe that it has a shared meaning among users. In the discussions we organized, more often than not the shallowness of the understanding of this concept was very evident" (p. 8). For information on the dominant international framework for "quality education" see the UNICEF website: http://www.unicef.org/girlseducation/index_quality.html.

9. The Egyptians are considered a subcategory of the Roma population who trace their roots to Egypt. The total number of Roma and Egyptian individuals living in

Albania is contested internally and externally. According to a 2002–2003 World Bank study, estimates of the Roma/Egyptian population ranged from 10,000 to over 200,000, or from 0.3% to 6% of the Albanian population.

10. The issue of "hidden dropouts" has been taken up in Albania by UNICEF and the local NGO, Development of Education Association. Pupils that do not physically drop out of school but are only "present for the purpose of roll call" and absent from class participation in all other ways are considered "hidden dropouts" (Sultana, 2006, p. 17). Their numbers are not measured as with pupils who actually leave the school, but researchers estimate that hundreds of thousands of Albanian students sit in class completely disengaged from learning.

ACKNOWLEDGMENTS

Funding for 2008 fieldwork in Moldova and 2009 fieldwork in Albania was generously provided by IREX Individual Advanced Research Opportunity fellowships to the authors. Meg P. Gardinier would also like to thank the National Security Education Program Boren Fellowship for research funding during 2008–2009. A version of this chapter was presented at the Comparative and International Education Society Annual Conference in Chicago, Illinois on March 4, 2010. The authors thank their fellow panelists for the encouragement and feedback, and Iveta Silova for her suggestions on earlier drafts.

REFERENCES

Albanian Council of Ministers. (2008). *National strategy for development and integration, 2007–2013*. Tirana: Republic of Albania Council of Ministers.

Albanian Ministry of Education and Science (MOES). (2005). *National education strategy, 2004–2015*. Tirana: Republic of Albania Ministry of Education and Science.

Anderson, B. (2006). *Imagined communities: Reflections on the origins and spread of nationalism*. London: Verso.

Anderson, E. (2005). Backward, forward, or both? Moldovan teachers' relationship to the state and the nation. *European Education, 37*(3), 53–67.

Apple, M., & Christian-Smith, L. K. (1991). *The politics of the textbook*. New York: Routledge.

Bartlett, L. (2003). World culture or transnational project: Competing educational projects in Brazil. In: K. Anderson-Levitt (Ed.), *Local meanings, global schooling: Anthropology and world culture theory* (pp. 183–200). New York: Palgrave Macmillan.

Cash, J. (2007). Origins, memory, and identity: 'Villages' and the politics of nationalism in the Republic of Moldova. *Eastern European Politics and Societies, 21*(4), 588–610.

Center for Democratic Education (CDE). (2006). *Education in Albania, national dossier: Indicators and trends*. Tirana: UNICEF.

CIA World Fact Book Online. (2010). Available at https://www.cia.gov/library/publications/the-world-factbook/geos/md.html. Accessed on February 8, 2010.

Council of Europe (COE). (2008). *Third Report on Moldova.* Strasbourg: European Commission against Racism and Intolerance.

Cuban, L. (1986). *Teachers and machines: The classroom use of technology since 1920.* New York: Teachers College Press.

Dhamo, M. (2003). *Stocktaking report on education for democratic citizenship: From policy to effective practice through quality assurance in Albania.* Tirana: Organization for Economic Cooperation and Development (OECD).

Heer, N. (1971). *Politics and history in the Soviet Union.* Cambridge, UK: MIT Press.

Ihrig, S. (2008). (Un)civic discourses and their discontents: Moldovanist and Romanianist conceptions of the nation and its citizens in current history textbooks and historiography in the Republic of Moldova. In: M. Heintz (Ed.), *Weak state, uncertain citizenship: Moldova* (pp. 150–163). Frankfurt: Peter Lang Press.

Keddie, N. (1971). Classroom knowledge. In: M. F. D. Young (Ed.), *Knowledge and control: New directions for the sociology of education* (pp. 133–160). London: Collier-Macmillan.

Luke, C., de Castell, S., & Luke, A. (Eds). (1989a). *Language, authority, and criticism: Readings on the school textbook.* New York: Falmer Press.

Luke, C., de Castell, S., & Luke, A. (1989b). Beyond criticism: The authority of the school textbook. In: C. Luke, S. de Castell & A. Luke (Eds), *Language, authority, and criticism: Readings on the school textbook* (pp. 245–260). New York: Falmer Press.

March, L. (2007). From Moldovanism to Europeanization? Moldova's communists and nation building. *Nationalities Papers, 35*(4), 601–626.

McNeely, C. (1995). Prescribing national education policies: The role of international organizations. *Comparative Education Review, 39*(4), 483–506.

Ministerul Educatiei si Stiintei. (1999). *Curriculum National Programe pentru Invatamintul Liceal: Stiinte socio-umane [National curriculum for high school humanities and social sciences].* Chisinau: Cartier.

Mungiu-Pippidi, A., & Munteanu, I. (2009). Moldova's "twitter revolution". *Journal of Democracy, 20*(3), 136–142.

Musai, B. (2005). Everybody's school. In: T. Bassler (Ed.), *Learning to change: The experience of transforming education in South East Europe* (pp. 85–93). Budapest: CEU Press.

Novoa, A., & Lawn, M. (Eds). (2002). *Fabricating Europe: The formation of an educational space.* London: Kluwer Academic Publishers.

Polyzoi, E., & Cerna, M. (2001). Forces affecting the implementation of educational change in the Czech Republic: A dynamic model. *Comparative Education Review, 45*(1), 64–84.

Rizvi, F. (2006). Imagination and the globalisation of educational policy research. *Globalisation, Societies, and Education, 4*(2), 193–205.

Rizvi, F., & Lingard, B. (2010). *Globalizing education policy.* New York: Routledge.

Silova, I. (2002). Returning to Europe: The use of external references in reconceptualizing minority education in post-Soviet Latvia. In: A. Novoa & M. Lawn (Eds), *Fabricating Europe: The formation of an educational space* (pp. 87–107). London: Kluwer Academic Publishers.

Solonari, V. (2002). Narrative, identity, state: History teaching in Moldova. *Eastern European Politics and Societies, 16*(2), 414–445.

Soysal, Y. (2002). Locating European identity in education. In: A. Novoa & M. Lawn (Eds), *Fabricating Europe: The formation of an educational space* (pp. 55–66). London: Kluwer Academic Publishers.

Steiner-Khamsi, G. (2002). Reterritorializing educational import. In: A. Novoa & M. Lawn (Eds), *Fabricating Europe: The formation of an educational space* (pp. 69–86). London: Kluwer Academic Publishers.

Steiner-Khamsi, G., & Stolpe, I. (2006). *Educational import: Local encounters with global forces in Mongolia.* New York: Palgrave Macmillan.

Sultana, R. G. (2006). *Facing the hidden drop-out challenge in Albania: Evaluation report of Hidden drop-out Project (2001–2005).* Tirana: UNICEF.

The World Bank. (1997). *Staff appraisal report: Republic of Moldova, general education project, 15967 MD.* Washington, DC: World Bank.

Tomiuc, E. (2007). Moldovan president sees solution to conflict with separatists. Available at http://www.rferl.org/content/article/1347680.html. Retrieved on April 9, 2010.

van der Leeuw-Roord, J., & Hiubert, C. (2002). *Raport [si Recomandarile] asupra vizitei de lucru in Moldova a delegatiei Asociatiei profesorilor de istorie din Europa (EUROCLIO) [Report [and Recommendations] from the working visit to Moldova by the Delegation of the Association of European History Teachers].* The Hague: EUROCLIO.

van Meurs, W. (2003). *Report: History textbooks in Moldova.* Strasbourg: Council of Europe.

REWRITING THE NATION: WORLD WAR II NARRATIVES IN POLISH HISTORY TEXTBOOKS

Magdalena Gross

INTRODUCTION

In anticipation of the 70th anniversary of the outbreak of the Second World War (WWII), Poland's largest newspaper, *Gazeta Wyborcza,* ran a story on the war nearly every day in the summer of 2009. That August also marked the 65th anniversary of the Warsaw Uprising. The event was commemorated over the course of three days. Men and young boys dressed in WWII army uniforms, rode in authentic war-era tanks and trucks, and reenacted numerous battles that occurred on the streets of Warsaw in August 1944.[1] Thousands of citizens gathered to experience the reconstructed battles that passed beneath department stores, fast food restaurants, and falafel stands. The commemorations made clear that WWII is a site of collective national memory that exists alongside a more globally integrated contemporary reality in Poland.

Many of the post-1989 history books under consideration in this chapter display a similar coexistence of discourses, reflecting global educational trends and narratives deeply rooted in both historical and contemporary meanings of national identity. In one 6th grade book published in 2001, for

Post-Socialism is not Dead: (Re)Reading the Global in Comparative Education
International Perspectives on Education and Society, Volume 14, 213–245
Copyright © 2010 by Emerald Group Publishing Limited
ISSN: 1479-3679/doi:10.1108/S1479-3679(2010)0000014011

instance, WWII is wedged between John Locke, the Polish Constitution, Nelson Mandela, and the late Polish Pope. The textbook compares Mandela to the Pope, for instance, by placing their leadership and struggle for human rights on common ground. Yet, the WWII narratives remain decidedly Polonocentric: Poles are heroes and Polish battles are fought by a taken-for-granted "Us," while Germans are "brutal aggressors"; Ukrainians are almost entirely absent, and the story of Polish–Jewish relations is neatly packaged under the heading "Polish Resistance." This chapter addresses the overarching question of how supranational and nation-level discourses regarding WWII coexist within the same official narrative space. My analysis is centered on three guiding questions: (1) How do WWII narratives in Polish textbooks portray Polish nationhood? (2) Thus, how is "Polishness" practiced through the narratives of this traumatic past? (3) How has this representation changed over time, given the political and geopolitical changes that have occurred over the last three and a half decades?

This chapter considers how WWII narratives and the representation of Polish nationhood both remain intact and change in Polish school history textbooks published between 1977 and 2008, as Poland transitioned from communism to democracy. Based on the analysis of history textbooks published during the 31-year period, this study reveals that educating youth about WWII in Poland focuses on reclaiming Polishness (*Polskość*) rather than on teaching universal understandings and citizenship. These findings can offer a glimpse into a larger phenomenon, namely the struggle of newly nationalizing states and communities that have been both victims and perpetrators of inhuman crimes to come to terms with their traumatic past. In an age where the language of "rights" – human rights, women's rights, indigenous rights, and diversity – has increasingly become the norm, how do nations portray to school-aged children a past littered with ethnic cleansing, deportations, and other brutal acts? An often overlooked resource in scholarship on Central and Eastern Europe (CEE), these textbooks provide a unique record of state-sponsored narratives of a catastrophic and divisive moment in human history.

BACKGROUND

By any measure, WWII was a cataclysmic event in Polish history. Poland was invaded in 1939, her lands divided between the Third Reich and the

Soviet Union. Over the course of approximately six years, hundreds of thousands of Poles were deported to *gulags* (forced labor camps), others died in battle, some starved to death, and another 250,000 were killed in the famous Warsaw Uprising. Altogether, six million Polish citizens perished during WWII. The lands between Berlin and Moscow also became killing fields for several national and ethnic groups – Jews, of course, in the largest numbers. Three million, or 50%, of all the Jewish victims in Nazi extermination camps were of Polish–Jewish origin, and the deadliest concentrations camps were on Polish soil. The complicity of local populations in the massacre of the Jews continues to plague national consciousness and politics across Poland and indeed across CEE today.

During communist rule, the history of WWII was silenced or misrepresented in Polish education. After 1989, the difficult political transition from Soviet-style authoritarianism forced the newly elected Polish government to navigate between the potentially diverging demands of its own society and those of international institutions (Zubrzycki, 2006, p. 12). Quite suddenly, Poland faced the task of rebuilding a nation-state to work in a global economy and in a climate of international integration promoted by the European Union (EU), while also having to redefine "Polishness" and Polish nationalism (Davies, 2005; Garton Ash, 2002; Michlic, 2002, 2006). On the one hand, it was imperative for the state to redefine itself and deal with previously censored WWII history. On the other, examining the traumatic past too closely threatened to undermine the new democracy (Garton Ash, 2002). Thus, post-socialist governments were often built on stories of wartime resistance and victimization while parallel local and international narratives of collaboration with the Nazis, interethnic killings, betrayal, and the plunder of one's very own neighbors were resurfacing.

In these last two decades, politicians and families alike have been struggling to come to terms with a dark past still very much alive in the region. This chapter focuses exclusively on state-sponsored educational narratives of WWII in Poland. It attempts to illuminate broader trends regarding the creation of nationhood through the writing of war narratives. Not only the waging of a war, but also writing and remembering of war have the power to shape its legacy (Lepore, 1999). War "almost always defines the boundaries of nations … enemies or allies … the binary of 'us' and 'them'" (Nozaki, 2008, p. 49). Perhaps even more importantly, war is often essential to the legitimization of a nation.

THEORETICAL FOUNDATIONS AND PERSPECTIVES

Narrative change in school textbooks and curriculum has been previously researched at many levels throughout sociological, educational, and historical literature. Here, I set my research against the backdrop of macro-sociological studies about global educational trends. I then ground my research in scholarship of nationalism and nationhood creation. The review of previous scholarship focuses primarily in three major areas that pertain to this research: (a) cross-national trends in textbook narratives that illuminate broader macro-trends in educational research; (b) case studies of national identity in history education both within and outside of the CEE region; and (c) research about WWII narratives in textbooks.

World Polity Perspectives

International influences and global norms have shaped both political and educational policy landscape in the CEE region after the dissolution of the former socialist bloc in 1989. In this context, the world polity perspective, or institutional sociology, has become an influential perspective in explaining large-scale educational transformations. As an example, some institutional scholars have analyzed cross-national changes in history, civics, and social studies textbooks over time; and such studies depict the diffusion of human rights issues and language as well as a wave of pan-European and multicultural language permeating school textbooks worldwide (Meyer & Jepperson, 2000; Ramirez, Suarez, & Meyer, 2006; Suarez, 2007; Ramirez, Bromley, & Russell, 2009). Furthermore, institutional scholarship notes that textbook narratives may be moving from nationalist and militaristic views of local histories to more global views of world history (Meyer, Boli, Thomas, & Ramirez, 1997). In particular, this group of sociologists (Meyer et al., 1997) note that "nations have traditions of piling up the skulls of their neighbors in war but these are no longer announced as goals ... Nation-states present themselves as not simply rational actors but rather nice ones at that" (p. 154). The authors utilize rigorous statistical data and coding schemes that allow for comparisons across nations and facilitate variable-oriented research. Given this perspective, a researcher could hypothesize that descriptions of war in textbooks will become more subdued over time, focused less on defining the "Us" and more on including victims and perpetrators and global perspectives within the context of wartime pasts.

However, the limitations of world polity perspective lie directly in its macro-comparative approach. While, on the one hand, macro-comparisons can create the illusion that a researcher can learn more by juxtaposing many variable cases (different countries, different histories, different politics), the drawback is that the large-scale comparisons cannot adequately capture nation-level discrepancies. Although informative, macro-comparisons can dilute the influence that particular histories, particular regions, and particular events have on educational practices and national narratives. Thus, in contrast to a world polity approach, I seek to understand what is distinctive about Poland and its description of WWII narratives in schoolbooks while also considering what is part of a larger set of concerns in CEE and the world. My research will undoubtedly lead to further questions that make sense to ask not only of Poland, but also of other national contexts.

Furthermore, although world polity research is longitudinal, the research can only make sweeping claims as to the influence that time has on educational trends. Therefore, a closer analysis of the influence that both communism and democracy have had on the creation of national narratives regarding Polish WWII history is an indispensible case study for further research regarding CEE in the long run. In sum, although I am keenly aware of the world polity influences, I also choose to seek a better understanding of the creation of nationhood in schoolbooks and other state practices through an analysis of recent scholarship on nationalism.

Nationalism, Nationhood, and Textbooks

This research builds on scholarship regarding national identity as a constructed category dependent on the creation and representation of an Other in national narratives (Gellner, 1983; Hobsbawm, 1994; Gellner & Breuilly, 2006; Halbwachs & Coser, 1992; Hobsbwam & Ranger, 1992). State-sponsored narratives can be one tool that create and uphold "imagined communities" (Anderson, 1991) through the preservation and/or creation of myths and symbols that restore or generate historical continuities (Gellner, 1983; Hobsbawm, 1994; Weber, 1976). However, my research extends these approaches in nationalism scholarship by rejecting the idea that nations are "things in the world," albeit socially constructed, still arising out of a set of particular historical trends and events considered to be modern. Rather I attempt to see nations and representations of nationhood as "perspectives on the world" (Brubaker, 2004). In this context, I approach the concept of nationhood not by considering *what is a nation*, but rather by asking, *"how is nationhood institutionalized within a state?"* (Brubaker, 1996, p. 16). I analyze how "Polishness" is practiced through textbooks, what descriptions are privileged, and how "Polishness" is narrated.

This study is grounded in analytic assumptions in line with sociologist Rogers Brubaker's scholarship on nationalism, nationhood, and nationality, which posits that all three are processes that are practiced by institutions in cultural spaces (Brubaker, 1996, pp. 17–23). In this way, the conception and creation of nationhood is evolving and crystallizing as a "practical category, as classificatory scheme, as cognitive frame" (Brubaker, 1996, p. 16). I focus on the concept of nationhood, not national identity, because *identity* implies personal understanding. Through an analysis of history textbooks I cannot actually know what children believe. Rather, I analyze the process of nationhood as it is presented through state-sanctioned history books.

Case Studies and National Identity

Case studies offer a detailed view of war narratives and national identity politics enacted in textbooks. Recent studies of Eastern European textbooks note a rising tide of nationalist language (Janmaat, 2004, 2005; Schissler & Soysal, 2005; Soysal, 2006). Janmaat (2004, 2005) argues that post-socialist Ukrainian textbooks advance an ethnocentric and historically continuous image of national unity (see also Kuzio, 2002). His scholarship operationalizes the concept of national identity from Hans Kohn's (1944) influential work on the East/West distinction in national identity formation in Europe. In particular, his analysis reifies the nation, which becomes an agent of history by demonstrating that the books tell the story of "the Ukrainians," thereby positing "Ukrainians" to be a kind of bounded group that could present themselves as either ethnic or civic conceptions. Historically speaking, it is not likely that many of the CEE countries developed strong civic nationalism, and, as such, categorizing the nation as a "thing in the world" distorts the analysis. Thus, this research diverges from Janmaat's approach as noted above. It does not understand nations as "things" but rather as "perspectives" enacted by institutional actors enabling the researcher to avoid imposing bounded categories in the analysis.

WWII in Textbooks

This study adds to the growing body of scholarship on WWII representations in textbooks. Michaels and Stevick (2009) interrogate national identity formation in post-Soviet Slovak and Estonian textbooks. They find that history is rewritten in post-socialist textbooks as the concept of Europe brings on new meaning and new geographic boundaries. "Europeanness" is used to legitimize the ethnocultural, exclusive national agendas that appear in those textbooks. Other scholarship has shown how the swift transition to democratic freedom affected history curricula in Estonia and the former USSR (Heyneman, 1998; Wertsch, 2002). These studies also show an increase in nation-centered narratives in official educational discourse. Researchers Foster and Crawford (2007) compiled an impressive set of essays that take textbook representations of WWII to be attempts by national elites to justify the course of war in their respective nations. Some chapters of this volume analyze different nations' depictions of WWII by looking at whether textbooks depict certain events (i.e., the bombing of Dresden) as acts of war or as war crimes. For example, American-led bombings often appear as strategic military moves rather than as acts of evil. In general, the studies are cross-sectional in scope, and therefore do not assess continuity and change in WWII depictions over time. The overarching point to which the authors return, time and time again, is that history textbooks are not neutral. This is not a new or original contribution. Furthermore, they seem to approach their text analysis with the mindset that textbooks have a direct influence over individual national identity, rarely demonstrating this with individual level data.

Regarding the Holocaust in particular, Western Europe, the United States, and some countries far removed from the war have been known to teach this part of WWII quite thoroughly. Foster and Crawford (2007) note that in Germany and Britain, Holocaust education is substantial. In particular, there is a "pervasive recognition of the German national past within ... the school curriculum where National Socialism and the Holocaust are compulsory aspects of the curriculum" (pp. 24–25). British textbooks portray the Holocaust as an ultimate evil, but also as an outcome of totalitarian and repressive regimes. The Holocaust in both countries becomes a transcending symbol representing evil and human rights violations, rather than a historical and particular moment in that nation's past. Still, other findings note that while Estonia did not adopt Holocaust education until 2002 (Stevick, 2009; Michaels & Stevick, 2010), in the form of Holocaust Day, Poland adopted the term Holocaust in their educational curriculum plan in the mid-1990s. Similarly, Holocaust education was implemented in Ukraine in 1996, but only nominally. In practice, in 2001, as noted by Himka (2007) regarding Dietsch's analysis of Ukrainian textbooks, "The books approved by the Ministry of Education ... all fail to mention the Holocaust" (p. 685). These textbooks occlude, avoid, or misrepresent the national Jewish story with regard to WWII. Although scholars and teachers are writing about and enforcing Holocaust education more prominently in Poland (Szuchta, 2008), the teaching of the Holocaust remains in its infancy in CEE states. And as some scholars have pointed out, this fact constitutes quite an irony, as the traumatic event in fact occurred in that territory (Foster & Crawford, 2007; Tych, 1997, 1999).

Summary and Contributions

Scholarship on textbooks in other regions of the world has indicated that sensitivity and attention paid to bloody pasts has been a recent and increasingly pertinent phenomenon in international politics (Tsutsui, 2009). With the post-WWII increase in global attention to human rights violations, many nations have been forced to confront their dark pasts in public discourse (Michlic, 2002). However, the studies do not attempt to tend to how the narratives – Holocaust or other – might have changed over time due to political transitions. Few educationalists in CEE have focused on the changing concepts of nationhood through the presentation of war narratives over a period of political change as a potential site of reconciliation, commemoration, or contest for EU member states and national minorities.

Whereas world-level analyses are helpful in recognizing global educational trends, case studies can add texture and nuance to textbook analysis and identify the changes that may be influencing the narratives. At the same time, they can shed light on nation-level phenomena that might even be in direct contrast to world-level changes. Furthermore, analyses over time, especially over a period of political change, have the potential to illustrate broader trends that have affected many countries in CEE. My work is influenced by macro-level analyses and the scripts for citizenship generated at this level, and although broad global changes are sure to influence the content of these texts, I am primarily interested in understanding the tension between macro-level changes and more locally centered historical legacies and their implications for imagining the nation. On a national level, the experience of war usually redraws geopolitical, ethnic, and national lines and provokes contests of memory and forgetting that reverberate for a long time in the public and private sphere. By utilizing scholarship on nationalism as well as mixed methods, this study will add to both theoretical and analytical scholarship, as well as provide innovative approaches to textbook analysis in the field.

SOURCES AND METHODS

Studying educational narratives is important because they are public records that can reflect what political elites, Ministries of Education (MoE), historians, and other interest groups have at some point deemed acceptable for children to "know" about their national past. They are historical documents that provide the researcher with a glimpse of state-approved sets of facts, stories, and myths intended for students to learn. The seven textbooks chosen for the study are all Polish MoE-approved and represent a sample of high school (HS) and middle school (MS) texts published between the years 1977 and 2006. Each chosen book was published during Poland's transition to democracy and/or EU accession. Previous scholarship has sought to identify phases of WWII memory in the region: The first phase directly after the war is called "living memory/memory's wounds" (1944/5– 1949), the second phase is referred to as "confiscated memory/memory repressed" (1950–1979), the third phase is "memory reanimation/ reconstructed" (1980–1988), while the fourth is known as "memory regained" (1989–2005) (Steinlauf, 1997; Traba, 2000). The textbooks were chosen to represent phases two, three, and four and are considered to be state-sponsored records of wartime historical past, not reflections of what children actually know.

Before 1989, there was a centralized education system and one major educational publishing house (*Wydawnictwo Szkolne i Pedagogiczne*). Therefore, the two textbooks published in 1977 and 1988 were widely used and distributed (Szuchta, 2008). After 1989, the education system became decentralized, though, in practice, history education has remained the province of the state. Young university-employed historians will often write textbooks, which are then submitted through publishers to an anonymous board at the MoE. Until 2009, the board was made up of older Polish historians as well as teaching, language, and other educational experts. A history book is blindly reviewed and approved unanimously by three people, two content experts and one expert of language and pedagogy. After their approvals, the book goes to print. The MoE provides a list of reviewers on a public web site so that authors can prepare manuscripts appropriately. Many authors and textbook publishers are in the market, and teachers can

Table 1.   Sources and Pages Analyzed.

Primary Title	Author	Date/ Abbreviation	Pages Analyzed
Historia 4. [History 4]	Roman Wapinski	1977HS	65
Historia: Dzieje Najnowsze 1939–1945. [History: Contemporary issues 1939–1945]	Tadeusz Siergiejczyk	1988HS	139
Historia 8: Trudny Wiek XX. [History 8: The difficult 20th century]	Tadeusz Glubinski	1993HS	72
Polska i Swiat po 1939 Roku: Historia dla Szkol Srednich Zawodowych. [Poland and the World after 1939: History for vocational secondary school]	Halina Tomalska	1999HS	110
Historia i Spoleczenstwo. [History and society]	Grzegorz Wojciechowski	2001MS	8
A to Historia: Podrecznik Historii i Spoleczenstwa. [Ah! This is history: A textbook for history and society]	Alicjia Pacewicz, Tomasz Merta	2006MS	11
Historia 3: Podrecznik Dla Gimnazium. [History 3: A textbook for junior high]	Grzegorz Wojciechowski	2008HS	28

choose their own texts from MoE-approved lists. In practice, however, certain history books, authors, and publishers are favored by the MoE.[2] Books in my post-1989 sample come from the most widely recognized publishing houses and are authored by MoE-favored historians.

In my analysis, I focused on representations of Poland and Poles during WWII, as my concern was with nationally embedded and state-sanctioned visions of Polish nationhood. Any issues not directly connected with this concern, for example, the story of America bombing Hiroshima or other similarly internationally significant WWII events, were left out of my analysis. Table 1 shows which specific pages are analyzed, as well as identifies the titles, authors, publication date, and school level for each textbook in this study, distinguishing between HS and MS textbooks.

This study combines quantitative and qualitative research methods. Quantitative methods help the researcher to find and count particular aspects of textbook content, while qualitative methods bolster these findings by adding texture to them and by facilitating the triangulation of those results (Creswell, 2009). Accordingly, this combined approach uses descriptive statistics and bias analysis with qualitative text analysis to interrogate the question of nationhood in textbooks in an innovative manner. The text is analyzed for changes in content and structure, as well as for shifts in narrative tone and perspective. At times the analysis is interpretive, and wherever possible I have leaned on previous scholarship or quantitative metrics to capture the inclusion of particular episodes, developments, or subgroups in the texts. Throughout the analysis, five major meta-codes arose; each is presented and explicated, and examples from the text are utilized for further evidence.

Quantitative Analysis

Through the use of descriptive statistics (frequencies, counts), I capture specific attributes in a thorough manner. For example, quantitative counts of frequencies of certain themes, words, or events in books allow for a comparison of how history is represented over time. I count number of pages dedicated to certain topics, whether or not a specific event is mentioned at all (e.g., The Warsaw Uprising), the number of open-ended and closed questions, and the number of times certain terms (e.g., "Holocaust" or "Gypsy/Roma") are mentioned.

This work is shaped by a 1972 content-analysis tool called Evaluation Coefficient Analysis (ECO), which was developed by David Pratt in order to reliably find and measure bias in school textbooks. In order to get an accurate reading of the attitudes and biases expressed with regard to specific groups in textbooks, the tool requires that the researcher identify all the evaluative statements that are expressed in the text (e.g., "patriotic Americans" or "German aggressors"). The researcher can consult a list of "positive, negative, and neutral" terms as listed in the ECO appendix. After the researcher identifies and lists the evaluative terms, s/he calculates the relative weight of positive versus negative and neutral terms to arrive at a score between 0.0 and 1.0. This locates the authors'/texts' "attitudinal position on a favorable–unfavorable continuum" (Pratt, 1972, p. 13). This method allows me to capture distinctions and changes in the texts and present them in a statistically accurate manner. Generally, I fold these findings into my discussion, while at other times I present charts and tables of exact counts.

Qualitative Analysis

To organize and bring meaning to the data, this research uses qualitative methods that include grounded theory focused coding (Charmaz, 1995; Corbin & Strauss, 1990) and narrative schematic templates (Wertsch, 2002).

In grounded theory, the "data collection and data analysis are interrelated processes ... [that] capture all relevant aspects of the topic as soon as they are perceived" (Corbin & Strauss, 1990, p. 6). The coding process involves two major steps: pass reviews and then pass coding. First, the author reads for content, narrative structure, and pedagogy of the textbooks (in my case, the WWII narrative found within), taking detailed "field notes" on each text and generating pages of observations. The second pass allows intersecting themes and concepts to surface. Overarching and repeating concepts are then placed into codes (Creswell, 2009; Corbin & Strauss, 1990). After the first and second pass analysis of my sample of Polish history textbooks, five major meta-codes arose: The Other, the Resister, the Enemy, the Hero, and the Child. It is through these five major meta-codes that I present my findings.

To further triangulate, I use textbook discourse analysis as presented by Wertsch (2002). Following his scholarship, I understand textbooks to be the "tools, or raw materials to be employed in organizing or reconstructing an account of the past" (Wertsch, 2002, p. 8). Wertsch (2002) uses what he calls *schematic narrative templates* to analyze changes in war stories in Soviet textbooks over time and through the political transition from an authoritarian state to a democratic one. His use of "templates" allows him to describe and analyze continuity and change in textbook narratives before and after the fall of communism in the former USSR. He considers a history textbook to be "not an accurate representation of the past, and instead the creation of an account of the past to serve the interests of the present" (Wertsch, 2002, p. 33). In particular, narratives deployed in the construction of a "usable past" could more accurately be seen as "cultural tools for remembering" (Wertsch, 2002, p. 57).

I utilize a template that reflects a Polish textual heritage and is uniquely national, the overarching thematic template of *Poland-the-Martyr-of-Nations*. In much Romantic literature and poetry of the late 19th century, Poland is portrayed as the "Martyr-of-Nations," a depiction that resulted from centuries of immense human losses during a series of lost wars and uprisings. Adam Mickiewicz, a Polish Romantic poet, wrote what might possibly be the most recited poem in Polish history (*Pan Tadeusz*), which captures the essence of this Martyrdom schema. British intellectual Timothy Garton Ash describes this trope as the "messianic allegory in which Poland, the 'Christ among nations', suffered, was crucified, but would rise again for Europe's redemption" (Garton Ash, 1989, p. 3; see also Davies, 2005 and Zubrzycki, 2006). This particular template affords flexibility in explaining certain historical events, implies little to no neutrality on behalf of participants, and depicts Poland as nonthreatening and a constant victim of history. It also offers a commonly felt and known story, or lens, through which Poles can identify. Rather than focusing on specific events and people, the Martyr-of-Nations schema allows the researcher to elucidate broad continuities and changes in the representation of Polish nationhood in the textbooks.

Some limitations to the study include the small sample size and the inability to know, with certainty, how common post-1989 books are in Polish classrooms. Further research must be done that includes more textbooks and some from before 1977, interviews with authors and teachers, as well as interviews and responses from school-aged children.

FINDINGS

The findings are presented in two major sections. The first provides a comprehensive view of the content of the textbooks presented, including the omission or inclusion of events and ethnic groups (see Table 2) as well as

Table 2. Inclusion of Events.

Event/People/Group	Book						
	1977HS	1988HS	1993HS	1999HS	2001MS	2006MS	2008HS
Molotov–Ribbentrop Pact, 1939			X	X	X		X
German Aggression, September 1, 1939	X	X	X	X	X	X	X
Massacre of Polish officers at Katyn, 1941		X	X	X	X	X	X
Warsaw Ghetto Uprising, 1943	X	X	X	X	X	X	X
Warsaw (non-Jewish) Uprising, 1944	X	X	X	X	X	X	X
Gulag or forced deportations and work camps in USSR territories			X	X	X	X	X
Concentration camps (general)	X	X	X	X	X	X	X
Auschwitz (general or as site of murder of Poles)	X	X	X	X			
Auschwitz (as a place of the murder of the Jews)			X	X	X	X	X
Holocaust or Shoah					X	X	X

continuities and changes that become evident through first and second pass coding. In the second section, the analytic themes and culturally relevant schema are presented through the five aforementioned meta-codes: The Other, the Resister, the Enemy, the Hero, and the Child.

Continuity

A few major trends and patterns emerge from first and second pass analysis (see Table 2). The Warsaw Ghetto Uprising (WGU), the Warsaw Uprising, Polish martyrdom at concentration camps, and the murder of Polish Jews are consistently represented across the sample to varying degrees. In general, Jewish persecution during WWII is represented as a Polish resistance story, a narrative in which Poles are shown to have saved Jews from Hitler's extermination policies (see Table 4). The invasion of Poland is described as an "aggression," and Poland is presented as a victim of unwarranted and brutal attack, isolated and abandoned by the West. The average soldier is a brave martyr, triumphant in his patriotism. Likewise, Polish civilians and civilian resistance fighters appear as heroes, the protagonists of the prominent story of Polish resistance. And yet, the nature of this resistance described in the text changes slightly after 1989, shifting from that of a Polish communist-led resistance to one led by the people through widespread "Underground State" and civilian networks.

Despite global trends and international pressure to diversify textbooks, national minorities and women are seldom mentioned in WWII histories found in textbooks. Though global attention to human rights violations increased in the years following WWII, this emphasis is not reflected in the WWII narratives of the textbooks considered in this study. For example, highly publicized events such as the Polish–Ukrainian civil war, which devastated parts of the Polish countryside between 1943 and 1944, are almost entirely omitted and when referenced are subsumed under generally "aggressive" acts of the Ukrainian Insurgent Army (Snyder, 2003).

Change

Although there is occasional evidence of outright falsification in pre-1989 textbooks, the manipulation of history typically occurs through blind spots or purposeful omissions. For example, there is no mention of the Soviet Secret Police (NKVD) organized killing of 22,000 Polish prisoner of war officers now known as the Katyń massacre (mentioned with ambiguity in the 1988HS book), or the Molotov–Ribbentrop Pact, the secret protocol between Hitler and Stalin to split Polish territories in 1939. Soviet deportations of Poles from Eastern Poland to the far reaches of Siberia and the Majski–Sikorski Pact of 1941 begin to appear only in post-1989 textbooks. After 1989, the *Armia Krajowa* (AK: Polish anti-Nazi resistance army) displaces the *Gwardia Ludowa* (GL: Communist Polish resistance army) as the main protagonists in the story of Polish resistance (see Table 4).

In line with global trends increasingly emphasizing the role of the child in the learning process (McEneaney, 1998), content on the children of WWII emerges prominently after 1999, a phenomenon that continues throughout the sample. Before 1989, textbook readers were expected to read military or official primary documents and answer closed questions. Later, primary source documents become more learner-friendly: Children are asked to empathize and engage with child protagonists in the stories. In the most recent books, published in the 2000s, children can read civilian letters as primary source documents.

The term "Holocaust" appears in Polish textbooks late by global standards (Bromley & Russell, 2010), but does emerge nonetheless by 2001. The coverage of the Jewish story and Polish–Jewish relations during WWII remains scarce, however (see Table 3). And the number of pages and space dedicated to the Holocaust and the Polish–Jewish question increases only slightly over time as the overall amount of pages and attention paid to the war itself decreases a bit. Few books in the sample admit that the three million Jews murdered by Nazis on Polish soil were Polish citizens.

Table 3. Total Pages and Percentages Dedicated to WWII.

Year	Total Pages	Pages WWII	Pages Poles in WWII	Pages Jewish Issues	Pages Remaining	Pages WWII as % of Total
1977HS	238	109	64	1	44	45.8
1988HS	239	239	137.5	1.5	100	100.0
1993HS	367	137	71	1	65	37.3
1999HS	477	133	106.5	3.5	23	27.9
2001MS	221	8	7	1	0	3.6
2006MS	168	17	7.5	3.5	6	10.1
2008HS	256	50	26.5	1.5	23	19.5

The Other

A major theme that arose in the books was the separation of the Jewish story from the Polish WWII story. In part, this is due to a long history of "otherizing" Jews throughout the European continent, but it is also a result of the creation of a unified Polish story that excludes Polish Jews. Between the 15th and 18th centuries and even earlier, the Jews of Poland became associated with the Other – an "unknown object of mystery, the possessor of secret lore, an alien being who ... had rejected the true faith and was implicated in the murder of God" (Steinlauf, 1997, p. 5). The image of Jew as "other" in Polish society has persisted until today. The changing perception of the Jew is intimately tied to Polish national identity, and thus the Holocaust remains a divisive history in the nation.

There are four major observations that emerge from Fig. 1, which is presented with correlating precise numbers in Table 3. First, the number of pages and detail in these books dedicated to WWII content is wide ranging, from over 100 pages to only eight (2001MS book). Second, the pages of

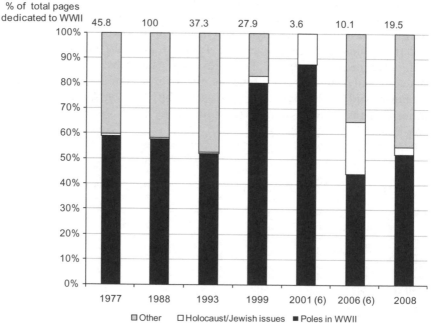

Fig. 1.   WWII Issues in Polish History Textbooks.

WWII content as a percentage of the total text decreases slightly over the years. Third, the number of pages dedicated to the Jewish story remain scarce (between only one and four pages of the entire book). Fourth, the HS books have a consistent amount of space committed to discussion of Polish–Jewish/Holocaust issues that is slightly greater than in the 6th grade books.

In the 1977HS book, the number of Polish–Jewish victims is subsumed into the overall Polish narrative. Jews are only passingly considered Polish citizens: "The result of the extermination politics of the occupier led to the deaths of 6,028,000 million Poles of which 2.7–3 million were said to have been Jews." (p. 73). Yet, in discussing the concentration camps, this same book avoids/omits describing victims as Jews: "On their territory, the Hitlerites created, among others, the concentration camp Oswiecim-Brzeznika, where 3–4 million victims were killed ... By the end of WWII, the Poles were the largest national group of prisoners at these camps, reaching 25–30% of the total"[3] (1977HS, p. 144). Although the text states that Poles were prisoners and not exterminated, there is no follow-up mention of the gas chambers or massacre of the Jews in these camps.

The Nuremberg trials are described in the concluding chapters of the 1977HS textbook. The text does not discuss Nazi crimes against the Jews, but rather emphasizes the evils of the Germans in language that extends to all humanity. Oddly, there is a brief section that calls attention to independence movements in Sudan, as well as a picture of Martin Luther King with a reference to the civil rights movement, indicating an awareness of global movements and perspectives in the communist era book. Regardless of these nods to global human rights issues, there is clearly a deeply embedded national slant in the book: The persecution of Jews is still omitted. Regarding Poland's own minorities, the book remains silent. The postwar mono-ethnic Polish population is taken for granted.

In general, the Jewish story is subsumed under the broad notion of Polish resistance, one presenting Poles as active in helping Jews to survive in some capacity. For example, in the 1988HS text the murder of ethnic minorities by Nazis is situated under the broad heading, "The development of freedom movements among Poles." The extermination is placed in the context of Polish resistance, clearly separating Polish and Jewish experience.

Still other descriptions are distorted or glossed over. The deportations to Siberia begin the discussion of the "final solution," which is described as the German murder and "Germanization" of Poles.[4] The explicit discussion of Jews and Roma occurs under a subheading titled, "The extermination of Poles, Jews and Gypsies" (1988HS, pp. 144–145). The author does not discuss the other groups for some pages and does not acknowledge that nearly 50% of Jewish victims in the Holocaust were Polish citizens.

In the 1988HS book, the concentration camps are a place of the martyrdom of Poles rather than a place of the extermination of the Jews. The Oswiecim (Auschwitz) camp is first identified as a prison camp, and then as a camp of genocide for Poles: "Each camp could kill from a few hundred to a few thousand people a day ... the Polish people also perished in camps outside of Poland" (p. 147). The author states that Jews and Gypsies (Roma) were slotted for death because they held the lowest ranking on the ethnic ladder envisaged by the Nazis. In the final paragraph of this section, the author adds that Jews were moved from ghettos and taken to camps to be killed, but 300,000 of them were saved – rescued, the implicit suggestion is, by Poles. This ambiguous and distorted presentation of the Holocaust and Jewish plight on Polish soil changed slightly after 1989.

In the few pages regarding concentration camps in the 1993HS book, the term *Auschwitz* replaces *Oswiecim* for the first time. *Auschwitz* being universally known as a place of the massacre of the Jews, this name change indicates a subtle, but notable, shift in textbooks' recognition of the Jewish narrative. Yet, the 1993HS book still obscures this plight. There is an image of the camp's "Work Will Set You Free" sign, under which the text does not mention the plight of Jews, but rather the extreme work conditions for Polish prisoners: "Work that was beyond human capacity was aimed at eliminating the Polish people ... the Hitlerites even created a camp for youth ... nearly 3,000 children were there and treated with brutality by the Germans" (pp. 253–256). One full page later, no longer under the concentration camp picture, two paragraphs take on the question of the Other: "Special treatment was allotted for Jews from the start of the occupation ... they were taken to ghettos, cut off from the rest of the city and watched by German police ... they were in terrible conditions, nearly 100,000 Jews died of starvation in the Warsaw Ghetto ... in late 1941 the Germans began the mass execution of Jewish men, women and children." Although the 1993 book treats the Jewish question more honestly (i.e., describing the initial differential treatment of Jews on Polish soil), the tone wavers with moral ambiguity. The Germans treated the Poles with "extreme brutality," at the same time, the Germans "began the mass execution" of Jews (with "less" extreme brutality, one wonders?). The result is the impression that Poles were as horribly treated, or possibly even more brutalized, than Jews.

By 2001 the term Holocaust is defined and used, yet the story is still one of the Poles and their resistance. Although the Nazis are portrayed as the perpetrators of Jewish massacres on Polish soil: "On Polish lands a couple million Jews perished. Even though the death sentence was a constant threat, Poles did not turn a blind eye. Thanks to this 120,000 were saved." (2001MS, p. 145). That the Poles "saved" Jews, and that furthermore the Jews are a distinct national group is communicated here.

In the 2008HS book, the term Holocaust is also used. The description of the event is more detailed here. The influence of some recent historiography regards the relative complicity of Poles in the genocide of Jews. But this Holocaust sections ends with the following caveat: "Most helped Jews despite the threat of the death sentence. ... Some cared but were too afraid to act. ... A small group that acted badly towards to Jews ... in Jedwabne some Poles murdered Jews" (2008HS, p. 143). Thus, although there is a brief attempt at redressing the past in the text, the narrative nevertheless maintains the national story separating Jews from Poles and singles Poles out as having saved the Jews – an acknowledgment of Poles' ambivalent relationship toward the massacre of the Jews.

In the 2006MS book, treatment of the Jews and Roma (although still largely portrayed as the Other) is markedly improved. The Gypsies (Roma) are mentioned four times, while Jews are mentioned 33 times, and although they are called a separate "nation," they are acknowledged as Polish citizens. The Holocaust is thoroughly discussed, Auschwitz is a place of Jewish murder as well as Polish suffering, and Jewish ghettos are described. The end of the book has a human rights section, and children are asked to imagine certain situations that are exacerbated by stereotypes. However, the terms "our" and "we" are used more than in other books – thus excluding minorities from certain parts of the WWII story: "our fight, our nation, our issue, our situation, our army" (2006MS, p. 101). Further, the book is particular in the manner in which it asks students interpret the Holocaust.

Fig. 2 depicts a 2006MS textbook exercise for students. It is, in fact, a follow-up lesson regarding censorship in the form of a letter written by a Polish prisoner to his family outside of a concentration camp. The personal letter asks the family general questions, and does not refer much to the conditions of the camp. Students are asked to empathize with the Polish prisoner, as well as to imagine what he may be not allowed to discuss – food rations, work conditions, and the murder of Jews on the other side of the camp. This exercise does not allow a grappling with the horrors of mass murder in the neighboring camp, and in some ways it defines Polish silence as a result of censorship, thus maintaining a separation of Poles and Jews within the narrative.

List z Oświęcimia

Auschwitz (Oświęcim), den: 15/2.1942.

*Moja kochana Żono, Dzieci i Wszyscy w domu! Dono-
szę Wam, że się już lepiej czuję lecz tęsknię za Wami i nie
wiem jak długo to potrwa. Jak się Wam powodzi w domu i co
słychać nowego? Piszcie proszę jak dawniej i dajcie odpowie-
dzi na moje listy. Przypominam Wam pszczoły. Już w marcu
trzeba je dożywiać. 1 część cukru, 2 części wody i 2–3 łyżki mio-
du. Zaangażujcie do tej pracy Dzięcioła lub Janka. Napiszcie proszę jak najprędzej, jak się Wam w domu i w gospodarstwie powodzi. Jak mówi Jadzia i jak się uczy Jureczek? Jak stoi sprawa
mojego majątku? Czy będzie na wiosnę dokończona? Co myśli
o tym Józiek? Co słychać nowego u Tadka? A co u rodziców? Co
w okolicy? Oddaję Was opiece Boga, pozdrawiam i całuję Was
wszystkich z całego serca*

*Wasz kochający Was Bolek
Przyślijcie mi znaczki pocztowe.*

Przeczytaj uważnie tekst oryginalnego listu pana Bolesława Wzorka, więźnia obozu koncentracyjnego
w Oświęcimiu. Wszystkie przesyłki z obozu i do obozu były cenzurowane (pamiętasz, przy jakich oka-
zjach zetknąłeś się ze słowem „cenzura"?). W listach nie wolno było pisać o prawdziwej sytuacji więź-
niów, o niewielkich racjach żywnościowych, braku ciepłych ubrań, szerzących się chorobach, śmierci
współwięźniów, głodzie, ciężkiej pracy ponad ludzkie siły, codziennym mordowaniu tysięcy Żydów w dru-
giej części obozu, odległej o 5 km Brzezince (nazwa niemiecka Birkenau).
O jakich sprawach mógł do swej rodziny napisać pan Wzorek? Jak myślisz, czy dokarmianie pszczół było naj-
ważniejszym problemem tego więźnia?

Fig. 2. Follow-Up Exercise for Children Regarding the Holocaust in 2006 Middle
School History Textbook. *Source: Author of excercize: Adam Czetwertyński.*
Reproduced with permission.

The Resister

The resistance theme is very strong in both Polish postwar culture
(Hobsbawm, 1994; Garton Ash, 1981; Davies, 2005; Judt, 2005) and in
Polish textbook narratives. In fact, resistance narratives have been strong
throughout all of Europe in the postwar years. As historian Eric Hobsbawm
(1994) states, "The legitimacy of post-war regimes and governments
essentially rests on their Resistance record" (p. 164). In particular, the
Polish underground state, or AK, was the strongest and most robust of all
European nations under occupation (Judt, 2005; Gross, 2006). The AK had
nearly 300,000 members at its peak during the war, and there were other
resistance organizations as well. The Polish government in exile in London,
the Polish communist underground resistance army, and other smaller
groups all created clandestine networks throughout occupied Poland.

In the 1977HS textbook, Poland is portrayed as standing up to defend the nation against the German aggressors (p. 71). However, this communist era book focuses on the smaller and less known resistance army, the GL, while the AK and the government in London are described as ineffective. The narrative in the 2008HS book remains remarkably similar: "Poles stood up to Hitler first" (p. 123) and the "organized state" of resistance is emphasized. In this text, civilian Poles are depicted as fighting against German and Soviet aggressors by surreptitiously not obeying orders and working as "slow as snails" (p. 149). Also, much attention is paid to the military resistance, with organizations such as the GL and AK referenced.

Finally, Poles represent "martyrs," "suffering heroes," or "civilians with a will to fight" in the 1977HS book. From what this text describes, it would seem as through not a single Polish person collaborated with the Germans: "Polish resistance was so strong, this singled out the Polish nation from all other nations in Europe – those countries did collaborate with the Hitlerites" (p. 79). Poles suffer, fight valiantly, and defend their country, making Poland unique among nations (a common cultural trope) while creating extreme enemy "others": Germans bestially murdering, Soviets idly standing by.

The plight of the Jews is subsumed throughout the sample into the story of Polish resistance. Table 4 illustrates how the story of Jewish wartime events is folded into the Polish resistance story. The table illuminates the structural aspects of the textbooks, while the exact quotes demonstrate, in detail, the nature of the narratives themselves. For example, until 2001, the WGU is consistently presented under the Polish resistance headings. Later, the WGU is awarded its own headings, often under a larger banner of Polish resistance. The excerpts below track this development over time:

On April 19th, 1943, the people of the Warsaw ghetto took hold of their guns to defend their dignity against the Hitlerite politics of genocide of the Jewish people. This uprising was met with the full and entire support of the Polish underground resistance, which from the start of the occupation gave the utmost support and overwhelming help to the Jewish people. Despite the possibility of the death sentence that awaited a Pole upon helping a Jew, thanks to the overwhelming support on behalf of the Polish citizenry over 100,000–120,000 Polish Jews were saved. (1977HS, p. 95)

... in 1942, Jewish orphans were sent to Treblinka. With them went a very famous pedagogue ... Korczak ... then there came to be a Polish help organization for the Jews by the initiative of a famous Polish writer Kossak-Szczucka ... called Zegota ... this organization was meant to bring help to Jews hiding beyond the ghetto and those isolated in the ghettos and work camps ... on 19 April 1943, with the hopes of

Table 4. Selected Coverage and Chapter Headings on WWII in Polish
History Textbooks.

Date	Selected Major Headings, Chapters, or Sections on Topics Covered on WWII	Major Headings, Chapters, or Sections in which the Polish–Jewish History Is Presented
1977HS	• German aggression on Poland: The start of WWII • The battle for the Polish nation and for freedom: Poland from 1939 to 1944	• Chapter 4: Under subheading "German occupation" • Second mention under "Resistance Movement in Poland"
1988HS	• War for the defense of Poland: 1939, the beginning of the Second World War • Time of the success of the fascist block • Poland under occupation • Development of the attempts at freeing the Polish Nation	• In the section: Development of freedom movements among Poles • Under subheadings: Extermination of the Polish Nation, Jews, and Gypsies
1993HS	• War for the Defense of Poland, 1939 • Poles and Poland in the war years • Polish government in exile from 1941 to 1943 • The Polish nation in battle with the occupier	• WGU is under: The Polish nation in battle with the occupier • Auschwitz and the concentration camps are a place of murder of Poles

1999HS	• The Second World War
	• German aggression on Poland in the start of WWII
	• Poland on outside of the homeland
	• Losses of people and possessions of Poles from 1939 to 1943
	• Polish political resistance and underground government in 1939–1943
		• Two brief mentions of Jews under subheadings:
		  – Losses of people and possessions of Poles
		  – Polish Political resistance and underground government in 1939–1943
		• Jews are mentioned under subheading: German politics with regard to the Polish people

2001MS	• Poles in the whirlwind of history • The greatest war in history • Poles under occupation • Genocide of the Jews • In the name of a free Poland	• Situated under: Genocide of the Jews
2006MS	• Chapter 12: WWII • Chapter 13: Poland during the time of WWII	• The term Holocaust appears in the WWII chapter • The WGU under: Poland during the WWII years

Table 4. (*Continued*)

Date	Selected Major Headings, Chapters, or Sections on Topics Covered on WWII	Major Headings, Chapters, or Sections in which the Polish–Jewish History Is Presented
2008HS	• Chapter 4: WWII • "Alone against two great powers" • "The triumph of the aggressors" • "Time of change" • "Poland under occupation" • "Unbroken curse" • "Poland fighting"	• Poland under occupation: Governance without law and with terror, the final solution of the Jewish question

liquidating the ghetto, SS men entered it. The Jews (Jewish Fighting Organization) began an unequal fight with them, using weapons that they obtained from Polish underground fighting organizations (AK). The fight in the Warsaw Ghetto lasted 28 days. And then the goodness and bravery in the Warsaw ghetto ceased to exist. The Germans burned it to the ground. About 600 fighters died under the ashes, and even a few dozen Polish fighters from underground organizations died, they were bringing help to the Jews. (1993HS, p. 285)[5]

... in the Nazi plans there was the liquidation of the entire Jewish nation ... the first ghettos were in Lodz ... in the Warsaw one, they locked in nearly 400 thousand people ... there they died of hunger ... on 19 April 1943, after most Jews were already taken to their death ... a group of 220 young fighters started an uneven uprising with the Germans. Poles offered some help, but in general this was a fight for Jewish dignity. ... not a big group of Poles helped the Jews despite the threat of the death penalty ... . (2006MS, pp. 105–106)

There is both continuity and change in these descriptions. Poles are presented as resistance fighters who helped their Jewish other. Over time, though, the inclusion of particular heroes (largely Poles who helped Jews) and an admission of perpetration against the Jewish community enter the textbooks, demonstrating a toning down of the resistance narrative with regard to the Jewish story, and a start toward reconciliation and admission of wartime atrocities.

The Hero and the Enemy

Images of "enemies" in the textbooks look remarkably similar. Their characteristics are either subhuman (bestial), or superhuman (evil). The enemy is characterized as composed of strangers with whom only extreme conflict is possible. Before 1989, Germans were portrayed as the ultimate enemy, explicitly described as "Hitlerites," "bestial," "aggressors," "plundering," and "the most murderous [of any group] in all of their acts." The Polish reaction to this evil–enemy–other was hatred: "The fight to protect Poland's freedom was a reaction to the massive hate that the patriotic Poles felt towards the Germans" (1977HS, p. 78). The extreme stance toward the Germans in textbooks before 1989 could be seen as the communist authorities' attempt to legitimize their regime and dehumanize Germans, as well as an attempt for the Polish nation to cope with the traumatic past. Soviets are rarely referenced as aggressors in these earlier texts, and when they are mentioned, they are referenced with a neutral or slightly positive tone.

After 1989, however, this shifts. The Soviets and the Nazi Germans are placed on a similar level. Where Germans or Nazis are mentioned, there is an attempt to mention the Soviets. Often, both are described negatively. By the 2008HS book, both German and Soviet armies are similarly described (p. 142). Hailed as a hero, the common soldier opposes the less competent military leaders. In the 1977HS book, Polish military leadership is ambiguously described and criticized. The author degrades the AK while praising the resistance and heroism of the less effective, smaller GL. This narrative choice is a response to Soviet-imposed controls – the texts cannot portray the often anti-Soviet Polish AK military leaders in a positive light. What results is a "mixture of nationalism and Marxism" (Geller & Nekrich, 1986, p. 295). Meanwhile, Jews and Gypsies, the Other, are neither heroes nor enemies.

Over time the use of terms like hero (*bohater*) diminishes in number, occasionally replaced with the overarching term "us" (2001MS, 2006MS, 2008HS), maintaining the exclusive nature of the Pole, without as much emphasis on their heroic behavior. In particular, in the 2006MS text, the term hero or heroism (*bohaterstwo*) is used in the context of how the Poles *fought*, rather than as a characteristic of who they *were*. For example, "[even in] the hardest battle, they did not give up ... they fought heroically," or "they protected *our* nation" (2006MS, pp. 101–103). As for the enemy, the Soviets and the Nazis are described as having "split up our country secretly" but their character is described with less openly aggressive language. Thus, the position of the Pole as a hero remains intact over the 31-year sample. The Germans remain the enemy, while the Soviets are added after 1989 as an enemy. The overall descriptive adjectives used to describe Poles, Germans, and Soviets is tempered over time.

The Child

The final meta-code of the "child" uses the national biblical parable of Poland-Christ-of-Nations as an explanatory frame. The representation of the child in Polish textbooks is an example of this culturally specific schema. The role of children in the war is introduced in 1993 through the plight of youth under the Nazis. For example, one image from the 1999HS text demonstrates how the battle for Polish nationhood begins to include children: An authentic poster from the Uprising calls children to fight. In the 1999HS text, there is no direct call for the student to analyze and empathize with the content, but the presence of the child as fighter, hero, and martyr are present.

By the 2006MS text, the role of the child has expanded. Youth participation in the uprising is emphasized, and the cartoon figure in Fig. 3 speaks directly to the student – "For me the Uprising was the greatest adventure of my life" – somehow likening the terror and destruction of this battle with a heroic act of giving up one's livelihood. By any historical measure, the Uprising was one of the bloodiest battles ever fought in Warsaw. In the course of three months, 250,000 Polish civilians perished due to the brutal treatment by the German army, as the Soviet army stood by and did nothing to help. This image directly reflects the common cultural schema in Polish life while simultaneously being hybridized with a global trend, namely, the increased role of the students in their own learning. The child-martyr-of-nations schema is so common, in fact, that it was mocked in Poland's popular political magazine (Fig. 4).

DISCUSSION AND CONCLUSION

After 1989, the Polish nation regained its freedom. That year opened the floodgates of war memory. The new government took down statues and rewrote textbooks, and the people were allowed to remember. However, throughout the 31 years that this sample covers, there has been a striking continuity in narrative with regard to WWII in textbooks, despite all the political upheavals. The story of Poland's ethnic Other remains largely intact: Very few pages in the books are dedicated to the Holocaust; Poles and Jews are presented as having distinct histories and experiences; and Poles are presented as having saved Jews and resisted German aggressors,

*A dla mnie dni powsta-
nia były największą
przygodą mego życia.*

i mój Tata, inw
mycał osełkę m
Po siedemna
drzwi we]
czyzna w
to był, nie
lała mojeg
le zamies;
Miałeı
cia, rozdz
kach, któı
ludzi, odr
do pracy,
prawie pi
wymiaru.
znawali s

**Największym marzeniem małego po-
wstańca było dostać prawdziwą broń
i walczyć jak starsi koledzy**

Fig. 3. "For Me, the Uprising Was the Greatest Adventure of My Life" (2006MS).
Source: Cartoon Image by Agnieszki Czyżewska. (Photographic Source: Archiwum
    Dokumentacji Mechanicznej.) Reproduced with permission.

Fig. 4.   Grandson to His Grandmother: "When I Grow up, I'd Like to Die in the Uprising too!" *Source:* Cartoon from *Polytika*, August 8, 2009.

while Roma are rarely mentioned. The cultural trope of "Poland-Martyr-of-Nations" is still extant also, although children play a larger role in the narrative as time wears on. Significant changes do occur, however. For example, the singular enemy presented before 1989, the Germans, gets a partner in texts after 1989 in the Soviets. Throughout the full sample of narratives, *Nationhood*, or "Polishness," is consistently presented as heroic – Poles having a unique system of underground resistance. Similar to the changing definition of enemies, though, before 1989 this resistance was Polish communist, while after it was distinctly national.

Polish WWII state-sponsored narratives remain largely ethnocentric over the sample. This is evidenced by an emphasis on deeply rooted and nationally specific meta-narratives that support the creation of a Polono-centric national identity. In general, educating youth about WWII in Poland is focused on reclaiming "Polishness" rather than on educating youth toward the global significance of the experience of WWII or toward global citizenship. And although, in general, the WWII narrative may be influenced by global trends in education as evidenced by the slight decrease in overall pages dedicated to the war, the use of the term "Holocaust," and the use of cartoons or role plays to encourage the student to participate in his/her own learning, these changes are mostly decorative, as main lines of narrative remain consistent, sticking to the accepted national version of the role that Poland and Poles played in WWII.

Importantly, the textbooks reflect a selective truth that, in part, mirrors or reflects common beliefs regarding the war. Polish books are national histories, histories influenced by a legacy of occupation, reflecting a stance that does not often include other groups. These are not state histories. Accordingly, Polish historians write the textbooks for other Polish historians and teachers to approve. It is possible that the inclusion of an outside evaluator might help to soften the bias that is presented in these texts. In fact, educational reform has been occurring as of 2009, and Poland plans to collaborate with international organizations and publishing firms to create new teaching materials.

Indeed, the Holocaust and Polish–Jewish wartime events, in particular, present a dual difficulty. First, state-approved textbooks and historians were, and still are, unable to treat the matter with objectivity because of questions about the complicity of local populations that have come to bear through the scholarship of émigré historians (Gross, 2001; Naimark, 2002). Second, the pre-1989 regime was at times openly anti-Semitic, purging Jews from universities in 1968. Even after 1990, the first democratically elected president ran his campaign with slogans such as "I am a Pole, through and through, from my grandfather's grandfather," openly referencing accusations that his opponent had Jewish ancestry.

Can nations come to terms with their dark past at all? I believe they can. As stated by émigré historian Gross in 2001: "Can we arbitrarily select from national heritage what we like and proclaim it as patrimony to the exclusion of everything else? If people are indeed bonded together by ... a kind of national pride rooted in common historical experiences. ... Are they not somehow responsible also for horrible deeds perpetrated by members of such an 'imagined' community?" (p. 135). Educational and political trends across the globe seem to be moving to address this general conundrum. There have been multiple commissions and conferences that encourage new educational programs to promote intercultural understanding and diversity. As early as 1973, the Georg Eckertt Institute established a Polish–German textbook commission specifically designed to combat the stereotyping in schoolbooks. In 1978, the International Congress on the Teaching of Human Rights took place, and by 1991 the Soviet Union dissolved. Two years later the World Conference on Human Rights declared that human rights education must be a central concern for the international community (Suarez, 2007).

On the national level, the 1980s brought on a revitalization of educational reform in response to the growing Solidarity movement in Poland. In late 1980, there was a meeting of historians against lies in Polish history books (*Wolnym Zgromadzeniu Polskiego Towarzystwa Historycznego w Zielonej Gorze*). This was quickly followed by another meeting in 1981 to propose changes in history books (Szuchta, 2008) that resulted in adding that Poles helped to save Jews into educational texts. In the 1990s, a new curriculum plan for history was created that included input from a Polish–Israeli commission, and in 1997 the Ministry of Education and the Jewish Historical Institute conducted a reexamination of Polish textbooks regarding their coverage of the Holocaust. By 2004, an optional Holocaust curriculum became available for free online (Szuchta & Trojański, 2004).

In stride with many global and national level changes in education as well as in the public sphere in Poland, educational reform has been shifting toward a greater emphasis on internationalism, cultural diversity, and generalized human rights. Although one would predict that textbook content would have evolved accordingly, becoming more open in its approach, it is nevertheless evident that, with regard to WWII narratives, the history books continue to emphasize a homogeneous national story.

It is possible that as time brings nations further from the events in WWII, it may become easier to be more inclusive in national agendas and narratives. But if history is any indication of what will come, narrative change may be difficult. Timothy Garton Ash (2002) reminds us that until recently remembering the nasty past used to be considered unpatriotic: "Historically advocates of forgetting are numerous and weighty. Just two days after the murder of Caesar, for example, Cicero declared in the Roman Senate that all memory of the murderous discord should be consigned to eternal oblivion … European peace treaties … called specifically for an act of forgetting. … The English Civil War ended with an Act of Indemnity and Oblivion" (p. 267). Additionally, in CEE, many nations forgot in order to protect their integrity and in order to be able to rebuild from the cataclysmic effect WWII had on the region in all facets of life (Deák, Gross, & Judt, 2000). As historian Tony Judt has stated, "Were it not for the long period of forgetting … many countries in Europe – east and west – would have had trouble putting themselves back together as politically stable units. But living a lie can be useful that way … it allowed time for divisions to heal … the fact that most European history textbooks pre-1980 are skimpy or even outright disingenuous about WWII should not simply provoke scorn or irony: There was a reason" (personal communication, January 20, 2010). And even now, with international organizations promoting the year of human rights and various commissions jointly creating textbooks, WWII in CEE remains a decidedly national history, full of Resisters, Heroes, and Villains that uphold, justify, or glorify national legacies through official narratives often at the expense of the experience of the Jews and the ethnic Other.

NOTES

1. The insurrection claimed the lives of 250,000 Polish civilians, inhabitants of the city of Warsaw, between August and September 1944.
2. Interview on January 25, 2010 with Alicjia Pacewicz, Director of CEO "Center for Citizenship Education" in Warsaw, Poland.
3. "Hitlerite" is a term utilized in most of the Polish textbooks. It distinguishes a Nazi German army-man from a non-Nazi German. Hitlerite has negative connotations. Also, utilizing the term "Oswiecim" rather than "Auschwitz," from a cultural standpoint, signals the martyrdom of the Poles, as it is the Polish name of the town closest to the camp.
4. A discussion with regard to German anti-Polish policies such as the *Volksliste* also appears here.
5. In 1980s education reform, a meeting of historians decided to add the names of certain civilian heroes to the Polish WWII narratives including two Jews: Janusz Korczak and Mordechai Anielewicz. Korczak was a doctor who walked with children to his death in Auschwitz, and Anielewicz was the leader of the Warsaw Ghetto uprising (Szuchta, 2008).

ACKNOWLEDGMENTS

Many thanks to Sam Wineburg for his critical eye as well as to Jan and Tomek Gross and Orysia Kulick for their brutal edits, and to Irena Gross and Elizabeth Buckner for their support. Special thanks to the Spencer Foundation Grant (200600003) and to Professors and Principal Investigators Francisco O. Ramirez, John W. Meyer, and Christine Min Wotipka. Finally, I would like to thank all members of the comparative workshop research group at Stanford University for their feedback. Any and all shortcomings that remain are my own responsibility.

REFERENCES

Anderson, B. (1991). *Imagined communities: Reflections on the origin and spread of nationalism* (Revised and extended edition). London: Verso.

Bromley, P., & Russell, S. G. (2010). Holocaust as history and human rights: Holocaust education in social science textbooks, 1970–2008. *Prospects: UNESCO's Quarterly Review of Comparative Education, 40*(1), 157–173.

Brubaker, R. (1996). *Nationalism reframed: Nationhood and the national question in the new Europe.* New York: Cambridge University Press.

Brubaker, R. (2004). *Ethnicity without groups.* Cambridge, MA: Harvard University Press.

Charmaz, K. (1995). The grounded theory method: An explication and interpretation. In: J. A. Smith, R. Harre & L. Van Landgrove (Eds), *Rethinking methods in psychology* (pp. 335–352). Newbury Park, CA: Sage Publications.

Corbin, J., & Strauss, A. (1990). Grounded theory research: Procedures, canons, and evaluative criteria. *Qualitative Sociology, 13*(1), 3–21.

Creswell, J. W. (2009). *Research design: Qualitative, quantitative, and mixed methods approaches.* Newbury Park, CA: Sage Publications.

Davies, N. (2005). *God's playground: A history of Poland* (Rev. ed.). New York: Columbia University Press. (In two volumes).

Deák, I., Gross, J. T., & Judt, T. (2000). *The politics of retribution in Europe: World War II and its aftermath.* Princeton, NJ: Princeton University Press.

Foster, S. J., & Crawford, K. (2007). *What shall we tell the children?* Charlotte, NC: Information Age Publishing.

Garton Ash, T. (1981/2002). *The Polish revolution: Solidarity.* New Haven, CT: Yale University Press.

Garton Ash, T. (1989). *The uses of adversity: Essays on the fate of Central Europe.* New York: Penguin Books/Granta.

Garton Ash, T. (2002). Trials, purges and history lessons: Treating a difficult past in post-communist Europe. In: J. W. Müller (Ed.), *Memory and power in post-war Europe: Studies in the presence of the past* (pp. 265–282). Cambridge, UK: Cambridge University Press.

Geller, M., & Nekrich, A. M. (1986). *Utopia in power: The history of the Soviet Union from 1917 to the present.* New York: Summit Books.

Gellner, E. (1983). *Nations and nationalism.* Ithaca, NY: Cornell University Press.

Gellner, E., & Breuilly, J. (2006). *Nations and nationalism.* New York: Blackwell Publishing.

Gross, J. T. (2001). *Neighbors: The destruction of the Jewish community in Jedwabne, Poland.* Princeton, NJ: Princeton University Press.

Gross, J. T. (2006). *Fear: Anti-semitism in Poland after Auschwitz: An essay in historical interpretation* (1st ed.). New York: Random House.

Halbwachs, M., & Coser, L. A. (1992). *On collective memory.* Chicago: University of Chicago Press.

Heyneman, S. P. (1998). The transition from party/state to open democracy: The role of education. *International Journal of Educational Development, 18*(1), 21–40.

Himka, J. P. (2007). Review on the 1032–1933 famine in Ukraine. *Kritika: Explorations in Russian and Eurasian History, 8*(3), 683–694.

Hobsbawm, E. J. (1994). *The age of extremes: A history of the world, 1914–1991* (1st American ed.). New York: Pantheon Books.

Hobsbawm, E. J., & Ranger, T. O. (1992). *The invention of tradition.* Cambridge, UK: Cambridge University Press.

Janmaat, J. G. (2004). The nation in Ukraine's history textbooks: A civic, ethnic or cultural cast? *Educate, 4*(1), 7–15.

Janmaat, J. G. (2005). Ethnic and civic conceptions of the nation in Ukraine. *European Education, 37*(3), 20–37.

Judt, T. (2005). *Postwar: A history of Europe since 1945.* New York: Penguin Press.

Kohn, H. (1944). *The idea of nationalism: A study in its origins and background.* New York: Macmillan.

Kuzio, T. (2002). History, memory and nation building in the post-Soviet colonial space. *Nationalities Papers, 30*(2), 241–264.

Lepore, J. (1999). *The name of war: King Philip's war and the origins of American identity.* New York: Vintage.

McEneaney, B. (1998). *The transformation of primary school mathematics and science: A cross-national analysis 1900–1995.* Unpublished Ph.D. dissertation, Stanford University, Stanford, CA.

Meyer, J. W., Boli, J., Thomas, G. M., & Ramirez, F. O. (1997). World society and the nation state. *American Journal of Sociology, 103*(1), 144–181.

Meyer, J. W., & Jepperson, R. L. (2000). The "actors" of modern society: The cultural construction of social agency. *Sociological Theory, 18*(1), 100–120.

Michaels, D., & Stevick, E. D. (2009). Europeanization in the 'other' Europe: Writing the nation into 'Europe' education in Slovakia and Estonia. *Journal of Curriculum Studies, 41*(2), 225–245.

Michaels, D., & Stevick, E. D. (March 2010). *Holocaust education in Estonia and Slovakia.* Unpublished conference papers. Comparative International Education Society (CIES), Chicago.

Michlic, J. B. (2002). *Coming to terms with the "dark past:" The Polish debate about the Jedwabne massacre.* Jerusalem: Hebrew University of Jerusalem, Vidal Sassoon International Center for the Study of Anti-semitism.

Michlic, J. B. (2006). *Poland's threatening other: The image of the Jew from 1880 to the present.* Lincoln, NE: University of Nebraska Press.

Naimark, N. (2002). The Nazis and "The East:" Jedwabne's circle of hell. *Slavic Review, 61*(3), 476–482.

Nozaki, Y. (2008). *War memory, nationalism, and education in postwar Japan, 1945–2007: The Japanese history textbook controversy and Ienaga Saburo's court challenges.* New York: Routledge.

Pratt, D. (1972). *How to find and measure bias in textbooks.* Englewood Cliffs, NJ: Educational Technology Publications.

Ramirez, F., Bromley, P., & Russell, S. G. (2009). The valorization of humanity and diversity. *Multicultural Education Review, 1*(1), 29–54.

Ramirez, F. O., Suarez, D., & Meyer, J. W. (2006). The worldwide rise of human rights education. In: A. Benevot & C. Braslavky (Eds), *School knowledge in comparative and historical perspective: Changing curricula in primary and secondary education* (pp. 35–54). Hong Kong: Comparative Education Research Centre (CERC) and Springer.

Schissler, H., & Soysal, Y. N. (2005). *The nation, Europe, and the world: Textbooks and curricula in transition.* New York: Berghahn Books.

Snyder, T. (2003). *The reconstruction of nations: Poland, Ukraine, Lithuania, Belarus, 1569–1999.* New Haven, CT: Yale University Press.

Soysal, Y. N. (2006). The construction of European identity 1945-present. In: S. Foster & K. A. Crawford (Eds), *What should we tell the children? International perspectives of school history textbooks* (pp. 113–130). Charlotte, NC: Information Age Publishing.

Steinlauf, M. C. (1997). *Bondage to the dead: Poland and the memory of the Holocaust.* Syracuse, NY: Syracuse University Press.

Stevick, D. (2009). Historical and cultural dimensions of resistance to Holocaust education policy in Central and Eastern Europe: The case of Estonia. *Canadian Diversity, 7*(2), 67–72.

Suarez, D. (2007). Education professionals and the construction of human rights education. *Comparative Education Review, 51*(4), 48–70.

Szuchta, R. (2008). Zaglada Zydow w edukacji szkolnej 1945–2000 na przykladzie analize podrecznikow do nauczania historii [*The genocide of the Jews in school education 1945–2000 on the example of analyzing textbooks fro teaching history*]. In: P. Trojanski (Ed.), *Auschwitz and the Holocaust: Dilemmas in Polish education.* Oswieczim: Panstwowe Muzeum Auschwitz-Birkenau.

Szuchta, R., & Trojański, P. (2004). *Holokaust: zrozumie dlaczego.* Bellona.

Traba, R. (2000). Symbole pamięci: II wojna światowa w świadomości zbiorowej Polaków. Szkic do tematu [*Symbols of memory: The Second World War in Polish Collective memory. A sketch of the topic*]. *Przegląd Zachodni, 1,* 52–67.

Tsutsui, K. (2009). The trajectory of perpetrators' trauma: Mnemonic politics around the Asia-Pacific war in Japan. *Social Forces, 87*(3), 1389–1422.

Tych, F. (1999). *Dlugi Cien Zagaldy* [*The long shadow of the holocaust*]. Warszawa, ZIH: Zydowsky Institut Historyczny.

Weber, E. (1976). *Peasants into Frenchmen: The modernization of rural France, 1870–1914.* Stanford, CA: Stanford University Press.

Wertsch, J. V. (2002). *Voices of collective remembering.* Cambridge, UK: Cambridge University Press.

Zubrzycki, G. (2006). *The crosses of Auschwitz: Nationalism and religion in post-communist Poland.* Chicago: The University of Chicago Press.

Textbook Sources

Glubinski, T. (1993). *Historia 8: Trudy Wiek XX* [*History 8: The difficult 20th century*]. Warsaw, Poland: Wydawnictwa Szkolne I Pedagogiczne.

Pacewicz, A., & Merta, T. (2006). *A to Historia: Podrecznik Historii i Spoleczenstwa* [*Ah! This is history: A textbook for history and society*]. Warszawa: Wydawnictwo Nowa Era.

Siergiejczyk, T. (1988). *Historia: Dzieje Najnowsze 1939–1945* [*History: Contemporary issues*]. Warsaw, Poland: Wydawnictwa Szkolne I Pedagogiczne.

Tomalska, H. (1999). *Polska i Swiat po 1939 Roku: Historia dla Szkol Srednich Zawodowych* [*Poland and the world after 1939: History for vocational secondary school*]. Warsaw, Poland: Wydawnictwa Szkolne I Pedagogiczne.

Wapinski, R. (1977). *Historia 4* [*History 4*]. Warsaw, Poland: Wydawnictwa Szkolne I Pedagogiczne.

Wojciechowski, G. (2001). *Historia i Spoleczenstwo* [*History and society*]. Poznan: Wydawnictwo ARKA.

Wojciechowski, G. (2008). *Historia 3: Podrecznik Dla Gimnazium* [*History 3: A textbook for junior high*]. Poznan: Wydawnictwo ARKA.

WHEN INTOLERANCE MEANS MORE THAN PREJUDICE: CHALLENGES TO LITHUANIAN EDUCATION REFORMS FOR SOCIAL TOLERANCE

Christine Beresniova

INTRODUCTION: LITHUANIA AT THE CROSSROADS

On March 11, 1990 Lithuania was the first Soviet Republic to declare its independence from the USSR. By the time the proverbial dust had settled, communism had seemingly gone out with a whimper and scholars from around the world were trying to account for what had happened. The sudden collapse of this seemingly monolithic system resulted in the need to reimagine "the entire conceptual arsenal" of theories and models used to understand life in the former Soviet region (Verdery, 1996, p. 38), and two research paradigms emerged to help make sense of this brave, new world. The first posited that the unwieldy, centralized mechanisms of the failed communist state would easily give way to a capitalist system, while the second suggested that post-Soviet governments and their citizens would retain a penchant for strong-armed authoritarian politicians and collective

Post-Socialism is not Dead: (Re)Reading the Global in Comparative Education
International Perspectives on Education and Society, Volume 14, 247–269
Copyright © 2010 by Emerald Group Publishing Limited
ISSN: 1479-3679/doi:10.1108/S1479-3679(2010)0000014012

living regardless of western guidance or exposure (Paxson, 2005, p. 6). Like all theories, these postulations were only intended to serve as guideposts, but now, almost 20 years later, they have failed to fully capture the complexities of the post-Soviet experience. Instead of a seamless capitalist conversion, or a wholesale return to the communist past, democratic reforms exist alongside communist nostalgia, and ethnic nationalism is institutionalized within policies espousing inclusive citizenship and social tolerance.

For many Lithuanians, being independent was synonymous with reclaiming their "rightful place" in Europe, and in order to ensure this aim, policymakers patterned political, economic, and social reforms on European Union (EU) expectations for accession (Pavlovaite, 2003, p. 202). Subsequently, the entire EU accession process took less than 14 years from start to finish, and at the time of the accession referendum in 2003, 91% of the Lithuanians who turned out to vote supported EU membership. However, even with the accession process fast becoming a memory, the long-term impacts of EU-centered reforms are still far from clear in Lithuania. In fact, once Lithuania officially secured EU membership in 2004, some policymakers started drafting policies that challenged the boundaries of the democratic values outlined in the Lithuanian Constitution and EU protocols.

Though rarely examined, Lithuanian education reforms are a salient site for mapping these intersections between international standards and local self-determination, especially reforms intended to promote tolerance and respect for diversity within Lithuania and the EU. Policies promoting tolerance education have additional significance in Lithuania because international media outlets and government reports have increasingly come to see Lithuania as a country filled with anti-Semitism, homophobia, racism, and intolerance. Examples of this can be found in myriad studies showing that many Lithuanians still overtly reject social mixing with different groups, or are unable to assess what constitutes discrimination according to some western standards.

For example, in 2000, a well-known survey conducted by a Lithuanian source reported that 22% of Lithuanians openly said they would not live next door to Jewish people or immigrants, and 94.2% of Lithuanians reported that they felt they had a legal right to be employed before immigrants did (in Republic of Lithuania, 2003, p. 11). In 2005, the European Monitoring Center on Racism and Xenophobia (EUMC) (2005) analyzed data taken over seven years in 25 EU countries and found that Lithuania had one of the highest overall rates of intolerance in the EU (with neighbors Latvia and Estonia scoring similarly). A 2006 report from United

Nations Committee on Ethnic and Racial Discrimination (International Convention on the Elimination of all Forms of Racial Discrimination [UNCERD], 2006) reported that discrimination against the Roma population in Lithuania had increased their rate of ghettoization and marginalization from mainstream society to levels much higher than previously thought (p. 89). In 2007, a survey conducted on racism and xenophobia in the EU by the European Union Agency for Fundamental Rights (FRA) (2007) expressed concern that Lithuania had yet to argue a single court case regarding ethnic discrimination, even though 20 complaints had been brought forward to the Equal Opportunities Ombudsperson Office (p. 32). And in 2008, a report by the Organization for Security and Cooperation in Europe (OSCE) (2008) reported that attacks against foreigners had increased in the city of Klaipeda, a common destination for international university students, and that tolerance themed marches for gay rights experienced considerable backlash and government censure across the country (p. 61).

However, an interesting counterpoint to these surveys is a recent Eurobarometer Survey (European Commission [EC], 2009) on discrimination in the EU, which revealed that only 26% of Lithuanian respondents felt that discrimination of any kind existed in Lithuania – the lowest percentage reported in all 27 EU countries. Thus, while no survey captures the total picture of a society, the discrepancies between these surveys raise concerns that, at the very least, discourses in Lithuania surrounding tolerance seem unimportant to individuals in their daily lives, or that, at worst, continued discrimination exists because the Lithuanian government actually "encourages it" (Beresnevičiutė, 2003, p. 10).

The role that policies for the promotion of tolerance can have in undermining their own aims is subtle and complicated. Some scholars suggest that the way "bounded" groups are created and labeled for policy formulation might actually serve to undermine the values of inclusion because they define people as being comprised of static attributes, what Foucault (1995) referred to as "carefully distinct singularities" (p.144). Stein (2004) writes that the very culture of policy making is built on creating problems in order to solve them, and that this culture results in "thought and action used to regulate and organize behaviors that construct a way of seeing those affecting or affected by the problem" (p. 5). Popkewitz (2000, 2001) shares similar sentiments about the nuanced pitfalls of policy construction, arguing that, in many cases, educational policies effectively foster the very differences that they simply claim to categorize. The negative consequence of labeling populations in this way is that by "recognizing someone's existence, one establishes the primary foundation on which someone's rights can be denied" (Muhic, 2004, p. 4). Brubaker (2004) also questions the outcomes of an intense political focus on multiculturalism, writing that the "the main challenge to the nation-state from multiculturalism and identity politics comes from a general disposition to cultivate and celebrate group identities and loyalties at the expense of state-wide identities and loyalties" (p. 120). These discussions are relevant for understanding the role that Lithuanian educational reforms play in "dividing" and "naming" populations before attempting to teach them how to live together again.

This chapter seeks to join discussions about how globalization, borrowing, and nationalism influence education – and vice versa – by examining how policymakers in Lithuania use policy as a normative political technology to simultaneously promote and challenge the boundaries of international standards for tolerance. There are many ways to analyze a policy. Some of the most common ways are to rate the feasibility of policy implementation, to quantify the measurable outcomes of a policy, or to assess the levels of rationality with which a policy was structured (Dunn, 2007). While all of these foci are important aspects of educational reform in Lithuania, this assessment takes a further step back to situate and analyze Lithuanian educational reforms within their broader cultural, political, and historical contexts. As Popkewitz (2008) writes, understanding the influence of politics on education is the act of making visible "the conditions that shape and fashion its principles about who we are and should be" (p. 316) – an illustrative point for understanding how educational reforms for tolerance in Lithuania have become both a tool of democratic identity formation, as well as a means of resisting it.

The findings in this chapter are based on a synthesis of international surveys, academic assessments, interdisciplinary theoretical frameworks, and discourses found in key Lithuanian education policies. The conclusions of this analysis argue that because many of the same technologies used to produce subjectivities also provide "the conditions for subverting the apparatus itself" (Butler, 1997, p. 100), Lithuanian policies for tolerance education are increasingly producing prejudice in the name of national sovereignty. Though unique in many ways, Lithuania's experience is a useful case study because reforms for tolerance exemplify Popkewitz's (2000) notion of *hybridization*, "an overlay or scaffolding of different discourses" (p. 5), as the transformations currently underway are not just a political realignment or an economic conversion, but are tools for a re-subjectivation of Lithuanian citizens based on the complicated intersections of EU norms and national self-determination.

POLITICAL TECHNOLOGIES: THE USE
OF POLICY, PRECEDENT, AND SCHOOL

Although democracy is now the reigning political paradigm in the world, all societies must be constructed and maintained through a variety of governing tools because no system can intrinsically "reproduce the precondition for its existence out of itself" (Feldmann, Henschel, & Ulrich, 2000, p. 20). Instrumental views of policymaking describe it as a top–down process based mostly on enforcement, but policymaking is more than an instrument that acts "upon" individuals as objects or deprives them of agency to make decisions for themselves; policy is a productive force – what Foucault (1991) called governmentality – and is part of a larger ensemble of relations, institutions, and actors that exercise power, define populations, and condition social frameworks within which individuals constitute and regulate themselves through processes of subjection and subjectivation (pp. 102–103). Consequently, legislation as a "technology of power" (Foucault 1997, p. 266) is increasingly used as an organizational tool for contemporary societies because it influences the way that individuals "construct themselves as subjects" (Shore, 1997, p. 4) and understand "distinctions, differentiation, and divisions" (Popkewitz, 2000, p. 20).

Every society has a definition of what constitutes an "educated person" (Levinson & Holland, 1996, p. 1), and most countries offer some form of state-supported education to foster specific skills and subjectivities for "making useful individuals" (Foucault, 1995, p. 211). In its most practical application, schools train workers so that they can participate in the national economy, but many policymakers and theorists now recognize that schools are influential for more than just vocational training; they are also "sites of intense cultural politics" where socialization is promoted and subjectivities are fostered to normalize certain political systems and norms (Levinson & Holland, 1996, p. 2). (Additionally, while education often encompasses more forms of learning than just school, this chapter uses the terms interchangeably to mean formal practices and policies.) With the rise of pluralist democracies, "being educated" has increasingly come to mean understanding, classifying, and acknowledging differences between people without denigrating them (Connell, 1994, p. 3).

The 1948 Universal Declaration of Human Rights passed by the UN is the "landmark document" (Connell, 1994, p. 9) for the institutionaliza-tion, dissemination, and support of principles related to tolerance, human rights, and education. The United Nations Educational, Scientific, and Cultural Organization (UNESCO) (1994) also regards tolerance education as their key instrument for providing skills that promote respectful interactions among people with differing viewpoints. In 1995, UNESCO drafted the *Declaration of the Principles of Tolerance* (1995a), which maintains, "tolerance is not only a cherished principle, but also a necessity for peace and for the economic and social advancement of all peoples" (p. 9). However, because "groupness is more a political construction than a social fact" (Brubaker, 1995, p. 108), UNESCO (1995b) also recognizes that respectful social interactions are learned, not innate, and it regards the promotion of tolerance education as "an urgent imperative" (p. 12).

Because tolerance is a widely accepted component of social stability (UNESCO, 1995b), and because schools are seen as exerting "very powerful influences on individuals" (Vogt, 1997, p. 28), the two have been combined to create education programs for tolerance and human rights throughout the expanding EU. In Lithuania, these aims have been taken up as "tolerance education," which is centered on both EU and locally perceived needs. Tolerance education is different from intercultural or multicultural education because its primary aim is to reduce antagonisms, and not to impose a sense of cultural appreciation on individuals. In fact, in order for tolerance to exist, an individual must actively dislike the thing that they are tolerating, and then they must make a choice to allow the disliked value, belief, or behavior to exist without interference, discrimination, or violence (Vogt, 1997). Thus, the concept of tolerance is much more pragmatic and less "celebratory" than many other ideals found in multicultural or intercultural education (though tolerance is a component of multiculturalism) (Mansfield & Kehoe, 1994, pp. 418–419).

Increasingly, tolerance has also become linked with legal protections, or "rights," but while legislation protecting a behavior, attribute, or belief *may* concomitantly lead to more tolerance for it, legislation usually exists to protect something regardless of its popularity (Vogt, 1997). Nonetheless, legislation is rarely the sole guarantor of social change. Connell (1994) notes in her report on tolerance in the EU that "policy refers to more than just drawing up proposals and getting legislation passed" (p. 17). Thus, as part of a tool for more comprehensive social change, tolerance education attempts to promote normative changes in individual attitudes without the threat of external sanctions. In other words, tolerance education teaches individuals that "in a functioning democracy, the self-regulating capacity of the citizens plays a pivotal role" (Feldmann et al., 2000, p. 20). However, it is important to note that the concept of tolerance is not only limited to contemporary "democracies." Lithuania has long been situated at the geopolitical crossroads of "east" and "west," and its capital city, Vilnius, has always been comprised of multicultural communities (Breidis, 2009). The current situation of intolerance in Lithuania has arisen in large part because the *groups* around which social tolerance is constructed, the *means* by which tolerance is promoted, and the *agencies* through which standards are judged have rapidly changed. Hence, it is within this new context of transformation that tolerance education in Lithuania has come to stand for more than just acceptance or social stability; it is increasingly equated with the power of the EU to dictate the norms of an individual nation-state – a possibility that Lithuania both accepts and resists in its educational reforms.

SOVIETIZATION AND EUROPEANIZATION

Various forms of schooling have existed in Lithuania for almost 500 years, but because Lithuania has historically been an agrarian society, most educational opportunities were consolidated in urban centers, limiting access by the more agrarian populations who maintained concomitantly low literacy rates. Lithuanian educational expansion was mostly seen in the last century when it was both an independent country and a territory subsumed under Russian and Soviet models of education. Following the treaty of Versailles (from 1918–1940), Lithuania experienced a brief period of independence, during which time schools explicitly embraced symbols of Lithuanian identity that had been forbidden for almost a century. However, at the beginning of World War II, Lithuania was annexed alternately by both the Soviets and the Nazis, and by 1945 the USSR absorbed occupied Lithuania's educational system into the Soviet Ministry of Education.

Throughout the Soviet Union, reforms increased educational accessibility, yielded higher literacy rates across, strategically implemented wide-sweeping Soviet character education (vospitanie), and inculcated subjectivities of the "New Soviet Man." The Soviet system was highly centralized, but each republic maintained its own ministry of education and specialized pedagogical schools to train local teachers (though content and form were strictly regulated). Some republics, like Lithuania, were even allowed to maintain some schools in their native language so long as they fulfilled a mandatory Russian language component that resulted in student mastery of the Russian language (Tomiak, 1992). Yet, while Soviet ideology was "supposed to replace nationalism, not be superseded by it" (Bunce, 2005, p. 407), the system of token concessions allowed Lithuanians (and other nationalities) to surreptitiously construct a productive form of ethnic nationalism based on the Soviet allowance for "semi-sovereign nationally defined units" (Bunce, 2005, p. 427). Thus, when Gorbachev implemented *perestroika* and *glasnost* in the 1980s, there was an immediate public resurgence of Lithuanian national identity, and Lithuanian schools deviated from ministry control to experiment with new educational methods and theories (Peck, 2000, p. 31).

In 1991 Lithuania was officially recognized as an independent country, and its new government set about drafting a democratic constitution, instituting a market economy, and fundamentally amending the educational system to sustain the transformation process. The first wave of transformation quickly revealed that major economic reforms had to be coupled with educational changes because Lithuania possessed relatively few natural resources for export and had virtually no industrialized mechanisms upon which to build and sustain industry. Without competitive educational reforms, the national and economic advancement of Lithuania would be at risk from other more developed capitalist systems (Organization for Economic Cooperation and Development [OECD], 2002, p. 3). In response to this, the government acknowledged that educational development of its human capital was "of exceptional importance" (MoES, 2008, p. 2). However, Lithuanian educational reforms were not only focused on economic prosperity, but they were also intended to secure EU accession by demonstrating just how "European" Lithuanians already were. As Steiner-Khamsi (2004) suggests, the perception of a "common international model of education" is often exaggerated or imagined (p. 4), but even "imagined" codes of standards and practices can produce very "real" influences on local practice.

The hybridization of EU and Lithuanian aims produced unique policy configurations in Lithuania, which simultaneously espoused international belonging and local exceptionalism. Although identities are multilayered and complementary rather than mutually exclusive (Popkewitz, 2000, 2001), Weiner (2009) found in her study on post-Soviet accession states, that "newer states come to resemble older ones in the EU order, legally and institutionally" (p. 305). Heather Grabbe (in Budryte, 2005) outlines a similar unidirectional shift occurring during the process of "Europeanization" (p. 3). During the accession process, new member states draft policies and implement reforms that demonstrate a "shared" commitment to EU aims, practices, and norms. If these reforms meet EU expectations then these countries are able to secure EU funding, guidance, and eventually, accession; however, once accession is achieved, these policies often cease to have the same currency in the lives of politicians or ordinary citizens as they did before accession.

Furthermore, it is important to note that while the European Community was originally organized as an economic confederation, the latter part of the 20th century was a time of European-wide identity construction designed to foster subjectivities associated with a "pan national People's Europe" of shared European symbols and values (Shore, 1997, p. 16). In fact, Shore (1997) posits that even as far back as the 1970s and 1980s "the [European] Commission was operating a de facto cultural policy long before the Maastricht treaty gave it the legal right to do so" (p. 46). Though individual citizens have embraced the identity project to only varying degrees, normative expectations for EU accession have been part of a larger project conceived to create "Europeans" out of a conglomeration of nation-states (Walkenhorst, 2008).

The 1992 Maastricht Treaty was considered a turning point because it created a category of "European" citizenship and identified education in individual nation-states as a potential instrument for promoting EU development (Shore, 1997; Bonnet, 2004). The Maastricht Treaty framed education as a predominantly "local" issue, but one of considerable interest to EU elites because of its contribution to the way that "normative categories are established and internalized" (Shore, 1997, p. 30). At the same time, EU guidelines for educational practice encouraged local policies to move beyond their prior foci on vocational training and qualifications to "issues of personal, cultural, and social development" (Novoa, 2000, p. 32; Novoa & Lawn, 2002, p. 3). The Barcelona Process, The Lisbon Treaty, and the Bologna Process further enhanced expectations for educational coordination and convergence across Europe (Bonnet, 2004). However, education as a tool for EU subjectivation also engendered forms of resistance in Lithuania, as some policymakers attempted to demarcate national limits on policies initially designed to secure European belonging.

EDUCATION REFORM FOR TOLERANCE IN LITHUANIA

Since 1991, Lithuania has passed 43 educational reforms, many of which rely on education to inculcate student behaviors, teach skills that benefit the individual and the state, foster national identity and cultural continuity, and instill democratic values. The three key education documents examined in this chapter are *The General Concept on Education in Lithuania* (1994; herein *The Concept on Education*), *The Law on Education for the Republic of Lithuania* (2006; herein *The Law on Education*), and *The National Education*

Strategy 2003–2012 (2008; herein *The Strategy*). There are also several other reforms that deal with the promotion of tolerance in more detail, including the *Education for All Action Plan* (2004) and *The Program Against Xenophobia, Intolerance, and Anti-Semitism* (2003), though they do not have the same weight as education law.

First drafted in 1992, *The Concept on Education* (Ministry of Education and Science [herein MoES], 1994) heralded the collapse of the Soviet Union as a "fundamental historic shift" in Lithuania that provided "a unique opportunity for Lithuania to join the community of democratic European nations" (p. 1). It further recognized that the corollary democratic realignment required "a change in the mental climate of the society" (p. 8) that could only be brought about through education. Another key document, *The Law on Education* (2006) further demonstrates the vast role that governmental elites envisioned for education in promoting new social and individual development. A main clause from its general provisions on education reads as follows:

> Education is a means of shaping the future of the person, the society and the State. It is based on the acknowledgement of the indisputable value of the individual, his right of free choice and moral responsibility, as well as on democratic relationships and the country's cultural traditions. Education protects and creates national identity. It guarantees continuity of the values that make a person's life meaningful, that grant social life coherence and solidarity, and that promote development and security of the State. (MoES, 2006, p. 1)

The desire to secure EU accession influenced policy makers to incorporate discourse from "the west" in reforms for both educational content and structure; therefore, it is quite common to find Lithuanian reforms "based on European cultural values," which *The Concept on Education* (MoES, 1994) describes as "the absolute value of the individual neighborly love, innate equality among men, freedom of conscience, tolerance, [and] the affirmation of democratic social relations" (p. 11). Additionally, it is interesting to note that the effects of the EU identity project are visible in the discourse of early Lithuanian reforms, which effectively categorize the sentiments of "Europe" as being representative of a cohesive whole. *The Law on Education* (2006) echoes similar policy sentiments referring to a "European" identity, charging education with the following responsibility:

> To convey to each person the basics of national and ethnic culture, the traditions and values of the humanistic culture of Europe and of the world, to foster the maturation of each person's national identity, moral aesthetic and scientific culture and personal outlook; to guarantee the continuity of ethnic and national culture, the preservation of its identity and continuous renewal of its values; to promote the nation's openness for interaction and dialogue with other cultures. (p. 5)

The inclusion of tolerance in many Lithuanian reforms started as both an international principle and a locally preventative measure. Because EU elites were concerned that post-Soviet conflicts would arise (as they had in Estonia and Latvia) between the now-dominant Lithuanian population and the newly deposed Russian "minority" that had once enjoyed dominant privilege, the inclusion of "tolerance" in Lithuanian educational reforms was a discursive commitment to the values of democratic pluralism that 60 years of belonging to Soviet precedent could not demonstrate. Steiner-Khamsi (2004) notes that the practice of borrowing "international" policies and standards is often used to "radically break with the past" (p. 71), as Lithuania did in distancing itself from Russian and Soviet practices to align itself with the West (Coulby, 2000, p. 13); yet, the relationship between many Lithuanian policymakers and the word "tolerance" changes substantially in the post-accession phase of policy reforms.

The commitment to European values, including tolerance, appears in *The Concept on Education* (1994), *The Law on Education* (2006), and in *The Strategy* (2008); however, because *The Strategy* (2008) was last of the three documents to be drafted, it has a slightly more pragmatic tone marking a shift away from "Europe" and back toward "the nation." *The Strategy* (2008) explicitly notes Lithuania's reliance on education as a tool for "striving to establish itself in the west," though the language of the document no longer conceptualizes Europe as an integrated, normative whole, instead it refers to mandates from specific European political entities, such as the EU Council, in place of "Europe" (p. 2). The aims have also moved away from values such as humanism to the development of knowledge, security, and economic development – all action points necessary for increased economic competition in a globalized world.

While there is a discursive shift in the way policies conceptualize "Europe," the promotion of tolerance has come to the fore as a specific educational aim in Lithuanian policy and discourse. In 2003, Lithuania drafted the *Program for the Fight against Intolerance, Xenophobia, and Homophobia* (2003) to report about the state of tolerance in Lithuania on the eve of EU accession. This program summarized prior activities, conferences, and civil society organizations working to put tolerance education on the map in Lithuania, and it further committed the Lithuanian government to promoting positive social relations based on "mutual understanding and a spirit of tolerance between different ethnic, confessional and social groups" (p. 3). Additionally, Article 5 of *the Law on Education* (2006) legislated that teaching tolerance in Lithuania is a fundamental requirement for the promotion of multicultural competence intended to "develop the abilities and experience needed by a person for competence as a citizen of Lithuania and a member of the European and global community, as well as of a multicultural society" (p. 5). *The Lithuanian Education for All [EFA] Action Plan* (2004) also espouses the commitment to teaching the "principles of 'learning to live together'" (p. 2) and outlines the plan for promoting social justice as the evaluation, review, and adjustment of Lithuanian educational content to better teach skills for "life-long learning, civic education, sustainable development, and cultural tolerance" (p. 4).

Generally, while education reforms in Lithuania have contributed to "public debate about racism and discrimination in Lithuania," (Andriukaitis, 2007, p. 42), one of the most significant tolerance education programs emerged from outside of educational policy discourse. In 1998, a Presidential Mandate created *The International Commission for the Evaluation of the Crimes of the Nazi and Soviet Occupation Regimes in Lithuania* (herein the Commission) to focus on research about the Nazi and Soviet invasions (1940–1991). As part of their mission, the Commission also undertook the creation of formal programs to educate students about the historical events that took place in Lithuania during the Nazi and Soviet periods. Due to the work of the Commission, over 50 Tolerance Education Centers (TECs) have been established in secondary schools throughout Lithuania as a permanent fixture for commemoration events and education activities designed to promote tolerance, empathy, and understanding. Teachers have been specially trained to staff the TECs, and the Commission also provides seminars and conferences for teachers to discuss broader themes related to history, education, pedagogy, and tolerance (Racinskas & Matoniene, 2004, p. 3). At the present time, the education project for tolerance is the only branch of the Commission still operating after a highly controversial governmental decision that caused Commission historians to abandon their research.

Nevertheless, while the TECs have been lauded in a Congressional briefing to the United States Commission on Security and Cooperation in Europe (Helsinki Commission, 2006, p. 9), there are many other aspects of social diversity that are not addressed in these centers. Additionally, concerns have arisen about the fact that the TEC programs are optional (leading some to speculate that only those already predisposed to tolerance self-select into these programs), and that attempts to teach tolerance through bounded, historical events will not be internalized by students if they are seen as being too disconnected from contemporary situations (Wills, 1996). Thus, while the government of Lithuania remains committed to tolerance, especially in discourse with international agencies, such as the statement to the UN that "the promotion of tolerance and non-discrimination was ... a key educational objective in schools" (UNCERD, 2006, p. 2), local reviewers of Lithuanian textbooks described a different situation, writing, "tolerance could, and probably should, be taught as a separate subject in school in Lithuania today" (Ruskas & Poceviciene, 2006, p. 453).

Despite the fact that there are successful programs, such as the TECs, that embody the discursive commitment to tolerance in Lithuanian educational policies, there are also aspects of reforms that exemplify what Bryan & Vavrus (2005) call the "contradictory effects of globalization" (p. 184), such as entrenched ethnic nationalism in response to perceived international interference in local norms. In Lithuania, perceptions exist that the EU controls "local" governance and attempts to limit aspects of cultural identity formation that would celebrate ethnic symbols. Even at the time of accession, Lithuania had a number of detractors who expressed reservations about joining the EU because they felt the suffering endured under the Soviets was historically ignored by "the west" (Krakovska, 2005, p. 41) and that in an alliance with the West, Lithuania would be perceived as a lesser state rather than an equal (Clark, 2006, p. 176).

Additional concerns have also arisen over the perceived "whole cloth" transfer of values from "west" to "east," like those of tolerance education, because of their failure to consider the reality of social, political, or economic situations in post-communist countries. As Shore (1997) notes in his research on EU identity, treaties that attempted to redefine people as "European subjects" "is not the same thing as forging a 'European subjectivity'" (p. 83). Subsequently, despite expressive educational reforms embracing EU values, EU accession has incited resistance to those norms – not because the norms are in and of themselves objectionable, but because they are perceived as an encroachment on the right to self-determination in a country still reeling from 60 years of occupation.

The most significant policy change has been the shift of national sovereignty into the place originally occupied by a general embrace of all things "European." For example, in the *Strategy* (2008) the same European values explicated in *The Concept on Education* (1994) appear almost verbatim, including the commitment to tolerance and the commitment to "developing determination and ability of an individual to follow these values in all walks of life" (p. 5), but the total transfer of a "European identity" is no longer as comprehensive as it was before. Instead, the entity whose values are now of primary importance is "the nation," only then followed by "Europe, and global culture" (p. 5). The promotion of a "national identity" also appears as one of the eight strategic goals for education in *The Strategy* (2008), and it further states in section 4 that in education "exceptional attention is given to patriotism of an individual, and building of its civil, cultural, and national identity" (p. 13). However, while the promotion of a national identity is not unheard of as goal in educational systems around the world, a review of *The Law on Education* conducted for the Open Society Institute aptly surmises the concern: "it begs the question, 'Whose values? Whose beliefs? And Who decides?'" (Crighton, 2002, p. 10).

The promotion of dominant cultural norms as part of a "hidden curriculum" is not new to any educational system; as Popkewitz (2000) notes "all discourses are dangerous ... but all discourses are not necessarily bad" (p. 20). Instead, the danger exists in policy's power to name populations, divide groups, and generate norms that serve to exclude rather than unite. Groups with strong identities often exclude other individuals from belonging through different social distancing mechanisms, such as xenophobia, ethnocentrism, and racism (Frėjutė-Rakauskienė, 2006, p. 14). The potential appearance of these exclusive outcomes is one of the concerns raised by Lithuanian educational policies that contextualize tolerance alongside ethnic identity construction. Zelvys (2004) suggests that Lithuanian education policy is attempting to achieve the appearance of human rights through a conflicting dichotomy that disguises an ethnic "return to the roots" with "borrowing from abroad" (p. 563). As such, this discursive sleight of hand allows token minority concessions while entrenching the norm of minority assimilation into dominant norms. Thus, while the commitment to tolerance is institutionalized in the aforementioned education documents, resistance to this discourse has also been institutionalized in policies that limit the scope of tolerance – limits that have become clearly entrenched in legislation related to nontraditional lifestyles.

SEXUAL ORIENTATION: THE LIMITS OF TOLERANCE IN LITHUANIA?

Smith (1991) notes in his research on national identity that attempts to create politically inclusive discourse can also sometimes result in dissent (p. 134), and because many Lithuanian policies passed during the pre-accession phase were designed to institutionalize EU values and discourse, there is continuing concern that the importation of ready-made western political formulas has resulted in a "mismatch" between international expectations and local needs (even if they share similar aims). Weiner (2009) has observed that over time "international" policies represent an affront to many individuals because the "forced fitting" of EU directives onto local legislation can "disable their utility and endanger the larger political and economic aims which such mechanisms seek to advance" (p. 307). Thus outcomes of EU accession requirements have been twofold in Lithuania, having produced programs such as the Tolerance Education centers, but also coming to show how "premature legislation can prove counter-productive" (Reekie, 1997, p. 191) if it leads to "backlash" against well-intentioned mandates (Kochenov, 2007, p. 2).

A prime example of the socially destabilizing consequences that can come from hastily drafted reforms to secure EU accession is Silova's (2006) landmark study on Latvian educational policies intended to fulfill democratic expectations for multiculturalism. While the EU charged Latvia with accommodating the cultural, educational, and political needs of their large minority populations – as they did in Lithuania – this aim was neither achieved by fostering new attitudes toward diversity, nor by drafting structural reforms; instead it was achieved through a discursive relabeling of the segregated school system that already divided Russian-language students from their Latvian speaking counterparts. Additionally, funding and policy promises for minority programs were quietly re-purposed when the backs of EU monitoring commissions were turned (pp. 146–147). Subsequently, similar to the situation in Lithuanian, Silova found that in Latvia, policies were discursively "committed" to fostering respect for minority rights, but in practice they further entrenched social division and promoted resistance by "teaching" students that Latvian society was founded on cultural competition rather than integration and tolerance for difference.

In Lithuania, a salient example of similar discursive maneuverings can be found in the *Law on the Protection of Minors against the Detrimental Effects of Public Information* (2009; herein *The Law on Minors*) prohibiting discussions about nontraditional lifestyles between same-sex couples any-where that minors frequent. Although Lithuania decriminalized homosexu-ality in 1993 and an influx of Western-influenced discourses introduced the concept of gay rights to Lithuania around the same time, Gay, Lesbian, Bisexual, and Transgender (herein GLBT) communities continue to be undermined by official discourses that marginalize their rights, such as their ability to "name" themselves in a public, or to enjoy equal citizenship rights and political protections (Tereškinas, 2002/2003, p. 207). An Open Society

Institute (OSI) (2002) report on Lithuania found that discrimination on the grounds of sexual orientation was still being perpetuated at the individual, social, and systemic levels (p. 12), and a US State Department *Country Report on Human Rights in Lithuania* (2004) found that "homosexuals suffer permanent social exclusion" (USDOS, 2004, p.10) – a situation that had not changed significantly by the 2010 report noting that "discrimination and persistent social exclusion of LGBT persons remain problems" (USDOS, 2010, p. 11).

Reingarde and Zdanevicius (2007) found that gender norms in Lithuania are still based on "legalized heterosexism" (p. 55) because the Constitution of Lithuanian still omits sexual orientation as one of the statuses legally protected from discrimination. Additionally, Sagatys (2010), who wrote a legal exegeses on the status of the word "family" in the Lithuanian Constitution, discovered that "the majority of leading political forces in Lithuania have thus far chosen to follow the classical, conservative interpretation of the concept of family," rendering even the possibility for same-sex relationships "altogether outside the scope of the discussion" (p. 184) – which he regards as "the most conservative family policy model in the history of Lithuania since the re-establishment of independence in 1990" (p. 193).

One of the reasons for this backlash in Lithuania, and its intention to limit tolerance to only some officially sanctioned groups, is due to the fact that many discussions over gay rights have been introduced from external influences, such as EU directives or international media, which has been regarded as an encroachment on national sovereignty. For example, in 2010 the first ever Baltic Pride March in Lithuania was cancelled a number of times before international pressure finally forced officials to allow it to proceed; following the march, two Lithuanian Parliamentarians (Petras Grazulis and Kazimieras Uoka) were indicted for attacking police officers securing the protection of Baltic Pride Marchers and inciting the antigay rights crowd because they felt the march was an inappropriate use of state resources; in 2007 Vilnius mayor Juozas Imbrasas banned a visit by an EU sponsored antidiscrimination truck tour making stops in 19 cities as part of the 2007 EU Year for Equal Opportunities because it advocated tolerance for gay rights; and the same year ads supporting gay rights were removed from Kaunas trolley buses because drivers refused to take these buses out on public streets. Such resistance to change illustrates the limitations of using legislation to affect social change when legislation itself is a product of the very society it is attempting to transform.

Reactions to policies limiting gay rights in Lithuania reached international proportions in July 2009 over the amendment added to *The Law on*

Minors (2009). Originally, the purpose of *The Law on Minors*, passed in 2002, was to "protect" minors from explicit manifestations of violence, torture, sex, obscenities, discrimination, and so forth by bringing media and discourse more in line with Western norms; however, the 2009 clause institutionalizing intolerance against homosexuality drew challenges from human rights advocates, including the EU Parliament, because it disregards the human rights of GLBT communities and limits free speech through its mandated silence on "homosexual, bisexual or polygamous relations" or discussions where "family relations are distorted [and] its values are scorned" (Republic of Lithuania, 2009, p. 6).

Authors of the amendment to *the Law on Minors* (2009) stated that the preemptive strike against discourses supporting nontraditional lifestyles was necessary because "the propagation of a nontraditional sexual orientation and exposure to information containing positive coverage of homosexual relations may therefore cause negative consequences for the physical, mental and, first and foremost, moral development of minors" (Amnesty International, 2008), but this reasoning causes the entire law to suffer from conceptual confusion. *The Law on Minors* (2009) categorizes manifestations of intolerance, discrimination, or mockery *as being detrimental* to minors (p. 2), but by banning discussions on homosexuality or alternative lifestyles, *The Law on Minors* (2009) is guilty of detrimental effects according to its own standards. Additionally, because schools are one of the most common places where children are exposed to "public information," the law is seen as a start down that slippery slope of social control over ideological values and promulgation of normative identities despite *The Concept on Education's* (1994) commitment to the notion that schools are intended to "help the individual discover universal human values" (MoES, 1994, p. 10), of which tolerance has already been demonstrated as an international standard. The ban also counters *The Concept on Education's* (1994) foundations for effective teachers, who are required to "base fostering and pedagogical interaction on dialogue, tolerance, respect, insistence on high standards and creativity" (p. 37).

Furthermore, forced silence about something is not the same thing as absence of that issue. Silence, what Foucault (1997) calls the "expurgation ... of the authorized vocabulary" (p. 301), can be as injurious as speech because inducements not to talk about certain matters speak volumes about cultural norms and acceptable behavior. Silence is itself a productive form of discourse, and "far from confined to the symbolic level of representation, [it] translates into everyday practice" (Stella, 2007, p. 161). Thus, while the EU Parliament has been partially successful in encouraging Lithuania to adopt less oppressive discourse against gay rights in *The Law on Minors*, the law still officially – even if silently – defines "normal" as a relationship between a man and a woman.

Subsequently, policies such as these have exacerbated social marginalization of alternative groups who fear for their survival and thus silence themselves. As Reingarde and Zdanevicius (2007) observe in their study on "coming out" in the workplace, examining gay rights at the individual level in Lithuania is deeply influenced by the official policies and discourses that label homosexuality as deviant and wrong, and research on marginalized sexual minorities continues to be difficult in Lithuania because "silence prevails" (p. 51). However, there is also an ironic component to *The Law on Minors'* (2009) intentions to curb public discussions about homosexuality because it has *produced* discussions, public protest, and international censure over the confused scope and seemingly impracticality of the Law. As Foucault (1997) saw during the Victorian Age, prohibitions on discourses about sex actually brought about the converse aim, "an institutional incitement to speak about it" (p. 302).

The Law on Minors was initially regarded as a rejection of difference, but it has increasingly come to serve as a challenge to "European" guidance on the boundaries of tolerance and human rights. As such, it highlights an important post-accession reality for states concerned about their right to self-determination: the EU pays relatively little attention to whether new candidates and member countries actually meet in practice the standards that are set out in pre-accession treaties (Kochenov, 2002, p. 3), and post-accession sanctions for EU countries that do not tow political and normative lines are minimal, if they exist at all (Weiner, 2009, p. 320). So, while the EU Parliament can issue proclamations or request legislative revisions, the primary political technology of the European Union is policy reform and discourse intended to bring about a subjectivation that encourages individuals to regulate themselves in favor of democratic behaviors – a regulation that works only if educational aims are unquestioningly absorbed by individuals, which they never are.

CONCLUDING REMARKS

Tolerance education is a complicated endeavor that must be considered in its historical, political, and social contexts. While EU dictates on human rights, democracy, and tolerance were supposed to provide easy legislative models for post-Soviet accession countries to follow, Weiner (2009) aptly summarizes that "while policies may go global, this does not mean that they will become local" (p. 320). Still, educational policy reforms in Lithuania show that while the perception of "European values" may have had a real impact on Lithuanian policymaking and discourse, the aftermath of accession-based policies is still far from understood, especially at the individual level. Additionally, further research is necessary to understand what it means to teach tolerance in the context of a Lithuanian national identity, or in the context of an EU identity for that matter. A "European" identity is no less constructed than the Lithuanian variant, and both are produced by relational forces borne from perceived global and local intersections. Hence, while the "carrot" of EU accession shaped the discourse of many Lithuanian educational reforms for tolerance, the normalizing gaze of the EU has not sufficiently produced "European" subjectivities in many Lithuanians – an aim yet to be realized in most EU member states. Nonetheless, the remaining question is not whether the EU identity project has been successful, but whether *The Law on Minors* exemplifies the failure of Lithuanian tolerance discourse because it entrenches strict boundaries on human rights into national policy, or whether it highlights the success of tolerance rhetoric because corollary resistance has emerged as a response to Lithuanian re-subjectivation in a "European" context. However, maybe the most important question is not *which* one prevails, but what it means for the future of tolerance education in Lithuania if the two outcomes cannot actually be separated from each other at all.

REFERENCES

Amnesty International. (2008). 2008 annual report for Lithuania. Available at http://www.amnestyusa.org/annualreport.php?id = ar&yr = 2008&c = LTU

Andriukaitis, G. (2007). *ENAR shadow report: Racism in Lithuania*. Brussels, Belgium: European Network Against Racism (ENAR).

Beresnevičiutė, V. (2003). Ethnic structure of contemporary society: Dimensions of social integration of ethnic groups of Lithuania. In: B. Voicu & H. Rusu (Eds), *Globalization, integration and social development in Central and Eastern Europe* (pp. 311–320). Sibiu: Psihomedia Publishing House.

Bonnet, G. (2004). Evaluation of education in the European Union: Policy and methodology. *Assessment in Education, 11*(2), 179–191.

Breidis, L. (2009). *Vilnius city of strangers*. Budapest, Hungary: Central European University Press.

Brubaker, R. (1995). National minorities, nationalizing states, and external homelands in the new Europe. *Daedalus, 124*(2), 107–132.

Brubaker, R. (2004). In the name of the nation: Reflections on nationalism and patriotism. *Citizenship Studies, 8*(2), 115–127.

Bryan, A., & Vavrus, F. (2005). The promise and peril of education: The teaching of in/tolerance in an era of globalization. *Globalization, Society and Education, 3*(2), 183–202.

Budryte, D. (2005). *Taming nationalism: Political community building in the post-Soviet Baltic States.* Hampshire, England: Ashgate Publishing Limited.

Bunce, V. (2005). The national idea: Imperial legacies and post-communist pathways in Eastern Europe. *East European Politics and Society, 58*(4), 406–442.

Butler, J. (1997). *The psychic life of power: Theories in subjection.* Stanford, CA: Stanford University Press.

Clark, T. D. (2006). Nationalism in post-Soviet Lithuania: New approaches for the nation of "innocent sufferers". In: L. W. Barrington (Ed.), *After independence: Making and protecting the nation in postcolonial and post-communist states* (pp. 162–186). Detroit, MI: University of Michigan.

Connell, H. (1994). *Education and tolerance.* Paris, France: UNESCO.

Coulby, D. (2000). Education in times of transition: Eastern Europe with particular reference to the Baltic States. In: D. Coulby, R. Cowen & C. Jones (Eds), *Education in times of transition* (pp. 8–22). London, England: Kogan Page.

Crighton, J. (2002). *Comments on republic of Lithuania draft law on education.* Vilnius, Lithuania: Open Society Fund Lithuania (OSFL).

Dunn, W. (2007). *Public policy analysis, an introduction* (4th ed.). Upper Saddle River, NJ: Prentice Hall.

European Commission (EC). (2009). *Discrimination in the EU: Special Eurobarometer.* Brussels, Belgium: Directorate General Employment, Social Affairs and Equal Opportunities and coordinated by Directorate General Communication.

European Monitoring Center on Racism and Xenophobia (EUMC). (2005). *Majorities' attitudes towards minorities: Key findings from the Eurobarometer and the European Social Survey.* Vienna, Austria: Manz Crossmedia Gmbh and Co KG.

European Union Agency for Fundamental Rights (FRA). (2007). Report on racism and xenophobia in the member states of the EU. Available at http://fra.europa.eu/fraWebsite/home/home_en.htm

Feldmann, E., Henschel, T. R., & Ulrich, S. (2000). *Tolerance: Basis for democratic intervention.* Gütersloh, Germany: Bertelsmann Foundation Publishers.

Foucault, M. (1991). Governmentality. In: G. Burchell, C. Gordon & P. Miller (Eds), *The Foucault effect* (pp. 87–104). London, England: Harvester Wheatsheaf.

Foucault, M. (1995). *Discipline and punish* (2nd ed.). New York, NY: Vintage Books.

Foucault, M. (1997). In: P. Rabinow (Ed.), *The Foucault reader.* New York, NY: Random House.

Frėjutė-Rakauskienė, M. (2006). Contemporary phenomenon of racism and its manifestations in public discourse. *Filosofia, Sociologija, 4*, 13–19.

International Convention on the Elimination of all Forms of Racial Discrimination (UNCERD). (2006). Summary record of the 1733 meeting. Available at http://www.unhchr.ch/tbs/doc.nsf/c12563e7005d936d4125611e00445ea9/f0da9e44ceb40f98c125712300534daa/$FILE/G0640568.pdf

Kochenov, D. (2007). Democracy and human rights – not for gay people? EU eastern enlargement and its impact on the protection of the rights of sexual minorities. *Texas Wesleyan Law Review, 13*(459), 1–4.

Krakovska, V. (2005). Evolution of the Lithuanian national identity in the European context. *Slovo*, *17*(1), 33–47.

Levinson, B. A. U., & Holland, D. (1996). The cultural production of the educated person, an introduction. In: B. A. U. Levinson, D. Foley & D. Holland (Eds), *The cultural production of the educated person: Critical ethnographies of schooling and local practice* (pp. 1–26). Albany, NY: SUNY Press.

Mansfield, E., & Kehoe, J. (1994). A critical examination of Anti-Racist education. *Canadian Journal of Education*, *19*(4), 418–430.

Ministry of Science and Education of The Republic of Lithuania (MOES). (1994). *General concept of education in Lithuania (English)*. Vilnius, Lithuania: MOES.

Ministry of Science and Education of The Republic of Lithuania (MOES). (2006). Republic of Lithuania Law on the Amendment of the Law on Education. Available at http://www3.lrs.lt/pls/inter2/dokpaieska.showdoc_l?p_id=281043.

Ministry of Science and Education of The Republic of Lithuania (MOES). (2008). Parliament of the Republic of Lithuania Resolution Re: The provisions of the national education strategy 2003–2012. Available at http://www.smm.lt/en/legislation/docs/Lithuanian%20Education%20Strategy%202003-2012.pdf

Muhic, M. (2004). Multiculturalism in Central and Eastern Europe: Challenge or threat? *The Anthropology of East Europe Review*, *21*(2), 1–8.

National Education Forum. (2004). Lithuanian "education for all" action plan. Available at http://planipolis.iiep.unesco.org/upload/Lithuania/Lithuania%20NPA%20EFA.pdf

Novoa, A. (2000). The restructuring of European educational space: Challenging relationships among states, citizens, and educational communities. In: T. S. Popkewitz (Ed.), *Educational knowledge: Changing relationships between the state, civil society, and the educational community* (pp. 31–51). Albany, NY: SUNY Press.

Novoa, A., & Lawn, M. (2002). Fabricating Europe: The formation of an education space. In: A. Novoa & M. Lawn (Eds), *Fabricating Europe: The formation of an education space* (pp. 1–14). Dordrecht, Netherlands: Kluwer Academic Publishers.

Organization for Economic Cooperation and Development (OECD). (2002). *Reviews of national policies for education: Lithuania; education and skills*. Paris, France. OECD Press.

Organization for Security and Cooperation in Europe (OSCE). (2008). Hate Crimes in the OSCE region – incidents and responses – Annual report for 2007. Available at http://www.osce.org/item/33850.html

Pavlovaite, I. (2003). Paradise regained: The conceptualization of Europe in the Lithuanian debate. In: M. Lehti & D. J. Smith (Eds), *Post-cold war identity politics* (pp. 199–218). Portland, OR: Frank Cass Publishers.

Paxson, M. (2005). *Solovyovo: The story of memory in a Russian village*. Bloomington, IN: Indiana University Press.

Peck, B. T. (2000). Education in the Baltic states: Historical and current context; the educational system in the 1990s. In: B. T. Peck & A. Mays (Eds), *Challenge and change in education: The experience of the Baltic States in the 1990s* (pp. 185–189). Huntington, NY: Nova Science Publishers.

Popkewitz, T. S. (2000). Globalization/Regionalization, knowledge and the educational practices: Some notes on comparative strategies for education. In: T. S. Popkewitz (Ed.), *Educational knowledge: Changing relationships between the state, civil society, and the educational community* (pp. 3–30). Albany, NY: SUNY Press.

Popkewitz, T. S. (2001). Rethinking the political: Reconstituting national imaginaries and producing difference. *International Journal of Education*, 5(2/3), 179–207.

Popkewitz, T. S. (2008). Education sciences, schooling, and abjection: Recognizing difference and the making of inequality? *South African Journal of Education*, 288(3), 301–319.

Racinskas, R., & Matoniene, S. (2004). Holocaust education as an instrument of building civil society in the 21st century. Presentation to the International Conference on Teaching the Holocaust to Future Generations, Jerusalem, Israel (August 8–11, 2004).

Reekie, A. (1997). European international control. In: D. J. West & R. Green (Eds), *Sociolegal control of homosexuality* (pp. 179–195). New York, NY: Plenum Press.

Reingarde, J. Z., & Zdanevicius, A. (2007). Disrupting the (hetero)normative: Coming out in the workplace. In: R. Kuhar & M. Takacs (Eds), *Beyond the pink curtain: Everyday life of LGBT people in Eastern Europe* (pp. 49–64). Slovenia: The Peace Institute.

Republic of Lithuania. (2003). Nacionaline kovos su netolerancija, rasizmu, ksenofobia ir homophobia programa, vykdant programa "parama igyvendiant nocionalini zmogaus teisu veiksmu plana." [The national fight against intolerance, racism, xenophobia, and homophobia, working program "support for the implementation of national human rights action plan"]. Vilnius, Lithuania.

Republic of Lithuania. (2009). Law on the protection of minors against the detrimental effects of public information. Available at http://www.iglhrc.org/binary-data/ATTACHMENT/file/000/000/319-1.pdf

Ruskas, J., & Poceviciene, R. (2006). What Lithuanian pupils learn about disability: Analysis of attitudes and content of textbook. Paper presented at the International Conference on Learning and Educational Media, Caen, France (October 26–29, 2005).

Sagatys, G. (2010). The concept of family in Lithuanian law. *Jurisprudence*, 1(119), 181–196.

Shore, C. (1997). *Anthropology of policy: Critical perspectives on governance and power*. London, England: Routledge.

Silova, I. (2006). *From sites of occupation to symbols of multiculturalism: Reconceptualizing minority education in post-Soviet Latvia*. Greenwich, CT: Information Age Publishing.

Smith, A. D. (1991). *National identity*. Reno, NV: University of Nevada Press.

Stein, S. J. (2004). *The culture of education policy*. New York, NY: Teachers College Press.

Steiner-Khamsi, G. (2004). Introduction: Globalization real or imagined? In: G. Steiner-Khamsi (Ed.), *The global politics of educational borrowing and lending* (pp. 1–6). New York, NY: Teachers College Press.

Stella, F. (2007). The right to be different? Sexual citizenship and its politics in post-Soviet Russia. In: R. Kay (Ed.), *Gender, equality and difference during and after state socialism* (pp. 146–165). Hampshire, England: Palgrave McMillan.

Tereškinas, A. (2002/2003). *Toward a new politics of citizenship: Representation of ethnic and sexual minorities in the Lithuanian media*. Vilnius, Lithuania: Open Society Institute.

The Open Society Institute (OSI). (2002). *Sexual orientation discrimination in Lithuania, Latvia, and Estonia*. Vilnius, Lithuania: OSI.

Tomiak, J. (1992). Education in the Baltic States, Ukraine, Belarus, and Russia. *Comparative Education*, 28(1), 33–44.

United Nations Educational, Scientific, and Cultural Organization (UNESCO). (1994). *Tolerance: The threshold of peace*. Paris, France: UNESCO.

United Nations Educational, Scientific, and Cultural Organization (UNESCO). (1995a). *Declaration of principles of tolerance*. Paris, France: UNESCO.

United Nations Educational, Scientific, and Cultural Organization (UNESCO). (1995b). *Promoting tolerance.* Paris, France: UNESCO.

United States Commission on Security and Cooperation in Europe (Helsinki Commission). (2006). Tools for combating anti-Semitism: Police training and Holocaust education. Presented at the Congressional Hearing of the Helsinki Commission, Washington, DC (May 9, 2006).

United States Department of State (USDOS). (2004). Lithuania: Country Reports of Human Rights Practices. Available at http://www.state.gov/g/drl/rls/hrrpt/2004/41693.htm

United States Department of State (USDOS). (2010). Lithuania: Country Reports of Human Rights Practices. Available at http://www.state.gov/g/drl/rls/hrrpt/2009/eur/136042.htm

Verdery, K. (1996). *What was socialism and what comes next?* Princeton, NJ: Princeton University Press.

Vogt, W. P. (1997). *Tolerance and education: Learning to live with diversity and difference.* Thousand Oaks, CA: Sage Publications.

Walkenhorst, H. (2008). Explaining change in EU education policy. *Journal of European Public Policy, 15*(4), 567–587.

Weiner, E. (2009). Eastern houses, western bricks? (Re)constructing gender sensibilities in the European Union's eastern enlargement. *Social Politics: International Studies in Gender, State and Society, 16*(3), 303–326.

Wills, J. (1996). Who needs multicultural education? White students, US history, and the construction of a usable past. *Anthropology and Education Quarterly, 27*(3), 365–389.

Zelvys, R. (2004). Development of education policy in Lithuania during the years of transformations. *International Journal of Educational Development, 24*, 559–571.

TRANSNATIONAL VITALITY OF THE FINNO-UGRIC IDENTITY IN ESTONIA: THE ROLE OF EDUCATION AND ADVOCACY IN A NEW GEOPOLITICAL CONTEXT

Kara D. Brown

INTRODUCTION

The Finno-Ugric identity, originally formulated by 19th century academics and nurtured as part of national-identity movements, has revived since the collapse of the Soviet Union (1991). This chapter explores the transnational vitality of the Finno-Ugric identity for Estonians in the post-Soviet era. In particular, I ask, "How has the Finno-Urgic identity remained meaningful in the contemporary geo-political context?" I draw on Schiffman's (2006) "linguistic culture" framework to understand the renewed relevance of the Finno-Ugric identity. I argue that the identity's continuing significance and renewed vitality stems from the new meanings that Finno-Ugric culture has taken on in the particular post-Soviet geopolitical context. I examine the key role of Finno-Ugric identity in Estonian efforts to sustain lesser-used-language (LUL) instruction domestically and to support its development internationally. By analyzing Estonia's varied experiences with LUL

Post-Socialism is not Dead: (Re)Reading the Global in Comparative Education
International Perspectives on Education and Society, Volume 14, 271–296
Copyright © 2010 by Emerald Group Publishing Limited
ISSN: 1479-3679/doi:10.1108/S1479-3679(2010)0000014013

advocacy and development, I explore how Finno-Ugric linguistic culture functions as a rich resource in developing Estonian national identity, in making statements of ethnic solidarity and in providing new methods for language revitalization.

Speakers of Finno-Ugric languages live in small, widely dispersed clusters between Central Europe and Kamchatka, from Hungary to the eastern edges of the Russian Federation. Linked by their non-Indo-European tongues, many of these speakers feel a sense of cultural affinity and shared linguistic heritage that transcends the geographic, linguistic, and cultural distances between them; these generally "small" nations find a sense of broader collective identity as Finno-Ugric peoples.[1] The Finno-Ugrians represent about 24 distinct nations and, counting the Samoyed-language speakers, number roughly 25 million people. Three European countries are Finno-Ugric nation-states: Finland, Hungary, and Estonia. These three countries include approximately 60% of the world's Finno-Ugric population. The remaining populations reside as minorities with varying degrees of autonomy in Europe and Russia.

Given the ethnic and geopolitical diversity of the Finno-Ugric community, this chapter concentrates on the relevance of this transnational culture with one nation, the Estonians. While the Estonian experience is by no means representative of or generalizable to the other Finno-Ugric nations, this case helps to illustrate the cultural framing of contemporary projects to promote LUL education from a unique vantage point. Estonia bridges the European and Russian Finno-Ugric worlds; Estonians have experience, on one hand, with the Russian empire and the Soviet Union as an Autonomous Republic, and, on the other hand, with independence (1918–1940 and 1991–current) and membership in the European Union (EU) (2004–current). Moreover, Estonia is the only Finno-Ugric state with a Finno-Ugric speaking minority, the Võro, who identify with the ethnic majority (i.e., the Estonians), yet are in the process of developing a regional-identity and school-based language program. Finally, Estonia's involvement with efforts to promote LUL education points to the intersection of this issue with foreign policy, domestic politics, and contemporary nation-building attempts.

I begin the chapter with a conceptual introduction to linguistic culture and a methodological overview of the research. I then provide an historical synopsis of the three phases of the development of the Finno-Ugric connection with particular attention to issues of language marginalization in the context of a shifting political landscape. I have divided the third section into three vignettes from Estonia to demonstrate the varied role of

Finno-Ugric culture in framing and addressing LUL education. I conclude with a consideration of the new meanings and significance of the Finno-Ugric culture, both in transnational and Estonian contexts.

THEORETICAL FRAMEWORK AND METHODOLOGY

The concept of "linguistic culture" (Schiffman, 2006) illuminates enduring aspects of the transnational Finno-Ugric connection. Schiffman (2006) posits linguistic culture as the "sum totality of ideas, values, beliefs, attitudes, prejudices, myths, religious strictures, and all the other cultural 'baggage' that speakers bring to their dealings with language from their culture" (p. 112). In this chapter, I extend the linguistic-culture concept beyond the state (Schiffman, 1996; Lo Bianco, 1999) to a regional, transnational level. Scholars have noted the strategic use of formal schooling to promote cross-border identities (Yanik, 2004) in European and Eurasian space, but the role of pan-Finno-Ugric linguistic culture has remained largely under-examined (for exceptions see the *Nationalities Papers,* 2001; Taagepera, 1999; Kasten, 1999).

"Being small" constitutes a defining element of Finno-Ugric linguistic culture. The modest scale of demographic and political power across the Finno-Ugric world informs the cultural sense of smallness. The population of the individual Finno-Ugric nations, excluding the Hungarians and Finns, number between one million and one hundred people (according to 2002 statistics, Table 1). Participation in a larger, yet exclusive, joint culture allows for academic opportunities and a sense of combined strength. An Udmurt student echoed the unity-in-smallness sentiment, "It [the connection between Finno-Ugric people] gives a chance for all of us who are members of small nations to feel that we are part of something bigger" (informal interview, October 22, 2004).[2] As members of less populous nations, Finno-Ugrians share a sense of cultural vulnerability. Former Estonian President Lennart Meri (1992–2001), famous for his Soviet-era texts and documentary films on the Finno-Ugric people, alluded to the common smallness of Finno-Ugric nations in his welcoming speech to the 3rd World Congress of Finno-Ugric People:[3]

> We should remember that against the background of the world or even against the background of Europe, all Finno-Ugric peoples, including Hungarians, Finns and Estonians, are small nations, subconsciously or consciously trying to protect their identity, their small island in the vast ocean of the Indo-European languages. (Meri, 2000)

Table 1. Population of Uralic People, 2002.

People	Population	Home Countries
Hungarians	15,000,000	Hungary, Romania, Slovakia, Austria, other
Finns	5,000,000	Finland, Sweden, Russia, Estonia
Estonians	1,000,000	Estonia
Mordvinians (Ezyas and Mokshas)	843,400	Russia
Udmurts	636,900	Russia
Maris	604,300	Russia
Zyryan Komis	293,400	Russia
Permian Komis	125,200	Russia
Karelians	93,300	Russia
Saamis	100,0000–50,000	Norway, Sweden, Finland, Russia
Nenetses	41,300	Russia
Khantys	28,700	Russia
Csángos	20,000	Romania
Mansis	11,400	Russia
Kvens	10,000	Norway
Vepsians	8,200	Russia
Selkups	4,200	Russia
Setos	3,200	Russia, Estonia
Besermans	3,000	Russia
Nganasans	800	Russia
Ingrians (Izhorians)	700	Russia
Enetses	300	Russia
Livonians	250	Latvia
Votians	100	Russia

Source: Fenno Ugria Asutus. (n.d.). The Finno-Ugric peoples. Available at http://www.fennougria.ee/index.php?id = 10947

Meri's statement also highlights the linguistic lens through which national leaders position Finno-Ugric people and policies of cultural protectionism.

In the case of Finno-Ugric people, linguistic vulnerability has shaped both the form and response to protectivist and assimilative language policies. Schiffman (2006) argues that language policy is "inextricably connected" to the concept of linguistic culture (p. 112). His sociocultural perspective on policy encompasses all the "decision-making about language" from the overt policies crafted at official levels to those "implicit, unwritten, covert, de facto, grass-roots, and unofficial ideas and assumptions" that influence policy implementation and appropriation (Schiffman, 2006, p. 112).

The linguistic Finno-Ugric culture of Europe and Russia constitutes the foundation for transnational involvement in the educational sphere. Branch (1993) highlights the historic influence of the Finno-Ugric linguistic culture in shaping policy development:

> The cultural and political perception central to that process [of 19th century identity formation] is the assumption that the speakers of Finno-Ugrian languages had a common origin and to some extent a common history and culture, and that this legitimized cultural and political activity based on the assumptions of a common origin. (p. 37)

Just as the Finno-Ugric linguistic culture helped to fuel academic efforts and social investment in early attempts to consolidate national-identity and develop nation-states, contemporary Finno-Ugric links also help to justify transnational and domestic advocacy in the educational sphere. The interconnection of policy and culture is also reflected in the Finno-Ugric response to assimilative efforts:

> Many Finno-Ugric tribes have already disappeared or are on the verge of extinction. … Usually it is said in such cases [or assimilation] that the choice was made voluntarily. Unfortunately the voluntary character of such a choice is but an illusion, as it was made under economic, political, demographic and educational considerations in a situation where a people had become a minority in their historical territory and lost control over the way they order their lives. (Rüütel, 2004)

In the post-Soviet context, the shared culture of linguistic endangerment bears a post-imperial imprint (Moore, 2006). Political leaders, like former Estonian President Rüütel (2001–2006), identify particularly in the marginalization of native languages, the effects of the Soviet colonial power when Finno-Ugric people became minorities "in their historic territory."

The rise in global English dominance further exacerbates linguistic vulnerability in this postimperial context. Although, as Raun (2009) posits, "At first glance it would appear that the position of the Estonian language, which survived the threat of Russification in the Soviet decades and also continued to be modernized as an effective means of communication" (p. 528), would be secure; since regaining independence in 1991, Russian and English continue to pose threats to the vitality of Finno-Ugric languages. A researcher at the Võro Institute, a government-funded organization helping to spearhead the regional-language revival in Estonia, sketched (see Fig. 1) a scene that powerfully conveys the multiple and layered threats to Finno-Ugric languages. The artist depicts two of the regional southeastern Estonian languages, Võro and Seto, in the mouth of the "Eesti Keel" (Estonian) fish. The "Русский" (Russian) fish consumes

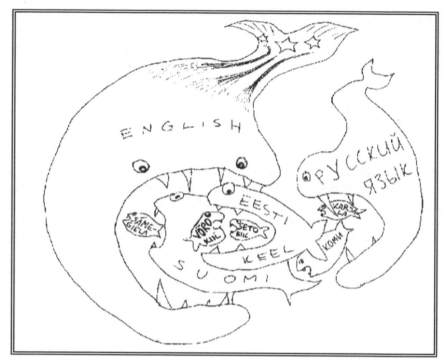

Fig. 1. Threats to Finno-Ugric Languages. *Source:* Image created by J. Sullõv (used with permission).

Karjala (Karelian) and Komi, two Finno-Ugric languages in the Russian Federation, while the Suomi (Finnish) fish swims in the middle eating Sámegiela (Sami). English, pictured with an impression of the US flag in its tail, sits on the far left on the verge of devouring Finno-Ugric languages both large and small. In this portrayal of the Finno-Ugric language feeding frenzy, the Võro Institute researcher captures not only the culpability of some of the larger Finno-Ugric languages in contributing to language endangerment, but also the significant threats posed by Russian and English.

In order to analyze the relevance of the Finno-Ugric identity in the post-Soviet era, I draw on data from document analysis and qualitative fieldwork conducted over the last decade in Estonia (1999–2009). Part of my research consisted of an analysis of documents culled from international, national, and regional levels concerning Finno-Ugric native-language instruction including: all Estonian Presidential speeches delivered at the central

Finno-Ugric events held since 1992, including the International Congress of Finno-Ugric Studies (1995, 1999), the Finno-Ugric Writers' Congress (1999), and the World Congress of Finno-Ugric Peoples (2000, 2004, 2008); Council of Europe (COE) documents and reports pertaining to the Finno-Ugric People of Europe and Russia; the resolutions of the World Congress of Finno-Ugric People (1996, 2000, 2004, and 2008); the Estonian government's three iterations (I, II, and III) of Estonia's Kindred Peoples Program (*Hõimurahvaste Programm*) and the Old Võrumaa (*Vana Võrumaa*) Cultural Program: 2010–2013. I have also incorporated data from semiformal interviews (2004 and 2008), reviews of the local Estonian press (2001–2010), and field notes from participant-observation in academic conferences and school-based research (2004, 2009). My research was conducted primarily in Estonian. Unless noted, I incorporated the official English translations of policy documents and speeches when possible.

HISTORICAL CONTEXT

The notion of a Finno-Ugric people emerged out of 19th century academic pursuits and national-identity projects. The Finno-Ugric culture has changed over the last 100 years and can be loosely divided into three over-lapping historical phases: (1) the birth of the Finno-Ugric culture through academic exploration and attempts at nation-building; (2) the Soviet-era consolidation and fracturing of Finno-Ugric culture; and (3) the rebirth and redirection of the Finno-Ugric connection through post-1991 cultural rapprochement. A brief overview of these phases positions Estonian efforts to sustain LUL instruction domestically and to support its development internationally.

The first phase, the birth of Finno-Ugric culture, spans the 18th and 19th centuries, encompassing academic exploration and the era of romantic nationalism. The concept of a Finno-Ugric connection, formulated, in part, by Hungarian and Finnish linguists after field research in Lapland and Russia, led to the development of Finno-Ugrian studies (or Finno-Ugristics) as an academic field of inquiry. Academic societies based on Finno-Ugric studies, including Finland's M. A. Castrén Society and Hungary's Reguly Society, consolidated the notion of Finno-Ugric kinship and brought together scholars across borders. The academic connections were strongest among the larger Finno-Ugric nations – Hungarians, Finns, and Estonians – but cultural bonds with the smaller Finno-Ugric people of Russia were also established primarily through academic linkages.

The academic foundation of the Finno-Ugric connection gained a political edge in the era of romantic nationalism revealing the intimate intertwining of the national and transnational elements of Finno-Ugric culture. Branch (1993) observes that scholars were driven in the mid- to late 1800s not only by the scientific curiosity of their predecessors, but also by an "emotional imperative, first, of cultural nationalism and later of political nationalism" (p. 40). The transnational Finno-Ugric linguistic culture emerged to play a feature role in the development of Finnish, Estonian, and Hungarian national identities in the 19th and early 20th centuries. Education helped to further consolidate national identities, particularly native-language instruction and the backlash to school-based Russification policies. Although political sentiment related to Finno-Ugric culture during this phase was primarily channeled to nation-building, covert critiques of Russian policy also emerged. Saarinen (2001) notes that Finnish scholars during this era foresaw in the Russian treatment of the Finno-Ugric people in the empire a possible parallel fate and privately condemned the Tsarist policies, "In their travel sketches and diaries, scholars severely criticized the Russian colonists, who, especially in Siberia, had brought the indigenous peoples neither culture nor religion, only demoralization and decline" (p. 44).

The second historic phase, a consolidation and fracturing of Finno-Ugric culture, emerged with the political reconfigurations of the early 20th century. The decade following the Bolshevik Revolution marked an early period of cultural consolidation for the Finno-Ugric people in the Soviet Union and Europe. For the newly independent states of Finland, Estonia, and Hungary, the 1920s brought a burgeoning of cross-border cooperation in the form of societies, associations, and Congresses, all in the name of Finno-Ugric links. For the Finno-Ugric people of the Soviet Union, the 1920s were "a time of national awakening" (Saarinen, 2001, p. 46). In general, the political will in both the newly independent Estonia and in the Soviet Union supported the development of national languages. Informed by efforts to secure national development (in Estonia) and to further cultural nationalism (in the Soviet Union), the 1920s marked a watershed in corpus and status planning for Finno-Ugric languages; standard written forms were developed for most of the languages, the government offered subsidized publication in native languages, and use of the languages expanded into political and educational spheres.

The introduction, support, and development for mother-tongue instruction established a foundation for national-identity sustenance through the later Soviet period. In Finland, Estonia, and Hungary, native-language education extended from kindergarten through the university. The use of the native language[4] as a medium of instruction (MOI) in the Soviet Union ranged, by the early 1930s, from having a strong presence in Mordvin schools, where by 1935–1936 mother-tongue instruction was offered through the tenth grade (Kreindler, 1985, p. 245), to being absent in other Finno-Ugric national schools like those of the Karelians, who never achieved Karelian MOI in their Autonomous Republic (Pyöli, 1998, p. 129).[5] A turning point and decline in native-language instruction occurred in the years leading up to and after World War II. For the Finno-Ugric people in Russia, the repressions of the late 1930s eradicated many of the gains in native-language education and, in several places, destroyed the native intelligentsia involved in language development (primarily through execution[6] and deportation). By the 1960s, many native-language schools were closed and the MOI shifted to, in some cases exclusively, Russian (Saks, 2006, p. 60). An exception to this Russification trend was the network of Mari and Mordvin native-language elementary schools (Lallukka, 2001, p. 19). After the Soviet Union's occupation of Estonia, its educational system was also used as a primary institution for Russification with an increased number of hours earmarked for Russian-language instruction in Estonian-medium schools.[7]

The expansion of the Soviet Union fractured and reconfigured transnational Finno-Ugric culture. The strong post-World War I Finno-Ugric academic networks and opportunities for Russian-based fieldwork were largely terminated from the late 1930s until Stalin's death, an era when "Pan-Finnism" was a serious charge (Kreindler, 1985, p. 249). As a result of Soviet rule, the networks supporting Finno-Ugric culture developed separately in Estonia, which became the Soviet center of Finno-Ugric studies, and in Finland, where Finno-Ugric research and academic growth continued without restriction, at times incorporating banned material produced by Estonians in the USSR. In the final years of the Soviet Union, with the ease of communication under glasnost, transnational communication strengthened particularly with Finland, and the Finno-Ugric people of the Soviet Union began to experience a second phase of national awakening.

The third phase, a rebirth of a transnational Finno-Ugric linguistic culture in the post-Soviet era, incorporates the scientific and academic activities reminiscent of the first phase,[8] but also grafts on an explicit political dimension to cultural and academic activities. Toomas Ilves, the current Estonian President, noted this cultural transformation in his 2008 speech at the World Congress of Finno-Ugric People in Khanty-Mansiysk

(Russia), "Language, and the presentation and development of languages, are truly important. But this can only occur successfully when we are engaged not in a narrow philological activity or garnishing for avcational [sic.] ethnography, but a socially encompassing, in other words political, theme" (paragraph 6). A new period of transnational political involvement with language maintenance, development, and education has begun with the collapse of the Soviet Union. Since 1991, the Finno-Ugric people of Russia and Europe have turned to international organizations in an attempt to protect national languages: "The World Congress confirms that protection of human rights, the rights of indigenous peoples and national minorities is not only the issue of the domestic policies of states but of the entire international community." The World Congress resolutions, in particular, advocate the use of international instruments, particularly the ILO Convention (No. 169) concerning Indigenous and Tribal Peoples in Independent Countries, and the European Charter for Regional or Minority Languages (ECRML) through calls for state ratification to protect the rights, cultures, and languages of minority and indigenous people.[9] Finno-Ugric scholars, language activists, and members of the Consultative Committee[10] now couch concerns about the non-state kindred people in global terms and concerns; regular references are made, for example, to the right to self-determination and the problems of indigenous people (Resolution of the 5th World Congress of Finno-Ugric Peoples, 2008, paragraph 2). Within this international framework, Finno-Ugric commitments to policies like mother-tongue instruction are discussed as a universal human right:

> Based on the principle that every human being has the right to get education in its own mother tongue, it is necessary to continue to support the establishment of educational facilities which apply mother tongue in the educational process (from basic to higher) and to expand their educational opportunities. (Resolution of the 3rd World Congress of Finno-Ugric People, 2000, point III)

The appeal to international commitments and global concerns marks the transformation in the presentation of Finno-Ugric culture as one linked with indigenous concerns and minority rights.

In addition to the role of international organizations in promoting and protecting the Finno-Ugric linguistic culture, the Finno-Ugric nation-states of Estonia, Finland, and Hungary have taken on explicit socio-political obligations vis-à-vis their non-state "kindred" people, particularly those living in Russia. The three countries' membership in the EU (Estonia and Hungary in 2004; Finland in 1995) brought new protections and resources for their national languages and fresh opportunities to infuse support for the non-state Finno-Ugric languages. The tripartite Finno-Ugric membership in the EU is conceived as one path to facilitate cooperation with Russia on issues of linguistic culture. For example, the Estonian parliamentary Foreign Affairs Committee has repeatedly called for ways "to deepen cooperation between the EU's Finno-Ugric member nations, that is Estonia, Finland and Hungary, and Russia to coordinate and implement through joint efforts state programs devised to help kindred peoples" (Estonian Review, 2006, paragraph 5). The three states have joined political forces in the EU and the COE to advocate for increased European attention to the monitoring of minority protections and the establishment of cultural programs for Finno-Ugric people in Russia. Evidence of this multilateral cooperation is the three-year program (2009–2011), "Minorities in Russia," sponsored by the European Commission, the COE, and the Russian Federation, to support Russia's native peoples. President Ilves (2008) readily takes credit for the Finno-Ugric States' influence in drawing Europe's attention to their kindred concerns:

> The European Union and its members are the motor that has driven the harmonization of protections for minority rights in Europe. And, we might now ask, would Finno-Ugric concerns be on the European agenda if Hungary, Finland, and Estonia were not members of the Union? Hardly. (Paragraph 34)

Finno-Ugric state advocacy with the COE has centered on concerns about the state of native-language education for their kindred people. Detailed reports (document no. 8126, 1998 and no. 11087, 2006) submitted to the COE's Parliamentary Assembly by Finnish and Estonian rapporteurs highlight problematic aspects of mother-tongue instruction in Russia.[11] The 1998 Report on "Endangered Uralic Minority Cultures" finds Russian to be the language of instruction in most of the Finno-Ugric autonomous areas with little, if any, native language MOI. The COE's Committee on Culture, Science and Education drew attention to five primary problems regarding Finno-Ugric native-language schools: (1) "lack of mother tongue education at all levels"; (2) "few hours of mother tongue instruction (less than foreign languages)"; (3) "Finno-Ugric languages are not compulsory for non-natives"; (4) "School closings in villages (Finno-Ugrics are village dwellers)"; and (5) "lack of learning materials of sufficient quality and in sufficient numbers" (Saks, 2006). The possible strategies to address this situation include increasing access to mother-tongue instruction at the elementary, secondary, and postsecondary levels; improving teacher-training in these languages; enhancing the quality and availability of native-language learning materials; and exploring immersion programs "in order to help children of Finno-Ugric peoples to recover fluency in their ancestral languages" (Council of Europe (COE), 2006, points 10.8–10.10). The World Congress's Consultative Committee echoes the COE suggestions and finds that "To preserve peoples, it is not enough to teach the native language as a separate subject. It is necessary to expand the network of national schools, and the first step, to increase the number of hours provided in the curriculum for teaching the national language" (Resolution of the 4th World Congress of Finno-Ugric Peoples, 2004, paragraph 16).

VIGNETTES

In the following section, I examine the key role of Finno-Ugric identity in Estonian efforts to sustain LUL instruction domestically and to support its development internationally. I provide three vignettes of Estonia's varied experiences with LUL advocacy and development, and explore the ways Finno-Ugric linguistic culture functions as a rich resource in developing Estonian national identity, in making statements of ethnic solidarity, and in providing new methods for language revitalization. The contemporary hurdles in maintaining the culture, including intractable educational systems and the distancing of contemporary school children from their kindred relatives, emerge as well from these overviews.

Vignette #1: Estonian State as Global Advocate

The Estonian government, in sustaining the Finno-Ugric linguistic culture, simultaneously invests in developing and defining contemporary Estonian identity. To be sure, Estonians are fully "European" in their state's commitment to freedom and democracy. President Ilves (2008), in his call for a new basis of cooperation across Finno-Ugric people, highlighted these shared European cultural elements of the state-based Finno-Ugric people, "cooperation will come to rest upon a strong foundation, upon common values. Hungarians, Finns and Estonians have chosen so-called European values, which today manifest themselves in the use of liberal democracy to order society" (paragraph 18). While European, the government also declares "... Estonians are Finno-Ugrians" (Kindred Peoples Programme, 1999–2004, p. 2). The identification with other Finno-Ugrians helps not only to define, but also to protect Estonian national identity:

> Besides the European segment, our culture is also based on our old Finno-Ugric folk culture having much in common with the cultures of other Uralic peoples. The kindred peoples form an inevitable cultural rear, the need for which is especially pressing today as cultural influences from the West have become predominant. (Kindred Peoples Programme, 1999–2004, point 0.1)

In this positioning of Estonia, the notion of "co-guardianship" emerges with the Eastern kindred peoples helping to guard Estonian culture from the powerful Western influences and, as I explain below, the Estonians helping to protect the Finno-Ugric cultures from Russification.

As both Europeans and Finno-Ugrians, the Estonian government recognizes its new responsibilities in the post-Soviet era; Estonia has become an advocate for non-state Finno-Ugric people. Former Estonian President Meri (1995) acknowledged this new role in his speech to the World Congress of Finno-Ugric People where he declared "our responsibilities ... are totally different from the romantic kindred peoples movement of the beginning of the century." As a Finno-Ugric nation-state, Estonia, along with Finland and Hungary, has a new obligation to channel the diplomatic and financial resources of the government to aid cultural preservation of the Finno-Ugric people, particularly in Russia. As the Estonian Parliament's Foreign Affairs Committee (Estonian Review, 2006) noted "Estonia has to express its support for Finno-Ugric people of Russia more forcefully and give stronger support to activities aimed at protecting their language and culture" (paragraph 3). The Estonian state has developed at least three different strategies, which I review below, to advocate for the development and protection of Finno-Ugric culture: Disseminating the Estonian model of national development, publicizing on the world stage Russia's treatment of Finno-Ugric people, and investing in a bilateral educational program.

One approach to sustaining the linguistic culture has been the dissemination of an Estonian model for national-identity development to non-state Finno-Ugric people. The Estonian government has identified historic parallels between the Estonians' early stages of national consciousness and the current development of Russian-based kindred people. This correspondence has inspired the government to promote the Estonian model as a possible path for cultural and national development. Former President Meri (1995) observed:

> Out of the 23 Uralic peoples only three have been able to establish their own states. Current social expectations of the Finno-Ugric people living in the Russian Federation can be compared to the feelings of national awakening among Estonians, Finns and Hungarians during the last century. They are looking at us. We have academic and even political responsibility to meet their expectations. (Paragraph 8)

In this Hrochian perspective on national development (Raun, 2003, p. 136), the Estonian government has an obligation to help raise "Finno-Ugrians' self-consciousness" (Estonian Review, 2006, paragraph 4) just as the Finns provided a model for the Estonians in the late 19th century (Raun, 2003, p. 134). The Estonian government has disseminated the model rhetorically at pan-Finno-Ugric meetings. President Ilves' (2008) delivered a bold call at the most recent World Congress for non-state Finno-Ugric nations to consider the Estonian example:

> Freedom and democracy were our choice 150 years ago, when not even the poets dreamt of an Estonian state. Many Finno-Ugric peoples have yet to make this choice. As a small aside it bears mentioning, particularly in light of the example of Estonia, that once you have tasted freedom, you will realize how much of it is sacrificed in the name of surviving or just 'getting by.' (Paragraphs 20–21)

In addition to this public invitation to consider the Estonian model, the government has earmarked funds for the material distribution of documentaries and other historic materials portraying the Estonian model: "Organisations and centres of Uralic indigenous peoples should be provided with video materials on Estonia. These should include copies of films made about Finno-Ugrian peoples as well as films on how Estonia gained independence, minorities in Estonia, Estonian economy. ... " (Kindred Peoples Programme, 1999–2004, point. 1.3, paragraph 3). In distributing these visual materials, the government embraces the notion that sharing Estonia's path to (re)independence and aspects of current statehood might help to enlighten and inspire the kindred people of Russia.

A second Estonian strategy for embracing its new responsibility for non-state kindred people is to draw global attention to Russia's treatment of Finno-Ugric people. The government has particularly focused on Russia's policy toward native-language education. From the Estonian government's perspective, an improvement in the native-language education helps not only to revitalize Finno-Ugric nations and languages, but also to support the democratic development of Russia. Former President Meri (2000) suggested that native-language education "would be a loyal way for the

Finno-Ugric nations to support the democratization of the Russian Federation with their cultural contribution and creativity. [The] Future always begins with education" (paragraph 5). Meri (2000) highlights in this proposal the notion that support for native-language education is not something threatening to Russia; in fact, investment in this policy reveals one's civic loyalty and commitment to the country's democratic future. A more critical tack was taken by Katrin Saks, an Estonian representative to the European Parliament (2006–2009) and the COE's Rapporteur on Finno-Ugric peoples in the Russian Federation (2003–2006), who offered this assessment of Russia's policy:

> The Russians have repeatedly emphasized that the problems of the Finno-Ugric people are not anything special, they are in the same situation as others. In this way, the Russians are right – all of the minorities have this problem because Russia, for some reason, does not believe in the possibility of multilingualism and plurality of identities. (Saks, 2008, p. 8)

In this passage, Saks used the universality of the Finno-Ugric plight to criticize the problematic aspects of Russia's policies toward other minorities.

A third state approach to cultural advocacy is the development of a bilateral program to assist in the cultural and educational development of Finno-Ugric people. The Estonian government has established and funded three iterations of the multiyear Kindred People's Programme (1999–2004, 2005–2009, and 2010–2014) similar to the Finnish state-sponsored bilateral program supporting linguistic cultural development and education of kindred people.[12] The program, framed initially as part of Estonia's contribution to the United Nations' Decade of Indigenous People (1995–2004), supports the linguistic and cultural development of Uralic (i.e., Finno-Ugric and Samoyed) people living in the Russian Federation and Latvia. Education plays a significant role in these programs with the Estonian government funding the education of over 100 Finno-Ugric students at Estonian universities since 1999.[13] The bilateral program also functions as a foreign affairs' tool. In part, the program strives to clarify and correct any Russian misunderstandings about the state of minority affairs in Estonia. The program states, "Via the Finno-Ugrians of the Russian Federation, a positive opinion of Estonia should be moulded. This would include sharing truthful information to the kindred peoples on the position of ethnic minorities in Estonia" (Kindred Peoples Programme, point 1.3, paragraph 3). This word-of-mouth diplomacy via education helps to counterpoint any misinformation and to illustrate the complementary purposes of supporting the development of Finno-Ugric linguistic culture.

Vignette #2: A Primer-Based Rapprochement

In addition to Finno-Ugric linguistic culture acting as a rich resource in protecting Estonian national identity and developing the state as a global advocate, language activists also draw on the culture to make statements of ethnic solidarity. As mentioned in the introduction to the chapter, Estonia represents a unique case to consider the sustained meaningfulness of Finno-Ugric linguistic culture since the state is home to two ethnic Estonian groups – Estonians who speak the standard language and the Võro, ethnic Estonians who typically speak both Estonian and, to varying degrees, the regional language of Võro. Similar to other small Finno-Ugric languages, Võro is endangered; it has experienced significant language shift over the 20th century with a decline in language transfer from generation to generation. Researchers estimate that 50,000 to 70,000 Estonians (approximately 5% of the ethnic Estonian population) speak the regional language, which has benefitted from 15 years of state financial support (1995–2010) to further revitalization and research. One of the primary avenues of state assistance is the subsidizing of a voluntary Võro regional-language program in about half of the schools in the region where the language is spoken.

As a small language in a state with an endangered official language, the Võro are sensitive to issues of ethnic solidarity, yet also strive to cultivate a distinct regional identity. Content analysis of core material used in elementary regional-language classrooms – the Võro-language primer, *ABC Kiräoppus* (Sullõv, Ülle, Kõivupuu, Reimann, & Hagu, 1998) and the companion teacher's guide to the primer, *ABC tiijuht' kiräoppusõ manoq* (Reimann, 2000) – illustrate the way text-based rapprochement with kindred people simultaneously functions to position the Võro as part of both the Estonian and Finno-Ugric communities through the use of familial terms and cultural parallels. By invoking the Finno-Ugric connection in instructional material, the Institute expresses the autochthonous community's membership in the Estonian "we," while also making connections, as a distinct group, with other "small" Finno-Ugric people in Europe and Russia.

The Võro are positioned as members of the Finno-Ugric language family through the careful development of linguistic and cultural connections. The Võro Institute recognizes that despite the general bond Estonians feel with kindred nations, both teachers and students may be unfamiliar with their Finno-Ugric relatives. The regional-language educational material encourages teachers to acquaint their class with other Finno-Ugric peoples, their stories, and their fates. The regional-language textbook serves as a tool of cultural rapprochement. The Võro-language teachers' guide urges teachers to bring Finno-Ugric people into the classroom to help students hear their stories first hand, "Every autumn there are kinship days (*hõimupääväq*). With the help of 'Fenno-Ugria' [an NGO-based in Tallinn] you can also invite singer-dancer kinsmen to your school. The teacher should speak about who these guests are, where they come from, and how they are our relatives" (Reimann, 2000, p. 54).[14] To assist in preparing students for these visits or other lessons incorporating kindred people, the Võro-language teachers' guide includes lists of additional recommended readings and web sites on Finno-Ugric peoples (Reimann, 2000, p. 60).

One of the ways textbook authors establish solidarity with Estonians and other Finno-Ugric nations is through the use of kinship language. Familial terms, like relative, family, and kinsmen, bridge the territorial distance between the Finno-Ugric people and evoke a bond based on language, and perhaps in the very distant past, blood.[15] The teachers' guide refers to the Finno-Ugric peoples as "our kinfolk" and "our relatives." The recommended questions for Võro-language instructors to pose in class reflect the extension of family terminology to other Finno-Ugric peoples:

> Who can name our kinfolk? Why are they considered to be our relatives? What do we have in common with them? ... Look on a map and find where our relatives live. How much time might it take to visit one or another of them? The most well known relatives are Finns. Do you know some Finnish words? What do you know about Finns? (Reimann, 2000, p. 157)

These questions reflect a strategy to regenerate the Finno-Ugric linguistic culture for a new generation (i.c., "Why are they considered our relatives?") and establish meaningful transnational connections in a new geopolitical order (i.e., "What do we have in common with them?"). Moreover, this passage underscores the unique connection between Estonians and Finns, who are the first among equals of Finno-Ugric kindred people.

An additional text-based strategy for establishing Finno-Ugric solidarity is through attention to cultural commonality. One shared element between the Võro and other Finno-Ugric speakers, according to the teachers' guide, is a universal belief system. "The Finno-Ugric people regard all that is around them equally and do not consider themselves to be superior to the rest of what was created" (Reimann, 2000, p. 110). The primer also points to the collective musical traditions of the Finno-Ugric people. A caption next to a photo of a Mari woman playing the zither, for example, highlights the common musical instruments of the two peoples, "The Mountain Mari Julia Kuprina plays the zither (*kannõld*) – in their language, zither (*kärsi*)" (Sullõv et al., 1998, p. 122). The juxtaposition of the Võro and Mari term for zither suggests that although the names differ, the people share the instrument and broader musical tradition.

A second common cultural element highlighted in school material is the Finno-Ugric sense of linguistic endangerment. Fateful stories of other Finno-Ugric nations function as a cautionary tale of what could become of related languages like Võro. The primer's closing story concentrates on a Kamas woman,[16] who speaks a language that is "a distant relative of the Võro-Seto language" and represents, to the story's author, a portentous tale for Finno-Ugric language-speakers and nations. The author, a well-known poet and author, Kauksi Ülle, recounts the details of a documentary featuring this Kamas woman she saw while a university student:

> An old Kamas woman stood alone in the middle of a mowed field and said something to herself that was almost soundless. The researcher, who was allowed to shoot the film, said that the old woman was saying something to her god because there was not anyone else left with whom to speak in her own language. I have this Kamas old woman on my mind whenever I speak, write, or teach Võro. She was also in front of my spiritual eye when I put together this ABC-book. I do not want this type of fate that she does not have another person with whom to speak her language. This is why you should speak your language as much as you are able. (Sullõv et al., 1998, p. 148)

The author, by invoking the image of the "last speaker," highlights personal responsibility in maintaining one's mother tongue. Thus, the primer story provides an example of the way transnational Finno-Ugric elements, represented here by the Kamas woman, serve to inspire and motivate local regional-language identity construction in southeastern Estonia.

Vignette #3: Language Nests as a Finno-Ugric Tradition

A final way the Finno-Ugric culture maintains relevance in the post-Soviet era is as a source for new methods of language revitalization. In particular, language nests, or immersion kindergartens, have emerged as a favored strategy to address Finno-Ugric language loss. The attempts of the Võro-language activists to found a language nest illustrate efforts to reshape "international trends ... to local ends" (Arnove, 1999, p. 3). Language nests are early-childhood education programs premised on the idea that an older person, who acts as language educator, speaks with a small group of children in his/her minority language; this native-language environment ideally helps to sustain the minority language by passing the language along to the next generation. The language nests, which originated in the 1980s in

New Zealand in an effort to revitalize the Maori language and then "traveled" to Hawaii as part of language renewal efforts, have quickly gained a foothold in the Finno-Ugric world as a potentially effective method to infuse early childhood education with native-language learning opportunities. The experiences of the Inari-Sámi (in Northern Finland) and Karelians (in Russia), in particular, have had great influence on regional-language nest experiments in southeastern Estonia. The Inari Sámi first experimented with language nests in 1993, opening programs in 1997. Karelian language nests, developed in cooperation with the Finns and modeled on the Inari experience, began in 2000 (Pasanen, 2009, p. 3). By 2004, two modified Karelian language nests had opened in Karelian villages (Mattheus, 2004), and, in September 2009, one Finnish and one Karelian language nest opened in the Karelian capital of Petrozavodsk.

Language nests have become the signature Finno-Ugric early-childhood language-learning method. The Finnish Government has emerged as a major proponent of the language nest approach and in 2006 began to finance (via its State kindred people's program) the development of language nests among Russia's Finno-Ugric peoples. The Finnish President, Tarja Halonen (2008, paragraphs 10–13) has acted as a major advocate of this method. In her welcoming speech to the 5th World Congress of Finno-Ugric People, Halonen concluded,

> ... we [the Finns] have learned to respect everyone's right to a native language and to understand that minority languages need support to survive and to develop as living languages. We have made particularly strong efforts to strengthen the position of the endangered Inari Sámi language. International cooperation has been a great help in this, as the much acclaimed 'language nest' method proved to be an excellent tool. ... Now we want to help others. In 2006, the Finnish Cultural Foundation launched a project to support the maintaining and saving of endangered Finno-Ugric languages in Russia. A decision has now been taken to extend this project by allocating more than one and a half million euros to the revival of small Finno-Ugric language communities. The tool used for this process is, once again, the language nest method.

Halonen's attention to the successful Finnish experience with the Inari Sámi and announcement of the allocation of financial support illustrates the leading role of the Finno-Ugric nation-states in providing a model for other states' investment in non-state kindred people. The Consultative Committee of the World Congress of Finno-Ugric People further endorsed language nests in its 2008 Resolution "to study the experiences of language revitalization for the Finno-Ugric and Samoyed minorities using the so-called language nest methods ... and develop its further dissemination" (paragraph 22).

The Võro-language nest idea emerged as a result of new, post-Soviet networks of Finno-Ugric educators and language activists. The educational ideas and experiments of other Finno-Ugric groups have informed the trajectory of several research and language projects since the Institute's foundation in 1995. When researchers and other activists became interested in developing a Võro-language nest in southeastern Estonia, they reached out to other Finno-Ugrians, especially the Karelians and Sámi, through visits (to the Karelian Republic of the Russian Federation), participation in conferences and casual communication in order to understand better the organization and impact of language nests. The Finno-Ugric experiences with language nests, as documented in papers such as Annika Pasanen's research report on the Inari Sámi, which was circulated to Võro Institute members in the early 21st century, serve not only as a useful project blueprint, but also as testimony to the language nest tradition among the Finno-Ugric peoples. The influence of the Finno-Ugric network on Võro language-nest planning is reflected in an NGO's application to fund language nests teachers' salaries, "The thought to create the Võro language nest arose in Karelia while visiting the Karelian language nests" (Ministry of Culture, 2010b). The rooting and pertinence of the language nest experience with other Finno-Ugric people adds familiar context and veracity to proposals to develop this approach in Estonia.

Regional-language nests in Estonia have emerged in a different form from their kindred counterparts in part due to the limitations imposed by existing educational and language laws. In Estonia, the pilot Võro-language nest, which opened in the fall 2009 for one day a week, is not part of the public-education system.[17] The language nest, a result of NGO and public institute cooperation (between the Võro Institute and the Hanja Men's Council), operates outside the public-education sphere, which allows teachers the freedom to maintain the one-language immersion approach. Within the public sphere, the exclusive use of the regional language is not possible; based on existing language laws, the state language (Estonian) must be offered in public schools even at the preschool level (also called "kindergarten" for three- to six-year olds in Estonia). Given these limitations, the Ministry of Education and Research would allow the establishment of a regional-language nest only with parallel Estonian instruction. Pasanen (2009) reports similar systemic troubles with developing language nests in Russia where preschool children are required to learn Russian as a state language, "Relying on this [the language regulation], the Karelian Education Ministry has not let the language nest work like they should with the children speaking only in the minority language from the beginning in their groups" (p. 3). Due to these Russian regulations, the Karelian-based language nests operate on a modified immersion model, but within the public sphere, with one teacher speaking to the children in Russian and the other in the target minority (i.e., Karelian, Finnish, etc.) language.

Although the organization of a Võro-language nest meets systemic limitations in the public sphere, the Estonian government had expressed ideological and financial support for native-language early childhood education through programmatic assistance. The Director of the Language at the Ministry of Education reflects this enthusiasm in his statement that the instruction of the "dialect language" to nursery school children is in "every possible way a positive phenomenon" if it is taught alongside standard Estonian and voluntarily (Mattheus, 2004). Currently, the Estonian Government translates this support for language nests into programmatic development and funding. The Old Võrumaa (Vana Võrumaa) Cultural Program: 2010–2013, for example, specifically mentions the program's intentions to support the widening of support for the use of Võro language on the basis of a language-nest or playgroup model (Ministry of Culture, 2010a, p. 10). The language nests' dependence on programmatic funds are evidence of the "competitive market model of language policy" in Estonia, "in which individuals or organisations in civil society compete to implement projects connected within a general programme framework developed by the Ministry of Culture" (Brown, 2009, p. 141). The market model makes language nests unstable, however, in part due to the lack of a comprehensive LUL language policy, but also, because programs can be canceled due to lack of funds, leadership, or support. The instability of language nests has been a concern in Finland as well where five ministries within the Finnish Government recently announced (June 2010) joint efforts to secure permanent state funding for the Sámi language nests (operating in Inari, Skolt, and Northern Sámi).

DISCUSSION AND CONCLUSION

The sustained pertinence and intellectual investment in the transnational Finno-Ugric identity illustrates the enduring cultural links across European and Eurasian space. The political reconfigurations following the collapse of the Soviet Union ushered in a new era in the development of the Finno-Ugric linguistic culture. European resources and the advocacy position of three independent Finno-Ugric states hold potential for infusing energy into this 18th century cultural idea. In this chapter, I have suggested ways that the Finno-Ugric identity has become newly relevant in the post-Soviet context from an Estonian vantage point. Conceptually, Schiffman's notion of a linguistic culture helps to frame the renewed sense of belonging, or at least, a return to the shared linguistic Finno-Ugric culture across different nations and ethnicities. A defining element of this culture is "being small," a common worldview informing a sense of linguistic vulnerability. For Estonia, independence, occupation, and membership in the EU have transformed the state's and nation's relationship to non-state Finno-Ugric peoples with the most recent political developments, bringing new resources and possibilities for international advocacy in multiple spheres.

The Finno-Ugric linguistic culture has survived and thrived in the 21st century, in part, due to the dynamic nature of the culture in Estonia. Rather than representing a staid, two century-old idea, Finno-Ugric culture changes and accommodates multiple expressions due to its broad, defining parameters. In the case of Estonia, I argue the Finno-Ugric linguistic culture remains relevant, in part, because it allows those who embrace it to accomplish several goals. The chapter's three vignettes illustrate the varied ways that establishing and promoting the Finno-Ugric connection also assist in (1) reaffirming Estonian national identity as both European and Finno-Ugric and positioning the state as global guardian; (2) transmitting messages of national solidarity and distinct regional identity; and (3) promoting new strategies for LUL education. These three snapshots provide evidence of the way that educational advocacy intersects with foreign policy, domestic politics, and nation-building.

Finally, this chapter suggests that the Finno-Ugric linguistic culture provides a basis for considering language education as a justified and active sphere for transnational involvement. A significant component in the renewed relevance of the Finno-Ugric linguistic culture is advocacy for education in native languages. The proposed use of Finno-Ugric languages as the MOI represents one strategy to address the progressive assimilation and cultural loss among the varied national groups of Europe and Asia. This analysis reveals, however, the ways the persistent politics of education threatens to thwart gains made via this strategy. Whether native-language instruction represents a challenge to existing notions of civic loyalty, contradicts the "logic" of voluntary assimilation, or runs counter to protective state-language policies, a shift in current educational policy signals a potentially potent, and in some cases, unwelcome, sociopolitical change. Tsui and Tollefson (2004) address the politics of an MOI shift:

"Medium-of-instruction policy ... is a key means of power (re)distribution and social (re)construction, as well as a key arena in which political conflicts among countries and ethnolinguistic, social, and political groups are realized" (p. 2). The vital intersection of Finno-Ugric linguistic culture and native-language instruction depends upon the continued redistribution of power and reconstruction of national identities in Europe and Asia.

NOTES

1. I use the term nation in this chapter to refer to a self-identified ethnic group; I am not using "nation" as a synonym for state. When the borders of the nation and state broadly overlap, I use the term nation-state as in the case of Estonia, Finland, and Hungary.

2. The student made this observation at the Võro Institute's annual conference, where the working languages were any of the Finno-Ugric language (without translation). Organizers included English as a conference language in 2005.

3. The World Congress of Finno-Ugric People is a gathering every four years in a different Finno-Ugric home territory of government authorities (including Presidents) and select international organizations to share status reports, deliver academic findings, and make policy recommendations. For more information of the Congresses in English see the Fenno-Ugria web page http://www.fennougria.ee/index.php?id = 10973.

4. The use of the term "native" for an ethnic group's national language becomes increasingly complicated during the 20th century as the mother tongue of more Finno-Ugric nations shifts to Russian. As a result of this change, a nation's "native" language might be Russian. Although this is the sociolinguistic dynamics common to several Finno-Ugric nations, when I use "native" or "mother-tongue" instruction in this chapter, I am referring to the language sharing the group's eponym.

5. National schools refer to a school that follows a curriculum that includes the native language and subjects related to the national group (e.g., history, literature, etc.).

6. Saarinen (2001) reports that in 1937 and 1938 all the writers belonging to the Mari Autonomous Soviet Socialist Republic were shot (p. 47).

7. Several area studies scholars note the detrimental impact of Krushchev's educational reforms of 1958–1959.

8. Among the examples of the scientific and academic activities of this third phase are the founding of the Finno-Ugrian Program at Tartu University (Estonia), the meeting International Finno-Ugric Students' Conference, and the regular gathering of Finno-Ugric Writers.

9. Finland and Hungary both ratified (in 1994 and 1995, respectively) and put the ECRML into effect (both in 1998). Russia signed the Charter in 2001, but has yet to ratify it; Estonia has not yet signed the ECRML.

10. The Consultative Committee, composed of an equal number of representatives from each of the Finno-Ugric peoples, refers to the coordinating body of the World Congress of Finno-Ugrian Peoples.

11. The COE has further addressed joint Finno-Ugric concerns in Recommendation no. 1775 (2006) and Resolution no. 1171 (1998), which highlight the decline in opportunities for native-language education.

12. As early as 1992, Finland had signed a treaty with Russia to support the Finnish kindred peoples through underwriting cultural and linguistic preservation programs; a state program of support, launched in 1994 from this initial agreement. Estonia's Kindred People's Program has been in effect since 1999.

13. The Kindred Programme III document provides (in Estonian) a useful overview of the ethnic background, site of enrollment, and completion rates for these students.

14. The Pan-Fenno-Ugrian Days, held in Estonia since 1988, and in some of the Finno-Ugric Republics of Russia as well, are traditionally celebrated on the third weekend of October. The days are full of concerts, literary evenings, cultural workshops, and exhibits.

15. To be sure, these terms are used in standard Estonian publications as well. An example of this particular use of language is the title of a newspaper article reviewing the highlights of the 2004 World Finno-Ugric Congress – Congress as a Family Reunion [Kongress nagu suguvõsa kokkutulek] (Mõttus, 2004).

16. Kamas was a Samoyedic language spoken in the Russian Federation. Like Estonian, Kamas is in the Uralic language family, but while Estonian is in the Finno-Ugric language group, Kamas in the Samoyedic language group. Both the Finno-Ugric and Samoyedic language groups constitute the Uralic language group (Raun, 1991, p. 5).

17. The first Võro-language nest opened in 2004, but, by the language-activists' own description, this was more of a one-language playgroup. For more on the history of Võro language nests, see http://keelepesa.haanimaa.ee/

REFERENCES

Arnove, R. (1999). Reframing comparative education: The dialectic of the global and the local. In: R. F. Arnove & C. A. Torres (Eds), *Comparative education: The dialectic between the global and the local* (pp. 1–24). Lanham, MD: Rowman and Littlefield.

Branch, M. (1993). The Finno-Ugrian peoples. In: L. Honko, S. Timonen & M. Branch (Eds), *The great bear: A thematic anthology of oral poetry in the Finno-Ugrian languages* (pp. 25–41). Helsinki: Finnish Literature Society.

Brown, K. D. (2009). Market models of language policy: A view from Estonia. *European Journal of Language Policy, 1*(2), 137–146.

Council of Europe. (2006). Recommendation no. 1775 Situation of Finno-Ugric and Samoyed Peoples. Available at http://assembly.coe.int/main.asp?Link = /documents/adoptedtext/ta06/erec1775.htm

Estonian Review. (2006). Parliament panel wishes Estonia to house Finno-Ugric Centre. Available at http://www.estemb.org/news/estonian_review/aid-2741. Retrieved June 7, 2010.

Halonen, T. (2008). Address by President of the Republic of Finland Tarja Halonen at the opening session of the V World Congress of the Finno-Ugric Peoples in Khanty-Mansiysk. Available at http://www.tpk.fi/Public/default.aspx?contentid = 177565&nodeid = 41416&contentlan = 2&culture = en-US. Retrieved on June 28, 2010.

Ilves, T. (2008). President of the Republic at the 5th World Congress of Finno-Ugric Peoples in Khanty-Mansiysk. Available at http://www.president.ee/print.me.pho?gid=115783. Retrieved on June 28, 2010.

Kasten, E. (1999). *Bicultural education in the north: Ways of preserving and enhancing indigenous peoples' languages and traditional knowledge.* Münster: Waxmann.

Kindred Peoples Programme. (1999–2004). (*Hõimurahvaste Programm: 1999–2004*). Available at http://www.ut.ee/Ural/ariste/proging.html

Kindred Peoples Programme III. (2010–2014). (*Hõimurahvaste Programm III: 2010–2014*). Available at http://www.fennougria.ee/index.php?id=18997.

Kreindler, I. T. (1985). The Mordvinian language: A survival saga. In: I. T. Kreindler (Ed.), *Sociolinguistic perspectives on Soviet national languages: Their past, present and future* (pp. 237–264). Berlin: Mouton de Gruyter.

Lallukka, S. (2001). Finno-Ugrians of Russia: Vanishing cultural communities? *Nationalities Papers, 29*(1), 9–39.

Lo Bianco, J. (1999). The language of policy: What sort of policy making is the officialization of English in the U.S.? In: T. Huebner, K. A. Davis & J. Lo Bianco (Eds), *Sociopolitical perspectives on language policy and planning in the USA* (pp. 39–66). Philadelphia: John Benjamins.

Mattheus, Ü. (2004). Lõunaeesti keele programm rõhub lastele [*Southern Estonian language program weighs on children*]. *Postimees, 5*(May 14), 14.

Meri, L. (1995). Speech by President Meri at the opening of the 8th International Finno-Ugric Congress in University of Jyväskylä on August 10, 1995. Available at http://vp1992-2001.vpk.ee/eng/PrinditavDokument.asp?ID=9348. Retrieved on May 26, 2010.

Meri, L. (2000). President of the Republic on the Opening of the 9th International Congress of Finno-Ugric Studies in Tartu. Available at http://vp1992-2001.vpk.ee/eng/PrinditavDokument.asp?ID=3768. Retrieved on May 26, 2010.

Ministry of Culture of Estonia. (2010a). (*Vana Võrumaa Kultuuriprogramm: 2010–2013*). [Old Võrumaa Cultural Program]. Available at http://www.kul.ee/index.php?path=0×214×1719.

Ministry of Culture of Estonia. (2010b). Riigieelarvelise Toetuse Taotlus. [Application for support from the State budget] (Document no. 1164). Available at https://kule.kul.ee/avalik/Vana_Vorumaa_KP/Vana%20vorumaa/Haanimiihhi%20novvokoda_palk.pdf

Moore, D. C. (2006). Is the post- in postcolonial the post- in post-Soviet? Toward a global postcolonial critique. In: V. Kelertas (Ed.), *Baltic postcolonialism* (pp. 11–43). New York: Rodopi.

Mõttus, A. (2004). Kongress nagu suguvõsa kokkutulek [*Congress like a family tree reunion*]. *Õpetajate Leht, 28*(August 21), 1.

Pasanen, A. (2009). Annika Pasanen: Keelepesade punumine Venemaal pole kerge [*Annika Pasanen: Weaving language nests in Russia is not easy*]. *Fenno-Ugria Teataja, 4*(October), 3.

Pyöli, R. (1998). Karelian under pressure from Russian – Internal and external Russification. *Journal of Multilingual and Multicultural Development, 19*(2), 128–141.

Raun, T. U. (1991). *Estonia and the Estonians* (2nd ed.). Stanford, CA: Hoover Institution Press.

Raun, T. U. (2003). Nineteenth- and early twentieth-century Estonian nationalism revisited. *Nations and Nationalism, 9*(1), 129–147.

Raun, T. U. (2009). Estonia after 1991. *East European Politics and Societies, 23*(4), 526–534.

Reimann, N. (2000). *ABC tiijuht' kiräoppusõ manoq [Guide to accompany ABC primer]*. Võru: Võro Instituut'.

Resolution of the 3rd World Congress of Finno-Ugric Peoples. (2000). Available at http://www.fennougria.ee/index.php?id = 16734. Retrieved on April 30, 2010.

Resolution of the 4th World Congress of Finno-Ugric Peoples. (2004). Available at http://www.fennougria.ee/index.php?id = 16734. Retrieved on April 30, 2010.

Resolution of the 5th World Congress of Finno-Ugric Peoples. (2008). Available http://www.fennougria.ee/index.php?id = 14478. Retrieved on April 30, 2010.

Rüütel, A. (2004). The President of the Republic at the Opening of the IV World Congress of the Finno-Ugric Peoples in Tallinn on August 16 2004. Available at http://vp2001-2006.vpk.ee/print.dokument.pho?gid = 52329. Retrieved on May 26, 2010.

Saarinen, S. (2001). The myth of a Finno-Ugric community in practice. *Nationalities Papers, 29*(1), 41–52.

Saks, K. (2006). Situation of Finno-Ugric and Samoyed Peoples. Council of Europe Parliamentary Assembly (Doc. 11087). Committee on Culture, Science and Education. Available at http://www.mari.ee/eng/scien/topical/Katrin_Saks_Report.html.

Saks, K. (2008). Katrin Saks jälgib soomeugrilasi rahvusvaheliselt areenilt *[Katrin Saks monitors the Finno-Ugric people from an international stage]*. *Fenno-Ugria Teataja, 1*, 4.

Schiffman, H. (2006). Language policy and linguistic culture. In: T. Ricento (Ed.), *An introduction to language policy: Theory and method* (pp. 111–125). Malden, MA: Blackwell.

Schiffman, H. F. (1996). *Linguistic culture and language policy*. London: Routledge.

Sullõv, J., Ülle, K., Kõivupuu, M., Reimann, N., & Hagu, P. (1998). *ABC Kiräoppus [ABC primer]*. Võro: Võro Instituut' ja Võro Selts VKKF.

Taagepera, R. (1999). *The Finno-Ugric republics and the Russian state*. New York: Routledge.

Tsui, A. B. M., & Tollefson, J. W. (2004). The centrality of medium-of-instruction policy in sociopolitical processes. In: J. W. Tollefson & A. B. M. Tsui (Eds), *Medium of instruction policies: Which agenda? Whose agenda?* (pp. 1–18). Mahwah, NJ: Lawrence Erlbaum.

Yanik, L. (2004). The politics of educational exchange: Turkish education in Eurasia. *Europe-Asia Studies, 56*(2), 293–307.

PART II
EDUCATION AND POST-SOCIALIST
TRANSFORMATIONS WORLDWIDE

THE RECONFIGURATION OF STATE–UNIVERSITY–STUDENT RELATIONSHIPS IN POST/SOCIALIST CHINA

Heidi Ross, Ran Zhang and Wanxia Zhao

The emergence of China on the global stage is balanced against the struggles of the Chinese to stage their arrival as postsocialist subjects. (Zhang & Ong, 2008, p. 1)

INTRODUCTION

The People's Republic of China might seem a coy partner to this volume's counterparts. Even though market socialism may represent a "counter-revolution" (Whyte, 2010a), China has not experienced an ideological rupture formalized in name since the one that made socialism stick, and that one was orchestrated by Mao Zedong, whose legacy still influences post/socialist China (Wright, 2010). How do we read the "post" of post-socialism when China's state/party complex has not retired its socialist label? Our answer is partially rhetorical: condition post/socialism with a back slash to denote the state's ambiguous attachment to socialism. Still, no matter how path-dependent, "illiberally adaptable" (Pei, 2006), or different *in kind* from other post-socialisms (Liew, 2005; Wright, 2010) and Mao's China (Gries & Rosen, 2004), Chinese post/socialism is not exceptional. Rather, it captures a

Post-Socialism is not Dead: (Re)Reading the Global in Comparative Education
International Perspectives on Education and Society, Volume 14, 299–327
Copyright © 2010 by Emerald Group Publishing Limited
ISSN: 1479-3679/doi:10.1108/S1479-3679(2010)0000014014

"symptomatic moment of our world at the present time" (Liu, 2009, p. viii). Its formation and multi-vectored present have been shaped by dominant forces of global integration – commercialization and consumption, individualism and privatization, and competition (Stromquist, 2002). There is no local China that is not also global, and that "glocal" reality is one of the defining characteristics of post/socialism – and post/socialist higher education.

A related characteristic of Chinese post/socialism is the state's distribution of opportunity and uncertainty. The Chinese Communist Party (CCP) has honed its social imagination, political agility, and "deliberate institutional ambiguity" (Ho, 2004, p. 109) to hang on to a hybrid, shape-shifting socialism-or-is-it-capitalism with Chinese characteristics. Simultaneously ruling the People's Republic with an authoritarian grip and embracing the global market, China's structural adjustment and growth stamina are all the more remarkable as they have been achieved "in the face of formidable obstacles including inefficient state enterprises, ambiguous property rights, irrational prices, primitive transportation, and outmoded banking and securities facilities" (Perry & Selden, 2004, p. 1). The tightrope that supports the CCP's successful (and to the public largely convincing) balancing act sways across a continent anxiously engaged in deciding "what is institutionalized and what is not, what is participation and what is resistance, who is a challenger and who is a polity member, what citizenship entails and who enjoys it" (O'Brien & Li, 2006, p. 66).

As long as reactions to such questions depend on where one stands, there can be no definitive answer to what it means to be post/socialist and Chinese (Zhang & Ong, 2008, p. 19). For some, China's "postsocialism seeks to avoid a return to capitalism, no matter how much it may draw upon the latter to improve the performance of 'actually existing socialism'" (Dirlik, 1989, p. 364). Others describe Chinese post/socialism as a pragmatically adaptive, politically repressed neo-liberalism aimed at "containing societal challenges and maintaining its political monopoly" (Pei, 2006, p. 46). Placing Chinese post/socialism in a comparative framework, still others focus on why the majority of Chinese citizens "accept authoritarianism" (Wright, 2010) without "strong feelings of distributive injustice, of active rejection of the current system, or of nostalgia for the distributional policies of the planned socialist era" (Whyte, 2010b, p. 64). Indeed, Wright (2010) and Whyte (2010a) similarly conclude that China's state-led development, late industrialization, and socialist legacy have shaped the public's view of government authority, social mobility, and tolerance of social inequalities in such a way that together they "are more conducive to political stability than to instability" (Whyte, 2010b, p. 197).

Lastly, China "defies easy categorization ... along a capitalist/socialist axis" (Wasserstrom, 2010, pp. 96–97), because it is a moving target. China's engagement with socialism began well back in the 19th century and embodied a search for an alternative to colonial modernity, bureaucratic socialism, and capitalist subordination (Lin, 2006). Chinese post/socialism in deed (not name) was officially ushered in by the Third Plenum of the 11th Party Congress in 1978, which gave a green light to on-the-ground reforms already apace, such as the de-collectivization of agriculture, the growth of town and village enterprises, and labor mobility. We focus primarily on post/socialism after 1989, because of the significance to global post-socialisms of Tiananmen, and because it was during the 1990s that state-directed neo-liberal policies from above, globalization forces from without, and strong demands for access and accountability from below created a "perfect storm" for higher education reform (Ross & Lou, 2005).

We limit our discussion to postsecondary education because worldwide it is the most globally integrated level of schooling and therefore ideally situated to illustrate the opportunities and uncertainties of post/socialism. This focus allows us to rescue the school from the nation and highlight the importance of globalization and transnationalism in creating and confronting post/socialist educational challenges. Specifically, we examine shifts in the state–university–student relationship, the educational equivalent of the key relational shift that justifies the "post" in Chinese post/socialism: the state–society–individual relationship that accompanies state efforts to steer a path between state control and institutional autonomy; individualism and collectivism; nationalism and global citizenry; and economic development-alism and equity.

As the quintessential "pedagogical state" (Kaplan, 2006), China provides a keen lens for viewing the intertwining nature of these shifts. Universal faith in the power of schooling to enhance individual and familial advancement places education at the forefront of social policy. Alongside China's version of "it's the economy, stupid," a school system that is perceived to enhance equality of opportunity, fairly reward merit and hard work, and deliver on social mobility is a potent symbol of state legitimacy, and CCP leaders rarely underestimate education's exchange value within the political/market economy.

In the following pages, we provide an introduction to challenges and achievements of Chinese higher education and suggest how these resonate with major characteristics of post/socialism. This background provides context for our discussion of state–university–student relationships through two case studies, one on the development of college student grievance and rights consciousness, and one on reforms in student services administration. When looked at from the point of view of the Ministry of Education (MoE), we see that appropriation and implementation of policies and regulations shaping student rights and services are in partial contradiction with state policies to accelerate economic growth and bolster party authority. From the point of view of universities, we see institutions grappling with how to deliver on forward-looking structures and actions while navigating between the state's policy mandates and growing expectations and demands of their student and business stakeholders. From the point of view of students, we see how constrained agency, uncertainty, and the power of the credential motivates social praxis. At all levels of the state–institution–student relationship actors are employing pragmatic improvisation (a salient feature of post/socialism) captured by the well-known Chinese proverb "groping for stones to cross the river" (Ross & Lou, 2005). This saying is an apt metaphor for the tentative searching by state, institution, and individual for a safe foothold in the post/socialist world.

POST/SOCIALIST HIGHER EDUCATION WITH CHINESE CHARACTERISTICS

There is almost no literature on Chinese education, let alone on the state–university–student relationship, that is analyzed from the perspective of post-socialism.[1] Given China's volatile past and current technocratic, developmentalist policy environment, contemporary scholars understandably (and ironically) steer clear of "politicized" analysis. That said, if we conceive of post/socialist scholarship as concerned with changing relationships among the state, society, and individual actors, as well as with refutations of orthodox essentialisms associated with economic determinism, class struggle, and history-as-stages (Kipnis, 2008), then four themes highly relevant to higher education emerge from general scholarship on Chinese post/socialism: *globalization, gradualism, civic society, and a critique of holism*. These themes help us explain interrelated educational trends that affect the state–university–student relationship: the globalization, "massification," and stratification of higher education; the redefined role of the state in university governance and management; educational marketization and privatization; and the quest for meaning and (e)quality in and through higher education.

Post/Socialism and the Globalization, Massification, and Stratification of Higher Education

Gerry Postliglione (2003) has noted that in China, "There is an abiding faith in an appeal to international standards (*guoji jiegui*) as a means of salvation within the new economy" (p. 162). Indeed, while during the early reform period China was "still entangled with the Maoist morality and reason" (Liu, 2009, p. 133), the past two decades have seen alternate technologies of state and self growing up in the "cradle of global materiality and productivity" (p. 141). Educators and policymakers regularly refer to "globalization" to approximate the pedagogical and social means they believe will ensure China's engagement in an international knowledge economy.

One such means has been the massification of higher education. Until the late 1990s China's educational system had a low center of gravity. The base of China's educational pyramid relative to that of other developing countries was massive, as a result of aggressive state action in universalizing basic education (Ross, with contributions by Jingjing Lou, Lijing Yang, Olga Rybakova, & Phoebe Wakhunga, 2005). The top of the pyramid, however, was very narrow. In 1990, 3% of Chinese 18- through 22-year-olds were studying in tertiary institutions, compared with 8% in India; fewer than 1 of every 100 citizens was a college graduate. With China's integration into the global economy and the state's concomitant policy to support development through science and technology, higher education entered a phase of unprecedented expansion. Demand by families for educational opportunities far outstripped supply, and policymakers, anxious to promote spending among savings-conscious families, understood that higher education was one of the few "commodities" for which parents would loosen their purse strings. The Chinese labor market also provided the younger generation rates of return for tertiary training that were much higher than those of their parents. China's higher education gross enrollment rate reached 15% in the early 2000s and is now nearly 25%.

Massification has sharpened the status hierarchy of tertiary schools and increased institutional diversification and stratification. From 1995 to 1998 mergers, targeted funding, and a reduction of institutions run by central ministries culminated in the creation of a group of Project 211 (100 elite universities in the 21st century) tier-one institutions that now includes 116 universities forming the core of China's advanced knowledge system. Preferential support has also been directed to 43 most elite "985" universities, which aspire to becoming world class institutions.

Post/Socialism, Gradualism, and the Redefinition of the State's Role in Governing and Managing Higher Education

One of the signatures of post/socialist reform has been "*gradualism*, Chinese style" (Perry & Selden, 2004; Gries & Rosen, 2004). China's dismissal of shock therapy and embrace of gradual reform is generally thought to have safeguarded relative social stability, co-opted social actors who might otherwise have been resisters or more likely just sidelined, promoted sustained economic growth, and shored up the CCP's legitimacy in the eyes of Chinese citizens. Gradualism has also been criticized by some scholars as a form of "development autocracy" that benefits elites and perpetuates "a quasi-totalitarian political system" (Pei, 2006, p. 1). Xin Liu (2009) links state developmentalism to a "triumph of statistical reason" whose presence in China means that "The case for socialism as an alternative possibility of being and becoming seems to be closed" (p. 57).

Indeed, in the context of higher education, pragmatic gradualism in practice has meant "neoliberalism" with Chinese characteristics, in which the state plays a critical role in making "use of the non-state sector and to mobilize market forces to finance education" (Mok, 2003b, p. 208). That the post/socialist state plays a guiding role as educational "architect" and "regulator" will surprise few readers who have followed the processes and conditions of educational decentralization worldwide. Decentralization defined as the redistribution of power and responsibility has not necessarily meant that states do less.[2] It means that their role as "education service providers" changes "from carrying out most of the work of education itself to determining where work will be done, by whom and how" (Mok, 2003a, p. 213).

Since 1978, the state's reorganization of education has been primarily to support the economic policies associated with market socialism. As power was gradually decentralized during the 1980s and 1990s, provincial and local governments were allowed to retain part or most of their revenues and to decide how to spend them. Simultaneously, educational policies promoting decentralization expanded to include: (1) the reduction of the center's regulation and provision of education service; (2) the devolution of responsibility and power to localities; (3) the diversification of resources (i.e., multiple channels of funding, including tuition); and (4) enhanced flexibility and autonomy in institutional governance. After the 1985 *Decision of the Central Committee of the CCP on the Reform of the Educational System*, which aimed to reduce excessive government control and give higher education institutions more autonomy, institutions began to generate nonbudgetary funds through tuition, contracts, international assistance, such as World Bank loans, and philanthropic donations. Since that time, policy calls upon the state to move from producing and controlling social services to building a more self-regulating socialist market and knowledge-based system (Mok, 2003a).

On the ground, students, parents, and teachers have had to adjust to a changing culture of higher education that emphasized private investment over public good. "Cradle to grave" social services were cut back as universities contracted out services. National, provincial, city, and institutional measures to help students afford college accompanied increases in tuition. Universities began to offer teaching and research assistantships, and initial plans for a national student loan program were put into place. As families absorbed an increasing share of college costs, graduates gained flexibility in job choice and place of residence.

From the perspective of the college administrator, decentralization meant that universities had to raise the majority of their operating funds, sometimes as much as 80%, from nongovernmental sources. Yet, the state retained control of enrollment, tuition, and faculty positions, leaving administrators limited power over a significant portion of both income and expenses. Although it is safe to say that governmental units remain the most influential actors in education policy formation, implementation, and appropriation of policy – in addition to pressures for reform – are driven by an increasingly diverse set of actors.

Post/Socialism, Civic Society, and the Marketization of Higher Education

Spurred by the depoliticization of society, growing institutional autonomy, and greater opportunity for subjects to act like citizens, a large literature has developed on Chinese civil society (Ross & Lin, 2006). Some social scientists remain skeptical of the extent to which China has a civil society (Yan, 2003), whereas others analyze how resisting but opportunistic bureaucrats came to support transnational exchanges in education and development assistance necessary to the flourishing of civil societies in a global age (Zweig, 2002). Harley Balzer (2004) suggests the appropriateness of an alternative concept, civic society, to describe the space of reciprocity between state and society in nations whose regimes once "demobilized independent social organizations while demanding participation in state-sponsored collectives, leaving populations both atomized and wary of organized social and political activity" (p. 243). This "managed pluralism" view of post/socialist society provides a useful way to think about the marketization of Chinese higher education and private institutions' "space" within it.

China's higher education expansion has taken place primarily in second and third tier institutions, and especially private institutions. Private universities and second tier colleges now comprise approximately 20% of the scale of higher education, and some predictions suggest that could climb to 60%. First established in the 1980s, private institutions received neither financial support from the state nor a clear legal framework in which to operate. Their rapid expansion in the 2000s has ratcheted up concerns about teacher and student qualifications, unstable funding, and lack of accreditation and oversight. As the job market for college graduates has sagged, the media, policy makers, and parents are scrutinizing college programs. As institutions of higher education are pressed to "prove" the value of their degrees and provide greater support to job-seeking graduates, the state is forced in turn to rethink its approach to managed pluralism in the increasingly diverse and stratified education sector.

Post/Socialism and the Critique of Holism in the Quest for Meaning and (E)quality in Higher Education

Illustrated by the notion of managed pluralism, which to succeed must maintain fluidly reciprocal state–society boundaries, is the post/socialist paradigm of *critiquing holism*. This pragmatic perspective eschews both the isms of socialist governance (e.g., collectivism) and the isms of liberalism (e.g., individualism), leaving the "self-animating subject" of our chapter's opening quote operating in a very ambiguous field.

The liveliest example in post/socialist thought of the simultaneous creation and destruction of holism is the heated, public, and transnational debate between China's neoliberals and neoleftists.[3] The most intriguing arguments associated with the debate are made in the name of avoiding isms, often by "left" leaning scholars, who are living up to the challenge posed by Burawoy and Verdery (1999) to develop post-socialist theory that captures disillusionment with the market and liberal democracy.

This debate can be disorienting to newcomers, because in China neoleftists are frequently cast as "conservatives" futilely trying to redeem the socialist legacy for a post/socialist world. In fact, the liberal/leftist argument is joined by a diverse group of scholars, some who wish to create a "broad social politics" to transcend socialism and capitalism; some who find collaboration between the socialist state and global capitalism despicable; some who see in the growth of affluence the market's leveling of the playing field (of power); and some who decry marketization for exacerbating social stratification, corruption, environmental degradation, and the commodification of personal life.

One interesting conclusion by a group of transnational anthropologists is that "the cross between privatization and socialist rule is not a 'deviant' form but a particular articulation of neoliberalism" which they call "socialism from afar" (Zhang and Ong, 2008, pp. 2–3). Essentially the argument is that neoliberalism in the hands of the post/socialist state becomes "a mobile set of calculative practices" for regulating from a distance the expression of citizens' self-interests (e.g., through consumerism and nationalism). Similar to Balzer's distinction between civil and civic society, the post/socialist state facilitates, through its controlled acceptance of the market, the reanimation of socialism by the "infusion of neoliberal values" into a freewheeling public (Zhang and Ong, 2008, p. 4). This conceptualization of socialism from afar begins to capture the reconfigured state–university–student relationship illustrated in our case studies, and how it truncates but does not eliminates the possibility for the success of any broad social politics.

Finally, since socialism has lost for most citizens a capacity to inspire, post/socialism is characterized by a search for meaning that has drawn individuals, institutions, and the state into a re-examination of China's "multi-stranded intellectual and political traditions" (Wasserstrom, 2010, p. 18) – from the re-emergence of traditional forms of spirituality and practice to the spread of Christianity. Most relevant to higher education is the reinterpretation of Confucian and Taoist traditions, as well as globally inflected scientific progressivism, for their guidance in addressing issues of virtue, relational harmony, distributive justice, sustainability, self-cultivation, creativity, and supra/national alliance. This search is captured in the 2000s debate about educational "quality" (suzhi), which the State Council declared in 1999 would govern education policy well into the 21st century. In public discourse *suzhi* has come to stand for everything from improved etiquette to higher test scores to global competence; for universities it implies nourishing within a hierarchical and competitive system a holistic approach in learning and students that will deliver high standards in the disciplines plus capacities for innovation.

Taken together, globalization, gradualism, civic society, and the critique of holism have reshaped the mission of universities. Before the 1990s, higher education was a public/state good designed to support the training of experts for socialist production. Universities were appendages of the state, which controlled policy, finances, and the management and distribution of human capital through the "manpower" plan. College graduates served the state and in return were recognized as bona fide persons of status, tenured civil servants.

As illustrated by our case studies, college enrollment no longer necessarily confers social status, legitimacy, and stability – nor even guarantees employment. College education is conceived of and treated as a private investment by students whose key relationship is with a particular institution, not the state. In regulating "from a distance" the state sometimes justifies this shift by positioning the student as an individual who through hard work and ability must negotiate market competition. Take the 2006 example of Wang Xuming, a MoE spokesperson. Calling post-compulsory education a form of consumption that "should depend on one's economic capability and intelligence," Wang explained, "It is natural that not everyone can afford excellent education resources. It is like shopping for clothing. A well-off man can go to a brand-name store to buy a 10,000 *yuan* suit, while a poor person can buy a 100 *yuan* suit from a vendor" (quoted in China Briefing, 2006). Comments like this one stretch to the breaking point the pact the Chinese people have made with the state to accept inequities as long as vehicles of equality of opportunity (i.e., a "fair" educational system) exist, and state policy is beginning to address access pressures. China's recently released *Blueprint 2020* for educational development across the next decade identifies equitable college admission procedures as a priority, but this is still in the context of larger goals of heightening "the global competitiveness of higher education" through the creation of "outstanding talents," "internationally renowned flagship disciplines," and "world class universities."

CASE STUDIES: POST/SOCIALIST RECONFIGURATION OF THE STATE– UNIVERSITY–STUDENT RELATIONSHIP

During the "socialist" period the key relationship structuring higher learning was between state and students. Universities as state agents had no independent legal status. In the post/socialist era a tripartite state–university–student relationship has emerged. The state has partially "withdrawn" from its relationship with students and begun to act like a regulator from afar. Simultaneously, the state/party complex continues to assert ideological preferences, mandating military training for first year students and courses in politics, and with the MoE and lower level education authorities encouraging graduates to teach in rural areas and join the military. The dominant university–student relationship is largely one of marketized, utilitarian exchange; students explain decisions to study a particular major or join the CCP as giving them an edge in the market. As paying clients students expect "services" from their university. However, especially in situations when students have institutional grievances, they also describe their relationships with universities through a discourse of benevolent paternalism. Asks one student, "How can a son challenge his father?" Both of the cases below portray universities as spaces in which students construct new modes of social being and interaction and see the university as part service provider, part authority.[4]

Legal Configuration and Reconfiguration of the State–University–Student Relationship (Case One)

State–Student Relationship in the Pre-reform Era

In the 1950s, soon after the founding of the People's Republic of China, the state launched a massive structural adjustment of higher education. Pre-liberation universities were regarded as the legacy of the Nationalist government, and their unarticulated structure with a heavy emphasis on humanities and law rather than science and technology was deemed unable to serve the needs of socialist economic construction. Guided by a manpower planning model, programs were streamlined and integrated across institutions. The higher education system of the Soviet Union served as the "golden example."

Previously private and missionary institutions were closed, assimilated, or transformed into public institutions; public universities were reshaped. In the span of several years, "imperial," "feudal," and "capitalist" universities became "socialist." The People's University, from which Soviet lessons were disseminated, became "the center and prototype of a new kind of higher education, designed to serve the socialist polity in a special way" (Hayhoe, 1996, p. 75). Absorbed into a structured "socialist bureaucracy" (Zhong & Hayhoe, 2001, p. 289) and subject to the vicissitudes of political change, universities and colleges had no independent legal status. They were mainly governed by state and CCP policies. Their curricula, especially those of the social sciences, followed the People's University Soviet model. Once students passed the college entrance examination and enrolled in a higher education institution, they were assured state-assigned employment on graduation and the formal identity of "state cadre" (Hayhoe, 1995, p. 133). Under these institutional arrangements, colleges and universities served as a gate to officialdom. Matriculation to college involved a student's implicit agreement to enter into an intimate, often life-long relationship with the state.

Legal Configuration of the State–University–Student Relationship by the Late 1990s

Educational transformation was an integral part of the "reform and opening-up" (*gaige kaifang*) policies of the reform era. Deng Xiaoping proclaimed that "education shall be geared to the needs of modernization, world, and future"; these three directions became the guiding principle of educational reform. "Socialist" education was no longer a field for class struggle or political mobilization but gateway to modernity and global integration. Two policy documents, issued in 1985 and 1993, paved the way for educational reform. The 1985 *Decision on the Reform of the Education System* advised changing the college admission and placement systems and allowing higher education institutions more autonomy. Colleges and universities were nudged toward the market and society and given modest decision-making powers. The 1993 *Program for Education Reform and Development in China* reaffirmed and deepened these reforms by defining higher education institutions as "self-governed legal entities" responsive to social needs, with rights and duties specified by law.

The policy of "governing education in accordance with law" (*yifazhijiao*) aimed at establishing a systematic body of educational law, and was accompanied by the enactment of a series of educational statutes. Among them, the 1995 Education Law and the 1998 Higher Education Law gave higher education institutions an independent legal status. According to Article 30 of the Higher Education Law, "an institution of higher learning has civil rights in accordance with law in civil activities and bears civil liability." Both the Education Law and the Higher Education Law recognized that educational institutions have rights and authorities over curriculum and instruction, student recruitment, the granting of awards, and punishments to students, teacher recruitment and personnel management, and financial accounts and assets management. Legislation carved out, from the previously huge bulk of the state, a fairly independent space for institutions and demarcated a legal boundary between them.

At the same time, relevant educational laws also defined the legal relationship between students on the one side and universities and/or states on the other. Article 42 of the Education Law afforded students the right to participate in various educational activities and to use educational facilities, equipment, books and materials; the right to scholarships, loans, and financial aid; the right to fair evaluation, diploma or certificate of study; and the right to appeal and litigation. Article 43 specified the duties of students, which include observing law, regulation, student conduct code, and university regulation; respecting teachers; and completing required learning tasks. According to Article 59 of the 1998 Higher Education Law, the state can establish scholarship, loans, and work-study programs, and higher education institutions and other organizations or individuals are also encouraged to do so. It is worth noting that Article 59 required higher education institutions to provide placement guidance and service to graduates. Based on the letter of the law, the state is no longer part of the placement process, and higher education institutions are responsible for providing placement guidance and services, not placement itself.

Another important legal document defining the state–university–student relationship is the 1990 *Regulation on Student Management in General Higher Education Institutions*, an administrative regulation passed by the Commission of Education (predecessor of MoE). The most comprehensive rule on students' relationships with universities or the state, the Regulation laid out specific rules on almost every facet of student life, including admission and registration, grading and evaluation, transfer, graduation, extra-curricular activities, and reward and punishment. It tightened control over student organizations and allowed universities to expel students for ideological or political reasons. Regarding student discipline, institutions were required to allow students to explain their situations during the disciplinary process, make the sanction decision available to students, and review the case if the decision was challenged by the student. If an expulsion was made based on political or ideological reasons, the decision must be reviewed and approved by government agencies in charge of higher education at the provincial level.

Paralleling the link between socialist economic construction and the reorganization of higher education in the early 1950s, educational reform in the 1980s and 1990s was tied to post/socialist reforms. A year before the release of the *Decision on the Reform of the Education System*, the Central Committee of the CCP issued the 1984 *Decision on the Reform of the Economic System*. The similarity of the two decisions' titles was no coincidence, and Section 9 of the 1984 decision concluded that, "As the reform of the economic system moves on, the reforms of the science and technology system and the reform of the education system become a more and more urgent strategic task" (p. 18). As recalled by Hu Qili (2008), the key drafter of the 1985 education decision, Deng Xiaoping believed that Section 9 was the most important section in the *Decision on the Reform of the Economic System*. Only a week after the passing of the 1984 economic reform decision, a governing board on the reform of science and technology and education systems had already been formed.

In summary, educational legislation in the 1980s and 1990s severed the university from the state – at least rhetorically – and established a tripartite relationship among state, universities, and students. But such legislation did not go beyond the goals of serving economic development and political control. Law was conceived of as an instrument of state governance (Law, 1999, 2002). From a process perspective, this wave of reform efforts started with policies of the CCP and acquired the form of law through immediately following legislation. Interestingly but not surprisingly, it was the CCP that laid the groundwork for the legal configuration of the state–university–student relationship. As the resulting statutes and rules were implemented by different levels of government, the reform was carried out in a top-down fashion. However, the system of law acquired a life of its own, and it was triggered and utilized by a new generation of university students, precipitating a legal reconfiguration of the tripartite relationship.

Legal Reconfiguration of the State-University-Student Relationship during the Past Decade
If the first two decades of the reform period were characterized by the resurgence of the university as an independent legal entity and the formation of a tripartite state–university–student relationship, the past decade has witnessed a reallocation of rights and duties within the tripartite relationship. In other words, there has been a "legal reconfiguration" of the state–university–student relationship. But this time the driving force for change came not from the state but from the students.

In 1999, Tian Yong, a student from the Beijing University of Science and Technology, challenged his university's refusal to grant him graduation and degree certificates ("Tian Yong v. University of Science and Technology Beijing: Trial Court Opinion," 1999). The branch in charge of administrative lawsuits at the Haidian District Court heard the case. According to the 1995 Education Law and the 1980 Regulation on Academic Degrees, China has a state diploma system. The court held that when a university grants a degree or a graduation certificate to a student, it is exercising upon "delegated authority" from the state. Therefore, it was the *administrative* law branch – rather than the *civil* law branch – of the Haidian District Court that had jurisdiction of the case. This case became the first administrative lawsuit over degree and graduation certificates in China (Interview with Tian Yong's lawyers). The application of administrative litigation to diploma disputes suggests that a higher education institution is acting like an "agent" of the state in granting graduation or degree certificates to a student. Meanwhile, the university also has an independent legal status and can become a named defendant in a lawsuit. Before the Tian Yong case, students' challenge of diploma refusal had not been actionable in China. The Tian Yong case marked the beginning of a new era in which the tripartite relationship was no longer exempt from judicial scrutiny.

The Beijing University of Science and Technology pleaded to the court that since Tian Yong had already been ordered to withdraw from the university because of "cheating" in an exam during his sophomore year, he was not eligible for graduation and degree certificates. Finding substantive and procedural flaws in the university's earlier decision on alleged cheating, the Haidian District Court ruled in favor of Tian Yong.

The procedural flaws the court found in the Tian Yong case are germane to our consideration of the state–university–student relationship. The court held that when a sanction that a university makes against a student has a negative impact on the student's right to education, the university should "directly deliver and announce the decision to the student" and "give the student an opportunity to defend," which in essence amounts to the principle of due process protection. Although the *Regulation on Student Management in General Higher Education Institutions* (1990) asked universities and colleges to make sanction decisions accessible to students and allow students to explain their cases, it did not make these clearly defined procedural requirements. At the time of the Tian Yong case, no other law formally afforded students these procedural rights. As recalled by one of the judges, it was largely the general judicial principle of "adequately protecting the rights and interests of parties involved" that guided her ruling (Rao, 2003). The Tian Yong decision transcended then existing legal configuration and provided more protection to the student. The court – an external reviewer outside the tripartite relationship – provided the student additional leverage. The fact that the opinion of the Haidian District Court was included in the *Supreme Court's Gazette*, the official publication by the highest judicial body in China, guaranteed the ruling legal significance.

As the first administrative lawsuit over graduation and degree certificates and as a case in which a student won his legal challenge against his university, the Tian Yong case was publicized widely in the media. Like the first block in a series of dominoes, it triggered and inspired a wave of legal challenges by students. One immediately following case was filed by Liu Yanwen, a former doctoral student of Peking University. After spotting a news report about the Tian Yong case, Liu filed a lawsuit against his former university on the same day (Interview with Liu). In 1996, the Academic Degree Committee of Peking University did not approve the decision to grant Liu the doctoral degree. Because receiving a relevant degree is a prerequisite for obtaining a graduation diploma at Peking University, Liu had neither the graduation certificate nor the degree certificate in hand when he left the university. From there started Liu's persistent efforts of appeal and petition. What made him most determined was not the fact that he was not granted the graduation and degree certificates but rather that he was given neither a reason for the refusal nor an opportunity to defend himself.

At the Haidian District Court, the judges sided with Liu ("Liu Yanwen v. Degree Evaluation Committee of Beijing University," 1999/2006). One rationale for the judgment was similar to that in the Tian Yong case. The university did not give Liu an opportunity to defend himself before the decision was reached; nor did the university deliver or announce the decision to him after the decision was made. The court judgment for the Liu Yanwen case reinforced the legal rationales established in the Tian Yong case, and the very fact that one of China's most prestigious universities became a "defendant" shook the foundations of the common belief that colleges and university were "unquestionable." The possibility that students and their universities could now be equal parties in a court of law was liberating and changed legal/cultural expectations across the state–university–student relationship.

After such legal challenges, the MoE (2003) issued a policy document addressing "school governance in accordance with law." In this policy, the MoE used legal terms and recognized certain protections in disciplinary processes as the "rights" of students, clarifying the ambiguous language used in the 1990 *Regulation on Student Management in General Higher Education Institution*. Specifically, the 2003 policy outlines the following requirements on student discipline: (1) as a general principle, a disciplinary action must have facts, adequate evidence, and solid legal basis; its process must follow required procedures; (2) a system of student appeal must be established within educational institutions to guarantee students' right to appeal; (3) at higher education institutions, a disciplinary decision must be approved by a chancellor's meeting and forwarded to and recorded by the educational agency supervising the institution; and (4) at higher education institutions, students' rights to know and to defend must be protected. The 2003 policy constituted official recognition of legal rights students had already begun claiming, and the state thereby adjusted the tripartite relationship by imposing new responsibilities on universities. However, because the 2003 policy was silent on the *legal details* for the protection of students' rights, universities and colleges controlled how and to what extent they would protect such rights.

Some universities have established their own rules on relevant procedures in student discipline (MoE, 2005), thus the procedural protection of student rights has been characterized by institutional initiatives and institutional design. Although a general requirement binds the state–university link in the tripartite relationship, diversity and uncertainty characterize the link between universities and students. In 2005, the MoE issued a new *Regulation on Student Management in General Higher Education Institutions*. It replaced the 1990 MoE regulation and made substantive modifications to the legal configuration of the state–university–student relationship.

With the 2005 MoE Regulation, the state further withdrew from immediate state–student relations, and the university–student relationship became more substantive. Although the 1990 Regulation specified standards for change of major, leave of absence, class retaking, and make-up exams, the 2005 Regulation leaves all such issues up to institutions (MoE, 2005). However, while institutions have acquired more substantive authority in student management, they are also subject to more procedural oversight of student discipline. For example, according to the 2005 Regulation, colleges and universities must hear defense from students or students' legal counsels before a disciplinary decision is made. A disciplinary decision must be in writing and include facts, rationales, and the decision itself. The decision must be delivered to the student. If the disciplinary action is expulsion, the decision must be recorded at the provincial level. The 2005 Regulation explicitly requires the procedures for student discipline to be "due," which is probably the closest approximation to "due process" in the entire Chinese legal system.

The 2005 Regulation fully incorporates the judicial standards established in the Tian Yong case and spells out institutional design for implementing general procedural requirements of the 2003 policy. It should be noted that the 2005 Regulation was enacted by the MoE as an administrative rule. Different from a policy, it is a recognized source of law and has the force of law in China, which means that institutions must abide by it. Thus, what characterizes the procedural aspect of the university–student link in the tripartite relationship is no longer institutional initiative and institutional diversity. It is rather a systematic set of state–imposed mandates as a legal minimum.

The 2005 Regulation has indeed established a system of legal account-ability. In addition to specific procedural requirements discussed above, the MoE has adopted two additional monitoring channels. First, it has a prior review system in place. All institutions, public and private alike, must formulate and align their university rules with the 2005 Regulation. The resulting university rules must also be submitted to the educational agency supervising the institution of record. Second, the two-layer appeal system required by the 2005 Regulation can serve as a post-review mechanism. An aggrieved student may bring his or her grievance first to a university-level appeal review board. If he or she is still unsatisfied with the review result, a further appeal to the provincial educational agency may be made. Although aggrieved students claim their rights, they are holding institutions accountable to the state at the same time.

In summary, the state–university–student relationship has been funda-mentally reconfigured over the past 10 years. The state has shown a tendency to withdraw from immediate student management and to regulate instead through procedural control and legal accountability. Students have acquired more rights, and universities have gained real authority over student management. The university–student link in the tripartite relationship has become more significant. Indeed, a "rights protection" (Fu & Cullen, 2008) movement or "rights revolution" (Lee, 2008) has elevated the student's position in the state–university–student relationship, indicating that state–society relations continue to adapt on the path of "reform and opening-up."

The Post/Socialist Student Services Administration
System: From Ideological Control to Multiple Functions (Case Two)

Student services administration is a developing concept in post/socialist China that has emerged with the expansion, diversification, stratification, and depoliticization of higher education, and the perception that education is an individual investment rather than a public responsibility. Reflecting case one's illustration of the state's reconfigured role in the tripartite state–university–student relationship, the state/party has given over some of its authority in student management to institutions, whose increasingly service-oriented role has broadened student affairs. Excepting academic affairs, student services administration deals with all affairs related to students, such as career guidance, psychological counseling, and financial assistance. Since 1949, the student administration system as developed through four periods, and ideological control and influence has waned as the service functions of universities have grown.

Until the end of the Mao era, student services administration was called student ideological and political work. The main task of student affairs was to shoulder CCP directed ideological and political education. In 1950, *the Provisional Rules for College and Universities* mandated that institutions as state agents should train professionals who would serve "the people" wholeheartedly through modern technology and advanced knowledge. Student services were to carry out political education, eliminate capitalist and feudal influences, and inspire in students the "correct" ideology of public service (Lin, Zhang, & Luo, 2008). Given these primary missions, student activities and graduate placement efforts were guided by and subordinate to national requirements for collective benefit.

The second period, from 1977 to 1981, has been called the period of "bringing wrongs to rights." CCP inflected ideological and political education was diluted by "moral education" and no longer drove all of student services management (Lin et al., 2008). Concomitantly, daily student affairs were largely decoupled from ideological and political work. Individual student needs were still largely ignored by the state (Lin et al., 2008).

During the next decade, the student services administration system became structurally and philosophically divided into student education, corresponding to ideological education, and student administration, which referred to daily student affairs (Lin et al., 2008). The former was still explicitly political; the latter was strengthened to establish an efficient and rational university structure (MoE, 1990).

Since the 1990s legislation and policies have provided institutions more autonomy in exchange for oversight. Coupled with the massification, marketization, and diversification of higher education, the student services administration system has become more comprehensive, with key functions of career guidance, psychological counseling, and financial assistance requiring specially trained personnel who assist an increasingly diverse and demanding student population (Lin, Zhang, and Luo, 2008). Though ideological education is still a part of student affairs, the definition of student services administration now approximates that which has been familiar in North America for decades: "colleges or universities administrate and guide students' nonacademic activities, provide nonacademic services to students and enrich the students' campus life, so as to encourage students to improve themselves" (Cai, 2000, p. 57). Supporting students as individuals with individual needs has become a key focus of the student administration system (MoE, 2005).

Marketization, Student Services Administration, and the State–University–Student Relationship

The development of student services administration parallels the interrelated reforms of market socialism and higher education more generally. As college costs and access have soared, many students are without the financial means to take advantage of post-secondary education. In the early period of "cost-recovery" financing, the MoE experimented with tuition charging in thirty universities in 1994, expanding the program to more than two hundred in 1995 and to all institutions in 1997 (Gui & Song, 2008). The result was the emergence of "impoverished college students" as a new service category. According to official statistics, there are 2,400,000 such students in China, 20 percent of China's undergraduate population (Pang, 2007), and financial support for them has become an important responsibility of student administration.

State guidance of student administration services is increasingly dominated by financial rather than political concerns. For example, in 1999 the state established a National Student Loan program for impoverished college students that was described as a "financial instrument to support education" (People's Bank of China, MoE and Ministry of Finance, 1999). Through the establishment of two national scholarship programs in 2007 (Ministry of Finance and Ministry of Education, 2007a, 2007b), universities were enabled to provide funds to their students directly through independent financial aid systems.

In tandem with financial assistance services, student placement systems have also changed as a result of educational marketization and expansion and increased institutional autonomy. In the pre-reform "centralist model" (Mok, 2002), student placement was controlled by the state. Seen as a kind of national property, university graduates were public resources allocated through the national plan. In contrast, as post-socialist citizens, recent graduates have career choice (Agelasto, 1998). This shift began in 1989 (Ren, 2008), and in 2002 the state confirmed a market-oriented graduate placement system (MoE et al., 2002). Placement "management" responsibilities gradually shifted from the central government to institutions (Mok, 2002), which in turn began providing students career guidance. The success a university had in placing graduates in the job market became a critical measure of its reputation and criterion for obtaining state funding (Mok, 2000). Supply and demand economics replaced manpower-planning, with significant consequences for university student management services. Whether seeking aid or jobs, students as individuals have become much more important in the state–university–student relationship.

De-politicization and the Persistence of the State/Party Role in the Student Services Administration System

In contrast to former socialist countries in Central and Eastern Europe, where ruling parties were overthrown and post/socialist reforms were begun in a ruptured policy environment, post/socialist policy reform in China has been orchestrated by the CCP (Law, 1995). As a result, political and ideologically driven education, while diluted, still persists as one task of the student administration system. Regulations in student administration from 1990 and 2005 share the general principle of "socialist direction" under the leadership of the CCP (MoE, 1990; MoE, 2005). Through 2006 MoE *Provisions for Developing Political and Ideological Instructors in Regular Higher Education Institutions*, universities are provided guidelines for insuring that student advising personnel, *fudaoyuan*, implement appropriate ideological and political education. Their principle responsibilities are to grasp university students' general political thinking and help them recognize and adopt "correct" values and a worldview in accordance with Chinese socialism (MoE, 2006). Even in a market-oriented placement system, the state tries to exert its influence. *Advice on Furthering the Reform of the Graduate Placement System* (MoE et al., 2002) proposed that graduate placement be guided by the "Three Represents"[5] for the good of the nation and social stability. Likewise, universities are called upon to encourage graduates to work in underdeveloped western regions and serve in grass-roots units. One of the purposes of the Tsinghua University Career Instruction Center, for example, is to guide students to choose "national-neediest" careers.

As a group that relies on financial aid to attend post-secondary schooling, impoverished students, relative to their peers, are potentially subject to greater political influence and pressure. For example, national fellowship programs privilege recipients who intend to pursue national-need majors, such as agriculture, forestry, and mining (MoF and MoE, 2007a; MoF and MoE, 2007b). In 2007, the State Council issued a policy of free education for students in teacher training institutions to encourage students with need to choose teaching-related majors. Furthermore, the policy requires students to work as primary or secondary teachers for more than ten years after graduation, or face fines and return all fees waived during their undergraduate studies (MoE et al., 2007). In 2009, MoF and MoE announced that the state would forgive impoverished students' loans if they agreed to serve in grass-roots units in underdeveloped regions of China for at least 3 years (MoF & MoE, 2009).

Impoverished College Students at Tsinghua University: Reactions to National Policies and University Administration

Tsinghua University is a first-tier institution whose impoverished students all receive enough financial aid to cover tuition and stipends (Tsinghua Alumni Association, 2007). Data collected from interviews with recipients of financial aid, including loans and university and national scholarships, indicate three trends in student responses to national financial aid policies and placement systems.[6]

First, impoverished students are more inclined to accept assistance or support from their university than from individuals or potential employers. Their priority choice is a student loan, however, as the transaction requires no indebtedness in the sense of obligation. Students want to be regarded as fully equal individuals with choices. When, a second year student, explained, "I prefer to accept national financial aid, because I can easily return back to society when I graduate. But if I receive money from other individuals, I will feel I am in debt to them and have to affiliate with them [in ways] besides money." Student loans are thus preferred as the simplest, cleanest option, because they involve nothing more than an economic transaction. As elite and entitled students (labels rightly or wrongly ascribed to all students able to enter Tsinghua), they are confident in their abilities to repay their loans and decline assistance that comes with strings attached. No student accepted the state's offer to repay their loans in exchange for working in underdeveloped regions.

Secondly, individual (as opposed to collective) "values" are dominant among students. Agelasto (1998) argued over a decade ago that as students picked up the costs of higher education and took increased responsibility for securing their own jobs they would rely on and assert their own values and concerns about career and future, and by definition become more powerful actors in the state–university–student relationship. In fact, most students affirmed that their aspirations were a result of individual or family interests. Socialism per se has little resonance for them. "To live in the city and find a good job," and "To earn enough money to provide families better lives" were the most common starting points. "National-need" guidance, prioritized by the university, has little influence on their plans. Chen, a fourth year student, said: "After four years of study we are not fools now. We know what will benefit ourselves. The university always encourages us to go to where the state needs us, but only when it is related to our own interests might it have some attractions."

In the context of individual choice and desire, economic and political power play different roles. On the one hand, economic power and influence is a clear factor shaping students' future choices. Most impoverished students agreed that economy/money will significantly influence or limit their futures. Yu is a second year student majoring in engineering. She wanted to study abroad but gave up the idea due to lack of money. "In reality," she said, "you have to consider money. Maybe I will have an opportunity when I earn some money." Chen said that to own his own business and earn money to help his family and rural communities is his life purpose.

That students prioritize economic considerations does not mean that state political priorities have disappeared. Rather, now they are asserted through political resources rather than ideological control. Like obtaining a college degree, membership in the CCP paves the way for advancement (Walder, Li, & Treiman, 2000). Li is a second year student from Xinjiang. His family hopes that he will become an officer in the state bureaucracy in order to help his siblings find good jobs. From the family's perspective state employment will allow Li to capitalize on his education and position for private ends.

In summary, though the state has acted to preserve its political authority and influence, ideologically directed guidance seems to have little impact on impoverished students who receive financial aid from the state and universities. They prefer taking on a "simple" debt that will leave their future paths unimpeded; other normative overtures and influence by the state is declined. Students' awareness of individual interests now dominate their relations with the state and universities. And as universities are gaining their rights to manage student services (Mok, 2002), state ideological or collective interests and control are fading.

CONCLUSION

As the state simultaneously practices and tries to shed its neo-authoritarianism (Pei, 2006), the "reconfiguration" of the state–university–student relationship differs from the "configuration" process in the first two decades of the reform era in several ways. First, the CCP-directed configuration process was characterized by national legislative effort, with key education statutes enacted. As a result, the status of universities was recognized and a system of educational law came into being. In contrast, the reconfiguration process has been fueled by bottom-up challenges and pressures from students (and parents) claiming rights and expecting services. Court rulings creatively expanded the boundary of students' rights and afforded students more procedural protection to think the previously unthinkable. Student claims and expectations gradually transformed administrative rule and student management services. Furthermore, discourse characterizing the two periods altered. In the configuration period, serving economic development was a salient purpose of educational reform. In the reconfiguration period, a discourse of protecting students' rights and meeting student needs has emerged (Gao, 2000; Zheng, 2000).

China's higher education system has been the largest in the world for over half a decade. It is the supplier of the world's largest pool of international students, second only to the United States in research productivity, and an increasingly influential referent for global educational reform. The system has moved in the last two decades from a free, elite, status-transforming system to a diverse, expensive, hierarchical, and over-stretched one in which "academic aspirations and the perceived importance of higher education outstrip both resources and an established academic culture" (Altbach, 2010, np).

The social outcomes of the state–university–student relationship during the next decade matter well beyond China's national boundaries. Policy makers and scholars worldwide look to China's education system for inspiration. Students who are emerging from China's universities are shaping global patterns of the production of knowledge, particularly in science and technology but also the social sciences and the humanities. Lastly, collaborative scholarly networks, deepened by the participation of Chinese intellectuals and students, have resulted in an explosion of research on state–society relations. China will be a leader in educational reform in the 21st century.

NOTES

1. One exception is a new publication about to be published by Andrew Kipnis (2010).

2. See Mark Bray's (2003) distinction among: "de-concentration" (the downward transfer of administrative tasks but not authority); "delegation" (discretionary transference of decision making power to other entities); and "devolution" (transference of authority to a unit with the power to act independently).

3. We apologize for simplifying the intellectual ferment in China since the opening of the reform period. Scholars in this debate draw their positions from a century of argumentation about Chinese reform/individualism and revolution/socialism, and the more senior of these start with Maoism as a theoretical discourse that simultaneously governed Chinese society and structured their own political imagination (Kipnis, 2008).

4. The first case study draws on document and media analysis, survey, and interview data collected from students at 10 universities, including both elite and

non-elite institutions, in 4 regions of China between 2004 and 2008, as well as data from key players in major educational disputes between 1999 and 2007. The second case study is based on document analysis and interview data collected from 2008 to 2009 from impoverished Tsinghua University students. Data collection and data analysis for the first case study were funded by the U.S. National Science Foundation (Grant No. 0719715) and China Times Cultural Foundation. Of course, any opinions, findings, conclusions, and recommendations expressed in this study are from the authors and do not necessarily reflect the views of any funding agency.

5. The "three represents" theory affirms that the Party should always represent the development needs of China's advanced social productive forces; always represent the forward direction of China's advanced culture; and always represent the fundamental interests of the majority of the population.

6. Because the interviews focus on impoverished students in Tsinghua University, findings may only help explain the actions of elite college students. Impoverished students in other types of colleges may have different experiences and/or less support, including financial assistance, from their institutions.

ACKNOWLEDGMENT

The authors wish to thank Yimin Wang, Indiana University, for her excellent help in developing a list of initial readings on post-socialism that inspired our thinking about the reconfiguration of Chinese higher education.

REFERENCES

Agelasto, M. (1998). Graduate employment: From manpower planning to the market economy. In: M. Agelasto & B. Adamson (Eds), *Higher education in post-Mao China* (pp. 259–280). Hong Kong: Hong Kong University Press.

Altbach, P. G. (2010). Academic fraud and the academic culture in China – and Asia. *Inside Higher Education*. Available at http://scholarsatrisk.nyu.edu/Events-News/Article-Detail.php?art_uid = 2243. Retrieved on August 2.

Balzer, H. (2004). State and society in tansition from communism. In: P. Gries & S. Rosen (Eds), *State and society in 21st century China: Crisis, contention and legitimation* (pp. 235–256). New York: RoutledgeCurzon.

Bray, M. (2003). Control of education: Issues and tensions in centralization and decentralization. In: R. F. Arnove & C. A. Torres (Eds), *Comparative education: The dialectic of the global and the local* (pp. 204–228). New York: Rowman & Littlefield Publishers.

Burawoy, M., & Verdery, K. (Eds). (1999). *Uncertain transition: Ethnographies of change in the postsocialist world.* New York: Rowman and Littlefield.

Cai, G. (2000). Gaoxiao xuesheng shiwu guanli gainian de jieding [*Concepts and definitions in student affairs administration*]. *Yangzhou Daxue Xuebao (Gaodeng Jiaoyu Ban)[Journal of Yangzhou University (Higher Education Edition)]*, 4(2), 56–59.

China Development Briefing (2006, April 4). *Education "like shopping for clothes."* Available at http://www.chinadevelopmentbrief.com/node/540. Retrieved on April 25.

Dirlik, A. (1989). Post-socialism? Reflections on "socialism with characteristics". *Bulletin of Concerned Asian Scholars, 21,* 362–384.

Fu, H., & Cullen, R. (2008). Weiquan (rights protection) lawyering in an authoritarian state: Building a culture of public-interest lawyering. *China Journal* (59), 111–127.

Gao Di. (2000). Fayuan: shuoli de zuihou difang [Court: the last place to seek a sound reason]. *Fazhi ribao [Legal Daily].*

Gries, P., & Rosen, S. (2004). *State and society in 21st century China: Crisis, contention and legitimation.* New York: RoutledgeCurzon.

Gui, F., & Song, G. (2008). 1994–2007 nian gaoxiao pingkun sheng zizhu yanjiu pingshu [*A synthesis of research on financial aid to impoverished college students (1994–2007)*]. *Xinan Jiaotong Daxue Xuebao (Shehui Kexu Ban) [Journal of Southwest Jiao Tong University (Social Science)], 9*(4), 62–69.

Hayhoe, R. (1995). An Asian multiversity? Comparative reflections on the transition to mass higher education in East Asia. *Comparative Education Review, 39*(3), 299–321.

Hayhoe, R. (1996). *China's universities, 1895–1995: A century of cultural conflict.* New York: Garland Publishing.

Ho, P. (2004). Contesting rural spaces, land disputes, customary tenure and the state. In: E. Perry & M. Selden (Eds), *Chinese society: Change, conflict and resistance* (2nd ed., pp. 93–112). New York: Routledge.

Hu, Q. (2008). Zhonggong zhongyang guanyu jiaoyu tizhi gaige de jueding chutai qianhou. [*Backgrounds of the drafting of the Decision on the Reform of the Economic System] Yanhuang Chunqiu [Yan-Huang Historical Review], 18*(12), 1–6.

Kaplan, S. (2006). *The pedagogical state: Education and the politics of national culture in* post-1980 Turkey. Stanford: Stanford University Press.

Kipnis, A. (2008). *China and post-socialist anthropology: Theorizing power and society after communism.* Norwalk, CT: Eastbridge Books.

Kipnis, A. (2010). *Governing educational desire: Culture, politics and schooling in China.* Chicago: University of Chicago Press.

Law, W. W. (1995). The role of the state in higher education reform: Mainland China and Taiwan. *Comparative Education Review, 39*(3), 322–355.

Law, W. W. (Ed.) (1999). Guest editor's introduction to new rules of the game in education in the People's Republic of China: Education laws and regulations. *Chinese Education and Society, 32*(3), 3–8.

Law, W. W. (2002). Legislation, education reform and social transformation: The People's Republic of China's experience. *International Journal of Educational Development, 22*(6), 579–602.

Lee, C. K. (2008). Rights activism in china. *Contexts, 7*(3), 14.

Liew, L. (2005). China's engagement with neo-liberalism: Path dependency, geography and party self-reinvention. *Journal of Development Studies, 41*(2), 331–352.

Lin, J. (2006). Class stratification and education in China: The rise of the new middle class and their impact on education. In: G. Postiglione (Ed.), *Education, stratification and social change in China: Inequality in a market society* (pp. 179–198). New York: M.E. Sharpe.

Lin, Y., Zhang, L., & Luo, X. (2008). Woguo gaoxiao xuesheng shiwu guanli de yanjin yu fansi [*The development and reflection of college student affairs management in China*]. *Zhongguo Dizhi Jiaoyu [Chinese Geological Education], 15*(1), 34–37.

Liu, X. (2009). *The mirage of China: Anti-humanism, narcissism, and corporeality of the contemporary world.* New York: Berghahn Books.

Liu Yanwen, V. (1999/2006). Degree evaluation committee of Beijing University. *Chinese Education and Society, 39*(3), 70–88.

Ministry of Education. (2003). *Guanyu jiaqiang yifazhixiao gongzuo de ruogan yijian* [Several Opinions on Reinforcing School Governance in accordance with Law].

Ministry of Education. (2005, March 29). The 4th Press Conference of 2005: Introducing the New Regulations on College Students Management in General Higher Education Institutions. Available at http://www.moe.gov.cn/edoas/website18/17/info9717.htm

Ministry of Education, China. (2006). *Putong gaodeng xuexiao fudaoyuan duiwu jianshe de guiding* [Provisions of establishing political and ideological instructors in regular higher education institutions]. Available at http://www.moe.edu.cn/edoas/website18/level3.jsp?tablename = 1225766841919187&infoid = 1225950963007592. Retrieved on June 12, 2010.

Ministry of Education, Ministry of Finance, Ministry of Personally, & the State Commission Office for Public Sector Reform, China. (2007). *Jiaoyubu zhishu shifan daxue shifansheng mianfei jiaoyu shishi banfa (shixing)* [The provisional measures for the implementation of tuition fee remission for students in teacher-preparation track in normal universities directly under MOE]. Available at http://www.gov.cn/zwgk/2007-05/14/content_614039.htm. Retrieved on June 12, 2010.

Ministry of Education, Ministry of Public Security, Ministry of Personnel, & the Ministry of Labor and Social Security, China. (2002). *Guanyu jinyibu shenhua putong gaodeng xuexiao biyesheng jiuye zhidu gaige youguan wenti yijian de tongzhi* [Advices on furthering the reforms of the job placement system for university graduates]. Available at http://www.moe.edu.cn/edoas/website18/53/info4253.htm. Retrieved on June 12, 2010.

Ministry of Finance & Ministry of Education, China. (2007a). *Putong benke gaoxiao, gaodeng zhiye xuexiao guojia zhuxuejin guanli zanxing banfa* [Provisional measures on the administration of the state-subsidized grant for students in academic and vocational higher education institutions]. Available at http://www.moe.edu.cn/edoas/website18/07/info29907.htm. Retrieved on June 12, 2010.

Ministry of Finance & Ministry of Education, China. (2007b). *Putong benke gaoxiao, gaodeng zhiye xuexiao guojia lizhi jiangxuejin zanxing guanli banfa.* [Provisional measures on the administration of the state-subsided "Inspirational Scholarship" for students in academic and vocational higher education institutions]. Available at http://www.gov.cn/zwgk/2007-07/03/content_670905.htm. Retrieved on June 12, 2010.

Ministry of Finance & Ministry of Education, China. (2009). *Gaodeng xuexiao biyesheng xuefei he guojia zhuxue daikuan daichang zanxing banfa.* [Provisional measures on the tuition and state-subsided student loan repayment for graduates of higher education institutions]. Available at http://www.gov.cn/gzdt/2009-04/21/content_1292076.htm. Retrieved on June 12, 2010.

Mnistry of Education, China. (1990). *Putong gaodeng xuexiao xuesheng guanli guiding* [Regulations to student affairs in higher education]. Available at http://www.moe.edu.cn/edoas/website18/level3.jsp?tablename = 1234&infoid = 886. Retrieved on June 12, 2010.

Mok, K. H. (2000). Marketizing higher education in post-Mao China. *International Journal of Educational Development, 20*(2), 109–126.

Mok, K. H. (2002). Policy of decentralization and changing governance of higher education in post-Mao China. *Public Administration and Development, 22*(3), 261–273.

Mok, K. H. (2003a). Globalisation and higher education restructuring in Hong Kong, Taiwan and Mainland China. *Higher Education Research and Development*, *22*(2), 117–129.

Mok, K. H. (Ed.) (2003b). *Centralization and decentralization, educational reforms and changing governance in Chinese societies*. Hong Kong: Comparative Education Research Centre, The University of Hong Kong, Kluwer Academic Publishers.

O'Brien, K. J., & Li, L. (2006). *Rightful resistance in rural China*. New York: Cambridge University Press.

Pang, L. (2007). Gaoxiao pinkunsheng xinli wenti chansheng de yuanyin ji jiaoyu duice [*The reasons for psychological problems of low-income college students and the relevant educational strategies*]. *Jiaoshu Yuren [Educator]*, *9*(8), 65–66.

Pei, M. (2006). *China's trapped transition: The limits of developmental autocracy*. Cambridge, MA: Harvard University Press.

People's Bank of China, Ministry of Education, and Ministry of Finance, China. (1999). *Guanyu guojia zhuxu daikuan de guanli guiding (shixing)* [The state regulations on the management of the student loan (for trial implementation)]. Available at http://www.gov.cn/ztzl/2005-12/30/content_143189.htm. Retrieved on June 12, 2010.

Perry, E., & Selden, M. (2004). *Chinese society: Change, conflict and resistance* (2nd ed.). New York: Routledge.

Postiglione, G. (2003). Universities for knowledge economies: Hong Kong and the Chinese mainland within globalization and decentralization. In: K. H. Mok (Ed.), *Centralization and decentralization, educational reforms and changing governance in Chinese societies* (pp. 157–172). Hong Kong: Comparative Education Research Centre, The University of Hong Kong, Kluwer Academic Publishers.

Rao, Y. (2003). Cong shenpan jiaodu tan shoujiaoyuquan de baohu yu faguan zeren [*Responsibilities for protecting and governing educational rights*]. In: Z. Zhan (Ed.), *Gaodeng Jiaoyu yu xingzheng susong [Higher Education and Administrative Litigation]*. (pp. 260–273) Beijing: Peking University Press.

Ren, Z. (2008). Beijing gaoxiao biyesheng jiuye gaige 30 nian [*The thirty years' reforms of the graduate placement system in Beijing higher education institutions*]. *Beijing Jiaoyu (Gaojiao) [Beijing Education (Higher Education)]*, *15*(Z1), 44–46.

Ross, H., & Lin, J. (2006). Social capital formation through Chinese school communities. In: E. Hannum & B. Fuller (Eds), *Children's lives and schooling across societies* (pp. 43–69). Greenwich, CN: JAI Press.

Ross, H., & Lou, J. (2005). "Glocalizing" Chinese higher education: Groping for stones to cross the river. *Indiana Journal of Global Legal Studies*, *12*(1), 227–250.

Ross, H. with contributions by Jingjing Lou, Lijing Yang, Olga Rybakova, and Phoebe Wakhunga. (2005). *Where and who are the world's illiterates: China*. (Background Paper for UNESCO Global Monitoring Report.) Available at http://portal.unesco.org/education/en/files/43542/11327151221Ross_China.doc/Ross_China.doc. Retrieved on June 12, 2010.

Stromquist, N. P. (2002). *Education in a globalized world: The connectivity of economic power, technology, and knowledge*. Lanham, MD: Rowman & Littlefield.

Tian Yong v. University of Science and Technology Beijing (1999). In *the Supreme People's Court's Gazette*. *4*, 139–143.

Tsinghua Alumni Association. (2007). Tsinghua daxue pinkun sheng zizhu qingkuang shuoming [The introduction of the financial aid system of Tsinghua University].

Available at http://www.tsinghua.org.cn/alumni/infoSingleArticle.do?articleId = 10005543. Retrieved on July 12, 2010.

Walder, A. G., Li, B., & Treiman, D. H. (2000). Politics and life chances in a state socialist regime: Dual career paths into the urban Chinese elite, 1949–1996. *American Sociological Review, 65*, 191–209.

Wasserstrom, J. (2010). *China in the 21st Century, what everyone needs to know.* Oxford: Oxford University Press.

Whyte, M. K. (2010a). *Myth of the social volcano: Perceptions of inequality and distributive injustice in contemporary China.* Stanford: Stanford University Press.

Whyte, M. K. (Ed.) (2010b). *One country, two societies, rural-urban inequality in contemporary China.* Cambridge: Harvard University Press.

Wright, T. (2010). *Accepting authoritarianism: State-society relations in China's reform era.* Stanford: Stanford University Press.

Yan, Y. (2003). *Private life under socialism.* Stanford: Stanford University Press.

Zhang, L., & Ong, A. (Eds). (2008). *Privatizing China: Socialism from afar.* Ithaca, NY: Cornell University Press.

Zheng Lin. (2000). Liu Yanwen su Beida yi'an panjue, yinqi zhuanjia xuezhe zhankai jilie tantao [Liu Yanwen v. Peking University was ruled by the trial court, incurring heated discussion among experts and scholars]. *Zhongguo Qingnian Bao [China Youth Daily].* Available at http://www.k12.com.cn/newspool/395.html

Zhong, N., & Hayhoe, R. (2001). University autonomy in twentieth-century China. In: G. Peterson, R. Hayhoe & Y. Lu (Eds), *Education, culture, and identity in twentieth-century China* (pp. 265–296). Ann Arbor, MI: University of Michigan Press.

Zweig, D. (2002). *Internationalizing China: Domestic interests and global linkages.* Ithaca, NY: Cornell University Press.

SOCIALIST, POST-SOCIALIST, AND *POST*-POST-SOCIALIST EDUCATION TRANSFORMATIONS IN NICARAGUA

Anita Sanyal

INTRODUCTION

This chapter explores post-socialist transformations in education in Nicaragua. While less commonly known to have been a full participant of the Cold War, Nicaragua's conflict with the United States during the 1980s was underlain by a socialist capitalist struggle, and the transitions in government in the following years represent important political movements away from and toward socialism.[1] For the better part of the 20th century, Nicaragua was a dependent capitalist state. Following an overthrow of the government, the socialist period existed from 1979 to 1989. The election in 1990 marked the beginning of Nicaragua's post-socialist period. Nicaragua makes a special case, however, because in 2007 it reelected the same government that was in power in the 1980s, thereby entering the current *post*-post-socialist period. Education policy under the current government represents an interesting mix of both socialist and capitalist elements. This analysis addresses the transformations that have occurred in education through the political transitions of the last 30 years and examines the

Post-Socialism is not Dead: (Re)Reading the Global in Comparative Education
International Perspectives on Education and Society, Volume 14, 329–349
Copyright © 2010 by Emerald Group Publishing Limited
ISSN: 1479-3679/doi:10.1108/S1479-3679(2010)0000014015

progress toward global goals in education. Specifically, it responds to the following questions: What are the post-socialist transformations that have occurred in education in Nicaragua? And, how have the directions of the reforms been shaped by international, national, and local political and economic factors?

The analysis is grounded in literature on the politics of education reform. This literature acknowledges the influence of political and economic factors on the design and implementation of reforms. Broadly, the international political–economic climate contextualizes the changing roles and relationships among various actors in education, including the state, ministries of education, and international agencies (Ginsburg & Cooper, 1991; Grindle, 2007). The complex dynamics among global actors in education are mirrored within countries in the ways reforms are initiated and carried out (Gershberg, 1999; Grindle, 2007), in the competing interests of various stakeholders (i.e., teachers' unions or local communities) (Gershberg, 2002; Torres, 1991), and in the roles of key individuals within ministries of education (Grindle, 2007).

In Latin America, most governments during the 20th century can be characterized as "dependent" states (Torres, 1991; Arnove, Franz, Mollis, & Torres, 1999), and this has reinforced deep social inequalities characterized by a small political elite and a mass of poor underclass. Marxist revolutionary movements have challenged these societal structures and envisioned broad social transformation. In the context of the Cold War and post-Cold War periods, the political and economic factors underlying relationships between international donors, the United States, and national governments have shaped the ways reforms have played out.

Education in post-Cold War Latin America has followed the dominant practices of international agencies and donors that have called for decentralization of the social sectors (Grindle, 2007). Decentralization, usually a process initiated at the locus of power, involves the redistribution of power from a central authority to a number of authorities (Bray, 1999). Decentralization policies are thought to increase the efficiency of education systems and to promote better quality of services since the local actors (i.e., teachers, school administrators) can be more directly held accountable for services they provide (Gershberg & Jacobs, 1998). In addition, decentralization policies that promote local financing of education are consistent with the calls for a reduction in government spending, which go hand in hand with broader economic reforms supported by international financial institutions (Carnoy, 1999). In Nicaragua, the specific education reforms and the nature of decentralization that have taken shape reflect political transitions and demonstrate the complex dynamics of the reform process.

The analysis in this chapter relies on qualitative inquiry methods to investigate the processes of education reform in the particular contexts of pre-socialist, socialist, and with an emphasis on post- and *post*-post-socialist eras in Nicaragua. This is carried out through a review of policy documents from the Nicaraguan Ministry of Education and international organizations (working in Nicaragua or more generally) as well as through literature reporting on research on educational policy in the context of Nicaragua. The analysis focuses on the nature of education reforms, the underlying ideologies represented by the reforms, and what they imply for the roles of various stakeholders in education. The document analysis is complemented by 14 interviews with different groups of stakeholders. Included in the interviews are ministry and former ministry officials, staff members from United States Agency for International Development (USAID) and other organizations, and rural primary school teachers. Insights from the interviews illuminate the internal political dynamics that underlie education reforms and detail the roles and relationships of the international community, the Nicaraguan Ministry of Education, and local actors in the education system.

This chapter is organized into sections according to political period followed by a discussion of the complex dynamics of reform. A brief presentation of education in pre-socialist (Somoza) Nicaragua and the first socialist Sandinista period provide foreground for more in-depth consideration of educational change in later transitions: Education during the post-socialist, politically conservative governments and the current Sandinista period. The discussion presents an analysis of three specific dynamics that highlight the multifaceted nature of the reform process: The Nicaraguan government's relationship with and the role of international donor organizations; differing notions of "local participation" in education that signify the shifting role of civil society; and continuities and discontinuities in ministry personnel and the policy process. The analysis is situated in a changing international climate and globalizing trends in education.

EDUCATION IN PRE-SOCIALIST NICARAGUA (THE SOMOZAS, 1936–1979)

The 43-year Somoza rule was the longest among the notorious Latin American dictatorships. During this period Nicaragua operated as a dependent capitalist state. The government maintained a political and economic relationship with the United States and the international capitalist donor community. The social structure greatly favored a very small elite, while greatly marginalizing large numbers of poor peasants. The donor relationship served the needs of the small Nicaraguan elite who were direct beneficiaries of national development, and the government functioned to maintain this social structure despite popular opposition. Under the Somozas, the country was "run like a family plantation" (Miller, 1985, p. 19). Social disparities were great, and corruption was common and overt. Reliance on key individual elites (through which relationships with the United States were maintained) and the National Guard (Somoza's army)[2] were the main forces that upheld the dictatorship (Walker, 1997). Together these factors created a national climate of political corruption, individual gain for the small number of elite families, and repressive and brutal forms of social control.

The education system overtly functioned to maintain the larger social structure of a very small privileged class and a mass majority of poor underclass (Miller, 1985). Students from upper class families who were enrolled in the education system went to private or church organized schools while not even half of the total Nicaraguan school age population was enrolled in school (Arnove & Dewees, 1991). Teaching standards in the public system were "notoriously low" and teachers who resisted or challenged the authority were reassigned to remote areas (Miller, 1985, p. 20). Twenty-eight percent of the teachers in primary schools and 78% in secondary school were under qualified (Torres, 1991). Rural development was grossly neglected and access to primary school was greatly limited. In smaller rural communities, political favorites were designated to teach in schools, but often did not show up for classes for the majority of the school year (Miller, 1985). Illiteracy reached 75% in some rural areas, and as Miller (1985) writes, it "was both a condition and a product of this overall system" (p. 20). The United States and the World Bank supported a development model based on export-oriented agriculture, which served to support this overall social structure by relying on a large pool of unskilled workers (Miller, 1985). Therefore, a public education system that would cultivate critically conscious citizens "made little sense in a society characterized by limited opportunity in the modern sector of the economy and constricted opportunity for political participation" (Arnove & Dewees, 1991, p. 93).

EDUCATION IN SOCIALIST NICARAGUA
(THE FSLN, 1979–1989)

In 1979, the *Frente Sandinista de Liberación* (FSLN), in an armed revolution led in part by future President Daniel Ortega, overthrew the dictatorship. The FSLN was inspired by the historic struggle of Augusto Sandino's crusade against the United States military presence in the late 1920s and in the student opposition to Somoza's repressive policies in the 1950s. Its priority was to empower the majority of the population that had been marginalized by the Somoza regime, which included all but the small capitalist class that controlled the majority of the country's industry and economic resources. The primary pillars of the FSLN platform were self-determination and sovereignty, democratic participatory governance, and collective involvement in national development (Arnove, 1995; Walker 1997). This new vision of national development saw beyond equity and economic growth to envision a broad social transformation, and was intended to unfold "in the short run [through] national reconstruction, and in the long run ... a transition to socialism" (Miller, 1985, p. 30). The FSLN, however, did not see themselves as specifically "socialist" (FSLN, 1986). They were explicitly nonaligned, and sought trading partners regardless of political and economic affiliation (Walker, 1997, p. 9). They wanted privately owned business, but resisted the monopolies held by very few private businesses. Rather they believed in community collectives that could exercise ownership over land or business (FSLN, 1986). They were interested in the development of a "mixed economy" wherein production would remain in the hands of the private sector through community collectives, but with increased government regulation (Walker, 1997, p. 9).

Education was of central importance for the FSLN. Ideologically, education was seen as a tool to promote the ideals of the new Nicaragua and to equip the population in areas of need according to the development agenda. To enact its belief that education is a human right and to instill a more equitable and egalitarian system, the FSLN aimed to "push a major campaign to immediately wipe out illiteracy" (FSLN, 1986, p. 16). This would be accomplished through free and obligatory basic education and by training more and better teachers "who have the knowledge that the present era requires, to satisfy the needs of [the] entire student population" (FSLN, 1986, pp. 16–17). Through mass education, people could learn the fundamental nationalist tenets of the Sandinistas and be inspired to be a part of the new national political project. The new tenets of education policy were hinged on incorporating the great majority as "active protagonists" in their own education and participants in national development (Arnove & Dewees, 1991).

Education during the FSLN years is known as having been very centralized, with curriculum, policy, and funding controlled at a central level. However, at the same time, the FSLN wanted mass local participation in education and there was opportunity for grassroots involvement and ownership through local collectives that provided education services for the community (Arnove & Dewees, 1991). In addition, there was a more significant, broader role for civil society. National Association of Nicaraguan Educators (ANDEN), the Sandinista teachers' union, had a strong leadership role in the education system and the Ministry of Education actively recruited the participation and involvement of students and other educated individuals to serve as teachers in the less developed rural areas (Hanemann, 2005). The ultimate goal was social transformation: To empower the population with skills and consciousness to critique and redefine the direction of development through the use of a Freirian pedagogical approach (Arnove, 1995). To those ends, the FSLN saw education as inherently and inextricably linked to the Sandinista political project (Arnove & Dewees, 1991; Miller, 1985).

Elsewhere in Latin America, structural adjustment programs promoted by international donors supported the reduction of government spending in order to deal with pressures from external debt. As governments limited their spending, the social sectors in many countries experienced cuts in spending. In Nicaragua, however, education spending increased until 1985 (Reimers, 1991). This was likely due to the emphasis the government placed on education early on and the priority it held for national development (Reimers, 1991).

The initial priority on education, however, quickly shifted. The U.S.-funded "Contra War"[3] further weakened the economy and cost many lives. Due to an escalation of attacks (including the destruction of schools), the strengthening of the U.S.-organized economic embargo, and a significant weakening of the (already weak) economy, by the late 1980s the government was increasingly supported by socialist countries such as the Soviet Union and Cuba. In addition, the political base of the FSLN was weakening because of the increasingly authoritative decision-making of the central government and the lack of space for political opposition (Wheelock, 1997). In order to cover costs, the government diverted an increasing proportion of its resources from the social sectors (including education) to defense (Arnove, 1986). Education suffered as a result, and the achievements made early on during the 1980s with the literacy crusade and mass education initiatives were not sustained.

EDUCATION IN POST-SOCIALIST NICARAGUA (1990–2007)

1989 saw the fall of the Berlin Wall, which signified the end of the Cold War, in Europe and elsewhere. For education, 1990 was a significant year as well. The World Conference on Education for All (EFA), which was held in Jomtien, Thailand, established education as a major global concern through the World Declaration on EFA (Inter-Agency Commission, 1990). EFA launched an ongoing global dialogue and directed attention to issues of educational access and quality as well as created a global climate encouraging international cooperation toward its goals by 2015.

In Nicaragua, the end of the Cold War was marked by the transition of power from the Sandinista revolutionary government to the right-leaning government of Violeta Chamorro. After a decade of conflict and severe economic decline, Chamorro came into power espousing economic revitalization and renewed relations with the capitalist donor community. Facing economic crisis and in the context of building international support – including from USAID (which reopened its Managua-based mission in 1990) – the Chamorro administration began a wave of neoliberal reforms aimed at stabilizing the economy by reducing government spending (Walker, 1997). In the social sectors, international donors were heavily promoting decentralization policies (Grindle, 2007). For education, this meant a reduction of the government role in the provision of education services, which had been an early emphasis of the Sandinista government. These reforms, as well as the increased involvement of the U.S. and other governments, donors, and NGOs set the stage for more specific education reforms that took place immediately after the change of government. They also contributed to setting a direction for education reform for the subsequent three governments up until 2007.

As relations with Western (i.e., capitalist) nations improved and their role in education development increased, the orientation in education also changed. The Chamorro era (including the subsequent governments) contrasted strongly on ideological grounds with the FSLN about the purposes and utilities of education. The new government critiqued the use of Sandinista revolutionary rhetoric and the reverence of Agusto Sandino and Carlos

Fonseca, symbols of the Revolution, in school curriculum. They emphasized traditional family and Christian values and morals as an important part of education that had been neglected during the 1980s (Kampwirth, 1997). From this perspective, the "social contract," the productive and cooperative relationship between parents and public schools, was seen as having eroded during the Sandinista years due to the extreme politicization of education (Arcia & Belli, 2001). The new minister of education, Humberto Belli, was a well-known, U.S.-educated conservative and religious opponent of the FSLN. He strongly promoted religious and values education as well as emphasized the need to increase accountability of teachers and schools. Belli's intent was to address these issues through major restructuring of education in two ways: Rewriting the curriculum and creating a system where teachers and schools could be held more accountable to parents. While he suggested a desire to create more stability for teachers, he also emphasized accountability of teachers' performance and that they should be more "fire-able and more accountable" (Humberto Belli, personal communication, June 12, 2009).

Belli was the main driver for the reforms that took shape immediately after the change of government. One of the major reforms undertaken by the new administration was the *Transformación Curricular*, a curriculum reform initiative that sought to rewrite the school curriculum to reflect the new post-Sandinista educational ideologies (MECD, 2000; Arcia & Belli, 2001). USAID had strong involvement in the reform through a 12 million dollar program that funded the complete replacement of the textbooks, though it did not significantly participate in the rewriting that was done by a select group at top levels of the Ministry (Walker, 1997). Later, also through USAID funds, other curriculum materials, including teachers' guides, were rewritten through the USAID BASE I Project, which also funded teacher training in the new curriculum (Academy for Educational Development [AED], 1998). These initiatives aimed at uprooting the revolution's ideological emphasis in the curriculum and teaching and emphasizing moral and values education based in Christian tradition.

The other major reform that was undertaken under Belli was a form of decentralization known as the *Programa de Autonomía Escolar*, the School Autonomy Program (ASP) (Arcia & Belli, 2001; King, Ozler, & Rawlings, 1999a, 1999b). School autonomy reflected new and contrasting ideas about local participation in education, the purposes of education, and in general rewrote the responsibilities of the central Ministry of Education and local communities. As one of the "most radical" forms of decentralization in education in Latin America, the ASP, which began in the secondary schools, involved the transfer of all responsibility of school management to school-based governing councils (*consejos directivos*). The councils were comprised of parents, school directors, local level ministry representatives, and teacher and student representatives (Gershberg, 2002). The central Ministry (not local educational ministry offices) was responsible for providing a cash transfer in a minimum amount per student directly to schools (Arcia & Belli, 2001). Beyond that, the governing councils had full decision-making authority over all school related matters including the hiring and firing of teachers, contextualizing curriculum for local contexts, and decisions about the use of cash transfers from the central Ministry (Gershberg, 1999). In addition, autonomous schools could and were encouraged to charge school fees to augment the per pupil funding they received from the government (Parker, 2005). The ASP was meant to make teachers and schools more accountable and increase the overall efficiency of the system under the assumption that local level participants and parents could allocate resources more effectively, thus increasing the quality of the system as well (Fuller & Rivarola, 1998). In transferring responsibility, the Ministry gave parents the majority vote on school councils (Gershberg, 1999). Teachers' unions, once strong voices in the system, had no place on the school councils (Gershberg, 2002). Shifting emphasis from the revolutionary ideology coupled with a consolidated interest in increasing accountability made teachers the subjects of reform. As noted by Aurora Guardian, an advisor to Belli and later Vice Minister of Education, teachers were the ultimate targets of the reform:

> If change on top doesn't reach the teachers, then it doesn't count. The key is teachers and teachers do not change easily. There are many different ways to teach reading, but teachers may not accept them. (Personal communication, June 14, 2009)

In some cases, however, the schools became such important parts of communities that some teachers even ran for local office (David Edgerton, AED Chief of Party, personal communication, May 29, 2009). This underscores potential for the effects of the ASP, but this was not a universal result. In many cases, the functioning of the school councils was varied and teachers and/or parents often felt subordinate to the school director (Fuller & Rivarola, 1998).

Due in part to the ASP's consistency with, and support for, a decreased government role in the provision of education, the ASP garnered strong support from the donor community. The World Bank and USAID were major actors in supporting decentralization. USAID funded and provided technical support for capacity building for decentralization at all levels of the Ministry (AED, 1998). Belli notes:

> Most of the time, we and the donors had the same philosophy and priorities. I was educated in the U.S. and shared the view. It was a high degree of coincidence with the U.S. and the [World] Bank ... since they had money, we could accept whatever they found they wanted to do. (Personal communication, June 12, 2009)

The ASP was not formalized in policy initially, nor was there much progress in the development of policy for the next few years. During the administration of President Arnoldo Alemán (1996–2000), there was a high degree of turnover at all levels of the Ministry of Education due to individual political interests. During the course of five years (1996–2001), the president appointed three different ministers. Interviews with key personnel in the Ministry during these years and later governments suggest agreement that the changes in staffing resulted in discontinuities in ministry policy and priorities. Belli noted that there could be "little continuity even between ministers in the same government and party, much less [after] major changes between parties" (personal communication, June 12, 2009). An example of a discontinuity regards the National Education Plan. Drafted by Vice Minister Tulio Tablada and others, the National Education Plan laid out a policy framework for the education system during the 1999 administration of Minister of Education Jose Antonio Alvarado – but the document never received final approval (Tulio Tablada, personal communication, June 13, 2009).

There was renewed momentum under Silvio de Franco (Minister of Education, 2002–2004). Under Belli, there was supposed to have been a two-pronged focus of the ASP. On one hand, it emphasized education management and governance, as modeled by the United States, but was also believed to result in improved quality of education. In practice, however, the emphasis was primarily on management and financing of education. There was little initial effort placed on addressing quality of teaching. This is consistent with Gershberg (2002) who notes that the quality of education is not necessarily linked to decentralized management of schools. As de Franco took over, he continued the focus on decentralized governance and worked on improving the participation of different actors in education (Silvio de Franco, personal communication, June 15, 2009). There was great variability in the performance of the ASP schools and the effectiveness and practices of the school councils.[4] Although the ASP had been in full function since 1993, it was only solidified into policy in 2002 with the *Ley de Participación Educativa,* the Education Participation Law (MECD, 2002b).

The law reinforced the roles and responsibilities of the councils and set up guidelines for how participation of the various stakeholders (parents, teachers, students, and local ministry representatives) should take place (MECD, 2002b). Throughout the ASP process, there was strong opposition from teachers' unions. The ASP helped to break the power that ANDEN (the Sandinista teachers' union) had during the FSLN but left no space for union voice on the school councils.

In 2000 and 2001, the Government of Nicaragua drafted an Interim Poverty Reduction Strategy Paper (GoN, 2000), followed by a Strengthened Growth and Poverty Reduction Strategy (GoN, 2001). These documents were drafted for the purpose of consideration for debt relief under the World Bank and IMF Highly Indebted Poor Country (HIPC) program and to help set priorities for governments and donor programs in the direction of economic growth and the reduction of poverty. Nicaragua, in 2004, was granted relief for 80% of its debt (Visser-Valfrey, Jané, Wilde, & Escobar, 2009). These papers subsequently formed the foundation for the *Plan Nacional de Desarollo* (National Development Plan, NDP) (GoN, 2005), which lays out a broad national development agenda. While these discussions were happening between the government and the international financial institutions, the Ministry of Education was engaged in a parallel effort to gain entry into (and later did) the World Bank's Fast Track Initiative (FTI), a funding program designed specifically to help poor countries achieve the goals of EFA (MECD, 2002a). As a part of this process, the Ministry of Education developed the *Plan Nacional de Educación 2000–2015*, a National Education Plan to be carried out by the EFA deadline of 2015 (MECD, 2001). The National Plan affirms commitment to the goals of EFA, is explicit regarding the necessity and role for international involvement in education, and reaffirms its commitment to a decentralized education system in which parents and communities play primary roles in its management (MECD, 2001).

In 2003, after a sector assessment and by presidential decree, a series of sector roundtable discussions involving the Ministry, international bi and multilateral donor organizations, and civil society members were launched to advance a "sector-wide approach" (SWAp)[5] (MECD, 2004). Under the direction of the Ministry, the SWAp would harmonize donor funds and programs toward the goals laid out in the National Education Plan (MECD, 2001). Finally, in 2006, the *Ley General de Educación* (General Education Law) was issued. It articulates a mission and vision for the education system, including an outline of the various modalities (primary/secondary/early childhood education, teacher education) and the qualities education seeks to develop in individuals (MECD, 2006). The policies developed between 2002 and 2006, despite the different emphases placed on reforms (or specific aspects of broader programs) by different ministries, reflect three broad policy goals of the Ministry of Education during this period: (1) to improve the relevance and quality of education with respect to appropriateness of curriculum and materials; (2) to improve coverage, stimulate demand, access, and equity; and (3) to improve governance, participation, and financial efficiency (MECD, 2004). While the international donor community was active immediately after the 1990 elections in Nicaragua broadly, and in education specifically, these documents and their related processes solidified in policy a role for the donor community in national development.

EDUCATION IN *POST*-POST-SOCIALIST NICARAGUA (2007–PRESENT)

Unlike some other stories of post-socialist states, the Nicaraguan case has a more recent chapter that might be loosely labeled *post*-post-socialist. In 2007, Daniel Ortega and the FSLN were reelected. As we will describe in this section, the current FSLN government demonstrates elements of socialist ideology, but maintains the basic structure of education from the previous governments. Currently, The Ministry of Education is unfolding its new policy agenda established under the leadership of Miguel De Castilla, the minister who only recently resigned (2007–2010). Despite the transition of government political orientation, continuities and dis-continuities remain. And there continues to be antimarket rhetoric in policy that is reminiscent of FLSN ideology of the 1980s. As De Castilla underscored, however, the policies themselves are not different from the previous governments – it is the "mechanisms" for carrying out policy processes that have changed (personal communication, June 12, 2009). Quality and local governance are still priorities, with a new strong emphasis on equity (Miguel De Castilla, personal communication, June 12, 2009).

De Castilla was highly critical of the Autonomous Schools Program and discontinued it upon taking office arguing that school fees imposed by autonomous schools restricted access for many poor families (Porta & Laguna, 2007; Miguel De Castilla, personal communication, June 12, 2009). In addition, the former minister leveled charges that schools acted like and "were treated like businesses" and of corruption in the use of government transfers (Miguel De Castilla, personal communication, June 12, 2009). De Castilla banned schools from generating extra funding and determined that all school costs are to be provided from the General Budget of the Republic (Jané, 2008). However, he continued to promote local participation through school clusters that allowed for community involvement in school governance and that provided opportunities for teachers within a cluster to collaborate (MINED Informa, 2010).

The Ministry has launched three major reform initiatives: A curriculum reform, through the process of *El Gran Consulta Nacional del Curriculum* (2007); the *Campaña Nacional de Alfabetización* (2007–2009); and the *Comisión Nacional de Planificación* (2007) to begin dialogue and the process of development of a *Plan Decenal*, a 10-year municipal level education plan (MINED Informa, 2010). These initiatives aim to achieve more education, better education, new (other) education, and participatory and decentralized management of education (MINED, 2007). The initiatives focus on the poor and most marginalized by the system through the introduction of a new (and what the MoE determined to be), more relevant curriculum that emphasizes lifelong learning and strengthens the different ethnic, cultural, and linguistic identities throughout the country (MINED, 2007). The policy goals also include language that aims to "rescue education from the hands of the market," to promote an education that is traditionally Nicaraguan, and to teach thinking skills that resist "ideological impositions" that act against the most poor (MINED, 2007, p. 9). Similar language, however, is not evident in the Ministry's more specific teaching policies. Detailed in policy are the new ideas that define good teaching and guides that target specific skills and strategies in each discipline (MINED, 2009a, 2009b). In relation to pedagogy, the Ministry asserts an emphasis on constructivist teaching (MINED 2009b). Guidelines and expectations for long-term and short-term planning for all levels of education are outlined for teachers and include specified criteria (including the integration of multiple modalities for learning and plans for garnering the participation of parents) (MINED, 2009a). The Ministry is attempting to reinforce good teaching by providing detailed scaffolds for teachers on how to assess knowledge of students in multiple ways, how to incorporate varieties of activities in class, and how to integrate problem-based teaching approaches (MINED, 2009a).

Finally, a "participatory and decentralized model" of education refers to the management of education in the hands of communities, while privileging the role of teachers. This is a renewed effort on the part of the Ministry to garner mass participation in education. A *nucleo*, or cluster system, forms school communities around a central school for the purposes of teacher training and professional development. Teachers within the *nucleo* also gather monthly to collaboratively plan, contextualize the curriculum, and address locally specific challenges (MINED Informa, 2010). These meetings are used to reflect on progress and modify plans according to successes and challenges experienced in the previous month maintaining focused attention to student learning outcomes (MINED, 2009a). Similarly, the municipality plays a large role. Municipal level 10-year education plans (in contribution to the national *Plan Decenal*) are now aligned with development projects and ground discussions with teachers, municipal level ministry officials, and other members of civil society – including parents – toward the development and improvement of the policy goals.

There are hints of the original ideological orientations of the FSLN in this new government. Recent minister De Castilla was explicitly "anti-capitalist" (MINED Informa, 2010), and the new goals for education espouse rhetoric resisting the influence of the market. This is in response to the movement toward the privatization of costs imposed by school fees under School Autonomy. The specific policies, however, reflect a more direct attention to student learning and the quality of teaching and learning processes. They value the development of critical thinking skills, multiple intelligences, and problem-based learning, and specifically oppose traditional teaching that relies on memorization (MINED, 2009a). The relationship between international donors and the government remains strong and significant. Recent minister De Castilla suggests that donor involvement should occur through ground level NGO programs and even direct involvement of NGOs with municipalities, rather than focusing on interactions with the central Ministry of Education (MINED Informa, 2010). He also recognizes organizations that engage in community level work as important civil society actors in education (MINED Informa, 2010).

DISCUSSION

The contrasting ideologies reflected in political transitions influence the different trends in education reform. These ideologies underlie differing positions regarding social sector spending and the responsibilities of the state and ministry, as well as the orientations and goals of the education system. The first FSLN government believed the government itself was responsible for promoting social transformation through education. They increased spending and spent much effort mobilizing the public around education. The "post-socialist" Chamorro government took the opposite approach by relying on individuals and communities (the school councils) to take up the responsibility for decision-making and provision of education.

Similarly, political ideology has helped to shape relations with the international donor community, which have had an important role in education development. That Nicaragua sought to decrease government spending in education worked in tandem with Belli's autonomous school program and decentralization efforts, which in turn, won strong international support. The new FSLN government maintains the ideological orientation of education benefiting the poor, which is consistent with the original revolutionary government. It also resists the market dynamics that play out with the imposition of school fees and instead favors a movement to socialize the cost of education under the national budget. However, it acknowledges the important role of the international donor community in education. This is a mixed perspective: In interviews, the recently resigned head of the Ministry of Education Miguel De Castilla has articulated a resistance to market forces, however the central focus of the reforms (beyond the shift toward public financing of education) do not reference the market. Rather, the focus seems to be the improvement of the quality of teaching and learning. At the same time, there is a continued emphasis on decentralized management of schools.

Although "local participation" was a central tenet in both the original FSLN government and the Chamorro administrations, its meaning has differed sharply across ministries. While the Sandinistas saw education as an avenue for mass participation in national development projects, the ASP saw local control and an education rich in Christian values as important to develop a moral citizenry (Gershberg & Jacobs, 1998). The Sandinistas envisioned participation through local community collectives that could be involved in debates, even at a national level, regarding the direction schools should take (Arnove, 1986). Belli, on the other hand, saw participation occurring at an individual level. He encouraged parent involvement above all other forms of participation such that parents could (and through a later legal framework did) have a majority voice in the daily workings of the school and classroom (Gershberg, 2002). The development and reinforcement of local participation in education through participatory decentralized management of schools is also a priority of the new FSLN government. However, this has taken on a different meaning than under the previous governments. Municipalities are an important locus of reform and policy-making, and are seen as active participants in defining the 10-year plans, working with local school councils, and potentially with direct dealings with NGOs seeking to do local education work (MINED Informa, 2010). Teachers have a renewed voice in the system under the current Ministry leadership. Under the FSLN during the 1980s, the Sandinista teacher union

(ANDEN) was a powerful voice and teachers themselves were leaders in the literacy campaign and other areas of education. Teachers' unions were not in support of Belli's ASP model because of the marginal influence they could exert (Gershberg, 2002). During an interview, Belli admitted that he missed an opportunity to generate support by not working with the teachers (personal communication, June 12, 2009). Under the current Ministry, in contrast, teachers and teaching seem to be of central importance. A full description of constructivist teaching, curriculum contents, and pedagogical approaches has been published (MINED, 2009a, 2009b). The Ministry has implemented the *nucleo* system, where teachers can network with other teachers in their cluster to collaborate and solve problems (MINED Informa, 2010). Furthermore, teachers are to be privileged voices in the planning of the 10-year municipal level plans. As of yet, there are no reports on how the process is working. It remains to be seen what comes of the form of decentralization initiated by the new FSLN, but the increased role and attention to teachers and equity hints to the possibility of new dynamics.

Discontinuities in personnel within the Ministry of Education are likewise important influences to policy.[6] Political fluctuations throughout have undermined the operations of the central Ministry and reveal two important outcomes. First, this demonstrates the Ministry's institutional weaknesses in policy development and implementation. Ministers and other high-level individual decision-makers were, and continue to be, the drivers of reform (Jané, 2008). The changes in high-level staff can be disruptive to the established inertia of reforms or fail to formally legitimize them in policy. Second, the curriculum reforms have caused discontinuities for teachers who have had to learn and relearn the curriculum, guides, and other materials with each change of government. In an interview conducted in 2007, teachers expressed frustration with having to relearn the curriculum and expectations once the new government was established (primary school teacher, personal communication, June 20, 2007). A similar discontinuity exists with local ministry officials who likewise must be reoriented to new reforms and new curriculum. This can create inconsistencies within the system in that understandings about what should happen in schools and classrooms frequently differ from the perspectives of different stakeholders in the system.

There have also been continuities. The presence of USAID is one of the forces promoting continuity of reform processes in the last 17 years starting with the BASE I and II projects (1994–1998 and 1999–2004) and continuing with the current Exelencia Project. The programs over time have shifted from a strong emphasis on curriculum and materials production, teacher training, and support for decentralization at all levels to a more consolidated effort toward education quality at the community, school, and classroom levels through the implementation of active learning methodologies (USAID, 2005). Additionally, the local support won by individuals has helped sustain the reforms, even when shifts have occurred at the central Ministry of Education. For example, Oscar Mogollón,[7] technical advisor for the BASE I and II projects and instrumental in scaffolding reform at very local levels, created a strong community and grassroots support for autonomy that functioned to strengthen and sustain it early on, even without a legal policy framework.

While the EFA has been in the political discussion from the outset and has been the focal point of much of the donor activity in education, especially relating to the National Education Plan and SWAp, the progress toward achieving the goals is mixed. There have been improvements mainly in early childhood education (ECE). Enrollment has increased from 28.8% to 55.2% between 2001 and 2008 (Visser-Valfrey et al., 2009) and its place within the education system is formalized in policy (MECD, 2006). Overall enrollment in primary school was reported as 84.1% – an improvement, but problematic since enrollment rates have been reported at 100% in most states (Porta and Laguna, 2007). And, there are persistent disparities between urban and rural primary enrollment rates (86.4% and 78.9%, respectively) (Lopez, 2007). Progress in learning outcomes is mixed. Scores have not significantly improved in the areas of standardized assessment (math and Spanish for 3rd and 6th grades in 2002 and 2006) (Lopez & Reyes, 2007). Improvements on these outcomes were more significant in urban areas, despite showing only a modest improvement, than in rural areas, where there is no clear improvement in scores (Lopez & Reyes, 2007). Finally, the scores for 6th grade are much less predictable than 3rd grade because of the consistent problem of students dropping out during the early primary school years (Lopez & Reyes, 2007). These results point to persistent problems in universal completion of primary school, equity and access to school, and to quality of education, three of the EFA targets.

The case of Nicaragua demonstrates that important transformations in education reflect the political transitions, both internally and within a wider global context, as the country has gone from a socialist to a post-socialist to the current *post*-post-socialist government. The changing roles of teachers, parents and communities, and the Ministry of Education reveal these complex dynamics within the country. The role of ideology as situated in a larger changing global context is significant because it has impacted the relationships between the government and the international capitalist donor community. These larger ideological and political–economic forces impact the concepts of "local participation" in education and the continuities and discontinuities affecting the policy process. What comes of the education reforms in the new Ministry and new international economic climate is yet to be seen, however, the mixed results on EFA goals suggest that providing universal access to education will continue to be a challenge.

NOTES

1. We use the term "socialist" to mean socialist ideology or tendencies represented in the governments. We do not imply a functioning socialist state along with this theoretical definition.

2. While beyond the scope of this chapter to discuss in great detail, it is important to note that Nicaragua – prior to the Somoza regime – already had a history of U.S. involvement and social opposition to that involvement. Augusto Sandino led an insurrection against U.S. Marine occupation between 1926 and 1932. The U.S. retreated from Nicaragua leaving Anastasio Somoza Garcia, who had trained under the marines, as commander of the National Guard. Augusto Sandino, after agreeing to disarm, was executed by the National Guard under Somoza in 1934. Sandino's legacy, along with his commitment to education as a tool for empowerment, makes up the ideological foundations of the Sandinistas.

3. The "Contras" were comprised of former National Guard members and other opponents of the revolutionary government. They were funded by the United States (who also participated in training) and operated from bases in Honduras.

4. For a more in-depth analysis of the Autonomous Schools Program, see Fuller and Rivarola (1998) and King and Ozler (1998) (see also King, Ozler, & Rawlings, 1999a, 1999b; King, Rawlings, & Ozler, 1996).

5. A sector-wide approach is a process by which governments, donors, and other stakeholders within the education sector come together to align activities and projects toward sector goals. For a greater discussion of SWAps in education, see UNESCO (2007).

6. This is evident even in the current Ministry as Miguel de Castilla stepped down in 2010.

7. Oscar Mogollón was among the founders of the Escuela Nueva rural school reform in Colombia, a model that has been adopted more widely in other countries in Latin America.

ACKNOWLEDGMENT

The author gratefully acknowledges the invaluable contributions of John Gillies, Kirsten Galisson, and Bridget Drury at the Academy for Educational Development who were responsible for conducting the interviews with ministry personnel and whose involvement was integral in the development of the chapter.

REFERENCES

Academy for Educational Development. (1998). *Final report: Nicaragua basic education project (BASE) 1994–1998.* Washington, DC: Academy for Educational Development.

Arcia, G., & Belli, H. (2001). La autonomía escloar en Nicaragua: Restableciendo el contrato social *[School autonomy in Nicaragua: Rebuilding the social contract]. PREAL* (21), 1–23.

Arnove, R. F. (1986). *Education and revolution in Nicaragua.* New York: Praeger Publishers.

Arnove, R. F. (1995). Education as contested terrain in Nicaragua. *Comparative Education Review, 39*(1), 25–53.

Arnove, R. F., & Dewees, A. (1991). Education and revolutionary transformation in Nicaragua, 1979–1990. *Comparative Education Review, 35*(1), 92–109.

Arnove, R. F., Franz, S., Mollis, M., & Torres, C. A. (1999). Education in Latin America at the end of the 1990s. In: R. F. Arnove & C. A. Torres (Eds), *Comparative education: The dialectic of the global and the local* (pp. 277–294). New York: Rowman and Littlefield Publishers, Inc.

Bray, M. (1999). Control of education: Issues and tensions in centralization and decentralization. In: R. F. Arnove & C. A. Torres (Eds), *Comparative education: The dialectic of the global and the local* (pp. 207–232). New York: Rowman and Littlefield Publishers, Inc.

Carnoy, M. (1999). *Globalization and educational reform: What planners need to know.* Paris: UNESCO/IIEP.

FSLN. (1986). The historic program of the FSLN. In: B. Marcus (Ed.), *Sandinistas speak: Speeches, writings, and interviews with leaders of Nicaragua's revolution.* New York: Pathfinder Press.

Fuller, B., & Rivarola, M. (1998). *Nicaragua's experiment to decentralize schools: Views of parents, teachers, and directors.* Washington, DC: The World Bank.

Gershberg, A. I. (1999). Education decentralization processes in Mexico and Nicaragua: Legislative versus ministry-led reform strategies. *Comparative Education, 35*(1), 63–80.

Gershberg, A. I. (2002). Empowering parents while making them pay: Autonomous schools and education reform processes in Nicaragua. Paper presented at the Woodrow Wilson Center Workshops on the Politics of Education and Health Sector Reforms. Retrieved from http://wilsoncenter.org/topics/docs/Gershberg_Paper.pdf

Gershberg, A. I., & Jacobs, M. (1998). *Decentralization and recentralization: Lessons from the social sectors in Mexico and Nicaragua.* Washington, DC: Inter-American Development Bank.

Ginsburg, M., & Cooper, S. (1991). Educational reform, the state, and the world economy: Understanding and engaging in ideological and other struggles. In: M. Ginsburg (Ed.), *Understanding educational reform in global context: Economy, ideology, and the state.* New York: Garland Publishing, Inc.

Government of Nicaragua. (2000). *Interim poverty reduction strategy paper.* Available at www.worldbank.org. Retrieved on June 30, 2007.

Government of Nicaragua. (2001). *A strengthened growth and poverty reduction strategy.* Available at www.worldbank.org. Retrieved on June 15, 2007.

Government of Nicaragua. (2005). *National development plan.* Available at www.worldbank.org. Retrieved on June 30, 2006.

Grindle, M. (2007). Reform despite the odds: Improving quality in education. *Revista Pensamiento Educativo, 40*(1), 131.

Hanemann, U. (2005). *Nicaragua's literacy campaign*. Hamburg, Germany: UNESCO Institute for Education.

Inter-Agency Commission. (1990). *World declaration on education for all*. Jomtien, Thailand: Inter-Agency Commission.

Jané, E. (2008). *Assessment of the sector-wide approach in the education sector in Nicaragua*. Paris: UNESCO.

Kampwirth, K. (1997). Social policy. In: T. W. Walker (Ed.), *Nicaragua without illusions: Regime transition and structural adjustment*. Wilmington, DE: Rowman and Littlefield Publishers, Inc.

King, E. M., & Ozler, B. (1998). What's decentralization got to do with learning? The case of Nicaragua's school autonomy reform. Paper presented at the American Educational Research Association. Retrieved from http://siteresources.worldbank.org/EDUCATION/Resources/278200-1099079877269/547664-1099079934475/547667-1135281552767/What_Decentralization_Learning.pdf

King, E. M., Ozler, B., & Rawlings, L. B. (1999a). *Nicaragua's school autonomy reform: Fact or fiction?* Washington, DC: The World Bank.

King, E. M., Ozler, B., & Rawlings, L. B. (1999b). *Nicaragua's school autonomy reform: Fact or fiction?* Washington, DC: The World Bank.

King, E. M., Rawlings, L. B., & Ozler, B. (1996). *Nicaragua's school autonomy reform: A first look*. Washington, DC: The World Bank.

Lopez, N. (2007). *Urban and rural disparities in Latin America: Their implications for educational access*. Buenos Aires, Argentina: UNESCO.

Lopez, R. R., & Reyes, C. N. (2007). *Informe de Resultados: Evaluacción Nacional del Rendimiento Academico de 3y 6 Grado 2002–2006 [Results report: National assessment of academic performance for 3rd and 6th grades, 2002–2006]*. Managua: MINED.

MECD. (2000). *EFA 2000*. Available at www.mined.gob.ni.

MECD. (2001). *Plan Nacional de Educacion [National Education Plan]*. Available at http://www.ilo.org/public/spanish/employment/skills/hrdr/init/nic_2.htm. Retrieved April 10, 2008.

MECD. (2002a). Education for All – Fast Track Initiative country proposal. Available at www.mined.gob.ni. Retrieved on May 26, 2009.

MECD. (2002b). *Ley de Participación Educativa [Education Participation Law]*. Available at www.mined.gob.ni

MECD. (2004). *Plan Común de Trabajo del MECD: Prioridades Estrategicas para el Periodo 2005–2008 [Ministry of Education Joint Work Plan: Strategic Priorities for the Period of 2005–2008]*. Available at www.mined.gob.ni. Retrieved on April 9, 2008.

MECD. (2006). *Ley 582, Ley General de Educación con Reformas [Law 582, General Education Law with Reforms]*. www.mined.gob.ni. Retrieved on June 15, 2007.

Miller, V. (1985). *Between struggle and hope: The Nicaraguan literacy crusade*. Boulder, CO: Westview Press.

MINED. (2007). *Politicas Para La Educación Basica y Media del Gobierno de Reconciliación y Unidad Nacional, Para el Período 2007–2012. [Education Policies for Basic and Middle School Education of the Government of Reconciliation and National Unity for the Period of 2007–2012]*. Available at www.mined.gob.ni. Retrieved on January 15, 2010.

MINED. (2009a). *El Planeamiento Didáctico y la Evaluación de los Aprendizajes. [Classroom Planning and Assessment of Learning]*. Available at www.mined.gob.ni. Retrieved on January 30, 2010.

MINED. (2009b). *Transformación Curricular, Paradigmas, y Enfoques Pedagogicos.* [*Curriculum Transformation, Paradigms, and Pedagogical Foci*]. Available at http://www. mined.gob.ni. Retrieved on January 15, 2010.

MINED Informa. (2010). *Entrevista con el Ministro de educación, Miguel De Castilla Urbina.* [*Interview with Minister of Education, Miguel De Castilla Urbina*]. Available at Foro Latinoamericano de Politicas Educativas: www.foro-latino.org. Retrieved on January 27, 2010.

Parker, C. E. (2005). Teacher incentives and student achievement in Nicaraguan autonomous schools. In: E. Vegas (Ed.), *Incentives to improve teaching: Lessons from Latin America.* Washington, DC: The World Bank.

Porta, E., & Laguna, J. R. (2007). *Education for All Global Monitoring Report 2008. Nicaragua: Country case study.* Paris: UNESCO.

Reimers, F. (1991). The impact of economic stabilization and adjustment on education in Latin America. *Comparative Education Review, 35*(2), 319–353.

Torres, C. A. (1991). The state, nonformal education, and socialism in Cuba, Nicaragua, and Granada. *Comparative Education Review, 35*(1), 110–130.

UNESCO. (2007). *Education Sector-Wide Approaches (SWAps): Background, guide and lessons.* Paris: UNESCO.

USAID. (2005). *BASE II Final Report.* Managua: MECD, USAID, AED, Juarez and Associates.

Visser-Valfrey, M., Jané, E., Wilde, D., & Escobar, M. (2009). *Mid-term evaluation of the EFA Fast Track Initiative Country Case Study: Nicaragua.* Cambridge Education, Mokoro, Oxford Policy Management. Retrieved from http://www.educationfasttrack.org/newsroom/focus-on/mid-term-evaluation-of-the-efa-fast-track-initiative/

Walker, T. W. (Ed.) (1997). *Nicaragua without illusions: Regime transition and structural adjustment in the 1990's.* Wilmington, DE: Rowman and Littlefield Publishers, Inc.

Wheelock, J. (1997). Revolution and democratic transition in Nicaragua. In: J. I. Dominguez & M. Lindenberg (Eds), *Democratic transitions in Central America* (pp. 67–84). Gainesville, FL: University Press of Florida.

STAYING THE (POST)SOCIALIST COURSE: GLOBAL/LOCAL TRANSFORMATIONS AND CUBAN EDUCATION

Noah W. Sobe and Renee N. Timberlake

In 1992, in the wake of the fall of the Soviet Union and the termination of a 30-year economic relationship, the Cuban government ratified a new constitution. In place of a statement asserting that Cuba "bases its educational and cultural policy on the scientific conception of the world, established and developed by Marxism-Leninism," the constitution was changed to indicate that educational and cultural policy was based on "the progress made in science and technology, the ideology of Marx and Martí, and the widespread Cuban progressive pedagogical tradition." This change to the text of the national constitution captures many features of post-socialist transformation in Cuba, the first notable element of which is that Marx (and socialism more broadly) hardly disappears from the scene. In fact, given the continued rule by Fidel Castro and his brother Raul as well as by the Cuban Communist Party over what is now nearly two subsequent decades, one can even question whether the designation "post-socialist" is appropriate to use in the Cuban context. Yet, the Cuba of 2010 is considerably different than the Cuba of 1990 and the aforementioned changes to the language of the constitution hint at the continuities and discontinuities between Cuba's "socialist" and "post-socialist" period.

Post-Socialism is not Dead: (Re)Reading the Global in Comparative Education
International Perspectives on Education and Society, Volume 14, 351–367
Copyright © 2010 by Emerald Group Publishing Limited
All rights of reproduction in any form reserved
ISSN: 1479-3679/doi:10.1108/S1479-3679(2010)0000014016

While Marx is not banished from the pantheon of official heroes, the position accorded to the 19th century Cuban nationalist Jose Martí (1853–1895) rises significantly. As we will discuss below, Cuban socialism has always been closely linked to ideas of national independence and the politics of establishing an "authentic" Cuban identity. However, over the last two decades the Cuban state has placed increased importance on national figures like Martí. In one part, this is clearly a regime legitimation strategy; yet, it also has important implications for how education in Cuba has been positioned and has navigated betwixt and between "local" and "global" pressures since the fall of the Soviet Union.

The Cuban case of post-socialist transformation is important to scholars of comparative and international education for reasons that go well beyond the need for comprehensive geographic/regional "coverage." Generally speaking, one might say that the Cuban case sheds light on the ways in which and purposes to which states use public education. This is an issue that has long been a mainstay of comparative education scholarship, but one that has recently garnered new attention because it appears to some observers that over the past several decades neoliberal political rationalities have altered the traditional contours of society–school relationships around the globe. The unique positioning of Cuba vis-à-vis neoliberal and state socialist modes of governance prompts our curiosity and interest in what the situation in Cuba might have to say (or portend) about contemporary educational transformations more broadly. As we discuss briefly below, there are uncanny points of contact between socialist theory – epitomized in Lenin's writings on state power and the "withering away of the State" – and certain liberal and neoliberal notions of autonomy and freedom (Valiavicharska, 2010). The governmental strategies of promoting and fashioning civic engagement as well as administering populations might not be as radically different between state socialist and liberal democratic regimes as has traditionally been thought (Sobe, 2007). Despite the North American tendency to view Cuba through Buena Vista Social Club lenses and see the island as a quaint and dated aberration, and as cut off from the "realities" of the contemporary global system, it will become clear across this chapter that contemporary Cuba is hardly "a land that time forgot."

The Cuban case of post-socialist transformation is also extremely instructive, both for what is anomalous about Cuban post-socialism and for what is similar to other post-socialist contexts. First, Cuba raises a set of questions regarding how social science and education researchers should conceptualize "transformation." A powerful corpus of political science theory and scholarship has long conceptualized post-socialist change in terms of a "transition." Principally grounded in the political changes experienced in Latin America and Southern Europe in the 1970s, this scholarship has tended to conceptualize post-authoritarian political and social transformation as a "path" along which nation states move as they become more and more successfully functioning democracies, that is, so-called "third wave democratization" (Carothers, 2002). The self-privileging teleology of the transition concept has long garnered criticism, and very early on scholars of the Soviet Union and East/Central Europe had vigorous debates about the (f)utility of drawing on a transitology problematic (Schmitter & Karl, 1994; Bunce, 1995). However, even leaving aside the question of the extent to which post-socialist change mirrors post-authoritarian transition in other parts of the world, the very idea that there is a master paradigm of post-socialist transition itself has been widely disputed (Gans-Morse, 2004; Silova, 2010). Nonetheless, in surveying post-socialist change globally, Herrschel (2007) suggests that unique to post-socialist transformations is the "comprehensive new start" which involves the establishment of completely new state structures, economies, and social formations (p. 5). Despite this emphasis on newness, Herrschel – like most other scholars – is also quite attentive to the profoundly important communist-era legacies. Of course, these legacies exhibit significant variation and are not at all the same from society to society. Nor are these legacies as if "dinosaurs" bound for extinction; rather they are themselves integrally constitutive of the new social, political, economic, and cultural formations that we have seen emerging since the fall of the Soviet Union (Burawoy & Verdery, 1999). Amidst all these complexities and debates, Cuba stands as a case of post-socialist (or at least post-Soviet) transformation that undoes any notion that there is a definite "path" to democratization and economic liberalization.

Second, within Cuba, the political and cultural discourse on change has fascinating contours that are notably different from what we can observe in other settings. Nostalgia for the pre-1992 period takes on an entirely different form than the campy "Ostalgie" of the former East Germany and the "Yugostalgia" found (though to a lesser degree) in the Yugoslav successor states. In part, this is due to the fact that within Cuba itself, the past two decades are seen as anything but a *post*-socialist period. From the viewpoint of the Castro regime, to acknowledge a deviation from the socialist mission would be to acknowledge the failure of *la revolución* and would signify a surrender to counterrevolutionary elements (Bönker, Müller, & Pickel, 2002). Yet, because *la revolución* in Cuba is conceived of by authorities as a process of social, economic, and cultural change, one might say that "transformation" itself has long been a self-defining feature of socialism in Cuba. As a result, some of the noteworthy changes in Cuba since the fall of the Soviet Union are downplayed in official discourses as continuity with the goals and principles of *la revolución* is emphasized, while other changes are explicitly framed as part of the necessary unfolding of *la revolución*. All of this means that in addition to thinking carefully about the social science framing of transformation as discussed in the previous paragraph, it is also important to pay attention to the ways that "change" and "transformation" are ideologically framed in Cuban political discourse.

This chapter focuses on the education sector in Cuba and we interrogate the questions about historical continuities and discontinuities and global/local dynamics that we have been raising by first discussing the history of education in Cuba, specifically its importance in the context of the 1959 revolution that brought Castro to power. Over the first three decades of socialist rule in Cuba, as we will detail, great strides were made in developing an education system designed to expand and equalize educational opportunities, particularly between urban and rural communities. The chapter then discusses the fall of the Soviet Union and what is called in Cuba the "Special Period in a Time of Peace," which was a time of great economic suffering and transformation but also shows the Cuban government's ability to adapt and persevere.

EDUCATION IN CUBA BEFORE THE "SPECIAL PERIOD IN TIME OF PEACE"

Prior to the 1959 revolution, Cuba's dependency on the United States was deeply entrenched, with the United States virtually controlling the island's economic and political institutions. Through military occupation (in the immediate aftermath of the Spanish–American war), missionary activity, and a plethora of consultant and aid/development projects, Americans had also been deeply influential in shaping the Cuban education system (Epstein, 1987; Yaremko, 2000; Sobe, 2009). Nearly all of Cuba's sugar cane crop was exported to the United States, which granted preferential economic treatment and supplied a steady stream of US tourists and gamblers. This arguably exacerbated severe economic gaps between urban and rural areas. It is important to note, though, that in comparison with its Caribbean and Central American neighbors, Cuba under the Batista regime had unusually high literacy rates and an unusually well-educated population. However, these accomplishments were severely limited to the urban and wealthy sectors of the population, while rural and poor Cubans had notably less educational access. Dissatisfaction with these disparities in educational opportunity, along with urban–rural inequalities more broadly, arguably in part led to the revolution and popular support for Castro's seizure of power.

Remedying these economic and educational achievement gaps was among the revolutionary leaders' primary goals. In one of the first widespread educational reforms, the Castro regime eliminated all private schools, converting them into public, free, equal access schools. In 1961, two years after seizing control and shortly after declaring Cuba a socialist country, Castro shut down all schools and mobilized teachers and students alike to take to the countryside to educate the rural population. The goal of this campaign was to eliminate illiteracy on the island. The year 1961 was declared the "year of education" and within nine months the illiteracy rate dropped from 21% to 3.9%, and by 1964, UNESCO had declared Cuba to be a territory free of illiteracy (Carnoy, 1990; Breidlid, 2007).

The Castro regime's early focus on education reform and the two-year gap between seizure of power and the official declaration of socialist orientation have important implications for what later occurred in the post-Soviet period. The extent to which Castro's revolution was from the outset, an anti-colonial, anti-dependency, and "national liberation" struggle is also extremely relevant for what has happened in Cuba in the 1990s and 2000s. Though some critics have maintained that in geopolitical terms in the early 1960s the Castro regime merely traded American tutelage for Soviet tutelage, it is nonetheless the case that the legitimacy claims and ideological posturing of the Castro regime were deeply rooted in ideas of national autonomy and independence. During the Cold War, the United States tended to view Cuba merely as a Soviet outpost, yet it is noteworthy that in Cuba, as in a number of African countries (and in contrast to East/Central Europe and Central Asia), socialism has long been closely associated with a *break* from external control/domination (Herrschel, 2007). With all this in mind, it becomes plausible to see the "nationalist turn" that the Cuban government has taken in the post-Soviet period not as a novel strategic development but as a consistent, if reinvigorated, emphasis.

During the first decade of *la revolución* the government sought to gain support by expanding educational opportunity and by harnessing schooling to produce citizens in the image of Che Guevara's vision of "the new socialist man." This individual was to be, among other things, driven by moral imperatives rather than by promises of material rewards, and was to exhibit a desire to function as part of a community of equals rather than as an individual (Kozol, 1978; Wald, 1978; Lutjens, 1996). In this project of refashioning collective consciousness, schooling was used in conjunction with other social institutions such as the Committees for the Defense of the Revolution (CDRs) that were established as, in essence, neighborhood associations with the mandate of fostering community-minded civic participation. By the 1970s, Guevarism in Cuba had been replaced by a somewhat more pragmatic form of market socialism associated with Soviet economist Evsei Lieberman. Ties with the Soviet Union were consolidated and in 1972 Cuba joined COMECON, the socialist world's trade and economic cooperation organization. Earlier attempts at completely leveling the educational system were suspended, and with increased allowance for material incentives in many areas of social life, Cuban education policy began to point toward elaborating and making improvements in a system that would develop targeted areas of higher education and would track high achieving primary students into secondary schools and others into vocational schools.

Achievements in the education sector are widely recognized as one of the Castro regime's notable accomplishments. Alongside expansion of educational opportunity at primary and secondary levels, Cuban higher education has expanded, with universities now appearing across the island, as opposed to simply in Havana as was the case before 1959. In certain areas of technical and medical education Cuba has become a recognized world leader and Eckstein (1997), for example, has argued that by the early 1990s Cuba faced the "diploma disease" problem of having an overeducated populace.

ECONOMIC COLLAPSE AND THE *PERIODO ESPECIAL EN TIEMPO DE PAZ*

At the time of the collapse of the Soviet Union, approximately 80% of Cuba's exports and 80% of Cuban imports were with the Soviet Union. Over the course of 1990, oil imports from the Soviet Union decreased to almost nil; Cuba's transportation networks and the heavily petroleum dependent agricultural sector ground to a halt. In point of fact, and tellingly for what would come next, the Cuban relationship with the Soviet Union had already begun to deteriorate in the mid-1980s. Castro had been strongly critical of Gorbachev's reform agenda, to such an extent that in the late 1980s, Soviet publications were banned in Cuba for being too critical of communism (Herrschel, 2007). By the end of 1991, the last of the Soviet military presence was withdrawn from the island and the close alliances that Cuba had with the socialist world evaporated (COMECON was disbanded in the summer of 1991). This precipitated an intense economic crisis in Cuba. Cubans remember the early 1990s as a time of hunger, helplessness, and general deprivation. A black market thrived and a literary scholar who has written on the Cuban fiction produced during this time notes that "the fierce competition for extremely scarce resources further cleaved a society already divided by suspicion and distrust, but also created a strong cohort-type consciousness based on the common experience of those years" (Hernández-Reguant, 2009, p. 2). Such a profound moment of economic and social change could well have portended significant political changes. But, while there were street demonstrations in Havana in August 1994 and political opposition movements that have gained visibility and momentum for short periods (such as the *Movimiento Cristiano Liberación*, or Christian Liberation Movement, closely tied to the Catholic church and the Varela Project which has been strongly supported by former East/Central European dissidents such as Václav Havel [Gershman & Gutierrez, 2009]), the Castro regime has nonetheless managed to maintain firm political control and rebuild a considerable measure of social and economic stability in the country.

In 1990, the Cuban government declared that the country had entered a "Special Period in a Time of Peace," which alluded to the contingency plans – a "Special Period in a Time of War" – established in the 1960s to respond to a US invasion. Food rationing was significantly increased and numerous austerity measures were introduced. Castro pledged to continue the Cuban state's commitment to socialism and began adding the phrase "*socialismo o muerte* (socialism or death)" to the exclamation "*Patria o muerte* (homeland or death)" with which he characteristically closed his speeches (Hernández-Reguant, 2009). Throughout this period, Castro pledged (and asserted) that health, education, and other social welfare programs were not being interfered with. As we noted at the outset of this chapter, the constitution was amended in 1992. In addition to placing additional emphasis on Cuban national heroes and traditions, the Cuban legal system was changed to enable the country to open up to foreign investors and international economic networks that had been excluded from the island for over 30 years. As Cubanologists off the island awaited the political change that was seen as a necessary accompaniment to these changes in economic policy, the Castro regime's incremental and experimental approach to introducing market-based reforms had, by the end of the 1990s, led both to a significant restructuring of the Cuban economy and to a reassertion or stabilization of political control by the Castro-led Cuban communist party. A momentary "flowering" of civil society initiatives in Cuba in the mid to late 1990s had been for the most part rolled back by the early 2000s. And, as Hernández-Reguant (2009) suggests, for a short period of time there was "broad space for autonomous social action" (p. 4). Although there is today a steadily growing presence of and significance to Cuban cyber activism (Timberlake, 2010), it is fair to say that whatever ambiguities and opportunities presented themselves in the confusion of the immediate aftermath of the fall of the Soviet Union were relatively rapidly stabilized and brought within the sphere of governmental control and regulation.

Since the 1990s the Cuban government has focused on three primary areas of economic development: developing tourism, revamping the sugar industry, and developing Cuba's biotech sector (Reid-Henry, 2007). Although – as we discuss in the following section – the expansion of tourism in Cuba has had the greatest effect on education, a brief examination of the post-Soviet growth of Cuba's biotech industry is instructive. Cuba's biotech sector was initially developed in the early 1980s with the mastery of the production of interferon, a protein that triggers the protective defenses of the human body's immune system. Cuban-produced interferon was used with great success in ending a Dengue fever outbreak in 1981 and Cuba began exporting it to world markets. Thanks to extensive government investments in research and the construction of a massive science park on the outskirts of Havana, Cuba had by the end of the 1980s developed the world's only meningitis B vaccine (a vaccination that, as of this writing, is still not available in the United States). As Reid-Henry (2007) discusses, in the 1990s the Cuban biotech industry increasingly moved in the direction of joint-ventures and market-driven pharmaceutical production and development, all of which provided a much needed source of hard currency for the government. The increasing globalization of Cuban biotech was not, Reid-Henry argues, a contradiction in terms that suggests Cuba was a victim of circumstance and "compelled" to develop this economic sector. Rather, this "in fact points up the success of Cuba's response to transition" (p. 451). As noted above, historical experience and circumstances mean that Castro's Cuba can easily represent itself as working toward a strengthening of Cuban independence. Nationalism has always been a tricky question for socialist theory because of the Marxist inclination to consider national identity a form of bourgeois false consciousness (Anderson, 1991; Hobsbawn & Ranger, 1992); yet the longstanding anti-colonial thrust of Cuban national identity projects means that a plausible claim can be made that both socialism and engagement with global capitalism are reconcilable in the Cuban context, in that both can be seen as furthering Cuban independence and strengthening the Cuban nation. From this perspective, the case of the biotech industry in

Cuba would then refute the view that transitional states are, necessarily, unusually vulnerable to the logic and power of global capital.

In the tourism sector, however, the trade-offs between "opening up" the country to the global tourist market and the Cuban state's traditional (socialist) commitments to ensuring the social welfare of its population become somewhat more acute. Nonetheless, we would argue that Cuba's turn to tourism is highly strategic and by no means merely the forced consequence of accidental or circumstantial vulnerabilities – even as it is hard to refute the fact that tourism in Cuba presents a double-edged sword for the Castro regime (Sanchez & Adams, 2008).

The upgrading of tourist facilities (hotels, beaches, airports) and, for example, the renovation/restoration of parts of downtown Havana so as to present a particular kind of "branded" touristic experience to visitors (Hill, 2007) presents a series of stark contrasts with the hardships and deprivations experienced by everyday Cubans. For instance, American journalist Corbett (2004) notes that when rice was priced at 50 pesos a pound in 1992, the Cuban government invested US$8 million into a golf course in the coastal resort town Varadero. The apparent contradiction with *la revolución*'s original principles of ensuring fair and equitable opportunity and treatment for all Cubans is further highlighted when we consider that initially this golf course, like many of the tourist facilities built through foreign joint-venture partnerships, was off-limits to Cuban citizens.

One of the more contentious features of the "Special Period" was the creation of a "dual economy" and what was described as "tourism apartheid." State salaries are paid in *pesos nacionales* whereas the tourism sector operates using a different currency, *pesos convertibles* (CUC) which were introduced in 1994 and are pegged to the US dollar. In the late 1990s and early 2000s the US dollar was also widely used as the currency of luxury shops and tourist facilities, though this practice was ended in 2004. For a number of years – just as tourist hotels, the Varadero golf course, and certain beaches were off-limits to them – Cuban citizens were officially prohibited from using the CUC currency. Over the past five years these restrictions have been eased and Cuba increasingly has a de facto dual currency system. In sum, since the beginning of the "Special Period" and continuing through the present, for ordinary Cubans, having access to foreign hard currency or CUC has frequently been essential for basic survival. The black market, remittances, and links with the tourist industry are the primary sources of hard currency; many researchers have commented that this has led to a notable worsening of the socioeconomic position of Afro-Cubans (de la Fuente, 2001). In general, the importance of foreign hard currency (or even possession of CUC), coupled with some, albeit limited, easing of restrictions on private ventures has led to the (re)emergence of socioeconomic class divisions on the island (Mesa-Lago & Pérez-López, 2005). In addition, the growth of Cuba's tourist sector has, according to some analysts, begun to introduce elements of consumer society in Cuba (Taylor & McGlynn, 2009), as there has been, through the influx of European and North American tourists, considerable undermining of governmental efforts to insulate Cuban society from the materialist and symbolic/lifestyle consumption practices that pervade contemporary global capitalism.

CUBAN EDUCATION IN THE "SPECIAL PERIOD" THROUGH THE PRESENT

The economic pressures of the post-Soviet period have created numerous pressures on the Cuban education system. Perhaps most prominent, at least in the 1990s, have been teacher shortages as educators have left the profession for work in the tourist industry. It is estimated, for example, that as much as 10% of the teaching force left the profession in 1993 to pursue employment opportunities connected with tourism (Lutjens, 2007). However, even with the resultant shortages and a controversial emergency teacher certification program, the Cuban education system has been found to be extraordinarily successful by numerous international standardized test measurements. In this final section of the chapter, we discuss the challenges of maintaining an education system sometimes alleged to be one of the gemstones of Castro's rule in the midst of an economic crisis and governmental reforms that are at times at odds with one another.

In 1997–1998, UNESCO's Latin American Laboratory of Educational Evaluation conducted an assessment and achievement survey of third and fourth graders in 13 Latin American countries. The results were startling, in that researchers found that the average score of the bottom quartile of Cuban students was higher than the average score of the top quartile of students in the rest of the region. Cuba's average test scores in both reading and mathematics were about two standard deviations above the regional mean (Willms & Somers, 2001; Lutjens, 2007). UNESCO retested Cuban students from five randomly selected schools and found the results held. Carnoy, Grove, and Marshall (2009) point out, however, that the five retest schools hailed from the original sample of 100 schools that had been initially selected by the government for inclusion in the study – an observation that points to the difficulty of reliably conducting research on the island given the government's level of control and strong desire to portray social welfare provision in Cuba as well above international standards (on this point, see also Epstein, 1979). In a 1998 article on the reliability of Cuban statistics, Aguirre and Vichot examined the statistics produced in UNESCO's yearly reports and concluded that while international independent statistics were reliable, those published by the Cuban government are not. As is the case with other social scientists studying Cuba (e.g., Mesa-Lago & Pérez-López, 2005), education researchers are forced to do a considerable amount of interpolating and hedging. All this considered, however, there is little doubt that Cuban students are more academically successful as compared to their Latin American counterparts.

In a 2009 book that tries to explain Cuba's "academic advantage" over wealthier neighbors such as Chile and Brazil, Carnoy et al. propose that it is a social environment in which educational achievement is highly valued that can be pointed to as responsible for the impressive academic performance of elementary school students in Cuba. Drawing on James Coleman's theory that academic success is related to the amount of support given to and value attributed to education in the family and in neighborhoods, these authors argue that the primary cause of such impressive academic achievement is "state-generated social capital." According to Carnoy et al. (2009), Cuba enacts this through "state interventions in children's welfare and a national focus on education," and in this way has created "a cohesive and supportive educational environment on a regional or national scale that creates learning benefits for all students" (pp. 14–15). Taking a long-term perspective similar to what some US scholars (e.g., Ladson-Billings, 2006) recommend when addressing the "achievement gap" that seems to stubbornly persist between test scores of black and white students in the United States, Carnoy et al. (2009) note that those Cuban students who participated in UNESCO's 1997 survey benefitted from 40 years worth of governmental policy focused on creating and maintaining an equitable education system. Given the government's efforts to equalize economic opportunity through mass education, families trust the state with their children and the state has created space for "the development of a youth culture and social norms wherein even lower SES groups value academic success" (Carnoy et al., 2009, p. 53). Taylor (2009) has documented that even in recent years there are still high levels of community trust in the state-run schools and proposes that his research supports Carnoy's thesis (which also appeared as Carnoy & Marshall, 2005).

Coming at these questions from a different angle, Lutjens (2007) proposes that the Cuban government under Castro can be considered a "caring state" that has convincingly demonstrated its commitment to fairness and egalitarianism and to norms of respect and responsibility. All of this, she proposes, has resulted in the creation of "a caring classroom" in which teachers are both "caregivers and embodiments of the new socialist person" (p. 175). Yet, characterizing Cuban classrooms and teaching practices with any measure of reliable generalizability proves extremely challenging given the state involvement in researchers' site selection. Nonetheless, alongside reports on researchers' officially sanctioned visits to Cuban classrooms (e.g., Coe & McConnell, 2004), we have occasional "unsanctioned" glimpses such as a lesson observed by two American literacy scholars (Worthman & Kaplan, 2001) who happened across an opportunity to see a teacher at work in a Havana primary school. They concluded that while the Cuban government characterized its literacy curriculum as one focused on dialogic exchange, the teacher questions they witnessed often contained a suggestive "correct" and ideologically driven answer.

In the Cuban case, both in the socialist and the "post-socialist" period it is extremely difficult to reliably study the school system. Despite the generally acknowledged and accepted successful performance of Cuban students on international assessments, there is considerable divergence in the research literature on how successful the Cuban government has been at maintaining quality in the education system over the past two decades. For example, Cruz-Taura (2003) of the University of Miami's Cuba Transition Project proposes that the education system, like other the pillars of Cuba's social welfare system, is "corroding at the base" (p. 10). Whether the Cuban education system is truly delivering on its commitments to the extent claimed by the government and some foreign researchers is a question that cannot be decisively answered as of yet. It is abundantly clear, however, that teacher shortages are one of the key challenges that the Cuban education system has faced since the fall of the Soviet Union.

As noted above, the departure of teachers from the education system began in the early 1990s. In 1999 the Cuban government increased teacher salaries by 30%, to the equivalent of approximately US$20 per month, which was still inadequate to compete with money that can be earned in the tourist sector (Breidlid, 2007; Lutjens, 2007). To address the continuing shortage of teachers, Cuba has created an emergency teacher certification program through which secondary and university students studying pedagogy can enter the classroom (as teachers "*emergentes*") after only one year of training/coursework. At the same time, Cuba has embarked on a campaign to bring modern information communication technology into the Cuban school. On the one hand, this can be seen as an effort to more adequately prepare students for a technologically driven economy (Lutjens, 2007), while, on the other, it can be seen as a desperate measure to ensure quality uniform learning and a concession to the shortage of teachers (Breidlid, 2007). Although televisions do not replace the presence of a teacher in the classroom, Breidlid (2007) argues that they are an attempt to compensate for the lack of experience the *emergentes* bring into the classroom. Prior to the creation of the *emergente* training programs, teachers studied for four to five years before entering the classroom; under the new system, students spend one year studying and then enter the classroom full-time under the loose supervision of an experienced teacher. The *emergentes* continue to take classes on weekends and over the summers until their coursework is finished. Although the program originally only sent *emergentes* into primary school, they are now being sent to secondary schools as well, which can create situations where, for example, there are 19-year-old *emergentes* teaching 17-year-old students. As Breidlid notes, teacher shortages that date to the beginning of the Special Period and the development of emergency teacher certification programs suggest the eroding of the high esteem that once might have been accorded to the teaching profession in Cuba. Thus, despite tight governmental controls, and – ironically – with some resemblances to the "retreat of the state" that we witness in neoliberal economic contexts in other sites, the experience of the last two decades appears to have undermined the ability of the government to foster the state-generated social capital that Carnoy et al. (2009) proposed to be supporting Cuba's culture of academic achievement. This does not deny the possibility, however, that this general social capital is persisting/ will persist through these transformations if it is indeed embedded at multiple social levels and in multiple institutions.

CONCLUSION

Post-socialist educational transformation in Cuba has as of yet not "settled" into any predictable pattern or path. Though they had been preaching the decay of the communist model across the Cold War, Western social scientists (almost across the board) famously missed the boat on predicting the fall of the iron curtain and the revolutions of 1989. Ex post facto explanations and theories to explain the "inevitability" of post-socialist transition immediately cropped up to fill the absence. While, as we noted at the outset and as this volume conclusively shows, careful examination of other post-socialist settings puts lie to the claim that there is a single transition path, the Cuban case – possibly more than other cases – shows that today, 20 years out, we are farther from "the end of history"/"the end of social science prognostication" than perhaps at any other moment. The fact that the Castro regime "mystifyingly" defies all predictions of its death, unviability, and obsolescence speaks to the uncertain, contingent, and nonlinear nature of social, cultural, economic, and political change in general.

One of us (Sobe, 2009) has argued that "historically speaking, modern schooling has been very much a state-centered enterprise – of government and for government" (p. 124). Thus, to focus too much on the ways that the Cuban communist regime uses schooling as a means of so-called "indoctrination" is to lose sight of the extent to which all forms of schooling (qua schooling) inscribe normative principles and regulate modes of reasoning and possibilities for "rational" or "acceptable" behavior – regardless of the political persuasion of the regime, agency, or institution involved. As noted above, Cuba's inaccessibility (but not its isolation – claims for which, we argued, are quite exaggerated) makes fine-grained, reliable, and valid research on classroom realities close to impossible. The challenge of the next decade will be to try to understand, as Cuba's transformations continue, what role(s), purpose(s), and techniques are ascribed to the educational system; what results or outcomes they produce; and how they too have transformed and continue to transform over time.

The Cuban post-socialist experience also allows us to overcome the misleading question that so often bedazzles political scientists: whether we can point to exogenous or endogenous forces as more responsible for the shape and pace of social, political, and economic change. Social scientists clearly need to move beyond a preoccupation with the question of whether global forces or local, cultural patterns and histories are more important. Both are. The question really needs to be: What combinations and sets of interaction between different sets of actors and institutions have shaped social, political, and economic trends and trajectories? On the one hand, the uniqueness of the Cuban post-socialist experience might suggest a powerful influence of local path-dependency. However, many commentators have advanced the entirely plausible argument that the Castros have only retained power, thanks to the militant agitation of the Cuban exile community in the United States as well as – for most of the past two decades – fierce opposition on the part of the US government. Cuba's attraction as a tourist destination and willingness to accept foreign investment has had a profound impact on the country across multiple sectors. One can say, then, that the situation does not reduce to determining whether "global" models or "local" models hold sway. Rather the task is to establish how what structures and patterns have emerged through multiple sets of interactions and the ways in which the Cuban government (and other actors) describe and acknowledge those interactions.

REFERENCES

Aguirre, B. E., & Vichot, R. J. (1998). The reliability of Cuba's educational statistics. *Comparative Education Review, 42*(2), 118–138.

Anderson, B. (1991). *Imagined communities: Reflections on the origin and spread of nationalism.* London: Verso.

Bönker, F., Müller, K., & Pickel, A. (Eds). (2002). *Postcommunist transformation and the social sciences: Cross-disciplinary approaches.* Lanham, MD: Rowman and Littlefield.

Breidlid, A. (2007). Education in Cuba – An alternative educational discourse: Lessons to be learned? *Compare, 37*(5), 617–634.

Bunce, V. (1995). Should transitologists be grounded? *Slavic Review, 54*(1), 111–127.

Burawoy, M., & Verdery, K. (Eds). (1999). *Uncertain transition: Ethnographies of change in the postsocialist world.* Lanham, MD: Rowman and Littlefield.

Carnoy, M. (1990). Socialist development and educational reform in Cuba: Education from poverty to liberty. In: B. Nasson & J. Samuel (Eds), *Education, from poverty to liberty.* Cape Town: Creda Press.

Carnoy, M., Grove, A. K., & Marshall, J. H. (2009). *Cuba's academic advantage: Why students in Cuba do better in school.* Stanford, CA: Stanford University Press.

Carnoy, M., & Marshall, J. H. (2005). Comparing Cuban academic performance with the rest of Latin America. *Comparative Education Review, 49*(2), 230–261.

Carothers, T. (2002). The end of the transition paradigm. *Journal of Democracy, 13*(1), 5–22.

Coe, G., & McConnell, J. (2004). The children of Cuba. *Young Children Journal, 5*(September), 1–7.

Corbett, B. (2004). *This is Cuba: An outlaw culture survives.* New York: Basic Books.

Cruz-Taura, G. (2003). *Rehabilitating education in Cuba: Assessment of conditions and policy recommendations.* Miami, FL: Institute for Cuban and Cuban-American Studies, University of Miami.

de la Fuente, A. (2001). Recreating racism: Race and discrimination in Cuba's "special period". *Socialism and Democracy, 15*(1), 65–91.

Eckstein, S. (1997). The coming crisis in Cuban education. *Assessment in Education, 4*(1), 107–120.

Epstein, E. H. (1979). Book review. Children of the revolution by Jonathan Kozol. *Comparative Education Review, 23*(3), 456–459.

Epstein, E. H. (1987). The peril of paternalism: The imposition of education on Cuba by the United States. *American Journal of Education, 96*(1), 1–23.

Gans-Morse, J. (2004). Searching for transitologists: Contemporary theories of post-communist transitions and the myth of a dominant paradigm. *Post-Soviet Affairs, 20*(4), 320–349.

Gershman, C., & Gutierrez, O. (2009). Ferment in civil society. *Journal of Democracy, 20*(1), 36–53.

Hernández-Reguant, A. (Ed.) (2009). *Cuba in the special period: Culture and ideology in the 1990s.* New York: Palgrave Macmillan.

Herrschel, T. (2007). *Global geographies of post-socialist transition: Geographies, societies, policies.* New York: Routledge.

Hill, M. J. (2007). Reimagining old Havana: World heritage and the production of scale in late socialist Cuba. In: S. Sassen (Ed.), *Deciphering the global: Its spaces, scales and subjects* (pp. 59–77). New York: Routledge.

Hobsbawn, E., & Ranger, T. (Eds). (1992). *The invention of tradition.* Cambridge: Cambridge University Press/Canto.

Kozol, J. (1978). *Children of the revolution: A Yankee teacher in the Cuban schools.* New York: Delacorte Press.

Ladson-Billings, G. (2006). From the achievement gap to the education debt: Understanding achievement in U.S. schools. *Educational Researcher, 35*(7), 3–12.

Lutjens, S. L. (1996). *The state, bureaucracy and the Cuban schools: Power and participation.* Boulder, CO: Westview Press.

Lutjens, S. L. (2007). (Re)reading Cuban educational policy: Schooling and the third revolution. In: I. Epstein (Ed.), *Recapturing the personal: Essays on education and embodied knowledge in comparative perspective* (pp. 163–194). Greenwich, CT: Information Age Publishing.

Mesa-Lago, C., & Pérez-López, J. (2005). *Cuba's aborted reform: Socioeconomic effects, international comparisons, and transition policies.* Gainsville, FL: University of Florida Press.

Reid-Henry, S. (2007). The contested spaces of Cuban development: Post-socialism, post-colonialism and the geography of transition. *Geoforum, 38,* 445–455.

Sanchez, P. M., & Adams, K. M. (2008). The Janus-faced character of tourism in Cuba. *Annals of Tourism Research, 35*(1), 27–46.

Schmitter, P. C., & Karl, T. L. (1994). The conceptual travels of transitologists and consolidologists: How far to the East should they attempt to go? *Slavic Review, 53*(1), 173–185.

Silova, I. (Ed.) (2010). *Globalization on the margins: Education and post-socialist transformations in Central Asia.* Charlotte, NC: Information Age Publishing.

Sobe, N. W. (2007). U.S. comparative education research on Yugoslav education in the 1960s and 1970s. *European Education, 38*(4), 44–64.

Sobe, N. W. (2009). Educational reconstruction "By the dawn's early light": Violent political conflict and American overseas education reform. *Harvard Educational Review, 79*(1), 123–131.

Taylor, H. L., Jr. (2009). *Inside El Barrio: A bottom-up view of neighborhood life in Castro's Cuba.* Sterling, VA: Kumarian Press.

Taylor, H. L., Jr., & McGlynn, L. (2009). International tourism in Cuba: Can capitalism be used to save socialism? *Futures, 41*(6), 405–413.

Timberlake, R. N. (2010). *Cyberspace and the defense of the Revolution: Cuban bloggers, civic participation, and state discourse.* Unpublished MA Thesis. Cultural and Educational Policy Studies, Loyola University Chicago, Chicago.

Valiavicharska, Z. (2010). Socialist modes of governance and the "Withering away of the state": Revisiting Lenin's state and revolution. *Theory and Event, 13*(2). Available at http://muse.jhu.edu/login?uri = /journals/theory_and_event/v013/13.2.valiavicharska.html

Wald, K. (1978). *Children of Che: Childcare and education in Cuba.* New York: Ramparts Press.

Willms, J. D., & Somers, M. A. (2001). Family, classroom and school effects on children's educational outcomes in Latin America. *International Journal of School Effectiveness and Improvement, 12*(4), 409–445.

Worthman, C., & Kaplan, L. (2001). Literacy education and dialogical exchange: Impressions of Cuban education in one classroom. *Reading Teacher, 54*(7), 648–656.

Yaremko, J. M. (2000). *U.S. Protestant missions in Cuba: From independence to Castro.* Gainesville, FL: University Press of Florida.

AFRICAN SOCIALISM, POST-COLONIAL DEVELOPMENT, AND EDUCATION: CHANGE AND CONTINUITY IN THE POST-SOCIALIST ERA

Diane Brook Napier

INTRODUCTION

Educational transformation was a crucial component of postindependence national development for most African countries, as a vehicle for cultivating literate and civil society, building new institutions, fostering development in all sectors, and creating new post-colonial identity. African socialism emerged as a continent-wide movement in which many countries adopted socialism in some form as a reactive, anticolonial, anticapitalist guiding ideology to overcome the legacy of colonial domination. In the post-socialist era, African socialism and its variants have been widely derided as "failures," alongside continued criticism of the failures of capitalism and democracy in achieving development goals and in producing a better life for all Africans. Educational transformations on the continent were influenced by these shifts toward new political models, which were themselves shaped by internal events within countries and by external events on the

Post-Socialism is not Dead: (Re)Reading the Global in Comparative Education
International Perspectives on Education and Society, Volume 14, 369–399
Copyright © 2010 by Emerald Group Publishing Limited
ISSN: 1479-3679/doi:10.1108/S1479-3679(2010)0000014017

global stage. However, educational transformations cannot be directly correlated with either socialist or capitalist/democratic regimes, as they were heavily influenced by events in other aspects of society, by individual leaders' philosophies, and by external influences. By the 21st century, the debate over the "failures" of both socialism and capitalism in Africa produced many questions about the optimal path for future development on the continent.

Across the continent, the role of the state was the key in guiding economic development and in enacting educational transformation. In efforts to avoid the capitalism associated with the colonial era, indigenized forms of socialism offered hope in the form of many basic tenets, such as equality, equity, and social justice that some saw as associated with traditional collectivism. However, as Berg (1964) anticipated, state policies framed with the rhetoric of socialism produced "economic dislocation" not development (p. 560). Patterns appeared in which lip service was paid to basic tenets of socialism. Variants and hybrid state forms emerged with socialism adopted as a label when politically and economically expedient and with many strategies and political realities embodying features of elitism and capitalism. These spilled over into educational transformations because the state shaped educational reform. In most newly independent states, the economy-education nexus was a major challenge because most countries were predominantly agricultural, and colonial rule left few people sufficiently trained, experienced, or educated to manage the economy. Kwame Nkrumah of Ghana asserted that capitalism was "too complicated a system for a newly independent nation" (quoted in Mohan, 1966, p. 221), but as history was to show, and as Berg (1964) noted for post-colonial African states, "socialism is not less but more complicated than a 'capitalist' or market system" (p. 556). Nonetheless, African socialism established itself as a phenomenon on the continent with imprints in many countries.

The goal of this chapter is to first consider the features of African socialism as a variant – or set of variants – in the wider movement of socialism, as African post-colonial states attempted to overcome the colonial legacy and to modernize. Secondly, the chapter contemplates the difficulties of implementing African socialism through the cases of educational transformations across the continent. I review the evolution of African socialism in its motives and origins, variants, and characteriza-tions (including education aspects) and consider some of the personalities who became its champions. I reflect on aspects of African socialism-in-flux and the "failure" of socialism as it lost credibility as a result of both internal and external events. Selected illustrations of African countries include some who barely dabbled in socialism, others that embraced socialism on a larger scale, and South Africa, which had socialism embedded within a "national democratic revolution" (NDR). I also consider aspects of continuity in African socialism. Following this, I review the empirical research on the challenges of educational transformation and the role of the state. I conclude by first considering the implications of the empirical research record of educational transformation to ponder what, if any, legacy of African socialism lies in the educational landscape across the continent today. Finally, I review the contemporary debate over the prospects for socialism, capitalism, and democracy as vehicles for future post-colonial development in Africa and the nature of a "vision" for a new Africa including continued emphasis on education as a key human resources development sector.

AFRICAN SOCIALISM AND EDUCATION: THEORETICAL PERSPECTIVES

Several interconnected perspectives inform this discussion. First, the global-to-local continuum underlies all (Arnove & Torres, 2007). African socialism emerged within the wider global movement of socialism. Some roots of the movement in Africa lay abroad and then fed into specific developments within African states. Remnants of the African socialist network remain in shared goals for contemporary Pan-African development and in alliances with Cuba and other countries. Secondly, a critical perspective demands observations about the domination, corruption, and exploitation that persisted despite the best efforts and the most allegedly enlightened new policies. In many cases, socialist ideals were manipulated to serve political agendas, and they were not infrequently abandoned when they failed to serve the political or economic purpose. Notions of the socialist "ideal" or the democratic "ideal" have to be juxtaposed with realities in a policy-practice dimension that contains many unintended outcomes alongside intended ones (Brook Napier, 2005b). Thirdly, in recent decades, the emergence of a global system of education and the phenomenon of policy borrowing and lending apply here (Wiseman & Baker, 2005; Phillips & Ochs, 2004; Stromquist, 2002; Zajda & Rust, 2009). Many or most African countries – including those espousing loyalty to African socialism – borrowed heavily from the West for educational reform ideas. This frequently resulted in unachieved goals and implementation problems when creolization of the imported ideas ensued, as described by Brook Napier (2003) and Jansen (2004) in South Africa, Anderson-Levitt & Diallo (2003) described in Guinea, and Stambach (2003) described in Tanzania.

Fourthly, elements of a post-colonial perspective inform the argument. This can be seen, for instance, in the concept of hybridity in forms of education system after independence and in various forms of government vis-à-vis ideology and agenda; in the notion of authenticity in the considerations of pure versus corrupted forms of "socialism"; in internal versus external perspectives; in the question of "who has the right to judge?" regarding the issue of widespread external criticism of African development policies in education and other sectors (and Afro-pessimism); and in the autochthonous call by Maathai (2009) that Africans need to take responsibility for their own development trajectory in future years.

Finally, the role of the state in public education runs through the discussion because newly independent states retained centralized institutional structures often reminiscent of their colonial predecessors, as Davidson (1992) and McGinn and Cummings (1997, pp 3–43) described, despite ideological shifts. In the immediate post-colonial era (largely the 1960s and subsequent decades), policies for socializing education were formulated as integral parts of the broader economic and political positions that defined African socialism. The state undertook responsibility for eradicating the colonial (capitalist, elitist) legacy and system of education, and socialism offered an appealing array of ingredients with which to build a new education system as part of a newly independent, economically productive country. However, the idealistic notions of this first period after independence became obscured as state reforms concentrated on economic development, whereas educational reforms were subordinated to this higher cause despite rhetoric to the contrary. Rising debt, corruption, and other factors intervened, redirecting the process and reshaping the role of the state regardless of ideology. In more recent decades, neoliberal reform policies for national development with heavy influence from abroad focused on economic needs and reductions in state spending that added new negative effects on educational reform policies and outcomes, on top of the failures from earlier decades, as noted by Weber (2002) for South Africa – with relevance for many other African states – and by Torres (2009) for countries worldwide. Weber (2002) described the role of the state in South African public education, wherein ambiguity and policy-ideology shifts wreaked havoc on initially well-intentioned policies. Morrow and Torres (2007) argued the "problematic [aspects] of educational reform must be situated in the context of contested relations between the state and social movements in the overall process of cultural reproduction and change" (p. 80). Applying this to the post-colonial African context, Morrow and Torres (2007) noted, "the state is an arena of confrontation for conflicting political prospects," which is faced with "contradictions and difficulties of carrying out unified and coherent actions that are within the parameters of a specific political project" (pp. 80–81). Their argument helps elucidate the apparent contradictions we see in the choices of many African states to adopt some rendition of "socialism," although with capitalist features and universal ingredients of educational reform. Consequently, multiple forces and sometimes contradictory goals shaped educational transformations in African countries, alongside and in addition to socialism and other labels of the state machinery. In the following section, I consider the evolution of African socialism as a movement with a complex variety of forms and features that unfolded in policies both ideal and real and that had many implications for educational transformations.

MOTIVES, ORIGINS, AND FORMS OF AFRICAN SOCIALISM

The overall motives for the emergence of African socialism can be summarized in terms of post-colonial decolonization imperatives including building egalitarian societies with solidarity, justice, and governments answerable to the people, promoting equitable development in all sectors, and restoring African identity and standing in the world order (Losch, 2008). As an anticolonial, reactionary, emancipatory path for development, socialism offered hope for a fresh beginning. With public ownership of the means of production, a strong central government was needed to ensure careful planning and use of resources to ensure independence from foreign markets (Ayittey, 1990; Mazrui, 1983). As Mazrui (1983) noted, there was a favorable climate for the blossoming of African socialism as the path to post-colonial development because of the "accumulation of frustrations with efforts to develop Africa through Western patterns of economic growth," and so it is not surprising that "most African governments soon after independence paid some kind of lip service to socialism" (p. 284). Because education had been an instrument of domination under colonial rule, educational transformation plans after independence quickly incorporated newly popular socialist ideas.

African socialism emerged in various forms, what Ayittey (1990, p. 3) called "African 'isms'," few of them pure, many of them corrupted, and some of them mixed with elements of capitalism and democracy. But essentially these versions manifested into two basic waves (Cohen & Goulbourne, 1991; Rosburg & Callaghy, 1979). A first wave of populist, pragmatic, "open" regimes resonating with communalism and local cultural traditions emerged during the early years of independence movements from the 1950s onward. This early period was exemplified by Leopold Sedar Senghor of Senegal (Senghor, 1964), Kwame Nkrumah in Ghana (often called the father of African socialism), Sekou Toure in Guinea, Modibo Keita in Mali, Amilcar Cabral in Guinea-Bissau, Kenneth Kaunda in Zambia, and Julius Nyerere in Tanzania (Apter, 2008; Ayittey, 1990; Mazrui, 1983). Ties to global powers benefited some aspects of economic development in these early years of independence. For instance, the Tanzania–Zambia railway was built with Chinese assistance during the 1970s (Azikiwe, 2009). Under these regimes, education was usually accorded a central role in plans for building a new nation because it was widely acknowledged that the population had suffered little or no adequate education and training under colonial rule – except in the training of a contingent for the civil service and in mission schools that offered quality education for some Africans (Brook, 1996).

By the 1970s, more militaristic scientific-socialist regimes emerged, constituting the second wave of African socialism. These decried traditional culture and sought to impose command economies with strong centralized political control. Nyerere's Ujamaa (familyhood) villages that had initially formed the core of a grassroots cooperative form of "first wave" socialism – with Education for Self-Reliance (ESR) featuring prominently (Nyerere, 1968) – became more characteristic of oppressive regimes of the second wave, in the enforced resettlement of thousands of peasants into cooperative communities (Young, 1982, pp. 114–115). The educational ideals of ESR in Tanzania, and variants in other countries, faded in these newer configurations of state leadership. Several states labeled as socialist, for instance, Uganda, Tanzania, and Ghana, "flirted with the principle of a one-party state," as Mazrui portrayed it (1983, p. 280), wherein ethnic divisions were seen as the principal rationale for needing a one-party state to overcome class struggle and colonial oppression. In fact, opposition parties were officially banned in these and many other African countries until the early 1990s. As Linton (1968) observed, the one-party state had "unique cultural relevance" to Africa (p. 1). Leaders such as Zambia's Kaunda and Tanzania's Nyerere saw socialism and a return to communal tradition as a rationale to rule without opposition (Kaunda, 1975).

Radical Marxist regimes emerged after fierce struggles to overthrow military juntas and extremely repressive colonial rulers, taking on more Leninist class-based rhetoric and using force to achieve objectives. In several instances, superpowers and their proxies were involved in these freedom struggles. Congo-Brazzaville was a military Marxist regime formed in 1969 under Marien Ngouabi. In Somalia, Mohammed Siad Barre established a military regime in 1970 with Soviet support. Others followed, in Benin with French support, and in Ethiopia in 1975, where a Leninist regime ousted Emperor Haile Selassie. Some of the most brutal struggles for freedom were fought against the Portuguese in Angola and Mozambique. In Angola, Cuban soldiers fought with the Soviet-backed Movimento Popular de Libertacao de Angola (MPLA), defeating the South African Defense Force (SADF) and the American-backed Uniao Nacional para a Independencia Total de Angola (UNITA) forces. In Mozambique, a bloody civil war gave birth to socialism once the FRELIMO party of Samora Machel gained victory over South African-supported RENAMO rebels in 1992. Educational reform agendas under these regimes continued to reflect post-colonial development goals seen elsewhere, but the devastating effects of the wars demolished much of functioning education.

In actuality, most regimes or governments adopted mixed economies with capitalist/democratic components infused into the overall socialist agenda or military regime. This, coupled with external influences regarding educational and economic development, leads one to caution against rigidly classifying any one regime or country. Many Afro-Marxist regimes desired Western economic ties and so remained politically socialist but economically neutral (Mazrui, 1983, p. 286). This hybridity in regime or government form parallels the hybridity in other aspects of post-colonial life, such as in race/ethnicity and individual identity and in indigenous versus colonial language use in literature and as instructional medium in schools (see collected writings in Ashcroft, Tiffin, & Griffiths, 2006). In many cases, countries shared national development priorities regardless of the chosen ideology. For instance, in Zambia, Zimbabwe, and Botswana, Brook (1992) noted parallel sets of core principles in their National Development Plans (NDPs) of "democracy, self reliance, egalitarianism, equity in development, and cooperation." They shared the development priorities of "rural (community) development" and "educational reform." Educational reform was presented as "education with production/partnership" under Zambia's socialist variant called "African Humanism" and in Zimbabwe's "Scientific Socialism," but also in Botswana's democratic approach under the Setswana slogans of "Kagisano" (cooperation, social harmony) and the "spirit of Therisanyo" (local participation/consultation). This lends some support to the argument that African socialism had roots in indigenous concepts of collectivism and people's rights in traditional African cultures, that it was really only the label "socialism" that was imported (Apter, 2008; Ayittey, 1990; Losch, 2008).

"Democracy" was a term variously and liberally used. For example, when Ghana's Kwame Nkrumah became an orthodox Leninist in later years, he advocated an "immemorial practice of democratic centralism" (Mohan, 1966, p. 227). In South Africa, founding principles for a new democracy were based on the ANC Freedom Charter that incorporated socialist principles (Weber, 2002). Some states became what were described as "one-party democracies." In Nigeria, Kenya, and later in South Africa, the overriding ideology was touted as "democracy," but the overwhelming dominance of a single party and leader, and ineffectual opposition parties, produced political strife and allegations of elitism and corruption. In South Africa, the socialist presence is seen in the South African Communist Party (SACP), which allied with the African National Congress (ANC) and other groups in the liberation struggle (Weber, 2002). The communist legacy prevails in strong labor unions such as the Congress of South African Trade Unions (COSATU) and the South African Democratic Teachers Union (SADTU) (Weizmann, 2003). Virulent anticommunist sentiment among conservative whites was another ingredient in the story of socialism and liberation in South Africa, as illustrated in the writings of Afrikaner philosophers such as Hans van Rensburg (Venter, 2008) and of Afrikaner hardliners who considered the liberation struggle to be a communist threat (Van Rooyen, 1994). The epithet "filthy communists" was often hurled at Cubans for their role in Angola defeating the white South African forces. Mandela himself was widely accused of being a "communist and terrorist." At his Rivonia Treason Trial on April 20, 1964, Mandela stated,

> For many decades communists were the only political group in South Africa who were prepared to treat Africans as human beings and their equals; who were prepared to eat with us, talk with us, live with us, and work with us. (quoted in Crwys-Williams, 1997, p. 16)

African socialism also had transatlantic roots, in the Negritude and Pan-Africanist movements that emerged in the mid-20th century. Edward Blyden is often credited as the father of early Pan-Africanism that incorporated socialist ingredients for African self-determination and communistic, cooperative society (Blyden, 1979, pp. 81–89). His ideas were rearticulated in the writings of Carter Woodson (1936) and by Du Bois (1965), who applied them to Africa in global context. Thereafter, they can be seen in the Negritude movement led by Leopold Sedar Senghor of Senegal (Apter, 2008; Mazrui, 1983). Kwame Nkruma's concept of "African Personality" was a Pan-African philosophy linking Africans and members of the African Diaspora in the early years of African socialism (see Brook Napier, 2008 for a summary of Pan-Africanism). The Cuban Revolution of 1959 and the leadership of Fidel Castro were additional international threads. Cubans participated in several liberation struggles on the continent including in Angola and the then-Belgian Congo. Che Guevara, who led guerilla fighters in support of the Congolese liberation movement in 1965, was among the international personalities who featured in the overall liberation story and the post-colonial legacy in Africa (Galvez, 1999). So-called Third World Marxist cultures linked revolutionary movements in Latin America (particularly those in Cuba and Chile) to anticolonial movements in Africa, particularly to those in Angola and Mozambique (Henighan, 2009).

Within Africa, a network of largely socialist solidarity developed. For instance, Tanzania became an operations base for liberation movements in Namibia, Zimbabwe, South Africa, and Mozambique, providing training grounds and organizational support, and a safe haven for freedom fighters in exile (Azikiwe, 2009). Mozambique supported freedom fighters in Rhodesia and South Africa. Zimbabwe (formerly Southern Rhodesia), Angola, and Libya supported the South African liberation struggle and gave haven to activists in exile. This legacy of mutual support within Africa and from abroad led Nelson Mandela to proclaim that "we will never renounce our friends" (who included Muammar Qadaffi, Robert Mugabe, and Fidel Castro) in recognition of their contributions to liberation in South Africa (quoted in Sampson, 1999, p. 562). These intracontinental ties also extended to education.

More recently, the concept of African Renaissance surfaced, linked to the New Plan for African Development (NEPAD) under the African Union (Brook Napier, 2008), to promote continent-wide economic and social development. South Africa aspires to take the lead in this effort and to be a broker of peace on the continent (Mbeki, 1998). This African Renaissance is a recent conception for post-colonial development, continuing the tradition of seeking continental solutions to development needs that emerged in earlier phases of Pan-Africanism and in the heyday of African socialism.

AFRICAN SOCIALISM IN FLUX: "FAILURE" OF AFRICAN SOCIALISM?

Many argue that socialism failed, that it proved to be anything but a panacea for all ills in post-colonial Africa (Ayittey, 1990; http://illvox.org, 2007). Some portray the change as socialism having "lost ground" (Saul, 2001; Meredith, 2005). Others render a harsher verdict: that socialism "failed" outright (see Bayart, 1993; Chabal & Daloz, 1999), also that socialism, liberalism, and neoliberalism were all ideologies imported into sub-Saharan Africa, and African politics was less about ideology than patronage. Considerations of the failure and legacy of socialism in Africa touch on economic, ideological, and political-military events as well as on the issue of lip service paid to socialism and other ideology while political and economic agendas and global influences drove the machinery of power. Because educational transformations were not always tied directly to socialism, one cannot directly correlate the trajectories of African socialism and educational transformations. From a post-colonial perspective, the apparent failure of socialism (and of capitalism in Africa, for that matter) presents a conundrum, in that external critiques need to be weighed with caution, against and alongside internal critiques of the history and the legacy.

Internal Developments

Several internal events contributed to the failure of socialism and to a growing crisis in general. Many leading political figures were deposed or they resigned, including Ghana's Nkrumah, ousted in a 1966 military coup, and Tanzania's Nyerere, who resigned as President in 1985 and from the ruling party Chama Cha Mapenduzi (CCM) in 1990. Most countries that espoused socialism experienced economic ruin, dictatorship and oppression, persistent poverty, and underdevelopment. Among these were Angola, Guinea, Guinea-Bissau, Mali, Burkino Faso, Ethiopia, Mozambique, Zambia, and Zimbabwe (Ayittey, 1990; Cohen & Goulbourne, 1991; http://illvox.org, 2007). Increasingly oppressive tactics by governments and their leaders eroded the popular appeal of socialist rhetoric. The lip service paid to the guiding principles of socialism compromised implementation of many plans for development and educational reform (Brook, 1992; Mhando, 2009).

In a statement to a Mexican reporter in 1991, Fidel Castro indicated the broader reality of failures: "They talk about the failure of socialism but where is the success of capitalism in Africa, Asia and Latin America?"

(quoted in Balfour, 2008, p. 165). Disintegration of incipient nation states, anarchy and militarism, and political violence felled chances for success in Congo-Brazzaville and Congo-Kinshasa,[1] Sierra Leone, and Sudan – to name a few (Ayittey, 1990). Reversals in position and cyclic patterns were the story elsewhere. For instance, in Cote d'Ivoire, the socialist faction La Racine enjoyed some revival even though the dominant Ivorian Popular Front (FPI) had previously moved away from socialism (Africa Research Bulletin, 2008). In Zimbabwe, the increasingly repressive regime of Robert Mugabe abandoned socialism in the early 1990s in the face of International Monetary Fund (IMF) stipulations for economic liberalization and debt relief, only to threaten reimposition of hard-line socialism a decade later (Peta, 2001). Buckle (2002) chronicled the tragic consequences for Zimbabweans, including the collapse of schooling. A complex picture emerged, of countries wrestling with tensions in and definitions of their governments and policies; of varied responses to internal events; of shifts to capitalist market-driven elements for the sake of aid or debt relief; of "democracy" emerging in a several forms; and of some sustained loyalty to socialism ingredients espousing popular participation and equality.

External Developments

In a classic illustration of the global-to-local continuum (Arnove & Torres, 2007), events outside Africa dealt African socialism a decisive blow. The fall of the Soviet Union and the communist bloc from 1989 onwards were watershed events impacting the continent. As socialism lost its political correctness and luster, and as the global geopolitical reconfiguration unfolded, Soviet markets, aid, and resources were undercut or lost. Somalia, Tanzania, Congo-Kinshasa, and Egypt were among the African countries impacted here. Even before this, normalization of relations between the US Nixon Administration and China caused a shift in relations that truncated Chinese support to Tanzania (Azikiwe, 2009).

Even beyond the fall of the Soviet bloc, global trends impacted African countries. Globalization embodied a set of effects including market liberalization; neoliberal economic development policies; a shared global discourse of "reform" in politics, economics, and education; and intensified international competitiveness for participation on the world stage (Baker & Wiseman, 2005; Stromquist, 2002; Torres, 2009; Zajda & Rust, 2009). World Bank and IMF structural adjustment policies (SAPs) imposed austerity measures on some 40 African countries by 1990 alone, with far-reaching ramifications in all sectors including education and healthcare (Tyler, 2006). In the 1990s and beyond, many African states attached themselves to the global trend of neoliberalism (Morrow & Torres, 2007; Torres, 2009). The results included adherence to economically driven neoliberal policies that perpetuated elitism and undercut educational development policies, as Weber (2002) and Vavrus (2003) described for South Africa and Tanzania, respectively. African states and other developing countries felt the pressure to compete in the global arena while striving to meet internal needs (Brook Napier, 2005b).

CONTINUITY: ENDURING LEGACIES AND NEW/RENEWED PRESENCES IN AFRICA

Despite the clamor about the "failure" of socialism in Africa, there are slender threads of continuity of the legacy, such as in support for enduring causes for social justice and equity, and in the spirit of programs like ESR. In Tanzania, although Mhando (2009) admitted that the philosophy of ESR was never fully implemented, he argued that ESR survived sufficiently to be present in the Tanzanian Education and Training Policy (ETP) of 1995 and in the 2009 ETP. However, the work of Vavrus (2003) on educational policy in Tanzania since the 1990s revealed the larger reality of disastrous effects of neoliberal reforms. The *spirit and idea* of ESR did become a legacy across the continent. Its elements that focused on self-determination, self-reliance, basic skills, and cooperative learning became embedded in programs variously labeled as Education with Production, Education with Partnership, on-the-job training, or skills development. In Botswana, the Brigades program was an early example of the legacy (Van Rensburg, 1974). Subsequently, vocational-technical programs focusing on basic survival skills and programs for advanced technical skills geared to workforce needs became prevalent in African countries and developing countries worldwide (King & McGrath, 2002).

Another aspect of continuity was the expeditious resurgence of socialism or communism, such as in its reimposition in Zimbabwe (Peta, 2001) and its continued presence in the new South Africa as the ideological underpinning of labor unions fighting for workers' rights and challenging neoliberal policies of the ruling ANC party (Weizmann, 2003). "Communist" or socialist factions in South Africa position themselves as voices of conscience in the debates over contemporary economic development policies, the persistent gap between rich and poor, and persistent elitism.

A third aspect of continuity lies in the persistence of rhetoric on socialist ideals for equality, self-determination, new Pan-African identity and new national identities within countries, and for multiculturalism and multilingualism. The African Renaissance, the contemporary Pan-African movement, and continent-wide economic development goals under NEPAD claim to incorporate elements of African socialism, even though they are heavily infused with elements of "democracy" and Western capitalism (Brook Napier, 2008). Neoliberal policies under the leadership of South Africa's President Mbeki received widespread criticism for being elitist and insensitive to real needs in areas such as education, poverty reduction, and health. Kersting (2009) declared NEPAD was a failed project, fraught with elitism.

The tradition of superpower involvement on the continent has continued. British, American, and Chinese interests – and multinational corporation operations – are extensive in military interventions and peacekeeping, telecommunications, mining and minerals/oil exploitation, technology, construction, transportation, and in publishing and education. The "new imperialists" are thus identified, with China's aggressive expansion particularly noted (*The Economist*, 2008).

In a more positive vein, there is continuity in some early alliances among freedom fighters, for instance, those that linked Cuba to liberation struggles in the DR Congo, Angola, and South Africa, holdovers from the Marxist era. Relationships among Fidel Castro of Cuba, Nelson Mandela of South Africa, Muammar Qadaffi of Libya, Robert Mugabe of Zimbabwe, Samora Machel of Mozambique, and Denis Sassou-Nguesso of Congo-Brazzaville were built on the shared colonial legacy and on common imperatives for liberation. Some of these bonds remain strong today, as seen in the lasting relationships between Mandela and Castro (Mandela & Castro, 1991; Mandela, 1994) and between Mandela and Sassou-Nguesso. South–south collaborations – as opposed to north–south collaborations in which post-colonial states of the south interact with superpowers of the north – have become established, linking Africa and the Caribbean, focused primarily on capacity-building and human resources development especially in education (Hickling-Hudson, 2004). Cuba is prominent in the movement, offering personnel, resources, material supplies, expertise, and scholarships to fellow post-colonial states including Jamaica, Venezuela, Botswana, Zimbabwe, Namibia, and South Africa. African students earn scholarships for study in Cuba in priority fields such as engineering and medicine. Brook Napier (2006b) described the ongoing ties between South Africa and Cuba regarding colonial legacy, capacity-building and development, and the long relationship between the leaders Castro and Mandela (Mandela & Castro, 1991). Cuba and Libya assisted South Africa in meeting critical needs for mathematics and science teachers and doctors in remote villages. As Henighan (2009) noted, while differences outweighed similarities among the various Latin American and African "Third World Marxist" cultures, the legacy of connections prevailed even after the end of the Cold War.

Finally, regarding continuity, anticommunist sentiment still runs strong among conservative white South Africans as ingrained suspicion of "communism." Disagreements here over the benefits and perils of "communism' and "socialism" will probably continue. Apter (2008, p. 6) noted policy issues still prevalent in Africa include the role of the state in regulating trade and in steering education and other human resources development; the growing inequalities associated with economic liberalization, including the widening gap between rich and poor; and the persistent presence of "tribalism" with periodic eruptions of xenophobia and ethnic violence. The emergence of new African elites, and the better life they garnered for themselves often at the expense of the masses, also possibly ensures the persistent appeal of socialist egalitarian rhetoric – in opposition to elitism and privilege, corruption, and poverty plaguing so many African countries, problems that socialism as well as capitalism failed to eradicate.

EDUCATIONAL TRANSFORMATIONS

The difficulties of implementing African socialism (indeed also democracy and so-called democratic revolutions such as the NDR in South Africa) are evident in the rather tortured history of post-colonial educational transformation across Africa. As Morrow and Torres (2007) explained, the state/education relationship repeatedly emerges as problematic and often contradictory for many countries. African educational transformation agendas were pulled by the popularity of "socialism," confused with or accompanied by "democracy," often driven by quick-fix imported reforms and fashionable ideas, and riddled with implementation problems. New versions of corruption and elitism emerged. Period-specific events as well as ongoing obstacles to development compromised educational transformations. Across the continent, a mosaic of educational transformations emerged, shaped by internal and external forces and by state policies that produced some success but many failures, as seen in the following overview.

African countries faced awesome challenges both during the years when African socialism enjoyed widespread popularity and in the post-socialist era. The initial double imperative to overcome the colonial legacy and to craft policies addressing development needs in education and other sectors tended to be steered by NDPs or some equivalent, such as South Africa's Reconstruction and Development Programme (RDP) (ANC, 1994). In the post-socialist era and the contemporary epoch of globalization, an even more daunting, *triple* imperative has emerged: not only to continue overcoming the colonial legacy but also to rethink the guiding principles for wise government and to counteract policies under socialism – or capitalism, or whatever combination happened to be the case – that had failed to produce lasting and desirable results; *and* thirdly, to be competitive globally while attending to internal needs.

Educational transformations rode a roller coaster of change, continuity, persistent challenges, cyclic patterns, and inertia. Comparative education research in Africa illustrates the manner in which post-colonial states wrestled with issues and challenges within national imperatives, battling history while reeling under the impact of new needs. Many of these – such as HIV/AIDS – did not even feature in the years immediately after independence. Others were intergenerational issues in the legacy of oppression impacting current educational priorities. In some cases (e.g., in Rwanda, Sierra Leone, Somalia, and Congo-Kinshasa/Zaire/DRC), repeated rounds of political instability and violence undermined efforts to rebuild education and other sectors. In other cases, education was sacrificed to liberation struggles. In Zimbabwe, government schools were largely nonfunctioning during the Chimurenga (War of Liberation), and in South Africa in particular, schools were rendered nonfunctional for many years under the slogan "liberation before education" (quoted in Brook, 1996).

There were common threads in educational development across the continent. To dismantle colonial education systems, and to install new "democratic" modern education systems, the broader agendas contained policy components to expand or upgrade facilities; indigenize curricula; build a competent local teaching force with appropriate teacher training and evaluation systems; address priority subject areas such as mathematics, science, and technology; and foster "selective traditional cultural revival" in indigenized social studies courses, indigenous language courses, and mother tongue instruction provisions. "Quantitative reforms" sought to expand access and democratize education, including children previously excluded under colonial systems. "Qualitative reforms" included curriculum reform, teacher training and professional development, and quality assurance and evaluation systems.

The African propensity for importing reform packages from the superpowers was part of a global phenomenon (Phillips & Ochs, 2004; Steiner-Khamsi, 2004). Educational transformation policies were built with ideas imported from Britain, the United States, Canada, and New Zealand for learner-centered, outcomes-based education (OBE), and incorporating notions of constructivism and progressive pedagogy, testing and content-area standards for accountability, multiculturalism, citizenship education, literacy, and skills development. International development aid programs played a key role, as did SAPs in which funds for education came with strings attached – for instance, in dictating the focus of projects or language of instruction or publication. As Brook Napier (2005b) and Jansen (2004) noted, implementation problems ensued as a result of too-rapid implementation of imported reforms without sufficient connection to local contexts and with insufficient training and support of teachers.

A host of unintended outcomes reflected the disequilibrium that many transformation policies produced. For example, in many countries, a shortage of qualified teachers led to widespread dependence on expatriate teachers and volunteer teachers, as countries failed to train teachers at rates matching the demand for teachers in expanding school systems. Expatriate teachers worked alongside legions of underqualified local teachers. In South Africa, the task of collapsing four racially segregated education systems into a single nonracial system involved "rationalization" of schools and teacher training colleges, resulting in retrenchments of many educators; yet, thousands of African children lacked access to school. Another imbalance was the problem of the "unemployed school leaver" as job creation and employment failed to keep pace with educational production in South Africa, Zimbabwe, and elsewhere (Brook Napier, 2003, 2005b).

Varying degrees of decentralized or devolved authority became desirable to break the tradition of inherited highly centralized systems. In an analysis of transformations in sub-Saharan African schooling, Naidoo (2005) concluded that the outcome was a mixed bag of successes and failures – that in much of the region, educational decentralization failed to occur either as rapidly as intended or with the desired impact on school conditions and student achievement. In most cases, hierarchical administrative structures still predominated. Naidoo (2005) argued that attempts to implement decentralization policies actually led to problems related to obstructive bureaucracy and to resource shortages rather than to empowerment and strengthening of local school systems and schools. Likewise, Brook Napier (2003) and Jansen (2004) noted that in South Africa, "centralized thinking" persisted not only among administrators and policy-makers but also among many teachers who resisted imposition of new initiatives under OBE.

Imported ideas were frequently creolized upon implementation – mangled into other forms, mediated or resisted, or rejected outright – resulting in many variants of the original ideas within and across countries. In separate studies (see Anderson-Levitt, 2003), Anderson-Levitt and Diallo, Brook Napier, and Stambach described how global ingredients of educational reform were creolized in Guinea, South Africa, and Tanzania, respectively. Brook Napier (2005b) provided a cameo of these in South Africa. The propensity for importing reform ideas extended from Egypt in the north across the entire continent to South Africa, creating educational landscapes difficult to classify as either "democratic/capitalist" or as "socialist."

Patterns of persistent challenges in education emerged, for all the efforts to modernize and "democratize." These included textbook shortages, crowded classrooms, underqualified and underpaid teachers, inadequate facilities, insufficient teacher training and support to implement reform initiatives, high levels of corruption and inefficient management, vertical and horizontal discordance in administration, and poor employment prospects for graduated students (Bajaj, 2010; Samoff & Carrol, 2007). Brook Napier (2005b) enumerated the educational challenges facing African post-colonial states and other developing countries with few – if any – outright successes, some disastrous failures, and with many cases of mixed results. Overall, however, there *were* advances in literacy in most countries *and* improvements in providing expanded access to schooling and basic education. In many cases, including in Zambia, Zimbabwe, and South Africa, the overall record of postindependence educational transformation was the emergence of a two-tier system of high-quality private schools and former white schools for the elite who could pay the fees, and inferior, chronically underresourced African schools for the rest (Bajaj, 2010; Brook Napier, 2005b).

Standard slogans for national development and educational reform emerged, such as African Humanism – Zambia's variant of socialism framed in explicitly humanistic terms (Kaunda, 1975) – and Zimbabwe's Scientific Socialism. Yet, Brook (1992) found that only in Zambia were "socialist principles" clearly discernible in curricula and policy documents, with genuine attempts to operationalize them in new indigenized social studies curricula. In contrast, in Zimbabwe, a decision was made at the highest educational policy level (by a western-educated leader) to retain the British Cambridge Syndicate syllabuses and examinations so that the best students could earn the internationally accredited Cambridge Certificate, and specific evidence of "socialist principles" was absent from curricula and materials. However, a lack of any real change was the outcome of years of reform in both countries' new education systems (Brook Napier, 2005a, 2005b). Jansen (1990) described how in Zimbabwe after independence, policies to indigenize the curriculum failed to materialize. Dorsey (1989) summarized the many problems Zimbabwe faced in resolving dilemmas of quality versus quantity and in attempting to rebuild education all but destroyed during the Chimurenga. In more recent years, repeated rounds of economic adversity, political turmoil, and oppression caused ruination in all sectors (Peta, 2001). The socialist years produced anything but an egalitarian society, as Dorsey predicted in 1989 and as Buckle (2002) subsequently chronicled.

In Zambia, despite sincere efforts to transform education, events *in addition to* the wane of socialism dealt the reforms a mortal blow (Brook, 1992; Brook Napier, 2005b). The collapse of the international copper market hobbled the economy and exacerbated poverty levels. SAPs siphoned resources from educational reform programs. These period-specific factors intersected with cyclic and ongoing patterns of adversity that undercut attempts to implement educational reforms and to improve living conditions. Repeated years of severe weather and floods washed out roads, obstructing contact with educators in remote areas and compromising implementation of new syllabuses (Brook, 1992). Endemic malaria consistently undermined whole rural communities. Idealistic reforms and implementation problems also contributed to the failures. Lulat and Clarke (1982) and Muyebaa (2001) described how the ambitious "Education for Development Plan" of 1976–1977 never materialized due to many implementation problems, but also because it was too focused on academic priorities, insensitive to needs in Zambian society. Muyebaa (2001) argued that after independence in 1964, each round of educational reform in the period 1964–2001 was handicapped by insufficient funding and by implementation obstacles, while Musonda (1999) called donor-influenced education reforms in Zambia a misfit with local needs. Bajaj (2010) demonstrated how intergenerational perspectives on secondary schooling in Zambia were shaped by these and other events, including the prevalence of HIV/AIDS, loss of hope for social mobility and success, and corruption.

Other cases in point add to the mosaic on the continent. Hanson (1988, 1990) and Reimers and McGinn (1997) described the bureaucratic inertia in Egyptian educational reform programs. In Sudan, Lynch (1992) exposed the farce of failed top-down reforms to indigenize curricula that completely ignored the Khalawi, Muslim institutions that had operated locally for generations. In Somalia, in the early 1980s, the Ministry of Education developed a Nomad Education Program incorporating American-style social studies for cultivating a new national identity through the teaching of social studies, first aid, and animal husbandry for nomads in the Guban Desert. However, the attempt to implement this centralized curriculum from Mogadishu was short lived in the country beset by anarchy and clan warfare (Brook & Brook, 1993). In relatively successful Ghana, Yeboah (1997) noted that although girls' participation in schooling expanded initially, in subsequent years, school quality and girls' declining performance led to increased dropout rates among girls. In Tanzania, Youngman and Ishengoma (1999) commented on the "imperiled promise of reform" due to a mismatch with local historical context and controversial initiatives imposed by multinational corporations, and Vavrus (2003) confirmed the negative effects of neoliberal policies. In a retrospective analysis, Mhando (2009) argued that in Tanzania, Nyerere's ideas for education were misinterpreted and that ESR was left to lie dormant while attention was given to adopting fashionable "new" ideas of learner-centered, OBE undergirded by constructivism. Mhando observed the irony that ESR in fact embodied many of these same ideas decades earlier. Yet, Tanzania's travails with socialism and ESR have to be juxtaposed against some of the enduring legacy of the spirit of ESR.

In South Africa, the achievements of the educational transformation agenda since 1994 have been widely acknowledged (Brook Napier, 2005b; Jansen 2004). However, many blocking factors obstructed reform implementation, and in remote areas such as northeast KwaZulu Natal, significant educational transformation was minimal (Brook Napier, 2005a, 2005b; Johnson, 1995). The powerful trade unions in South Africa were accused of hampering reforms by staging crippling strikes, some of which severely impacted education in forcing school closures and compromising learners' chances for adequate preparation for the matriculation examinations in 2008 (Kane-Berman, 2009). Blocking factors were also cited in connection with questionable sustainability and effectiveness in Kenya, for example, in the Kismayu School Improvement Program (SIP) in the early 1990s (Capper, Nderitu, & Ogala, 1997).

There are some elements of success, in particular, transformation stories. Botswana had a fairly stable record of post-colonial development and educational transformation under democratic rule (Brook, 1992; Brook Napier, 2005b), and Vlaardingerbroek (1998) reported positive results in student participation and performance as well as success in HIV/AIDS awareness programs; yet, the record was not so positive in preparing girls for self-employment. Large, multiple-country aid projects promoted specific elements of educational transformation in African and other developing countries. For instance, Liberia participated in the Instructional Management by Parents, Community, and Teachers (IMPACT) Project that produced a number of "success factors" (Cummings, 1986). Reimers and McGinn (1997) reported on a project in Namibia that succeeded, thanks to stakeholder participation. Hickling-Hudson (2004) and Brook Napier (2006a, 2006b) described Cuban capacity-building programs in South Africa and Zimbabwe in "south–south collaborations," but Brook Napier (2006b) reported the strong opposition to Cuban educators by South African teachers who feared the outsiders were stealing jobs.

There were also patterns across the continent in subject area offerings. The global priority subjects of mathematics, science, technology, and English became priorities in Africa too. Programs cultivating new forms of national identity and citizenship became popular as well: Kubow (2007) described these in South Africa and Kenya; Waghid (2007) described education for democratic citizenship and cosmopolitanism in Egypt; and Nordvelt (2008) reported on education for literacy and civil society in Senegal. In Botswana, high school Development Studies syllabuses were variants of social studies courses, and in South Africa, Integrated Studies became popular as interdisciplinary courses with multicultural and indigenized content (Brook, 1991, 1992). Skills development and vocational/technical education – once denigrated as inferior – enjoyed a revival for relevance and employability (King & McGrath, 2002). Many countries developed bilingual or multilingual programs to accord indigenous languages equal standing with English or French, while wrestling with appropriate policies for mother tongue instruction and equitable instructional medium choice and dilemmas of English dominance associated with global competitiveness. Brock-Utne and Skattum (2009) assembled research on these issues in Francophone Africa and Anglophone Africa, and Brook Napier (2006a) discussed these for South Africa.

Another common feature was competition for resources among human resources development areas. Educational reforms vied for resources with needs in areas such as healthcare (including HIV/AIDS, malaria, and tuberculosis), exploitation of children, poverty reduction, housing, crime and justice, jobs, and water supply. Even in relatively successful Botswana, educational development needs competed with gross inequities between rich and poor, and with environmental conservation needs. For illustrations of tensions between education and healthcare demands, see Nordvelt (2010) on Namibia and Swaziland; Kamat (2008) and Vavrus and Seghers (2009) on Tanzania; Bajaj (2010) on Zambia; and Brook Napier (2009a) on South Africa.

African post-colonial higher education transformation formed part of the global convergence of higher educational institutions (Anderson-Levitt, 2003; Baker & Wiseman, 2005, 2008). Africans followed the global trend: to become internationally competitive, introduce global systems and standards, and undo the colonial hierarchy composed of historically disadvantaged African institutions and superior former-colonial institutions – regardless of ideological labels on the governments in question (Saint, 1992; Zeleza & Olukoshi, 2004). As Holland (2010) noted for Malawi, and Jansen (2005) for South Africa, in other African states too, complexities of context and interactions generated an array of institutional configurations nationally and regionally in response to external/global influences as well as to internal needs.

Countries still plagued by political instability, violence, and corruption include Zimbabwe, Congo, Rwanda, Sierra Leone, Sudan, Liberia, Nigeria, South Africa, and Kenya. Their violent historical legacies impact education. Sierra Leone tries to educate former child soldiers to help them become self-sufficient and productive in normalized lives (Betancourt et al., 2008). In South Africa, secondary schooling for Africans was largely sacrificed to the liberation struggle, leading to the mourning of a "lost generation" (or two) of students who never had the chance to complete their schooling (Brook, 1996). In post-genocide Rwanda, teaching history to the current and next generations in ways appropriate for different ethnic groups is an important goal (Freedman, Weinstein, Murphy, & Longman, 2008). Revisionist histories depicting *African* achievements were among the first investments in curriculum reform in Zambia and Zimbabwe after independence (Brook, 1992), but as Altbach (1971) noted, multinational textbook publishing companies are among the powerful global corporations that continue to exploit Africans and African markets.

What are the implications of the empirical research record regarding the educational aspects of African socialism and educational transformation? What, if any, legacy of African socialism lies in the educational landscape of today and tomorrow across the continent? The educational transformation efforts described earlier suggest that noble ingredients such as equality, equity, and social justice often espoused under the banner of socialism fell victim to influences and events that were more powerful in shaping educational transformations. Global imperatives for educational reform, the popularity of imported reform packages from western superpowers, opportunities for international aid, neoliberal reforms and SAPs, and the positions taken by western-educated political leaders became driving forces shaping the educational policies of states whether they were avowedly socialist or otherwise. As Weber (2002) and Torres (2009) observed, neoliberal economic development spilled over into education policies and created conditions perpetuating elitism and inequity in spite of basic postindependence achievements such as educational expansion and curriculum reform. Pressing internal problems of economic planning, party organization, and official responses to political, economic, military, and economic crises (to name a few) frequently sabotaged educational reforms. The failed promises of socialism appear in the stories of Zambia, Zimbabwe, and Tanzania: three examples of economic development and educational transformation gone awry under socialism but also buffeted by global influences and interconnecting events. The legacy of African socialism is a set of tenuous threads encapsulated in a complex history.

PROSPECTS FOR 21ST-CENTURY TRANSFORMATION?

What is the nature of the debate over socialism and other vehicles for development in the 21st century? One feature here is the lack of a single clear path for achieving longstanding goals for equality, self-determination, sustainable development, civil and peaceful society, and a better life for all. Much of the debate centers on visions that risk being more rhetoric than reality or on speculations about hybrid forms of government.

Recommendations for a return to socialism are absent in international measures of African countries' progress in building "democratic institutions," for instance, under NEPAD and the African Peer Review Mechanism (APRM). As Jeffrey (2010) criticized in South Africa, there is no point in trying "to make ideology trump pragmatism and practicality," while "crises in education, health, and elsewhere go unresolved" (p. 1). The United Nations global indicator system of Millennium Development Goals (MDGs) places high importance on education (UN, 2007a). As Maathai (2009) noted, considerations of the prospects reasonably include the manner in which African post-colonial states address MDG targets as well as Education for All (EFA) targets in basic literacy and schooling (p. 10). Some 25 African countries are on the list of the 50 "least developed countries" (LDCs) in which education and technical knowledge are critical for future development (UN, 2007b). Ideology aside, the future mandate features educational needs as high priorities, continent-wide.

There is some agreement that a new epoch of neoimperialist domination is unfolding and that current EFA, international aid programs, and global imperatives amount to a "recolonization" of African minds anew (Brock-Utne, 2000; Torres, 2009), a new generation of "black man's burden," as Davidson (1992) portrayed the colonial inheritance. Saul (2005) described the "next liberation struggle" against the march of globalization and neoliberalism, whereas Tyler (2006) called it the new "scramble for Africa." Contemporary penetration of the continent is an issue also, one example being China's inroads into African agriculture (Brautigam & Xiaoyang, 2009) and its thirst for natural resources (*The Economist*, 2008).

Conversely, Guest (2004) and Maathai (2009) urged consideration of the success stories on the continent as models for other countries to emulate. They pointed to Botswana's prosperity and peacefulness; the avoidance of all-out civil war in South Africa, thanks to negotiations; Uganda's turnaround of the spread of HIV/AIDS through education programs; and the rebuilding of Rwanda, Mozambique, Angola, the DR Congo, and many other countries that should not go unnoticed in the midst of critique regarding failed programs. There is also continuity and hope in the south–south collaborations among post-colonial states.

Among philosophical conceptions and visions for future development in post-socialist era Africa, a return to socialism outright is missing. Many writers contemplate forms of hybrid governance, or they offer abstract "visions." Arrighi (2002), Chabal and Daloz (1999), Henry (2007), and Kiros (2007a) were among those who noted that Africa was in a state of "crisis." Kiros (2007b) suggested that the Egyptian conception of "maat" (wisdom) included features of justice that might serve development with citizen participation in a new form of "moral economy." Irele (2007) emphasized the need for "political reconstruction" and "democratic revival in Africa" (p. 25). Bond (2007) framed the issues over hybridity in South Africa as "creative tensions between neoliberal problems and a desire for genuine social democratic solutions" (p. 125). Williams (2009) acknowledged the likelihood of hybrids: coexistence of capitalism and socialism and the extension of civil society and the state in the economy. Maathai (2009) framed a positive, empowering vision for Africa, claiming that development is not in the hands of multinational corporations, international aid, or the superpowers, but in the hands of Africans themselves, and that the task is also one of "reclamation" of what is essential and valued, incorporating traditional African values into future development (pp. 288–289). Mwaafrika Felder (2008) resonated with Maathai in arguing that Africans must define their *own* brands of democracy, socialism, or "whatever type of government that they may invent" (p. 13). Nelson Mandela invoked Havel in his vision for a new South Africa, and as Matustik (1993) summarized, the ideas of Havel, Habermas, and Kierkegaard fuse in an idealized vision of "multiculturalism without ethnocentric and national hatred, postnational identity without homogenization of regional culture, and deliberative democracy undistorted by imperial world order or by fragmentation and anomie" (p. 252).

Such a vision for post-colonial Africa in the coming decades might materialize in any number of forms – but through what exactly? Renewed socialism? Blended socialism and democracy? Outright capitalism and neoliberal policies? Or through a return to traditional conceptions of collectivism and equality? It is futile to speculate. Invoking history, future decades will likely see a persistent complex of mixed arrangements according to political agendas of those in power. The African Renaissance (Mbeki, 1998) and NEPAD are unproven as effective vehicles for continent-wide development. As in the birth of African socialism, sociophilosophical arguments are seducing, but they do not assure sound policies or concrete outcomes. The dilemma of ideal-versus-real surfaces once again.

A new generation of charismatic and enlightened leaders – another Mandela, Nyerere, or Nkrumah? – might restore faith in government and reforms for lasting change in education and other sectors through attainment of targets such as the MDGs. In South Africa, however, while current President Zuma enjoys both popularity and notoriety, prospects are debated in light of the "Zuma Era" ambiguities (Kane-Berman, 2009).

Educational development in the coming years will continue to compete with challenges that have raised the stakes, including HIV/AIDS, political violence and instability, and refugees and migrations. South Africa has the strongest economy on the continent, but reels under the impact of these and other challenges (Brook Napier, 2009a, 2009b). Whether future transformation is linked to socialism or capitalism, or Maathai's vision of "reclamation," African states share with other post-colonial states and former Soviet bloc states the triple imperative of overcoming the colonial legacy, rebuilding on the mixed record of the past, and juggling internal and external demands. A question posed by Morrow and Torres (2007) seems pertinent here: "How will processes of global creolization affect ... peripheral societies [– including African states –] especially with respect to educational stratification, elite formation, and cultural change?" (p. 96). Will African states actually "reclaim" responsibility for their own future development in education and other sectors?

Renewed hope for future decades might entail rethinking internal and regional needs in Africa rather than being preoccupied with global competitiveness (Postlethwaite & Kellaghan, 2008, p. 29). Lost hope and the demoralizing effects of perceived "failure" might be the worst enemies, as Bajaj (2010) noted among Zambian students, and as Brook Napier (2003, 2009a) recorded in teachers' struggles to adapt to reforms. Socialism in some dimension – if only as continued lip service – might prevail in Africa and in the global landscape as long as some of its tenets oppose greed, individualism, elitism, and exploitation – even though the legacy in Africa reveals that nominally socialist regimes perpetuated these problems. One truly enduring legacy lies in the instrumental value of education and the persistent efforts of legions of educators and students across the continent. These should be remembered, aside from politics, ideology, and economics.

NOTE

1. Congo-Kinshasa is distinguished from its neighbor state Congo-Brazzaville. The original Belgian Congo became independent as the Congo, and then later it become the state of Zaire, then the Democratic Republic of Congo, or DRC, as it is currently called. Some writers differentiate between Congo-Brazzaville (Congo) and Congo-Kinshasa (the Congo) in usage.

REFERENCES

African National Congress. (1994). *The reconstruction and development programme: A policy framework*. Johannesburg: ANC.

Africa Research Bulletin. (2008). Cote d' Ivoire in Brief. *Africa Research Bulletin: Political, Social and Cultural Series, 45*(1), 173–186.

Altbach, P. (1971). Education and neocolonialism. *Teachers College Record, 72*(4), 543–558.

Anderson-Levitt, K. M. (Ed.) (2003). *Local meanings, global schooling: Anthropology and world culture theory*. New York: Palgrave McMillan.

Anderson-Levitt, K. M., & Diallo, B. B. (2003). Teaching by the book in Guinea. In: K. M. Anderson-Levitt (Ed.), *Local meanings, global schooling: Anthropology and world culture theory* (pp. 75–97). New York: Palgrave McMillan.

Apter, A. (2008). In: W. A. Darity, Jr. (Ed.), *Socialism, African. International Encyclopedia of the Social Sciences*. Farmington Hills, MI: Thomson Gale, Cengage Learning, USA: Macmillan. Available at http://www.encyclopedia.com/doc/1G2-3045302514.html. Retrieved on October 8, 2010.

Arnove, R. F., & Torres, C. A. (Eds). (2007). *Comparative education: The dialectic of the global and the local*. New York: Rowman and Littlefield.

Arrighi, G. (2002). The African Crisis. New Left Review 15, May–June 2002, 5–36.

Ashcroft, B., Griffiths, G., & Tiffin, H. (Eds). (2006). *The post-colonial studies reader*. London: Routledge/Taylor and Francis.

Ayittey, G. B. N. (1990). The end of African socialism? Lecture to Heritage Foundation. Available at http://www.heritage.org/Research/Lecture/The-End-of-African-Socialism. Retrieved on January 24, 1990.

Azikiwe, A. (2009). Julius Nyerere: Pioneer in the liberations of Africa: Reviewing the Tanzanian experience 10 years since the passing of Mwalimu, October. Workers World. Available at http://www.workers.org/2009/world/julius_nyerere_1105/. Retrieved on October 8, 2010.

Bajaj, M. (2010). Intergenerational perspectives on education and employment in the Zambian Copperbelt. *Comparative Education Review, 54*(2), 175–197.

Baker, D. P., & Wiseman, A. W. (Eds). (2005). *Global trends in educational policy.* Amsterdam: Elsevier Science, Ltd.

Baker, D. P., & Wiseman, A. W. (Eds). (2008). *The worldwide transformation of higher education.* Amsterdam: Elsevier.

Balfour, S. (2008). *Castro* (3rd ed.). Edinburgh: Pearson Education Limited.

Bayart, J-F. (1993). *The state in Africa: The politics of the belly* (2nd ed.). Cambridge: Polity.

Berg, E. J. (1964). Socialism and economic development in tropical Africa. *The Quarterly Journal of Economics, 78*(4), 549–573.

Betancourt, T. S., Simmons, S., Borisova, I., Brewer, S. E., Iweala, & de la Soudiere, M. (2008). High hopes, grim reality: Reintegration and the education of former child soldiers in Sierra Leone. *Comparative Education Review, 52*(4), 565–587.

Blyden, E. (1979). Extracts from African life and customs. In: J. A. Langley (Ed.), *Ideologies of liberation in black Africa, 1856–1970: Documents on modern African political thought from colonial times to the present* (pp. 78–87). London: Rex Collings.

Bond, P. (2007). South Africa between neoliberalism and social democracy? Respecting balance while sharpening differences. *Politikon, 34*(2), 125–146.

Brautigam, D. A., & Xiaoyang, T. (2009). China's engagement in African agriculture: "Down to the countryside". *China Quarterly, 199*, 686–706.

Brock-Utne, B. (2000). *Whose education for all? The recolonization of the African mind.* New York: Falmer Press.

Brock-Utne, B., & Skattum, I. (Eds). (2009). *Languages and education in Africa: A comparative and transdisciplinary analysis.* Oxford: Symposium Books.

Brook, D. L. (1991). Social studies for multicultural education: A case study of a racially integrated school in South Africa. *Georgia Social Science Journal, 22*(1), 1–10.

Brook, D. L. (1992). *Social studies and national development in Botswana, Zambia, and Zimbabwe.* Unpublished doctoral dissertation, University of Georgia, Athens.

Brook, D. L. (1996). From exclusion to inclusion: Racial politics and educational reform in South Africa. *Anthropology and Education Quarterly, 27*(2), 204–231.

Brook, D. L., & Brook, G. A. (1993). Social studies for Somali nomads. *The Social Studies, 84*(1), 5–13.

Brook Napier, D. (2003). Transformations in South Africa: Policies and practices from ministry to classroom. In: K. Anderson-Levitt (Ed.), *Local meanings, global schooling: Anthropology and world culture theory* (pp. 51–74). New York: Palgrave McMillan.

Brook Napier, D. (2005a). Beyond the Apartheid-Post-apartheid divide in South Africa: A view of transformation in a remote KwaZulu Natal village. Paper presented at the 49th annual meeting of CIES, Palo Alto, CA.

Brook Napier, D. (2005b). Implementing educational transformation policies: Investigating issues of ideal versus real in developing countries. In: D. P. Baker & A. W. Wiseman (Eds), *Global trends in educational policy* (pp. 24–59). Amsterdam: Elsevier.

Brook Napier, D. (2006a). Rethinking imperatives for teaching indigenous languages in South African schools: Implementation dilemmas and realities. Paper presented at the 50th annual meeting of CIES, Honolulu, Hawaii.

Brook Napier, D. (2006b). Education, social justice, and development in South Africa and Cuba: Comparisons and connections. *Education and Society*, *24*(2), 5–23.

Brook Napier, D. (2008). Pan-Africanism. In: J. Hartwell Moore (Ed.), *The encyclopedia of race and racism* (Vol. 2, pp. 399–402). Farmington Hills, MI: Thomson-Gale/McMillan Reference International.

Brook Napier, D. (2009a). Comparisons are odious? South Africa's struggles to compete globally, and to meet internal educational needs. Paper presented at the annual meeting of CIES, Charleston, SC.

Brook Napier, D. (2009b). Pan-African – Mediterranean connections and challenges in education, social justice, and development. Paper presented at the IV Mediterranean Society of Comparative Education Conference, Rabat, Morocco.

Buckle, C. (2002). *Beyond tears: Zimbabwe's tragedy*. Johannesburg: Jonathan Ball.

Capper, J., Nderitu, S., & Ogala, P. (1997). *The school improvement programme of the Aga Khan Education Service, Kenya at Kismayu, Western Kenya: Evaluation report*. Geneva: Aga Khan Foundation.

Chabal, P., & Daloz, J-P. (1999). *Africa works: Disorder as political instrument*. London: James Currey.

Cohen, R., & Goulbourne, H. (Eds). (1991). *Democracy and socialism in Africa*. Boulder, CO: Westview Press.

Crwys-Williams, J. (Ed.) (1997). *In the words of Nelson Mandela*. London: Penguin.

Cummings, W. K. (1986). *Low-cost primary education: Implementing an innovation in six nations*. Ottawa: International Development Research Centre.

Davidson, B. (1992). *The black man's burden: Africa and the curse of the nation state*. London: James Currey.

Dorsey, B. J. (1989). Educational development and reform in Zimbabwe. *Comparative Education Review*, *33*(1), 40–58.

Du Bois, W. E. B. (1965). *The world and Africa: An inquiry into the part which Africa has played in world history*. New York: International Publishers.

Freedman, S. W., Weinstein, H. M., Murphy, K., & Longman, T. (2008). Teaching history after identity-based conflicts: The Rwanda experience. *Comparative Education Review*, *52*(4), 663–690.

Galvez, W. (1999). *Che in Africa: Che Guevara's Congo diary*. Melbourne: Ocean Press.

Guest, R. (2004). *The shackled continent: Africa's past, present and future*. London: Macmillan.

Hanson, E. M. (1988). Administrative reform and the Egyptian Ministry of Education. Unpublished manuscript.

Hanson, E. M. (1990). Administrative reform and the Egyptian Ministry of Education. *Journal of Educational Administration*, *28*(4), 46–62.

Henighan, S. (2009). The Cuban fulcrum and the search for a transatlantic revolutionary culture in Africa: in Angola, Mozambique and Chile, 1965–2008. *Journal of Transatlantic Studies*, *7*(3), 233–248.

Henry, P. (2007). (for Ato Sekyi-Otu). Africana political philosophy and the crisis of the postcolony. *Socialism and Democracy*, *21*(3), 36–59.

Hickling-Hudson, A. (2004). South-south collaborations: Cuban teachers in Jamaica and Namibia. *Comparative Education*, *40*(2), 289–311.

Holland, D. (2010). Waves of educational model production: The case of higher education institutionalization in Malawi, 1964–2004. *Comparative Education Review*, *54*(2), 199–222.

Irele, F. A. (2007). The political kingdom: Toward reconstruction in Africa. *Socialism and Democracy*, *21*(3), 5–35.

Jansen, J. D. (1990). The state and curriculum in transition societies: The Zimbabwean experience. Paper presented at the annual meeting of the Annual Meeting of CIES, Anaheim, CA.

Jansen, J. D. (2004). Importing outcomes-based education into South Africa: Policy borrowing in a post-communist world. In: D. Phillips & K. Ochs (Eds), *Educational policy borrowing: Historical perspectives* (pp. 199–220). Oxford: Symposium Books.

Jansen, J. D. (2005). *When does a university cease to exist? Fortieth Alfred and Winifred Hoernle Memorial Lecture, 17 November 2004*. Johannesburg: South African Institute of Race Relations.

Jeffrey, A. (2010). *Ideology versus practicality. Fast facts*, April 20. Johannesburg: South African Institute of Race Relations.

Johnson, D. (1995). Introduction: The challenges of educational reconstruction and transformation in South Africa. *Comparative Education*, *31*(2), 131–140.

Kamat, V. (2008). This is not our culture! Discourse of nostalgia and narratives of health concerns in post-socialist Tanzania. *Africa*, *78*(3), 359–383.

Kane-Berman, J. (2009). South African mirror: The Republic in the Zuma era. Presentation to SAIRR membership, Johannesburg, South Africa.

Kaunda, K. (1975). The future of nationalism. In: G.-C. M. Mutiso & S. W. Rohio (Eds), *Readings in African political thought* (pp. 468–477). London: Heinemann.

Kersting, N. (2009). New nationalism and xenophobia in Africa – A new inclination? *Africa Spectrum*, *1*, 7–18.

King, K., & McGrath, S. (2002). *Globalisation, enterprise and knowledge: Education, training and development in Africa*. Oxford: Symposium Books.

Kiros, T. (2007a). Introduction: The African post-colonial state in crisis. *Socialism and Democracy*, *21*(3), 1–3.

Kiros, T. (2007b). Moral economy: An original economic form for the African condition. *Socialism and Democracy*, *21*(3), 171–179.

Kubow, P. K. (2007). Teachers' constructions of democracy: Intersections of western and indigenous knowledge in South Africa and Kenya. *Comparative Education Review*, *51*(3), 307–328.

Linton, N. (1968). Nyerere's road to socialism. *Canadian Journal of African Studies*, *1*.

Losch, D. (2008). Socialism in Africa. *Intereconomics*, *25*(6), 300–306.

Lulat, Y. G.-M., & Clarke, R. (1982). Political constraints on educational reform for development: Lessons from an African experience. *Comparative Education Review*, *26*(2), 235–253.

Lynch, P. D. (1992). Educational change and the "Khalwa" in the Sudan: Reform reformed. *Journal of Educational Administration*, *30*(4), 53–62.

Mandela, N. R. (1994). *Long walk to freedom: The autobiography of Nelson Mandela*. Boston: Little Brown.

Mandela, N. R., & Castro, F. R. (1991). *How far we slaves have come! South Africa and Cuba in today's world*. New York: Pathfinder.

Maathai, W. (2009). *The challenge for Africa: A new vision*. London: William Heinemann.

Matustik, M. J. (1993). *Postnational identity: Critical theory and existential philosophy in Habermas, Kierkegaard, and Havel*. New York: The Guilford Press.

Mazrui, A. A. (1983). Political engineering in Africa. *International Social Science Journal*, *35*(2), 279–294.

Mbeki, T. (1998). *Africa: The time has come. Selected speeches.* Cape Town: Tafelberg.

McGinn, N. F., & Cummings, W. K. (1997). Introduction. In: W. K. Cummings & N. F. McGinn (Eds), *International handbook of education and development: Preparing schools, students, and nations for the twenty-first century* (pp. 3–43). New York: Elsevier/Pergamon.

Meredith, M. (2005). *The fate of Africa: A history of fifty years of independence.* New York: Public Affairs.

Mhando, E. (2009). Belated perspectives on education for self-reliance, November. Paper presented at the IV International Mediterranean Society of Comparative Education Conference, Rabat, Morocco.

Mohan, J. (1966). Varieties of African socialism. In: R. Saville & J. Miliband (Eds), *Socialist register* (pp. 220–266). London: Merlin Press.

Morrow, R. A., & Torres, C. A. (2007). The state, social movements, and educational reform. In: R. F. Arnove & C. A. Torres (Eds), *Comparative education: The dialectic of the global and the local* (pp. 79–100). New York: Rowman and Littlefield.

Musonda, L. W. (1999). Teacher education reform in Zambia … Is it a case of a square peg in a round hole?. *Teaching and Teacher Education, 15*(2), 157–168.

Muyebaa, K. C. (2001). In search of a curriculum for sustainable development in Zambia, July–August. Paper presented at the 9th BOLESWA International Educational Research Symposium, Gaborone, Botswana.

Mwaafrika Felder, N. (2008). Kenya: Post-traumatic colonization syndrome. *New York Amsterdam News*, January 17–23, p. 13.

Naidoo, J. (2005). Education decentralization in Africa: Great expectations and unfulfilled promises. In: D. P. Baker & A. W. Wiseman (Eds), *Global trends in educational policy* (pp. 99–124). Amsterdam: Elsevier.

Nordvelt, B. H. (2008). Producing literacy and civil society: The case of Senegal. *Comparative Education Review, 52*(2), 175–198.

Nordvelt, B. H. (2010). Schools as agencies of protection in Namibia and Swaziland: Can they prevent dropout and child labour in the context of HIV/AIDS and poverty? *Comparative Education Review, 54*(2), 223–242.

Nyerere, J (1968). *Ujamaa: Essays on socialism.* London: Oxford University Press.

Peta, B. (2001). Mugabe sets out plans to impose hardline socialism. *The Independent*, October 16. Available at http://www.independent.co.uk

Phillips, D., & Ochs, K. (Eds). (2004). *Educational policy borrowing: Historical perspectives.* Oxford: Symposium Books.

Postlethwaite, T. N., & Kellaghan, T. (2008). *National assessments of educational achievement.* Paris; Brussels: UNESCO/IIEP; IAE.

Reimers, F., & McGinn, N. F. (1997). *Informed dialogue: Using research to shape education policy around the world.* London/Westport: Praeger.

Rosburg, C., & Callaghy, T. (Eds). (1979). *Socialism in sub-Saharan Africa: A new assessment.* Berkeley, CA: Institute of International Studies.

Saint, W. S. (1992). Universities in Africa: Strategies for stabilization and revitalization. World Bank Technical Paper no. 194. Africa Technical Department Series, World Bank, Washington, DC.

Samoff, J., & Carrol, B. (2007). Education for all in Africa: Still a distant dream. In: R. Arnove & C. A. Torres (Eds), *Comparative education: The dialectic of the global and the local* (pp. 357–388). New York: Rowman and Littlefield.

Sampson, A. (1999). *Mandela: The authorized biography*. Johannesburg: Jonathan Ball/ HarperCollins.

Saul, J. (2001). *Millennial Africa: Capitalism, socialism, democracy*. Trenton, NJ: Africa World Press.

Saul, J. S. (2005). *The next liberation struggle: Capitalism, socialism, and democracy in Southern Africa*. Scottsville: University of KwaZulu Natal Press.

Senghor, L. S. (1964). *On African socialism*. (M. Cook, Trans.). New York: Praeger.

Stambach, A. (2003). World-cultural and anthropological interpretations of "Choice Programming" in Tanzania. In: K. M. Anderson-Levitt (Ed.), *Local meanings, global schooling: Anthropology and world culture theory* (pp. 141–160). New York: Palgrave McMillan.

Steiner-Khamsi, G. (Ed.) (2004). *The global politics of educational borrowing and lending*. New York: Teachers College Press.

Stromquist, N. P. (2002). *Education in a globalized world: The connectivity of economic power, technology, and knowledge*. Lanham, MD: Rowman and Littlefield.

The Economist. (2008). A ravenous dragon, March 15. Special report on China's quest for resources. *The Economist*. Available at http://www.economist.com.

Torres, C. A. (2009). *Education and neoliberal globalization*. New York: Routledge.

Tyler, R. (2006). Africa and the perspective of international socialism. Parts 1 and 2. World Socialist Web Site (WSWS). Available at http://www.wsws.org/articles/2006/mar2006/ afr1-m25.shtml. Retrieved on March 25, 2006.

United Nations. (2007a). *The millennium development goals report*. New York: United Nations.

United Nations. (2007b). *The least developed countries report: Knowledge, technological learning, and innovation for development*. Geneva: United Nations Conference on Trade and Development (UNCTAD).

Van Rensburg, P. (1974). *Report from Swaneng Hill: Education and employment in an African country*. Uppsala: The Dag Hammerskjold Foundation.

Van Rooyen, J. (1994). *Hard right: The new white power in South Africa*. London: I.B. Taurus.

Vavrus, F. (2003). *Desire and Decline: Schooling amid crisis in Tanzania*. Bern: Peter Lang.

Vavrus, F., & Seghers, M. (2009). Critical discourse analysis in comparative education: A discursive study of "Partnership" in Tanzania's poverty reduction policies. *Comparative Education Review, 54*(1), 77–103.

Venter, A. (2008). Die politieke Ortuigings van Hans van Rensburg (1898–1966): Kontinuiteit en Verandering *[The political convictions of Hans van Rensburg (1898–1966): Continuity and change]*. *Tydskrif vir Geesteswetenskappe [Journal of Human Sciences], 48*(1), 41–57.

Vlaardingerbroek, B. (1998). Challenges to reform: Botswana junior secondary school science teachers' perceptions of the development functions of science education. *International Journal of Educational Reform, 7*(3), 264–270.

Waghid, Y. (2007). Educating for democratic citizenship and cosmopolitanism. *South African Journal Higher Education, 21*(5), 584–595.

Weber, E. (2002). Shifting to the right: The evolution of equity in the South African government's development and education policies, 1990–1999. *Comparative Education Review, 46*(3), 261–290.

Weizmann, H. (2003). Re-building the movement in South Africa. *Socialism Today, 71*. Available at http://www.socialismtoday.org/71/southafrica.html, Accessed on October 8, 2010.

Williams, M. (2009). Reimagining socialist futures in South Africa and Kerala, India. *Journal of Asian and African Studies, 44*(1), 97–122.

Wiseman, A. W., & Baker, D. P. (2005). The worldwide explosion of internationalized education policy. In: D. P. Baker & A. W. Wiseman (Eds), *Global trends in educational policy* (pp. 1–22). Amsterdam: Elsevier.

Woodson, C. (1936). *The African background outlined: Or, handbook for the study of the Negro.* Washington, DC: Association for the Study of Negro Life and History.

Yeboah, A. (1997). Precious beads multiply: Family decision making and girls' access to primary schooling in Ghana. *International Journal of Educational Reform, 6*(4), 412–418.

Young, C. (1982). *Ideology and development in Africa.* New Haven, CT: Yale University Press.

Youngman, D. J., & Ishengoma, J. M. (1999). Educational equity in Tanzania: The imperiled promise of reform. *Journal of Education, 181*(1), 59–73.

Zajda, J., & Rust, V. (Eds). (2009). *Globalisation, policy, and comparative research: Discourses of globalisation.* Dordrecht: Springer.

Zeleza, P. T., & Olukoshi, A. (Eds). (2004). *African universities in the twenty-first century.* Dakar, Senegal: Council for the Development of Social Science Research in Africa (CODESRIA).

BEYOND POST-SOCIALIST CONVERSIONS: FUNCTIONAL COOPERATION AND TRANS-REGIONAL REGIMES IN THE GLOBAL SOUTH

Tavis D. Jules

INTRODUCTION

The collapse of the socialist bloc in 1989 has led to multifaceted transformations globally. Although most research has focused on the plethora of educational changes and challenges in the former socialist countries of Southeast/Central Europe and the former Soviet Union (Eklof, Holmes, & Kaplan, 2005; Silova & Steiner-Khamsi, 2008; Steiner Khamsi & Stolpe, 2006), there have been rather modest debates on the impact of post-socialism on the emerging markets of the Global South. Yet, the ruptures caused by the collapse of the socialist bloc and the flows brought about by the intensification of economic globalization during the 1990s have had serious implications for small developing states in the Caribbean Community (CARICOM).[1] Affected by debt fatigue, political fragmentation/ideological pluralism (as reflected in competing socialist and capitalist ideologies), as well as numerous attempts at internal renewal and

Post-Socialism is not Dead: (Re)Reading the Global in Comparative Education
International Perspectives on Education and Society, Volume 14, 401–426
Copyright © 2010 by Emerald Group Publishing Limited
ISSN: 1479-3679/doi:10.1108/S1479-3679(2010)0000014018

experimentation, CARICOM states attracted the attention of the super-powers in the early 1970s because of their perceived "high geo-strategic significance" (Searwar, 2001, p. 377). Of particular concern was how CARICOM would react to the massive alteration of the global institutional landscape in a post-Cold War epoch.

Although the countries of Southeast/Central Europe and the former Soviet Union were forced to rethink their sociopolitical futures in light of the posthumous rise of a single mono-economic model, the events of 1989 opened a wide array of opportunities for CARICOM as a regional assemblage to develop and promote its own imperatives in the Global South. In doing so, CARICOM member states utilized the non-economic policy process of functional cooperation to draw lessons from each other's experiences as they attempted to reposition themselves in a new geopolitical space. In the mid-1980s, CARICOM's post-socialist transformations began with the collapse of bilateral socialist relations with the former Soviet Union and Cuba combined with the disintegration of national experiments with strands of socialism in Guyana, Grenada, and Jamaica. These policy alterations paved the way for educational reform through regional cooperation. In the area of education, such cooperation began with the creation of an Advisory Task Force on Education (1989) by CARICOM heads of government to examine the state of education regionally among CARICOM's member states. Before 1989, CARICOM members could not have undertaken such a task because of ideological pluralism, i.e. the ideological differences (including various forms of socialist and capitalist ideologies) between member states that stemmed from their differing economic and political beliefs. From the Caribbean perspective, post-socialist transformation in education became grounded in the efficacy of the global political events of 1989 and a regional push toward integration, democracy, capitalism, and free market principles.

Thus, as the socialist bloc disintegrated in Southeast/Central Europe and the former Soviet Union, CARICOM experienced the deepening of integration as the then 13 member states sought to survive in an era filled with a new ex ante rhetoric about "knowledge management" and the new competencies that Caribbean citizens should inculcate. What became apparent to the member states of CARICOM was that if they were to endure the contagion of globalization in a post-Cold War world, they needed to intensify their integrative efforts. As a result, CARICOM underwent a shift from the regional balkanization of the 1980s to the regional harmonization of the 1990s as a way toward stimulating regional and national economic development in the Caribbean. In essence, post–Cold

War hysteria and polarization fertilized regional isomorphism in the Global South. Given the "fundamental global changes which had overtaken the community in spite of the gains in national building of reform," educational reform ranged from the "development of physical and financial capital ...; to [the] development of human capital" (Strachan, 1996, p. 7). Findings demonstrate that a shift from national isolation to regional harmonization in education became the way forward to stimulate regional and national economic development by creating a laundry list of munificent platitudes and a petite à la carte of educational choices. This paradigmatic shift was the core underpinning of the Grand Anse Declaration and Work Programme for the Advancement of the Integration Movement of 1989[2] that "recognize[d] the primary importance of Human Resource Development (HRD) and the expansion of scientific and technological capability to the modernization of the regional economy" (CARICOM, 1989, p. 1). The prospects for innovation through information technology were seen as having momentous potential for economic growth and development since member states acknowledged that they "are conscious that people, rather than institutions, are the creators and producers of development" (CARICOM, 1989, p. 1).

This chapter will examine the Caribbean experience with post-socialism as an example of a new type of a "trans-regional regime" in the Global South (Jules, 2008). Regimes are seen as "principles, norms, rules, and decision-making procedures around which actors' expectations converge in a given area of international relations" (Krasner, 1983, p. 1). Trans-regional regime indicates a large intra-regional organization or institution whose members are sovereign countries contributing resources to the development of that group of countries through a regional mechanism. They facilitate the exchange of policy ideas and act as multilevel governance institutions by responding to the gaps and inability of national governments to control global, regional, and transnational economic processes. A trans-regional regime exists to create common regional policies that benefit its members. Although CARICOM is solely nation-state driven, with the end of the Cold War, it embarked upon a shift in its focus, concentrating on harmonizing the positions of its member states so that they can rebut the various challenges associated with economic globalization. Moreover, given the region's past, it has opted for deeper regionalism instead of federalism and political unification because harmonization among CARICOM's member states allows the sovereign states of the region to pool their resources (West Indian Commission, 1992).

In understanding why post-socialist reforms at the national levels had direct repercussions regionally, this chapter examines educational policy-making at the discursive level through the analysis of ten national policies from the regional and international perspective coupled with in-depth interviews with regional policy-makers. Although other chapters in this volume document the nuances of post-socialist transformation across different contexts, this chapter delves deeper into how national and regional ideologies aided educational reform among CARICOM countries in light of the 1989 events by providing a historical background to understand the justification and impetus for educational reform and the policy mechanism of lesson-drawing used to facilitate theses educational reforms.

POLICY DISCOURSE AND POLICY REFORM

In CARICOM's context, educational policy exists within a "fabricated policy space" (Nòvoa & Lawn, 2002) that seeks to construct a borderless educational space. In understanding the unintended consequences of the post-1989 era, policy-making at the discursive level is examined, since national policies articulate vital expressions of social power because they epitomize the values of authoritative actors and institutions whose knowledge about the social world are echoed in these texts (Ball, 1990). Thus, this chapters considers discourse as seen through the Foucauldian perspective: [discourse] "can be said, and thought, but [is] also about who can speak, when, where and with what authority" (Ball, 1990, p. 17). The data presented stems from an analysis of national and regional educational policy texts that shows how discursive distinctions are negotiated since they are governed by differences in power structures (Wodak, 2005). The analyses of national educational policies of CARICOM members illuminate sites of isomorphism and contestations in the region that allowed for members to draw lessons paving the way for post-socialist transformations.

Policy texts are seen as sites of resistance as they illustrate traces of diverse discourses and ideologies that compete with each other for power. Fairclough (1995) argues that the definition of *text* should be broadened to include both written and spoken discourses; in what follows in this chapter, text exclusively signifies written discourse. Fairclough (1995), citing Bakhtin (1981), argues that text is part recurrence and part formation, and that texts are sites of tension between centripetal and centrifugal pressures. In other words, the tension between centripetal and centrifugal tendencies in discourse is the push and pull between "official" discursive energies that can impose uniformity and order on the world versus "unofficial" energies, those tending toward heterogeneity and disorder. It is this tension that can be reflected in an institution's genres, that is, ways of acting. In understanding the process of text production, distribution, and consumption, a thematic approach to policy analysis is utilized because a textual analysis cannot be isolated from an examination of the institutional and discursive contexts within which texts are embedded. Textual approaches focus on the syntactical structure of documents, whereas thematic approaches focus on both the syntax and content.

In order to understand the impacts of 1989 regionally, if any, educational policies written during the 1990–1996 policy cycle were analyzed. This policy period was chosen because in 1989 the Grand Anse Declaration was endorsed by the heads of government of CARICOM to create a platform for sweeping regional changes ranging from education to economic liberalization. A content analysis of 10 educational policies (the Bahamas, Barbados, Dominica, Guyana, Grenada, Jamaica, Montserrat, St. Kitts and Nevis, St. Vincent and the Grenadines, and Trinidad and Tobago) during the 1990–1996 period was done.[3] The content analysis focused on discourse production in text by examining an international policy framework, the World Declaration on Education for All (UNESCO, 1990), and regional educational policy, the Future of Education in the Caribbean (CARICOM, 1993), against all national educational policies written during this period. In using a thematic categorical analysis, themes and thematic categories were created based on a qualitative reading of the regional policy and the international framework. These themes were then coded against national policy discourse. A theme-based approach to content analysis located the existence, occurrence, and congruence of a specific category of a theme when comparing national policies with a regional policy and the international framework. Once a theme from the regional policy or the international framework was found in national documents, a qualifying marker was assigned and it was categorized as a congruence. Additionally, supplemental interviews were conducted with key policy officials between May and November 2007 to aid in the interpretation of primary data collected.

HISTORICIZING FUNCTIONAL COOPERATION

During the 1980s, the Reagan Administration referred to the Caribbean as a "circle of crisis" (Jagen, 2001, p. 69), since as one crisis was being resolved another was beginning. CARICOM's response to the impact of 1989 lies in how it spent the 1980s dealing with the 1973–1974 oil crises, ideological pluralism, and the subsequent imposition of Structural Adjustment

Programs (SAPs) under the World Bank (WB) and International Monetary Fund (IMF). Taken together or separately, these events profoundly altered the region during the 1980s, and the demise of socialism in the former Soviet Union and in Southeast/Central Europe created greater regional expectation of a borderless educational space. The institutional transformations of the 1980s began in the aftermath of the oil and recession crisis of 1973–1974 and the 1977 oil shock, causing the terms of trade and interest rates to decline and thus creating a period of intra-CARICOM protectionism as states scrambled to preserve their balance of payments. This crisis had wide structural effects because it conjoined with the then problems of the international capitalist system – "the rising oil prices and falling commodity process and the world inflation and recession" (Hall, 2001, p. xiv).

The second institutional transformation was political fragmentation or "ideological pluralism," a phrase coined by CARICOM leaders in the early 1980s signifying the varying developmental ideologies of member states. It began with the failure of the Conference of Heads of Government of the Caribbean Community (CHGCC) to meet between 1975 and 1982 owing to national differences and became a de facto condition when CARICOM's foreign affairs ministers embraced it to preserve the fabric and integrity of the region. Ideological pluralism became prominent in the 1980s after Guyana guided by President Linden Burnham,[4] Jamaica aided by Prime Minister Michael Manley,[5] and Grenada under Prime Minister Maurice Bishop[6] opted for socialism in contradistinction to the rest of the region that maintained Western liberal democratic principles (Hall, 2003). The mid-1970s became an era of optimism for the New International Economic Order (NIEO) and New World Information Order (NWIO). Subsequently, Prime Minister Errol Barrow's[7] "friends of all, satellites of none" nonalignment foreign policy objectives allowed Barbados, Jamaica, Guyana, and Trinidad and Tobago to established diplomatic relations with Cuba under the Air Services Agreement in 1972. These countries had different reasons for bilateral ties with Cuba. The issue of the large numbers of Barbadian and Jamaican nationals living in Cuba without representation at that time was of concern to these governments. In Guyana's case, Cuba acted as a strong military ally, as the country faced the constant eruption of border tensions with Venezuela.[8] Moreover, ties to Cuba provided political and economic support as Jamaica implemented democratic socialism, Grenada enacted revolutionary socialism, and Guyana moved from a cooperative republic to a socialist republic (Rose, 2002).

In 1971, cooperative socialism began when the Guyanese government embarked upon a policy of expanding state property by nationalizing the commanding heights, that is, the key economic sectors, and placing 80% of the economy under governmental control (Hall, 2001). The intention was that Guyana should rid its economy of the effects of "dependent capitalist development" (Rose, 2002, p. 60). The notion was that Guyana should be self-reliant and egalitarian by allowing economic power to be controlled by all Guyanese. The objectives of cooperative socialism in Guyana were the creation of employment opportunities, equal distribution of incomes, equitable geographic distribution of economic activities, and the attainment of self-sustained economic growth (Lee, 2000). By 1976, Guyana and Jamaica were grappling with the effect of the world inflation and recession, rising oil prices, chronic food shortages, falling sugar prices, growth in public expenditure, and balance of payment problems. These factors saw these countries pursuing aggressive socialist policies – the expansion of the state sector and social welfare programs – by promoting an active role for the state in the form of state-capitalist oriented development.

Jamaica's response to these problems was democratic socialism, as President Manley argued that the neoclassical economics caused the island's economic dependence and that socioeconomic salvation lay in "reducing or eliminating its economic dependence on the metropolitan powers" (Rose, 2002, p. 245). For Manley, democratic socialism, an alternative to path to development, was based on the "single touch tone of right and wrong" and a belief in the Christian ideals of equity for all of God's children (Rose, 2002, p. 245). In 1979, the first coup d'état in the English-speaking Caribbean occurred in Grenada under the Marxist-Leninist New Jewel Movement. This paved the way for revolutionary socialism under President Bishop, which was supported by Guyana and Jamaica. Bishop's aim was to rebuild Grenada's economy in wake of the economic destruction caused by Eric Gairy's government between 1967 and 1979. Revolutionary socialism embraced the socialist theory of noncapitalist development and the principles and doctrine of Marxism-Leninism (Rose, 2002). It was aimed at creating a "patriotic, politically aware and educated Grenada" based on a mixed economic module of development guided by capitalist principles that nationalized industries, restructured land tenures, and controlled wages and price (Rose, 2002, p. 331). The 1983 United States-led invasion of Grenada sanctioned by CARICOM members to contain "socialism to one country" soured regional relations (Lewis, 2001, p. 46). Regionally, this kind of balkanization effect created centrifugal policy forces in education as the prospect of deeper disintegration loomed on the horizon. By mid-1980, Cuban-CARICOM relations declined and other countries in the hemisphere began to re-examine their bilateral relationships.

With the collapse of individual national economies across the region, the third institutional metamorphosis occurred through the normative patterns created by SAPs, that is, liberalization of domestic and foreign trade, privatization/disinvestment of inefficient public enterprises, and other international stabilization programs across the region. SAPs implemented by the WB and the IMF were aimed at increasing economic competence so that the domestic supply of goods and services produced would increase. Instead, SAPs created a crisis situation regionally as the import bills ballooned, unemployment soared, real wages declined, currencies devalued, budget deficits increased causing drastic budgetary reductions in expenditure on goods, and social services and employment costs created retrenchment in the public sector. Additionally, contractions occurred in public sector investment programs and restricted spending on other projects. SAPs aimed at eradicating socialism under the guise of neoliberalism by blending aspects of Thatcherism and Reaganomics together. In the Caribbean, Thatcherism was implemented through neoliberal policies: diminished state interference, free market economy, monetarist economic policy, privatization of state-owned industries, lower direct taxation and higher indirect taxation, and a reduced welfare state. On the contrary, Reaganomics consisted in part of hefty budget cutbacks in domestic programs and extensive tax cuts for individuals and international businesses. The theory of supply-side economics – producing development by motivating a better delivery of goods and services and thereby creating jobs – was a basis of this approach along with combating inflation and controlling government-spending deficits.

By 1989, having experienced all three of the aforementioned pestilences – the oil crisis, ideological pluralism, and SAPs – Caribbean governments became determined to steer their economies away from socialism as well as economic and social breakdowns by shifting toward a new development path while adapting to major external and internal shocks in their economic system. As member states sought to build consensus, the new development path spun an overabundance of regional declarations and understandings, as well as a general consensus about how to deal with exogenous influences. Consequently, they realized that the deterioration in terms of trade services, increased food shortages, protracted fiscal deficits, and contraction in imports and economic growth had to be addressed. Against this milieu, member states began to reform their educational systems utilizing the process of functional cooperation to stimulate regionalism. As Girvan (2001) notes:

> The tendency towards ideological and policy convergence among member states due to debt and adjustment crisis of the 1980s; to the collapse of the Socialist experiments in

Jamaica, Grenada, and Guyana; and to the end of the Cold War ... were developments that paved the way for a regional consensus on the necessity of market oriented policy reforms in domestic economic management and for its correlated 'Open Regionalism', as the model of regional integration. The shift was initiated in the Nassau Understanding of 1984. (p. 1)

That being so, the Nassau Understanding (CARICOM, 1984) argued that the regional solution to these problems and socialist experiments was a better-educated populace since national governments needed to strengthen their educational system at all levels by offering "opportunities for the acquisition of skills that will directly contribute to the modernization and development of the economy" (p. 6). Fundamental changes at the global level created conditions in which economic well-being became increasingly dependent on the availability of a highly educated and highly skilled labor force capable of being retrained to meet international demands (Hall, 2003, p. xiii). Pressures to reform educational systems in the mid-1980s allowed functional cooperation to thrive. Cooperation was further intensified as the confidence of respective member states declined with the "flight of human and financial capital, reduced production and productivity and the emergence of a large underground sector in the economy" (CARICOM, 1984, p. 2). Against this backdrop of the Nassau Understanding (CARICOM, 1984), the Kingston Declaration (CARICOM, 1990) spoke of the importance of human resource development (HRD) and sustainable development. In making a case for a greater increase in HRD, the Barbados Consensus (CARICOM, 1985) pointed out the shortcomings of the regional education systems by noting that when compared with other emerging markets the literacy rate of high school enrollment was almost 100%, yet the availability of skills available quantitatively or qualitatively was inadequate to create economic development.

Post-socialist transformations were initiated at the regional level when the groundwork for selecting and identifying educational indicators was laid out in the 1984 Nassau Understanding and culminated in 1995 with the Regional Workshop on Education in Guyana. Internationally, three major conferences re-emphasizing the importance of "education in the development of human capabilities, and the capacity of nations to pursue and sustain development efforts" (CARICOM, 2003, p. 52) were held during the 1990–1996 policy period. The first, the World Conference on Education for All by UNESCO in 1990, provided a framework for countries to review and assess developments in basic education. The second, the International Conference on Population Development (ICPD) by UNFPA in 1994, reaffirmed human development as an important and valuable resource of nations since it is essential for sustainable development and people's well-being. ICPD observed that education allows individuals to gain access to knowledge as it serves to "empower women, improve the quality of life of the working population, to produce genuine democracy and reduce fertility, morbidity and mortality, which if left uncontrolled could nullify development efforts" (cited in CARICOM, 2003, p. 52). The third, the World Summit for Social Development by the United Nations in 1995, adopted a Plan of Action to attain universal and equitable access to education. Together, these conferences produced goals and actions related to education in the Caribbean concerned with eradicating illiteracy, universal access to quality basic education for girls, women, children, youths, adults and persons with disabilities, nonformal education programs for young people, curriculum restructuring, linking labor markets to education policies, and eliminating gender disparities and creating gender relevant policies (CARICOM, 2003). The conferences also contributed indirectly to post-socialist transformations since they focused on the free market philosophy, democratization, human rights, and choice, thus reinforcing neoliberal principles at the regional level as members sates wanted to be seen as modern and free.

The CHGCC 10 (1989) was held against a changing international background inspiring interstate relations premised on trust and deeper cooperation in seeking solutions to national and regional policy issues. CHGCC 10 emphasized the need for member states to strengthen the integration movement further by adopting coordinated national and regional economic policies in response to continuing efforts by Canada, Mexico, and the United States to create a North American Free Trade Area (NAFTA) for themselves. This lead to a substantial restructuring of trade, monetary aid, and investment relations in the hemisphere. In acknowledging the global trend toward greater intra-regional cooperation, CARICOM leaders argued that hemispheric transformation created new, far-reaching policy opportunities that could be achieved through the deepening and widening of the integration movement and by achieving increasingly higher levels of efficiency (CHGCC 13, 1992). In sum, regionalism became typecast as a panacea rooted in the heightened consciousness of international partnerships and a new willingness to cooperate in the search for solutions to national problems, such as the abuse and trafficking of narcotic drugs, external debt, and HIV/AIDS. Simultaneously, the globalization of the world economy was creating new centers of economic power, with nation-states combining into large economic groupings and unified markets.

POST-SOCIALIST TRANSFORMATION: INTENSIFIED COOPERATION 1990–1996

The disintegration of national experiments with socialism in Guyana, Grenada, and Jamaica laid the foundation for post-socialist transformations by forcing CARICOM members to cooperate after the collapse of the bipolar international system. The window of opportunity for post-socialist reform in the region first opened after the failure of cooperative socialism in Guyana, a failure stemming from the consequences of imposed state ownership and the control of its national resources which failed to produce prolonged growth as the leading economic sectors of sugar, rice, and bauxite declined from inefficient and administrative mismanagement. In Guyana, cooperative socialism had become a strategy for controlling the state apparatus. Although Jamaica was critical of Western capitalism, democratic socialism collapsed there as living conditions worsened along with the failure to reduce the unyielding economic dependence on the IMF as the government was forced to implement loan conditionalities when it sought to bailout its central bank. IMF conditions clashed with socialist policies. In Grenada, revolutionary socialism had made great inroads in the first three years through land reform and improvements in the social services; however, in it fell apart in Grenada because of the unfeasibility of nationalizing industries while seeking financial assistance from Western countries. Moreover, the small and fragile economy of Grenada, sustained by tourism and foreign capital, could not nourish noncapitalist developmental principles (Rose, 2002). Although these three countries directly experimented with socialism, the other 10 CARICOM countries had direct and indirect contact with socialism via their bilateral ties with Cuba, Venezuela, Chile, and Nicaragua.

Given the historical context that led the region to fend off exogenous influences, the 1990–1996 policy period became characterized as a period of intensified functional cooperation because it was premised upon internal educational reformation through a discourse of compliance purging the region of the principles of socialism. Functional cooperation, the non-economic principle of integration, is enshrined in the Original Treaty of Chaguaramas (CARICOM, 1973) and the Revised Treaty of Chaguaramas (CARICOM, 2001). It is intended to create the efficient operation of common services and activities for the benefit of the people; accelerated promotion of greater understanding among the people; the advancement of their social, cultural, and technological development; and intensified activities in areas such as health, education, transportation, and telecommunications. It operates within a rules-based enterprise, such as the Caribbean Single Market and Economy (CSME), advancing specific aspects of the Community's agenda (CARICOM, 2007). Therefore, it refers to the common services and activities carried out by the region. Intensified functional cooperation occurred when internal and external educational reform pressures ignited deeper regional integration, and it manifested in the mutual drawing of lessons regionally and cross-nationally to survive. Following the definition provided in the Revised Treaty, functional cooperation within the context of education is deemed as "intensified activities in areas," rather than the "efficient operation of common services and activities," occurring in varying degrees of intensity across the Community (CARICOM, 2001). Its forms include, but are not limited to: meetings and other types of interaction aimed at arriving at decisions about the planning and implementation of shared services or other regional activities (an example of the most basic form of cooperation); coordination of the actions of individual member states so that, once agreement is reached on general principles, member states may proceed to apply them on a bilateral basis; unifying action that goes beyond the adoption of common principles applied at the level of member states; and creating a single policy space (short of political and economic integration) that may be managed supra-nationally (Task Force on Functional Cooperation, 2008).

The final regional educational policy by the Advisory Task Force on Education, *The Future of Education in the Region*, was derived from consultations in each member state and it allowed lessons to be drawn from individual national objectives and connected them to regional outcomes. As member states undertook educational reforms, they kept the "goals" of the larger regional objective of creating ideal Caribbean citizens to function within the CSME (Jules, forthcoming). When the Standing Committee of Ministers Responsible for Education (SCME) 7 (1988) "agreed that a process of inquiry, diagnosis and design be pursued in the region in a attempt to consciously and systematically prepare for the short, medium and long term challenges of education" (p. 19), it paved the way for an intensive process of regional collaboration to develop and re-orient the educational systems of the member states. Functional cooperation re-emerged in the form of "collaborative dialogue" (Innes & Booher, 2003) engendering non-economic integration intended to (1) increase the efficient operation of common services and activities, (2) heighten internal understanding of cooperating states and the advancement of their social, cultural, and technological development, and (3) intensify and operationalize activities in non-economic areas such as education and health. The final comprehensive regional educational policy encapsulated the issues and concerns that were to be addressed if the region was to successfully confront the challenges that continually emerged at regional and international levels. Moreover, it articulated the policy goals that were supposed to guide member states toward greater integration.

Given this intensified cooperation, CARICOM focused on functional or non-economic activities, such as education, creating inward isolation for member states. When member states sought to draw lessons from each other they sought to mitigate transactional costs spent in negotiation efforts, including time, personnel, money, prestige, and even power, which is sometimes lost with bargaining concessions (Jules & Sa e Silvia, 2008). This reduction of transaction costs utilized "services and resources or other forms of cooperation that are not necessarily based on legal instruments, constructs or constraints or on the tenets of economic integration" (CHGCC, 2007). In effect, transaction costs did indeed become lower since the lesson-drawing method advocated efficiency, cost-sharing, and a collective commitment to improving the human condition (Brewster, 2003). Cooperation reduces the transaction costs associated with reaching and carrying out agreements, which in turn depends on further direct cooperation (Jervis, 1999). Although member states, in their attempts to avoid external threats, ultimately lowered these costs, lesson-drawing was premised upon mitigating exogenous policy factors. During this period, once trade barriers and legal protocols were removed as reform pressure took root across the region, intensified functional cooperation moved beyond traditional bilateral and multilateral intra-state collaborative efforts. It stemmed from outside the realm of traditional South–South cooperative efforts in that it promoted alliance intended to counter regional disintegration and balkanization. As a collaborative effort, it strove toward one goal: integration through social cohesion. The regional education policy produced in 1993 was the glue that held this together while showing to the rest of the world and international institutions that post-socialist transformations had taken place regionally. Through social cohesion, intensified functional cooperation gave rise to horizontal sectoral amalgamation. Functional cooperation created the chimera of an elusive virtual solitary policy space that was voluntary for its collaborating states.

Post-socialist ramifications led to intensified functional cooperation aimed at greater economic integration through coordinated policies, procedures, and practices defined by principles of efficiency and effectiveness. Efficiency, or "hard principles," reflected the tangible economic results produced by functional cooperation. Principles of effectiveness, the "soft principles" of intensified functional cooperation, were those based on the humanitarian and a common identity elements fostered by functional cooperation. They benefited the region through the harmonization of strategies that allowed for a greater quality of life by reducing poverty, improving health, increasing opportunities for acquiring knowledge and skills, creating avenues for employment, reducing the demand for drugs, and placing an emphasis on culture to forge social cohesion out of economic, geographic, and ethnic diversity. Intensified functional cooperation became the efficient method for collaborative efforts to forge national policies, procedures, and strategies that would derive common outcomes mutually beneficial to all member states, while at the same time deepening psychological and historical relations. It allowed for the efficient operation and autonomy of member states. Therefore, intensified functional cooperation between states focused on and dealt with the externalities that arose from increasing interdependence. In other words, intensified functional cooperation was driven by interdependence and gave rise to greater sectoral harmonization.

Regional post-socialist transformations were triggered by external forces and operationalized through the various modalities of functional coopera-tion.[9] Lessons at the national to regional level were premised upon activities among member states, among the institutions themselves, from institutions to member states, and from the CARICOM Secretariat to member states. Accordingly, these modalities centered on sharing policies and programs, disseminating information, developing human resources, and monitoring and evaluating. According to the Task Force on Functional Cooperation (2008), the dissemination of relevant data and other information on the Caribbean to the people of the region is an important objective of functional cooperation since it provides a better understanding of the Community's achievements and allows the region's people to predict the impact of policies/changes. An essential prerequisite in the region is increased cooperation among member governments and regional institu-tions in order to establish reliable systems for data collection and dissemination. Given the availability of modern technology, this was accomplished without having to create an excessive institutional capacity. The sharing and adopting of common policies has been an important formula for ensuring the success of functional cooperation.

In sum, the 1990–1996 policy period is categorized as a period of intensified functional cooperation. It is evident that the first modality was present: member states were sharing policies and programs with each other. This sharing of resources resulted from external influences pressuring the region to reform. As educational reform pressure spread, member states began to disseminate information at the national and regional levels in the form of the Nassau Understanding (CARICOM, 1984), the Grand Anse Declaration (CARICOM, 1989), and the Kingston Declaration (CARICOM, 1990). All three of these regional frameworks spoke of the importance of human resources development. The Nassau Understanding (CARICOM, 1984) contextualized human development within the framework, which expounded that "the acquisition of skills will contribute toward development and modernization" (p. 4). The Grand Anse Declaration (CARICOM, 1989) called for "the upgrading of human resource at all levels and enhancing scientific and technological capability" (p. 3), and the Kingston Declaration (CARICOM, 1990) conceived of HRD as the "central element of regional and national development strategies" (p. 1). Overall, member states were forced to evaluate their own educational policies during the collaboration process.

POLICY TSUNAMI, SPACE, AND TIME

Dolowitz and Marsh (1996) argue that policy transfer includes "lesson-drawing" (Rose, 1993), "policy band-wagoning" (Ikenberry, 1990), "policy borrowing" (Cox, 1999; Steiner-Khamsi, 2004), "policy shopping" (Freeman, 1999), "systematically pinching ideas" (Schneider & Ingram, 1988), and "social learning" (Common, 2004; Haas, 1992). Although educational transfer occurred during a different policy period within CARICOM (see Jules, 2008), it is argued that lesson-drawing, one tenant of policy transfer, was used to engender economic harmonization during the 1990–1996 period. Lesson-drawing during this period laid the foundation for policy transfer to occur later (Jules, 2008). Lesson-drawing is defined as "a program for action based on a program or programs undertaken in another city, state, or nation or by the same organization in its own past" (Rose, 1993, p. 21). Internal policy discontentment within a member state serves as a catalyst to stimulate policy change and induces policy-makers to pursue other policy alternatives. Policy aggravation becomes apparent when policy reforms suffer from internal differences resulting from disequilibrium between policy targets and successes. Thus, policy ignorance initiates the search for policy actions when solutions are not derived locally, propelling countries to explore across time and space to see how comparable challenges have been resolved elsewhere. Lesson-drawing depends on who searches and how a search is conducted, because organizations and countries do not have brains, but rather cognitive systems and memories in the form of information-receiving and information-gathering capacities (Hedberg, 1981). Although moving ideas from one country to another can be difficult, "international brokers of ideas depend upon national conditions in member countries becoming so unsatisfactory that their governments are driven to look abroad for lessons" (Rose, 1993, pp. 68–69). In this context, lesson-drawing as a policy tool is used during certain distinctive policy eras to facilitate policy renewal.

In the 1980s, given CARICOM's scope and mandates, lesson-drawing became the central policy tool aided by functional cooperation to facilitate deeper regionalism. Lesson-drawing is a practical policy tool for action since lessons can be drawn from both positive and negative experiences, as well as across time (from a given region's past experience) and space (from other regions). The extent of learning ranges from total duplication to adaptation (taking different starting-points into account), in making a hybrid from the exporting and importing region, extracting some aspects of an export program or policy and applying them internally, or simply using lessons from other regions as a broad inspiration for policy change (Rose, 1993). The starting-point for lesson-drawing is learning from the past in one's own region or nation-state. Lessons are more likely to be borrowed from other regions if the exporting region shares similar policy conditions (particularly economic, since there is a question of affordability), geographical borders, and ideology. In the case of CARICOM, these pre-existing conditionalities surfaced during the 1990–1996 policy period. Although lesson-drawing is not straightforward, states may choose to mimic other states that are "nearest," and policy conditions will differ from one country to another.

As a policy tool, lesson-drawing requires concepts, which are the policy ideas that are named, the questions that are asked, and the answers that are derived by policy-drawers. Concepts provide a common point of reference both for the policy-drawer and the drawee, that is, policy-originator, and are variables that are subject to analysis. Concepts are the stipulations of what the problems are and what solutions are sought. Fluency in the conceptual vocabulary is a precondition for drawing lessons. A lesson is not a disjointed set of ideas; neither does it require a cause-and-effect model showing how a program designed elsewhere can be achieved if adopted (Rose, 1993). Although a multiplicity of factors influences lesson-drawing (namely power, resources, expert opinions, and political values), transferability is a distinguishing feature. Lesson-drawing is a set of actions that governments consider in the light of experiences from elsewhere. Consequently, lesson-drawing has four analytical stages. First, lesson-drawing involves the search for programs that have worked elsewhere. Second, it abstractly conceptualizes the cause-and-effect from what is observed. Third, a lesson is fashioned on the basis of what is observed. Finally, the observed lesson from elsewhere undergoes evaluation and its application in a new setting is determined. A core element in lesson-drawing central to this CARICOM mission is that of desirability. The desirability of a program speaks to whether a program from elsewhere is technically feasible. A lesson that is being drawn is only considered desirable if it is consistent with the values and goals of the policy-drawer.

In sum, the global reverberations of 1989 caused a policy tsunami creating the right environment to draw lessons. Lesson-drawing among CARICOM states was a political mechanism that allowed members to pursue different developmental strategies in light of the rise of ideological pluralism during the 1980s. It gave members the feeling of security while they sought deeper ways to integrate. The drawing of lessons from elsewhere within the region rather than the transferal of individual policies was an act of externalization. In this way, national best practices and good governance modules were highlighted during national consultations and used domestically as a source of legitimacy for post-socialist reforms.

Drawing Lessons through National Consultations

Regionally, the genesis for post-socialist transformations began to take shape when SCME 7 (1988) agreed to embark on a "coherent and conscious, and systematic program of inquiry, analysis, diagnosis, and design" (p. 12). Lesson-drawing took the form of national consultations, which were central to the development of a common regional educational policy. As the process of functional cooperation intensified and took root, the Advisory Task Force on Education created in 1988 held national consultations on education across the region between 1989 and 1993. The core functions of the Advisory Task Force were to outline and manage the activities and events required in a continuing process of regional consultation and analysis. Through consultations, the Advisory Task Force drew lessons on education from member states that later became the backbone of national policies. These activities required involving relevant constituencies and drawing upon widespread views of objectives, content, and arrangements that were appropriate to contemporary needs and anticipated challenges. Drawing lessons was a common strategy that dealt with the challenges of educational policy reform. This response was triggered by anxiety to reform national education, which during this policy period utilized a process of intra-collaboration within the region in the form of intensified synergies and coherence that was desirous of intra-lessons. This process synchronized policies, processes, and procedures, and led ultimately to the post-socialist reforms nationally during this period. Lesson-drawing during the 1990–1996 policy period was a self-conscious act by national governments. In the case of CARICOM, lessons were drawn from the past and present experiences of member states to combat the challenges of the future. Thus, lesson-drawing became normative in that it was a "prescription to adopt a measure drawn from another, a statement about what ought to be done" (Rose, 1993, p. x). The experience of seeing a program in effect in another place showed that it could be realized elsewhere. Lesson-drawing started with the realization that policy challenges were not unique to a specific domain since "it is often easier to see similarities between the same policy area in different states or countries than to find similarities within a country" (Rose, 1993, p. 2). In this sense, lesson-drawing became a tool that Caribbean policy-makers utilized when confronted with a policy crisis. The need for quick-fix policy answers led policy-makers to look over the fence in order to find policy solutions.

The analysis of policy documents illustrate that national consultations became arenas of information-sharing, in which the Advisory Task Force on Education obtained insights on key educational issues, concerns, plans, and program for the development and improvement of educational systems across the region. Policy lesson-drawing during these consultations took the forms of hybridization, synthesization, and inspiration. Inspiration from an existing program allowed for the combination of recognizable elements of that program (hybridization) with the familiar elements of a different program into a distinctive whole (synthesization). This was typified during the Barbados consultations in 1993 when the Advisory Task Force noted that the concerns expressed by Barbados at various educational levels were common across the region (SCME, 1993). During the consultation process, the levels of education identified and the concepts – common points of reference both for the policy-drawer and the policy-drawee – of lesson-drawing within the Caribbean context were: pre-primary, primary, secondary, and tertiary, curriculum, measurement and evaluation, and planning. Additionally, the members of the Task Force on Education urged national education officials to document, for the benefit of other member states, two successful educational ventures in Barbados: the amalgamation of schools and the introduction of computers in primary and secondary schools. This documentation of experiences from abroad is an illustration of the analytical stages of lesson-drawing. First, consultations provided examples of programs that had been successful. Second, as in Barbados, the cause-and-effect was problematized. Third, a lesson, how to do this in another setting, was derived. Finally, the observed lesson from elsewhere underwent evaluation and its application in a new setting was determined in line with the final creation of regional policy.

The example of Barbados' experiences shows how policy lesson-drawing became applicable across time and space. In evaluating the Barbados experience, lessons were drawn because the members of the Advisory Task Force saw how the program operated in Barbados and, therefore, they could make hypotheses about its likely future effects in other member states. Rose (1993) refers to this process as the "fungibility" of a program, indicating the capability of a program to be constituted into other contexts. The fungibility of a policy was not based on total replication, though, rather policy prescriptions were treated as universally valid, since a system described in the model was expected to work in the same way irrespective of time and space. Fungibility became applicable to the CARICOM not only experience in that all member states shared the common goals, but also in that, as member states mitigated transactional costs, they relied upon and learned from each other and the lessons of their past. "In this way the existence of common problems [was] defined in terms sufficiently abstract so that generic solutions appear applicable everywhere" (Rose, 1993, p. 35). Thus, as CARICOM continued integrating, it became easier for programs to be transferred from one country to another (Jules, 2008).

The policy analysis showed that national consultations helped member states to recognize the importance of geographical propinquity in drawing lessons. Because neighbors are a convenient source of ideas, policy-makers may choose the neighbors that are nearest when concerned over a given policy area (Rose, 1993). Lesson-drawing through cross-national consultations was used to address the specific problem of "the relationship between education and development" (SCME, 1988). This period was distinguished from others in that pressure to reform educational systems caused structural changes at the national and regional levels. As Rose (1993) points out, "when structural changes occur, what worked before no longer works as it once did" (p. 5). Functional concerns then, such as education, created opportunities for learning from the experiences of other nations. In this way, lesson-drawing cut across territorial boundaries. As Rose (1993) notes, "interdependence creates a demand for the strongest form of lesson-drawing, namely the adoption of a common policy by different governments" (p. 11). Moreover, functional interdependence provoked a common response from two or more different governments for dealing effectively with a problem (Rose, 1993). As national consultations progressed, three analytical operational bases emerged:

(1) Regionalism: an ideal, a resource, and a style of operation appropriate to a situation of similar systems and common needs, conducive to the goal of and commitment to regional integration and building a Caribbean Community.
(2) Education objectives and curricula: the new and renewed objectives required and the concomitant provisions in education.
(3) Partnership in participation: the desirability of pooling resources to more efficiently relate to the new and renewed objectives (SCME, 1990, p. 11).

In this way, member states sought to understand how common influences across educational systems might produce similar effects. To this extent, the Advisory Task Force emphasized that the need for sharing information and collaboration to avoid duplication of efforts and maximize the use of available resources. Prominence was further placed on the necessary education requirements for an ideal Caribbean citizen (Jules, forthcoming). Moreover, when policy-makers searched for lessons across international boundaries, there was no limit to the distance traveled. Trans-regional regimes such as CARICOM encouraged the exchange of ideas between member states sharing the same historical, economic, social, and cultural outlook. This permeability, as in the case of national consultations, led to policy "leapfrogging" (Rose, 1993), in which national governments coordinated a response to common policy problems across the region. In this case, policy leapfrogging occurred when the national policy arena was extended to consider the regional space. Thus, it assumed that "national differences in institutions [were] less important than functional interdependence" (Rose, 1993, p. 107) of educational problems. By the mid-1990s, several CARICOM members were undergoing education reform to prepare their citizens to work in the knowledge economy. For example, by 1991, the original seven countries of the Organization of Eastern Caribbean States (OECS) had drawn up a compulsory subregional educational reform strategy called the Foundations for the Future (FFF) of the OECS Education Reform Strategy (OECS, 1991). Belize soon followed with education reforms aided by World Bank funding, and by 1997, the Bahamas, Barbados, and Trinidad and Tobago had established Education Task Forces or Commissions. During this time, Guyana and Jamaica also started to implement educational reforms that addressed the efficacy of

SAPs. From a national perspective, the educational reforms of the 1980s and 1990s were successful throughout in achieving high enrollment rates at pre-primary levels, universal primary education, the availability of secondary education, the creation of a regional university and several national colleges and universities, and secondary school assessment instituted by the Caribbean Examination Council (CXC).

CONCLUSION

The impact of 1989 generated a policy tsunami of new experiences in educational policies, performances, and strategies with the collapse of socialist experiments in Guyana, Grenada, and Jamaica. The beginning of the 1980s saw ideological fragmentations within the Caribbean, allowing member states to follow different developmental models. In the early 1980s, CARICOM was contaminated by debt fatigue, ideological pluralism, internal renewal, experimentation, structural reform, and policy cessation. However, the policy alterations in the global landscape stemming from the collapse of the Berlin Wall, the end of the Cold War, and the influence of Thatcherism and Reaganomics indirectly affected the region. For CARICOM member states this period coincided with debt created by extensive borrowing in the 1970s and 1980s because of two oil crises and SAPs creating varied debt service ratios, ranging from 3.4% in Barbados to 50.7% in the Bahamas according to 2004 economic data.

In demonstrating the efficacy the aftershocks of post-socialist transformations, this chapter argues that the removal of competition between the different internal systems – between Marxism/socialism and capitalism and their potential developmental trajectories – created a universal atmosphere and attitude in the post-1989 policy period paving the way for needed educational reform across CARICOM as leaders realized that their "small states remained subject to stresses and pressures directly and indirectly, [and] of a military political and economic nature" (CHGCC, 1983, p. 1). Furthermore, the chapter illustrates that the subsequent failure of the Cold War systems and postures, the demise of the Brezhnev doctrine, and the familiarity of the policies of *glasnost* and *perestroika* that crystallized the relaxation of East–West tensions created a regional reform atmosphere in CARICOM countries. The pressures of 1989 led to new coping strategies and conceptual tools: competitive advantage, competencies building, and human resource development. In the wake of global restructuring and the efficacy of post-socialism on the region, CARICOM countries sought to develop economically, and they invested in education to fuel this develop-ment. Development came to be seen as an evolutionary process in which countries progressed through an identified series of stages to become modern (Turner & Hume, 1997). Therefore, post-socialist alterations became the mechanism that allowed CARICOM to transform itself from a dormant institution to a viable trans-regional regime. The post-1989 period ushered in a period of internal exploration in the form of intensified functional cooperation aided by the policy tool of lesson-drawing through cross-national consultations. These consultations in education were a coping apparatus that allowed the region to move beyond the bifurcated international system with the realization that harmonized policies, strategies, and performances were needed to create a regional souk and economic space, a prerequisite for economic development. This expansion signaled more coherent networks of cooperation in functional areas such as education.

Arguably, the disillusionment with the Soviet Union led to several transformations globally; among the region of CARICOM countries it created a discourse of compliance based on deeper regionalism to purge member states of their socialist experiments and ties. Using CARICOM as an archetype, this chapter has demonstrated how this complex phenomenon allowed policy-makers to draw lessons through the use of time, space, and discourse along with knowing "when" and "how." Although other contexts may present different challenges, political settings, and grand narratives, this snapshot shows that the reverberations of 1989 have had far-reaching consequences in the Global South. It argues that considerations of the ramifications of 1989, often dismissed as merely an "Eastern European experience," need to take into account the spiral effect that the year's events had on educational policy-making in various regions around the globe.

NOTES

1. The Caribbean Community (CARICOM) refers to 12 independent island-nations: Antigua and Barbuda, Bahamas, Barbados, Dominica, Grenada, Haiti, Jamaica, Montserrat, St Kitts and Nevis, St Lucia, St Vincent and the Grenadines, Trinidad and Tobago, and the 3 mainland Caribbean countries of Belize, Guyana, and Suriname. In 1989, CARICOM had 13 Anglophone members. Today CARICOM comprises 15 member states, 13 Anglophone members and 1 Dutch (Suriname) and French (Haiti), and 5 associate members (Anguilla, Bermuda, British Virgin Islands, Cayman Islands, Turks, and Caicos). The Organization of Eastern Caribbean States (OECS) founded in 1981 is a subregional entity of CARICOM since all OECS full members are members of CARICOM. Today, OECS is an

eight-member group comprised of Antigua and Barbuda, Commonwealth of Dominica, Grenada, Montserrat, St Kitts and Nevis, St Lucia, St Vincent and the Grenadines. Anguilla and the British Virgin Islands, however, are associate members of the OECS.

2. The Declaration of Grand Anse was signed at the Tenth Meeting of the Conference at Grand Anse, Grenada in July 1989 and set out the path for the Community toward the 21st century. The declaration focused on transforming CARICOM into a single market and economy and on the establishment of the Caribbean Court of Justice (CCJ) while laying the foundation for revisions to the 1973 Treaty of Chaguaramas. The declaration also created the space to facilitate "Open Regionalism": the liberalization of internal markets for goods, services, and factors of production is combined with opening up the region to the rest of the world. Thus, the Grand Anse allowed member states to bring the Caribbean Single Market and Economy (CSME) into effect through the formulation and execution of sectoral policies.

3. Educational policies for Antigua and Barbuda, Belize, and St. Lucia were not available for this period.

4. Prime Minister from 1964 to 1980 and President from 1980 to 1985.

5. Prime Minister between 1972–1980 and 1989–1992.

6. After the 1979 Coup d'état, self-proclaimed Prime Minister from 1979 to 1983.

7. Errol Barrow was Premier of Barbados from 1961 until 1966. After leading the country to independence from Great Britain (1966), he became Prime Minister until 1976. He first declared the "friends of all, satellites of none" foreign policy stance in a speech to the Barbados National Assembly in 1966.

8. During the 1800s, Venezuela and British Guiana both laid claim to a large tract (five-eighths of present-day Guyana) between the Essequibo River and the mouth of the Orinoco River. In 1899, a court of arbitration awarded more than 90% of the disputed area to British Guiana. However, in the early 1960s, Venezuela reasserted its claim to the disputed territory. On October 12, 1966, Guyana discovered that Venezuelan military and civilian personnel had occupied the Guyanese half of Ankoko Island in the Cuyuni River. In July 1968, Venezuela's extended its territorial waters to 12 nautical miles off its coast including the disputed region. On January 4, 1969, disturbances occurred in the Rupununi region of southern Guyana. In February 1970, Guyanese and Venezuelan forces skirmished for several days leading Venezuela to close its border. Relations between Guyana and Venezuela slowly improved throughout the 1970s and 1980s.

9. The Caribbean Examination Council (CXC) and the University of the West Indies are often highlighted as great examples of the operationalization of functional cooperation in education.

REFERENCES

Bakhtin, M. (Ed.). (1981). *The dialogic imagination: Four essays.* (C. Emerson and M. Holquist, trans.). Austin, TX: University of Texas Press.

Ball, S. J. (1990). *Politics and policy making in education.* London, UK: Routledge.

Brewster, H. (2003). *CARICOM single market and economy assessment of the region's support needs*. Georgetown, Guyana: CARICOM.

CARICOM. (2007). *Needham Point declaration*. [Online]. Available at http://www.caricom.org/jsp/communications/meetings_statements/declaration_on_functional_cooperation.jsp

CARICOM. (1973). *Original Treaty of Chaguaramas*. Georgetown, Guyana: CARICOM.

CARICOM. (1984). *The Nassau understanding: Structural adjustment and closer integration for accelerated development in the Caribbean Community*. Georgetown, Guyana: CARICOM.

CARICOM. (1985). *Barbados consensus on development of local and regional entrepreneurship and skills in the member states of the Caribbean Community*. Georgetown, Guyana: CARICOM.

CARICOM. (1989). *Grand Anse declaration*. Georgetown, Guyana: CARICOM.

CARICOM. (1990). *The Kingston declaration*. Georgetown, Guyana: CARICOM.

CARICOM. (1993). *The future of education in the Caribbean*. Task Force on Education. Georgetown, Guyana: CARICOM.

CARICOM. (2001). *Revised treaty of Chaguaramas*. Georgetown, Guyana: CARICOM.

CARICOM. (2003). *The Rose Hall declaration on regional governance and integrated development*. Georgetown, Guyana: CARICOM.

Common, R. (2004). Organizational learning in a political environment: Improving policy making in UK Government. *Policy Studies, 25*, 72–97.

Conference of Heads of Government of the Caribbean Community (CHGCC). (1983). *Communiqué of the Fourth Conference of Heads of Government of the Caribbean Community*. Port of Spain, Trinidad and Tobago: CARICOM.

Conference of Heads of Government of the Caribbean Community (CHGCC). (1989). *Communiqué issued at the conclusion of the Tenth Meeting of the Conference of Heads of Government of the Caribbean Community*. Grand Anse, Grenada: CARICOM.

Conference of Heads of Government of the Caribbean Community (CHGCC). (1992). *Communiqué issued at the conclusion of the Thirteenth Meeting of the Conference of Heads of Government of the Caribbean Community*. Port of Spain, Trinidad and Tobago: CARICOM.

Conference of Heads of Government of the Caribbean Community (CHGCC). (2007). *Communiqué issued at the conclusion of the Twenty-Eighth Meeting of the Conference of Heads of Government of the Caribbean Community* (Available at http://www.caricom.org/jsp/communications/communiques/28hgc_2007_communique.jsp). Needham Point, Barbados: CARICOM.

Cox, R. (1999). Transfer and models of welfare reform. Paper presented at the Conference on Global Trajectories: Ideas, International Policy. Florence, Italy.

Dolowitz, D., & Marsh, D. (1996). Who learns from whom: A review of the policy transfer literature. *Political Studies, XLIV*, 343–357.

Eklof, B., Holmes, L., & Kaplan, V. (Eds). (2005). *Educational reform in post-Soviet Russia: Legacies and prospects*. Frank Cass, London: Cummings Center for Russian and East European Studies.

Fairclough, N. (1995). *Critical discourse analysis*. London: Essex Pearson Education.

Freeman, R. (1999). Policy transfer in the health sector: A working paper. Available at http://www.pol.ed.ac.uk/research/working_paper1.html

Girvan, N. (2001). Rally round the West Indies. In: K. O. Hall (Ed.), *Remarks at the launch of the Caribbean community: Beyond survival*. Kingston: Ian Randle. Available at http://www.acs-aec.org/About/SG/Girvan/Speeches/reinventccom_eng.htm

Haas, P. (1992). Introduction: Epistemic communities and international policy coordination. *International Organization, 46*(1), 1–35.

Hall, K. (2001). *The Caribbean community: Beyond survival.* Kingston, Jamaica: Ian Randle.

Hall, K. (Ed.) (2003). *Re-inventing CARICOM: The road to a new integration.* Kingston, Jamaica: Ian Randle.

Hedberg, B. (1981). How organizations learn and unlearn. In: P. C. Nystrom & W. H. Starbuck (Eds), *Handbook of organizational design* (pp. 3–27). New York: Oxford University Press.

Ikenberry, J. G. (1990). The international spread of privatization policies: Inducement, learning, and policy bandwagoning. In: E. N. Suleiman & J. Waterbury (Eds), *The political economy of public sector reform and privatization* (pp. 81–110). Boulder, CO: Westview Press.

Innes, E. J., & Booher, E. D. (2003). Collaborative dialogue as a policy making strategy. In: M. A. Hajer & H. Wagenaar (Eds), *Deliberative policy analysis: Understanding governance in the network society* (pp. 33–60). Cambridge: Cambridge University Press.

Jagen, J. (2001). The Caribbean in 2000: Challenges and opportunities. In: K. Hall (Ed.), *The Caribbean community: Beyond survival* (pp. 69–77). Kingston, Jamaica: Ian Randle.

Jervis, R. (1999). Realism, neoliberalism, and cooperation. *International Security, 24*(1), 42–63.

Jules, D. T. (2008). *Re/thinking harmonization in the Commonwealth Caribbean: Audiences, actors, interests, and educational policy formation.* Doctoral dissertation, Teachers College, Columbia University, Columbia.

Jules, D. T. (forthcoming). Trans-regional regimes and globalization in education: Constructing the neo-Caribbean Citizen. In: I. Silova, & D. Hobson (Eds), *Globalizing minds: Rhetoric and realities in international schools.* Greenwich, CT: Information Age Publishing.

Jules, D. T., & Sa e Silvia, M. (2008). How different disciplines have approached South–South cooperation and transfer. In: H. Williams & K. Downey (Eds), *South–South transfer* (pp. 1–13). New York: Society for International Education, Teachers College.

Krasner, S. (Ed.) (1983). *International regimes.* Ithaca, NY: Cornell University Press.

Lee, F. J. T. (2000). *The evolution-involution of "Co-operative Socialism" in Guyana, 1930–1984* (Available at http://www.franz-lee.org/files/coopguy.html#_Toc19952339). Merida, Venezuela: Pandemonium Electronic Publication.

Lewis, V. (2001). Major tasks for the 1980s. In: K. Hall (Ed.), *The Caribbean community: Beyond survival* (pp. 43–51). Kingston, Jamaica: Ian Randle.

Nòvoa, A., & Lawn, M. (Eds). (2002). *Fabricating Europe: The formation of an education space.* Dordrecht, the Netherlands: Kluwer.

OECS. (1991). *Foundation for the future: OECS education reform strategy.* Castries, St. Lucia: OECS Secretariat.

Rose, E. A. (2002). *Dependency and socialism in the modern Caribbean: Superpower intervention in Guyana, Jamaica and Grenada, 1970–1985.* Oxford: Lexington Books.

Rose, R. (1993). *Lesson drawing in public policy.* Chatham, NJ: Chatham House.

Schneider, A., & Ingram, H. (1988). Systematically pinching ideas: A comparative approach to policy design. *Journal of Public Policy, 8*(1), 61–80.

SCME. (1988). Report of the Seventh Meeting of the Standing Committee of Ministers Responsible for Education (REP. 88/7/53 SCME). CARICOM, Georgetown, Guyana.

SCME. (1990). Report of the Eighth Meeting of the Standing Committee of Ministers Responsible for Education (REP. 90/8/38 ME). CARICOM, Port of Spain, Trinidad and Tobago.

SCME. (1993). Report of the Second Special Meeting of the Standing Committee of Ministers Responsible for Education (REP 93/1/38 ME [Spec.]). CARICOM, St. John's, Antigua and Barbuda.

Searwar, L. (2001). Diplomacy and survival. In: K. Hall (Ed.), *The Caribbean community: Beyond survival* (pp. 377–381). Kingston, Jamaica: Ian Randle.

Silova, I., & Steiner-Khamsi, G. (2008). Introduction: Unwrapping the post-socialist educational reform package. In: I. Silova & G. Steiner-Khamsi (Eds), *How NGOs react: Globalization and education reform in the Caucasus, Central Asia, and Mongolia* (pp. 1–42). Bloomfield, CT: Kumarian Press.

Steiner-Khamsi, G. (2004). In: *The global politics of educational borrowing and lending* (pp. 201–220). New York: Teachers College Press.

Steiner-Khamsi, G., & Stolpe, I. (2006). *Educational import in Mongolia: Local encounters with global Forces*. New York: Palgrave Macmillan.

Strachan, G. (1996). *Study commissioned by CARICOM Secretariat of an analysis of the science and technology proposal promoting productive employment for poverty eradication in the creative and productive citizen in the 21st century*. Georgetown, Guyana: CARICOM.

Task Force on Functional Cooperation. (2008). *Final report of the task force on functional cooperation*. Georgetown, Guyana: CARICOM.

Turner, M., & Hume, D. (1997). *Governance and administration and development: Making the state work*. West Hartford, CT: Kumarian Press.

UNESCO. (1990). *World declaration on education for all*. Paris: UNESCO.

West Indian Commission. (1992). *Time for action: Report of the West Indian Commission*. Kingston, Jamaica: University of the West Indies Press.

Wodak, R. (2005). The discourse-historical approach. In: R. Wodak & M. Meyer (Eds), *Methods of critical discourse analysis* (pp. 63–94). London: Sage Publication Limited.

AUTHOR BIOGRAPHIES

Olga Bain teaches at the Graduate School of Education and Human Development at George Washington University, Washington, DC. Her research interests include educational policies in post-socialist countries, internationalization and globalization of higher education, faculty productivity and women's advancement in academia, and higher education financing. Olga Bain has consulted for the American Council on Education, the Academy of Educational Development, the International Research and Exchanges Board, the Council of Europe, the Salzburg Seminar, and others. She authored the book *University Autonomy in the Russian Federation since Perestroika* (2003, RoutledgeFalmer) as well as book chapters and articles in peer-reviewed journals. She holds a Ph.D. degree in social foundations of education, comparative and higher education from the University at Buffalo, NY, and a candidate of sciences degree in sociolinguistics from St. Petersburg University, Russia.

Christine Beresniova is currently completing her Ph.D. in international and comparative policy studies at Indiana University. Her research focuses on education and national identity in the Baltic States. Recently, Christine served as a coinvestigator on a UNESCO-sponsored project studying student attitudes toward diversity in the Baltic States, Finland, and the United States (2009). Additionally, she has presented her research at the Comparative and International Education Society (2007; 2008; 2010), the Association for the Advancement of Baltic Studies (2008; 2010), and the Educational Symposium for Research and Innovations (2008). Christine received her M.A. in international education from George Washington University and her B.A. from Sarah Lawrence College.

Kara D. Brown is an assistant professor in the Educational Studies Department at the University of South Carolina. She focuses her research on language policy, immigration, and educational segregation in Central and Eastern Europe. Brown's current research examines the role of teachers and parents in experimenting with immersion language policy in Estonian kindergartens. A second funded project concerns international teacher recruitment and the global economy in South Carolina. Brown serves as an instructor for both undergraduate preservice teachers and graduate students, teaching the Social Foundations of Education courses as well as Comparative and International Education and Introduction to Qualitative Research Methods. Her research has been funded by the Spencer Foundation, Fulbright, the International Research and Exchanges Board (IREX), and the University of South Carolina's College of Education. Brown's publications have appeared in *Anthropology & Education Quarterly*, *European Education*, and *European Journal of Language Policy*, as well as in several edited volumes.

Eduard Dneprov is the former Minister of Education of the Russian Federation who ushered in major reform in the early 1990s. He is former Director of the Federal Institute for Educational Planning at the Ministry of Education of the Russian Federation and professor of history at the University of the Russian Academy of Education. He has published widely on the history of education, policy, and reform in the Russian Federation.

Olena Fimyar is a Ph.D. candidate at the Faculty of Education, University of Cambridge, UK. Olena's personal and professional involvement in Ukrainian education has informed her research interest in studying educational policy and policy-making. Olena's Ph.D. thesis entitled "Educational policy-making in post-communist Ukraine: Rationalities, subjectivities, power, a Foucauldian perspective" employs Foucauldian conceptions of power and (neo)liberal mentalities of government – governmentality – to examine the recent educational policy developments in postcommunist Ukraine. Preliminary findings of the study appeared in "The (un)importance of public opinion in educational policy-making in post-communist Ukraine: Education policy 'elites' on the role of civil society in policy formation" in *Civil Society in Central and Eastern Europe: Successes and Failures of Europeanisation in Politics and Society* (2010, S. Fischer and H. Pleines, eds.); "Educational policy-making in post-communist Ukraine as an example of emerging governmentality: Discourse analysis of curriculum choice and assessment policy documents (1999–2003)" in the *Journal of Education Policy* (2008); and "Using governmentality as a conceptual tool in education policy research" in *Educate ~ The Journal of Doctoral Research in Education* (2008), reprinted as "Governamentalidade como Ferramenta Conceitual na Pesquisa de Politicas de Educacionais" in *Educação & Realidade* (2009).

Meg P. Gardinier is a Ph.D. candidate in the Department of Education at Cornell University. She holds a master's degree in international educational development from Teachers College, Columbia University (2002). She worked in the field of peace and human rights education for several years with a range of domestic and international organizations including schools, NGOs, and the United Nations. Meg contributed to the 2001 publication, *Learning to Abolish War: Teaching Toward a Culture of Peace* by Dr. Betty Reardon and Alicia Cabezudo. During 2003–2004, Meg researched educational change in Albania with a Fulbright fellowship. Her current research focuses on analyzing how global educational models become localized in particular social and institutional contexts. Her work addresses issues related to education policy and practice in the area of democratic citizenship and human rights education. Her wider research interests include educational reform in postcommunist societies, the role and identity of teachers, pedagogy and performative aspects of teaching, teacher training, the politics of the curriculum, international education policy, international institutions, global diffusion, and localization.

Magdalena Gross is a doctoral candidate in international comparative education at Stanford University. She holds an M.A. in teaching and is also pursuing an M.A. in history at Stanford. Her research interests include the intersection of historical memory and history education in post-war countries in East Central Europe with a particular focus on Poland and World War II history. Her work includes text analysis of Polish history textbooks and other curricula. During the summer of 2010, she interviewed Polish teachers and completed archival research at the National Library of Poland. She also taught a summer program to Polish high schoolers regarding war memory, art education, tolerance, and identity.

Irina Horga, Ph.D., is principal researcher in the Evaluation and Educational Politics section, Institute of Educational Sciences (ISE) in Bucharest, Romania. She also works as an educational evaluator and policy analyst. Her research focuses on education politics, with a focus on religious education, rural education, and vocational education.

Robert J. Imre teaches international relations at the University of Newcastle in Australia. He has recently co-authored two books examining the phenomenon of global terrorism and is currently writing a book on the topic of global multiculturalism as a comparative political initiative. Dr. Imre is also writing two other collaborative book manuscripts: one on global civil society and the governance state, and another on the problem of regime change. He has also just completed a research project examining the rise of the radical right in Central Europe. Dr. Imre has worked in a number of nation-states including South Korea, Canada, and Hungary.

Tavis D. Jules received his doctorate of education from Teachers College, Columbia University in 2008 in international educational development. For the past five years, Tavis has been working and teaching in areas of education policy in different educational contexts ranging from Eastern Europe to Africa to Latin America and the Caribbean. His major research area is understanding the influence of endogenous and exogenous actors on educational policy formation within the Caribbean Community (CARICOM) and their efficacy upon the Caribbean Single Market Economy (CSME). Tavis's other research interests include educational externalization, policy isomorphism, human rights, and gender parity. He is currently the Head of Knowledge and Communications at the Globally Responsible Leadership Initiative Foundation.

Zsuzsa Millei lectures at the University of Newcastle in the sociology and politics of education and in early childhood education. Her research is located in an interdisciplinary field and examines the ways in which ideologies and contemporary governance constitute the subjects of education. Based in comparative frameworks and individual case studies, her published work explores classroom discipline, government policies and initiatives, the use of political concepts in education, and curriculum and pedagogical discourses under different political ideological regimes.

Monica E. Mincu is an assistant professor/researcher in the Faculty of Education, University of Torino, Italy. Her principal research and teaching experience is in the field of comparative and international education, with an emphasis on East European education and teacher training. She is the author of several publications on post-socialist education reforms, the politics of education in cultural contexts, and teacher education. Her last co-edited book (with Maria Teresa Tatto) is *Reforming Teaching and Learning: Comparative Perspectives in a Global Era* (Sense Publishers and WCCES, 2009).

Diane Brook Napier was born and raised in South Africa, where she received her undergraduate education. She is a naturalized American citizen, residing in the United States. She is a associate professor in Comparative and International Education, in the program of social foundations in Social Foundations of Education at the University of Georgia (UGA), and a member of the African Studies Institute as well as the UGA Costa Rican Faculty. Her research and teaching interests focus on postcolonial educational reform policies, democratic transformation policies and implementation issues in sub-Saharan Africa (especially South Africa), and in other developing countries including Costa Rica, Cuba, and the United

Arab Emirates. Her research focuses on issues of globalization of education, reform policy/practice and implementation, race, ideology, language, justice/injustice, human resources development (education, health, housing, labor, and migration refugees), environmental issues, and teacher education.

Eleoussa Polyzoi is a professor of education at the University of Winnipeg in Manitoba, Canada. Her areas of research interest include comparative international research, at-risk youth, refugee education, respiratory health of young children, transformative educational leadership, and developmental studies. Dr. Polyzoi has published extensively and has completed international research in Eastern Europe, Russia, and Greece.

Heidi Ross is director of the East Asian Studies Center and professor of Educational Leadership and Policy Studies at Indiana University. She earned her B.A. in Chinese Language and Literature at Oberlin College, an M.A. in education/applied linguistics at the University of Michigan, and a Ph.D. in educational foundations, policy, and administration at the University of Michigan. Dr. Ross has taught and consulted at numerous institutions in East Asia, has served as president of the Comparative and International Education Society, is co-editor of *Comparative Education Review*, and served as chair of Educational Studies and director of Asian Studies at Colgate University. Ross has published widely on Chinese education, gender and schooling, and qualitative research methodology. Her books include *China Learns English* (Yale), *The Ethnographic Eye* (Garland), and *Taking Teaching Seriously* (Paradigm). She is currently leading two field-based projects in the PRC, one on student engagement in Chinese higher education and the other on girls' educational access and attainment in rural Shaanxi.

Anita Sanyal is a lecturer at the University of Maryland where she received her doctorate in international education policy in 2009. Her dissertation focused on the implications of education policy for rural primary school teachers in Nicaragua. More broadly, her research concerns the effects of education policy on teachers and teaching and the politics of education reform both in the United States and internationally. She is a former high school teacher and has designed and conducted professional development programs for teachers in Nicaragua and the United States. She currently teaches in the teacher education program and consults with organizations working in international educational development.

Iveta Silova is a Frank Hook assistant professor of comparative and international education in the College of Education at Lehigh University,

Pennsylvania, USA. Her research and publications cover a range of issues critical to understanding post-socialist education transformation processes, including professional development of teachers and teacher educators, gender equity trends in Eastern/Central Europe and Central Asia, minority/ multicultural education policies in the former Soviet Union, as well as the scope, nature, and implications of private tutoring in a cross-national perspective. Her books include *Globalization on the Margins: Education and Post-Socialist Transformations in Central Asia* (Information Age Publishing, forthcoming in 2010), *How NGOs React: Globalization and Education Reform in the Caucasus, Central Asia, and Mongolia* (Kumarian Press, 2008; with Gita Steiner-Khamsi), and *From Sites of Occupation to Symbols of Multiculturalism: Re-conceptualizing Minority Education in Post-Soviet Latvia* (Information Age Publishing, 2006). She is the co-editor (with Noah W. Sobe) of *European Education: Issues and Studies* (a quarterly peer-reviewed journal published by M.E. Sharpe).

Noah W. Sobe is associate professor of cultural and educational policy studies and associate director of the Center for Comparative Education at Loyola University Chicago. His scholarship focuses on globalization and education and on the trans-local circulation of theories and practices of teaching and learning. He has published articles in journals such as *Harvard Educational Review, European Education, Educational Theory, Current Issues in Comparative Education (CICE),* and *Paedagogica Historica.* He is the author of *Provincializing the Worldly Citizen: Slavic Cosmopolitanism and Yugoslav Student and Teacher Travel in the Interwar Era* (2008) and the editor of *American Post-Conflict Educational Reform: From the Spanish-American War to Iraq* (2009). Noah also serves as the co-editor (with Iveta Silova) of *European Education: Issues and Studies* (a quarterly journal published by M.E. Sharpe).

Renee N. Timberlake holds a M.A. degree from Loyola University Chicago in cultural and educational policy studies with a concentration in comparative and international education. In her research, she has focused on the education of marginalized populations and the effects of violence on education and children, specifically in boarding schools for Native American children and in Latin America. She is currently researching the effectiveness of the No Child Left Behind mandated Supplemental Educational Services in the Chicago Public Schools with the Wisconsin Center for Education Research.

Elizabeth Anderson Worden is an assistant professor at American University in Washington, DC. Worden earned a Ph.D. in international education from New York University in 2006. Worden's primary research examines the role of teaching history in national identity and the development of a post-Soviet nation in the Republic of Moldova, and the implications for other transitional states. She is currently working on a book manuscript, *Finding the Nation: Memory, Identity, and History in Moldova*. Her recent publications include " 'They are the Priests': The Role of the Moldovan Historian and its Implications for Civic Education" published in 2007 in *Compare: A Journal of Comparative Education* (Volume 37, Issue 3). Her research interests are history teaching, history textbooks, citizenship education, nationalism and national identity, education in the former Soviet Union, and international exchange.

Ran Zhang is assistant professor at Peking University. She received her undergraduate degrees in law and economics at Peking University and an M.S. in international and comparative education at Indiana University. Her dual Ph.D. degree in educational policy studies with a focus on educational leadership and in educational psychology with a focus on inquiry methodology is also from Indiana University. Zhang has received numerous honors for her scholarship on educational law, including grants from the U.S. National Science Foundation and the China Scholarship Council. Her diverse publications include comparative scholarship on educational law and the legal rights of teachers, students, and children.

Wanxia Zhao is a doctoral student in educational policy studies with a concentration in comparative and international education at Indiana University, Bloomington. She obtained her B.A. degrees in history and economics from Peking University, and an M.A. degree in educational economics and management from Tsinghua University, Beijing. Her research concerns higher education in the context of socialist transformation in contemporary China. Her academic papers have been published in *China Higher Education* and *Tsinghua Journal of Education*, among other academic journals in China.

INDEX